The U.S. Army War College
Guide to the

Battles of Chancellorsville & Fredericksburg

D1167411

Wilderness Church. The right of Howard's line was in the distance over the Hawkins buildings at the right. (USAMHI)

The U.S. Army War College
College
Guide to the

Battles of Chancellorsville & Fredericksburg

Edited by Dr. Jay Luvaas
and Col. Harold W. Nelson

Harper & Row, Publishers, New York
Grand Rapids, Philadelphia, St. Louis, San Francisco
London, Singapore, Sydney, Tokyo, Toronto

A hardcover edition of this book was published in 1988 by South Mountain Press, Inc. It is hereby reprinted by arrangement with South Mountain Press, Inc.

Library of Congress Cataloging-in-Publication Data

The U.S. Army War College guide to the Battles of Chancellorsville & Fredericksburg/Jay
Luvaas, Harold W. Nelson, editors.—1st Perennial Library ed.
    p. cm.
    Reprint. Originally published: 1st ed. Carlisle, Pa.: South Mountain Press, 1988.
    Includes index.
    ISBN 0-06-097252-1
    1. Fredericksburg, Battle of, 1862.   2. Chancellorsville, Battle of, 1863.
3. Fredericksburg and Spotsylvania County Battlefields Memorial National Military
Park (Va.)—Tours.   4. Historic sites—Virginia—Fredericksburg Region—Guide-books.
I. Luvaas, Jay.   II. Nelson, Harold W.   III. Army War College (U.S.)   IV. Title: US
Army War College guide to the Battles of Chancellorsville & Fredericksburg.   V. Title:
Battles of Chancellorsville & Fredericksburg.
E474.85U47   1989
973.7′3—dc20   89-45104

89 90 91 92 93 FG 10 9 8 7 6 5 4 3 2 1

CONTENTS

MAPS

ACKNOWLEDGEMENTS

All of the books in this series are the result of the support we receive from many people. In this instance General Carl Vuono, Chief of Staff, U.S. Army, inspired us to transform incomplete notes used for annual War College trips into fully-developed staff rides for his senior colleagues first in the Training and Doctrine Command and later on the Army Staff. His enthusiasm matched that of Secretary of the Army John O. Marsh, who has been a driving force behind the expanded use of the historical staff ride throughout today's Army.

At Carlisle Barracks we enjoyed the supportive command environment of Major General Howard Graves, the Commandant; Colonel Don Lunday, the Director of Academic Affairs; and Colonel David Hansen, our Department Chairman. Our fellow military history teachers have been of greater assistance with each passing year by continuing to offer outstanding classroom instruction (with little help from us) while assuming ever-larger loads as leaders on the numerous staff rides to Gettysburg and Antietam that Army organizations seek. Roy Strong has been much more than the representative of the War College Foundation in this endeavor, taking an active interest in every aspect of our publishing efforts—efforts that would be fruitless without the resourcefulness and creative skill of John Kallmann, our publisher, who has again given us the quality product every author hopes to see. Much credit for unseen dimensions of quality in our work also goes to Susan Chirico, who kept a busy office on track while we spent too many days on battlefields.

No one is counting those days, but we fear our wives may soon start. We thank them for their forbearance, and rejoice that they tolerate our enthusiasm for battlefield projects that demand more time with each passing month. Both Linda and Janet know that we seek neither fame nor fortune.

We owe a special debt to Mrs. Alice Pratt Milliken, who contributed the letters of her grandfather, James Pratt, Thirty-fifth Regiment, Massachusetts Volunteer Militia, who survived the assault against the stone wall.

No battlefield guide could be completed without the help of knowledgeable people on the scene. Will Greene, Robert Krick, and many other National Park Service professionals have been tremendously helpful, and the staff at Wilderness Resorts rendered us a unique service by giving us access to their property until we could devise a way to show off Hazel Grove from Park property. Everyone who walks old battlefields with us helps us learn, so let's get on with it.

Jay Luvaas
Harold Nelson

INTRODUCTION

After the battle of Antietam, September 17, 1862, the Confederates withdrew to Winchester, Virginia, where General Robert E. Lee hoped to rest and resupply his weary forces. "Our stragglers are being daily collected," he assured President Jefferson Davis. "We have plenty of beef and flour for our troops, hay for our horses, and some grain." With new conscripts from the recently liberated counties in Virginia and an improved capacity of the Commissary Department to collect stores to sustain future operations, Lee would have liked to make a fresh advance upon Hagerstown "and endeavor to defeat the enemy at that point." In his judgment this would have been the best move from a purely military point of view. He hesitated to attempt it, however, because his army no longer exhibited "its former temper and condition" and he calculated that the risk would be great "and a reverse disastrous."[1]

Major General George B. McClellan, commanding the Army of the Potomac, was far more reluctant to resume active military operations. He needed time, he explained to President Abraham Lincoln, to reorganize his army. "The army corps have been badly cut up and scattered by the overwhelming numbers brought against them" at Antietam, "and the entire army has been greatly exhausted by unavoidable overwork, hunger, and want of sleep and rest." He needed to rebuild his means of transportation, fill up the old skeleton regiments and appoint officers to supply "the numerous existing vacancies."[2] On October 1, Lincoln visited McClellan in his headquarters near Sharpsburg, more "to urge the General to advance" than to utter compliments. Several days later he ordered McClellan to cross the Potomac and either fight Lee or drive him south. McClellan, however, first wished to build up his supplies and establish a supply line, and his excuses and pleas for time added to Lincoln's impatience. When the General on October 25 justified the failure of his cavalry to move because of "sore-tongued and fatigued horses," an exasperated President replied: "Will you pardon me for asking what the horses of your army have done since the battle of Antietam that fatigues anything?"[3]

On October 26 McClellan ordered two divisions of the Ninth Corps plus cavalry to cross the Potomac at Berlin, *east* of the Blue Ridge mountains, leaving the Twelfth Corps to guard Harpers Ferry, and in the next few days the rest of the Ninth Corps, followed by the First and the Sixth, crossed on the pontoon bridge. "We occupy Leesburg," he reported to the President. "I am much pleased," Lincoln responded. "When you get *entirely* across the river, let me know." McClellan's plan of campaign during this advance

> was to move the army, well in hand, parallel to the Blue Ridge, taking Warrenton as the point of direction for the main body, seizing each pass on the Blue Ridge by detachments as we approached it, and guarding them after we had passed as long as they would enable the enemy to trouble our communications with the Potomac. It was expected that we would unite with the Eleventh Corps and Sickles' division near Thoroughfare Gap. . . . It was my intention if, upon reaching . . . any . . . pass, I found that the enemy were in force between it and the Potomac in the Valley of the Shenandoah, to move into the valley, and endeavor to gain their rear. I hardly hoped to accomplish this, but did expect that, by striking in between Culpeper Court-House and Little Washington, I could either separate their army and beat them in detail, or else force them to concentrate as far back as Gordonsville, and thus place the Army of the Potomac in position either to adopt the Fredericksburg line of advance upon Richmond, or to be removed to the Peninsula, if, as I apprehended, it were found impossible to supply it by the Orange and Alexandria Railroad beyond Culpeper.[4]

On November 5, while advancing toward Warrenton, on the Orange and Alexandria Railroad, McClellan was relieved from the command of the Army of the Potomac. "Had I remained in command," McClellan wrote in his final after-action report of Antietam," I should have made the attempt to divide the enemy . . . and could he have been brought to a battle within reach of my supplies, I cannot doubt that the result would have been a brilliant victory . . .[5]

The new commander was Major General Ambrose E. Burnside, who had commanded the Right Wing of the Army of the Potomac in the Maryland Campaign. Burnside initially had declined the offer out of loyalty to his friend McClellan and because he did not feel competent to direct a large army, but the prospect that it would then be offered to Major General Joseph Hooker, whom Burnside disliked, induced him to change his mind. In the measured words of Col. G. F. R. Henderson, later the biographer of Stonewall Jackson, Burnside, "though unwilling to accept the responsibility, was unfortunately for himself and the army unable to refuse it."[6]

This is probably unfair; at the very least it was looking backwards from the unimaginative assaults against the Sunken Road at Fredericksburg. Burnside was widely liked and respected. He had conducted successful coastal operations at Roanoke Island—where the Confederates were offered no terms "but those of unconditional surrender" a full week before Grant used similar language at Fort Donelson[7]—and at New Bern earlier in the year, while at Antietam his performance over the most difficult terrain on the battlefield was better than that of the other Union corps commanders, although much of the credit probably belongs to a subordinate who actually commanded the Ninth Army Corps. Moreover, this congenial and honorable outsider was not identified with any of the rival factions in Pope's old Army of Virginia or the Army of the Potomac. McClellan, in his initial report of the Maryland Campaign dated October 15, 1862, stressed "the difficult task" he had assigned to Burnside in carrying the bridge across the Antietam and concluded: "It became evident that our force was not sufficient" to enable Burnside's advance "to reach the town, and the order was given to retire." There is not the faintest suggestion here that Burnside's performance was wanting. It was only later, in his *second* official report written the following August, that McClellan blamed "My Dear Old Burn" (as he frequently addressed him in official correspondence prior to the Maryland campaign) for the failure to win a great victory. No mention here of the difficulties of the terrain. McClellan's order to Burnside to attack was now dated two hours earlier than before, from 10 a.m. to 8, and Burnside was accused of one needless delay after another. In this revisionist report Burnside moved forward only when prodded by McClellan's Inspector General; had he advanced "with the utmost vigor," McClellan concluded, "our victory might thus have been much more decisive."[8]

Burnside proposed immediately a reorganization of the army by dividing it into three wings, each of two army corps. He had nominally been in command of the Right Wing, comprising his old Ninth Corps and Hooker's First Corps, and in fact had fought the battle of South Mountain on September 14 as a wing commander. At Antietam, however, circumstances—perhaps aided by Hooker's manipulations—had separated these corps and it is difficult to feel Burnside's hand on events. The reasons for the new organization were probably administrative rather than tactical, although the move was justified on both accounts. Burnside wanted "to do away with the very massive and elaborate adjutant-general's office" at army headquarters "and require these wings and corps to correspond directly with Washington" in interior matters.[9] There is no evidence that one of the lessons he learned at Antietam was the folly of piecemeal attacks by corps and divisions, nor is it clear that by inserting an administrative headquarters between two tactical commands he had given much thought to the role played in battle by this new link in the chain of command.

Burnside, however, had obviously given much thought to coming operations, for on the day he assumed command he revealed his concept for the campaign:

> To concentrate all the forces near this place [Warrenton], and impress upon the enemy a belief that we are to attack Culpeper or Gordonsville, and at the same time accumulate a four or five days' supply for the men and animals; then make a rapid move of the whole force to Fredericksburg, with a view to a movement upon Richmond from that point.[9]

He reasoned that even if he managed to engage Lee successfully in the vicinity of Culpeper, "the enemy will have many lines of retreat for his defeated army" and would probably reach Richmond in sufficient strength to force another battle there, while pursuit would be precarious because of problems in maintaining a long and vulnerable line of communications along the railroad. A move by way of Fredericksburg, on the other hand, would place the army on the shortest route to Richmond—"the great object of the campaign," would "render it almost impossible for the enemy to make a successful move upon Washington by any road on this side of the Potomac," and—an interesting thought—would make it "hardly probable" that Lee would "attempt any serious invasion of Pennsylvania at this season of the year." Burnside asked for a build up of supply trains at Aquia Landing and he telegraphed for pontoons and bridge materials to enable a crossing at Fredericksburg.[10]

The Right Grand Division, commanded by Major General Edwin V. Sumner, marched at daylight on November 15 and reached Falmouth two days later, but the pontoons had not yet arrived because of mismanagement in Washington, and to cross the rising Rappahannock on the only available ford—where large rocks provided stepping stones for men but would have greatly hindered the passage of wagons and guns—was considered too risky. The other two Grand Divisions, commanded by General W. B. Franklin and Joseph Hooker, followed several days later. By November 20 there were 110,000 Union troops concentrated at Falmouth.

Lee, who had sent Longstreet's corps to Culpeper when it became clear that McClellan was moving east of the Blue Ridge, initially left Jackson's corps in the Valley until the Union objective could be ascertained. "Should you find that the enemy is advancing from the Potomac east of those mountains, you will cross by either gap that will bring you in best position to threaten his flank and cut off his communications." "You must keep always in view the probability of an attack upon Richmond . . . when a concentration of forces will become necessary."[11] On November 10 he ordered Jackson to prepare to rejoin Longstreet, and a week later, alerted by cavalry scouts that Sumner's corps was moving in the direction of Falmouth, he sent Longstreet's corps to Fredericksburg. About November 26 Lee directed Jackson to advance toward Fredericksburg.

By this time Burnside's intentions were clear.

* * *

The ensuing battle of Fredericksburg and the campaign of Chancellorsville were remarkable in several respects. The first offers a rare example of a river crossing under fire and street fighting, the second an uncommon instance of mounted cavalry attacking infantry, and both reveal the problems of mounting a serious attack at night. More to the point, with the introduction of what later became known as 'hasty intrenchments,' these battles represent a significant stage in the evolution of Civil War tactics.

It has often been asserted that the Civil War was the first of the modern wars because of the introduction of trench warfare. This requires some explanation, for it was not trenches *per se* that made it a modern war, but the way in which they were used. The earthen fortifications that protected Washington and Richmond varied only in detail from the defenses of Sebastapol half a dozen years earlier and of Yorktown in 1781, and only in the material of construction did they differ to any significant degree from works that had surrounded nearly every important city in Europe since the eighteenth century. The intrenched camps at Centerville, Carnifex Ferry, and Camp Nelson, were similar in purpose and construction to Bunzelwitz and any one of a dozen other intrenched camps of Frederick the Great or his Austrian opponents. The siege lines at Yorktown, Vicksburg, Petersburg, Charleston, Fort Morgan and Atlanta followed faithfully the principles and many of the details established by the French Engineer Vauban nearly two centuries earlier, and the defenses that would line the south bank of the Rappahannock in the winter of 1862–63 differed little in purpose or basic design from the Lines of Stollhofen, Brabant, or the Ne Plus Ultra Lines that had confronted the Duke of Marlborough in the War of the Spanish Succession, the much-publicized Lines of Torres Vedras that saved Lisbon from the French in 1810, or of the river lines that Napoleon ordered constructed to defend his conquests in Italy and Germany. Indeed, the Washington defenses were based upon the works of Torres Vedras, even to the extent of computing the size of the garrison required. As the Chief Engineer, U.S. Army, reported of the Washington Defenses in December 1861,

> The theory of these defenses is that upon which the works of Torres Vedras were based, the only one admitted at the present day for defending extensive lines. It is to occupy the commanding points within cannon range of each other by field forts, the fire of which shall sweep all approaches. These forts furnish the secure emplacements of artillery. They also afford cover to bodies of infantry. The works may be connected by lines of light parapets, or the ground. . . . may be so obstructed that the enemy's troops cannot penetrate the interval without being exposed . . . to the destructive effects of the artillery or musketry fire of the forts. . . . No less an authority than Napoleon says that, aided by fortifications, 50,000 men and 3,000 artilleymen can defend a capital against 300,000 men, and he asserts the necessity of fortifying all national capitals.[12]

And Winston Churchill, in writing of the Ne Plus Ultra Lines that stretched from the English Channel to Valenciennes in 1710, describes a situation not unlike that facing Hooker when he assumed command of the Army of the Potomac after Fredericksburg:

> The whole of this ninety mile front was fortified . . . for the effective manoeuvring of a field army. The many marshes . . . were multiplied and extended by numberless dams. . . . The watersheds between the rivers were held by strong ramparts with deep ditches . . . in front of them, and frequent redoubts or strong points. Behind the line . . . was a thorough system of lateral roads and bridges, and . . . depots for use in emergency were established.[13]

To Brigadier General Gouverneur K. Warren, Chief of Topographical Engineers in the Army of the Potomac, Lee's Lines of the Rappahannock must have seemed scarcely less imposing.[14]

Even before military operations had commenced in 1861, both sides had resorted to earthworks to protect railroad junctions and bridges, military camps, mountain passes or river crossings. Practically every town along a railroad in Missouri was fortified, Kentucky was dotted with intrenched camps where new regiments were assembled and trained, and mountain passes in Kentucky and western Virginia were defended with intrenchments. The purpose of these early works was to guard against surprise, compensate for lack of troops, and perhaps to make the best use of poorly trained soldiers, for Civil War officers were quick to appreciate that "raw troops will more nearly equal the efficiency of trained ones in defending positions than in general field service and active operations."[15] "Place the militia soldier on his natural field of battle, behind a breast work, and an equilibrium between him and his more disciplined enemy is immediately established," Professor D. H. Mahan had taught at West Point, while a current *Hand-book* began a chapter on "Field Fortifications" by defining field works as "any constructions which have for their object to impede the advance of an enemy, or to enable an inferior force to maintain their position against the attack of a superior number."[16]

Several battles had already occurred where earthworks previously had been constructed—First Bull Run, Pea Ridge, and Seven Pines—but for one reason or another had played no role in the fighting. Following their surprise at Shiloh, where neither Grant nor Sherman had ordered the construction of earthworks to protect their camps, the Union forces, now under Halleck, virtually dug their way to Corinth. "Since leaving . . . Shiloh we have occupied and strongly intrenched seven distinct camps," Sherman noted: the men "have sprung to the musket or spades according to the occasion." The purpose of this labor was to enable his men to "hold our camp against any amount of force that can be brought against us." Later in the campaign another Union General instructed a subordinate to throw up intrenchments, "to work upon them as soon as your force is in line and continue the work rapidly. They must be so far completed to-night as to be capable of making a good defense in the morning."[17]

Such works were constructed to defend camps, and thus in purpose— if not in details of construction—they differed from what later became known as "hasty intrenchments."[18] The latter were intended not only to strengthen the defense but also to minimize casualties; often they were constructed in the presence of the enemy, sometimes even under fire. This was the foremost tactical innovation of the Civil War.

Hasty intrenchments as such appear to have been introduced during the battle of Gaines Mill (June 27, 1862), when a line of log breastworks was erected by order of Colonel J. A. Gove, Twenty-second Massachusetts Volunteers. Gove caused a similar barricade to be thrown up by the regiments in front.

> This was scarcely done before the enemy opened a well-directed fire from a battery on this position. Here was tested Colonel Gove's military knowledge and foresight. The shell burst directly in front of the regiment, and many lives would have been lost, if no more serious

consequences involved, had it not been for this barricade. The enemy seemed determined to have this position, for they rained metal enough into this piece of woods to drive out any body of troops were they unprotected. The battery ceased its work for a short time to enable a large body of infantry which they pushed forward to seize this position. They met such a reception that but few lived to tell the tale.[19]

This was not the only Union regiment that utilized "hasty intrenchments" on this occasion, but the attention it attracted in after-action reports suggests a new technique on the battlefield. Ironically Col. Gove was killed trying to rally his troops when neighboring regiments, which had not taken adequate measures to protect themselves, fell back and his position was outflanked. Several days later a similar barricade was constructed at the battle of Fraser's Farm.

No hasty intrenchments were constructed at Second Bull Run, although Jackson's corps utilized an unfinished railroad cut and embankment to serve the same purpose, and at Antietam there was the example of the Bloody Lane, which was described as a "rifle pit" in some Union reports. Although this was due to years of erosion rather than an hour or two of hasty construction, it functioned nicely as a rifle pit until the position was outflanked and enfiladed. Then it looked more like a burial ditch.

Longstreet's rifle-pits and epaulements, which stretched from the river near Taylor's hill as far as south Howison Hill (Stop 4) may have been constructed for the same purpose as Sherman's lines in the approach to Corinth, but after the battle no one could doubt the value of hasty fortifications not only in defending a position but in saving lives. In the Chancellorsville campaign it became almost automatic: when a soldier stopped he dug or felled trees. At Zoan Church Lee, known derisively as the "king of spades" because he employed troops to labor on the Richmond defenses, for the first time ordered the construction of a line of hasty intrenchments as he moved out to meet Hooker, while at Gettysburg a Union corps commander responsible for the defense of Culp's Hill "ordered at once a breastwork of logs to be built, having experienced their benefits at Chancellorsville."[20]

In this respect, at least, what happened at Fredericksburg and particularly at Chancellorsville served as a watershed in the evolution of infantry tactics. After these battles hasty intrenchments—known variously as trenches, rifle-pits, breastworks, or field fortifications—became an active element in battle. A similar evolution occurred with the western armies. In Sherman's view,

> earth-forts, and especially field-works, will hereafter play an important part in wars, because they enable a minor force to hold a superior one in check for a *time*, and time is a most valuable element in all wars. It was one of Prof. Mahan's maxims that the spade was as useful in war as the musket, and to this I will add the axe. . . . When the enemy is intrenched, it becomes absolutely necessary to permit each brigade and division of the troops immediately opposed to throw up a corresponding trench for their own protection in case of a sudden sally. We invariably did this in all our recent campaigns.[21]

* * *

Probably no battle in the Civil War offers the modern soldier as much to think about as Chancellorsville. The battle demonstrates "in the most striking fashion the profound influence of the commander on the battle."[22] The Union committed more soldiers, supplies, money and better equipment than did the Confederacy, and yet Lee won. Today's soldiers, acutely aware of the preponderance of most of these factors facing NATO forces in Europe, are likely to ask "how"?

Why did Hooker lose? His performance reminded one modern soldier of Clausewitz' "very profound" words to the Prussian Crown Prince:

> The minute we begin carrying out our decision a thousand doubts arise about the dangers which might develop if we have been seriously mistaken in our plan. A feeling of uneasiness, which often takes hold of a person about to perform something great, will take possession of us, and from this uneasiness to indecision, and from there to half measures are small, scarcely discernible steps. . . . We cannot take this uncertainty too seriously, and it is important to be prepared for it from the beginning. After we have thought out everything carefully in advance and have sought and found without prejudice the most plausible plan, we must not be ready to abandon it at the first provocation. . . . We must tell ourselves that nothing is accomplished in warfare without daring: that the nature of war certainly does not let us see at all times where we are going; that what is probable will always be probable though at the moment it may not seem so; and finally, that we cannot be readily ruined by a single error if we have made reasonable preparations.[23]

The modern soldier who replays Hooker's decisions from beginning to end during this campaign, especially if he considers alternatives that Hooker should have explored, is almost bound to learn something about his profession.

Both armies displayed fine fighting qualities at the regimental and brigade levels. Some disparities in overall performance can be attributed to assigned missions, leadership, and tactical situations, but both armies performed relatively well at the minor tactical level.

In both battles the Union commander attempted to work his will over a long distance in offensive operations. Thoughtful soldiers ask how much more difficult this is than to conduct a coherent defense. The offensive commander must devise a plan, organize his forces, and then adjust both plan and forces as his subordinates act. Since Burnside and especially Hooker developed plans with some merit but failed to execute properly, modern officers can ask what role the staff and command structures of their armies played in the outcome. This question is especially germane to these two battles because Hooker had both the time and the opportunity to modify the structure he inherited.

And if it is more difficult to control the offensive than the defensive, how can we explain the brilliant success of Lee's army as it drives Hooker back across the Rappahannock? His staff and organization do not appear to be dramatically superior. How then do we account for his superiority? Has his length of time in command allowed him to develop subordinates who can exercise his will even when poorly articulated or attenuated by distance? Obviously he was more successful in making known his intent, but is this the secret of Wilcox's maneuvers throughout the Chancellorsville campaign?

Certainly Wilcox displayed unusual initiative in interpreting the situation confronting him in light of his understanding of the "big picture" — his commander's concept — and then acting on that knowledge. But even at the highest levels both battles are centered on the value of the initiative — how to keep it or, once lost, how to regain it. Burnside inherited a situation in which his army had lost the initiative, and he never really regained it even though he had assumed the offensive in crossing the Rappahannock. In contrast, Hooker enjoyed the initiative until his army began to clear the Wilderness on May 1, but by nightfall he had fallen back to his intrenched lines and the initiative had passed to Lee. When did that loss become irreversible? What actions by each commander caused the initiative to change sides? What, if anything, might Hooker have done to regain it?

There are no definitive answers, but it is essential to ask these and similar questions if our study of the art of war is to have enduring value.

Much has been written about how the industrialization of warfare has expanded the battlefield. At Fredericksburg both armies rested at the end of fairly short rail-based supply lines, so we see the effect of that expansion in the traditional sense in the battle there. The long defensive lines and the massive attacking forces are both impressive.

At Chancellorsville the battlefield expanded in an exciting new way. Using deception, rapid movement, careful planning and meticulous organization, Hooker maneuvered an enormous mass of men, animals, and equipment over long distances—going "off the map" or beyond the bounds of the "expected" battlefield to turn his enemy's position, which is why some soldiers had trouble distinguishing between the battle and the campaign.

By one of the ironies of military history, the "surpriser" was surprised by the same trick—a march to attack a flank. Both armies were willing to risk breaking major elements away from a base to expand the battlefield and gain advantage over their adversary. Modern soldiers must continuously study this fundamental of maneuver warfare.

The modern soldier is trained to use infantry, armor, artillery and aviation in concert, so that the strength of one "combat arm" offsets a weakness of another. The Civil War commanders employed horse, foot, and artillery, but their employment concepts were not built upon explicit recognition of this modern notion. Early in the war they tended to give minor tactical commanders a small force of cavalry and a battery or two of artillery to supplement an infantry formation as an instinctive response to a need that was not well understood.

By 1863, however, both armies were groping toward the realization that melding forces of different capabilities under a single low-level commander dissipated combat power, reduced flexibility, and deprived higher commanders of an ability to use the peculiar capabilities of each arm decisively. Organization reform is but the first step toward resolving this problem, for commanders at the higher levels must learn how to use the new formations to best advantage. Who decides where they should be deployed? When should they be employed? When does control pass from the combined arms commander to the commander of the single combatant arm? Infantry cannot survive all battlefield situations without support from artillery or cavalry, but how is the infantry commander assured of receiving minimal protection from these other arms?

Studying these two battles together lets us see both armies learning from experience—and the innovations of their opponents—as they adopt new organizational structures and learn how to use them.

A soldier can gain greater understanding of modern doctrine by studying old campaigns. *FM 100-5*, for example, states that "to insure success, AirLand Battle doctrine concentrates on—

- Anticipating the enemy.
- Indirect approaches.
- Deception and effective OPSEC.
- Speed and violence.
- Flexibility and reliance on the initiative of junior leaders.
- Rapid decision-making.
- Clearly defined objectives and operational concepts.
- A clearly designated main effort.
- Actions throughout the depth of the battle area.[24]

To read and merely memorize is useless: to reread and meditate is the beginning of understanding; but to follow Lee on May 2 is to see the doctrine come alive.

Lee and Jackson did not see themselves as old soldiers; they considered themselves modern soldiers,[25] and today's officers will quickly learn to identify with them.

Several years ago the authors were among a group of historians at Carlisle Barracks tasked to develop a list of battles in history where one side "had fought outnumbered and won." Obviously Chancellorsville was prominently on the list that dutifully made its way to the Pentagon. None of us had the courage, unfortunately, to point out the obvious: whatever gave Lee the victory, it works best when Hooker is the opposing commander.

1. *The War of the Rebellion: a Compilation of the Official Records of the Union and Confederate Armies* (128 vols., Washington: Government Printing Office, 1887), XIX, Part 2, pp. 626–27.
2. *O.R.*, XIX, Pt. 2, pp. 342–43.
3. *O.R.*, XIX, Pt. 2, p. 485; T. Harry Williams, *Lincoln and his Generals* (New York: Alfred A. Knopf, 1952), pp. 172–74.
4. *O.R.*, XIX, Pt. 1, p. 87.
5. *O.R.*, XIX, Pt. 1, p. 89.
6. Lieut.-Colonel G. F. R. Henderson, *The Campaign of Fredericksburg: A Tactical Study for Officers* (3rd ed., London: Gale and Polden, Ltd., n.d.), p. 2.
7. *O.R.*, VII, p. 161; IX, p. 87.
8. *O.R.*, XIX, Pt. 1, pp. 31, 63–65.
9. *O.R.*, XIX, Pt. 2, pp. 553–4. Although General Orders 184 was issued on November 14, Burnside's proposal to the Chief of Staff was dated November 7.
10. *O.R.*, XIX, Pt. 2, pp. 552–54.
11. *O.R.*, XIX, Pt. 2, pp. 686, 706.
12. *O.R.*, XI, Pt. 1, pp. 107–8.
13. Winston Churchill, *Marlborough: His Life and Times* (2 vols., London: George G. Harrap and Co., Ltd., 1947), II, 838.
14. See Warren's *Report*, below, pp. 121–123, 138, and Chancellorsville Stop 2.
15. *O.R.*, VII, p. 902.
16. D. H. Mahan, *A Complete Treatise on Field Fortifications* (1836, reprinted New York: Greenwood Press, 1968), p. vii; Robert L. Viele, *Hand-book for Active Service* (New York, D. Van Nostrand, 1861), p. 92.
17. *O.R.*, X, Pt. 2, pp. 103, 200, 233–34.
18. Those interested in the subject should read Major Arthur L. Wagner, "Hasty Intrenchments in the War of Secession," *Papers of the Military Historical Society of Massachusetts: Vol. XIII, Civil and Mexican Wars, 1861, 1846* (Boston: 1913), 129–53; Capt. W. C. Johnson and Capt. E. S. Hartshorn, " The Development of Field Fortification in the Civil War," *Professional Memoirs Corps of Engineers, United States Army* VII, (1915), pp. 570–602.
19. *O.R.*, XI, Pt. 2, pp. 301, 304, 175, 188.
20. Milo M. Quaife, ed., *From the Cannon's Mouth: The Civil War Letters of General Alpheus S. Williams* (Detroit: Wayne State University Press, 1959), p. 226.
21. *Memoirs of Gen. W. T. Sherman* (2 vols., New York: Charles L. Webster and Co., 1891), II, 396–97.
22. . Lieutenant General Hamilton H. Howze, "The Battle of Chancellorsville," The Kermit Roosevelt Lecture, May 21, 1962. Howze-Hawkins Family Papers, Archives, p. 33. U.S. Army Military History Institute, Carlisle Barracks, Pa.
23. *Ibid.*, pp. 29–30.
24. *Field Manual No. 100-5* (Washington: Headquarters Department of the Army, May 1986) p. 33.
25. Although the phrase is borrowed from an observation applied to the Greeks by Col. Oliver L. Spaulding in his delightful *Pen and Sword in Greece and Rome* (Princeton: Princeton University Press, 1937), we believe that Col. Spaulding would approve. As director of the Historical Section of the War Plans Division when the section was transferred to the US Army War College, Colonel Spaulding likewise led staff rides to Chancellorsville.

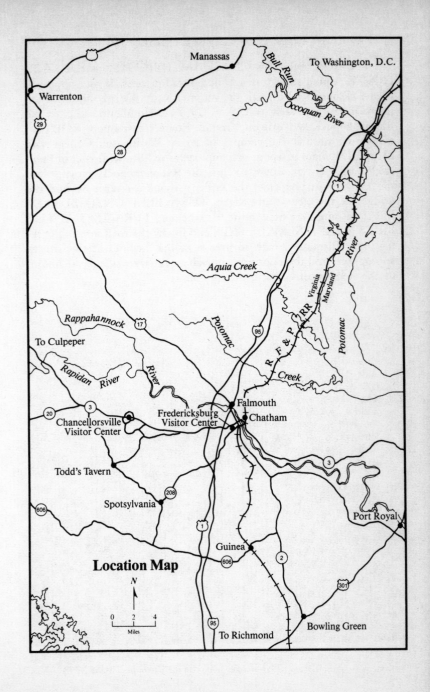

Location Map

N

0   2   4
Miles

The tour begins on **CHATHAM HEIGHTS**, at the **LACY HOUSE**, which served as a Union Headquarters. If you approach Fredericksburg on I-95, exit on Virginia Route 3 eastbound into the town. If you approach on U.S. 17, use I-95, southbound to cross the Rappahannock and exit on Virginia Route 3 eastbound. ROUTE 3 takes you through the campus of Mary Washington College and becomes William Street as you approach the historic district of Fredericksburg. Stay on Route 3 across the Rappahannock, moving into the left lane as you cross the bridge. About 250 yards beyond the bridge, at the next traffic light, **TURN LEFT ONTO BUTLER ROAD** (Route 664). Stay in the left lane, and **TURN LEFT AT THE BROWN PARK SERVICE SIGN** and follow the road into the parking area. Dismount, take advantage of the facilities at this site as appropriate, and then position yourself on the river side of the house, on the steps or terrace near the cannons.

Lacey House, Chatham Manor, the headquarters of Maj. Gen. Sumner. This location had telegraph communications with other key points on the Union lines. (USAMHI)

OBSERVATIONS
FREDERICKSBURG

You are now at CHATHAM MANOR. Known also to Union soldiers as the Lacy House, after its wartime owner, this building served as the headquarters of Major General E. V. Sumner, commanding the Right Grand Division, Army of the Potomac, during the battle of Fredericksburg. Army headquarters was located at the PHILLIPS HOUSE, which then stood on higher ground about a mile to the northeast.

In the Chancellorsville campaign CHATHAM was used briefly as temporary headquarters for subordinate commands and also as a communications center. On May 2 a telegraph line was pushed forward from this house to the headquarters of Major General John Sedgwick, then located across the river in the outskirts of Fredericksburg. Maj. Gen. Joseph Hooker had already moved his headquarters to Chancellorsville, but he was in telegraphic communication with his chief of staff, who remained in camp near Falmouth to coordinate the flow of information, supplies, and the movements of Sedgwick's Left Wing.

At the time of the battle of Fredericksburg the bridge across the Rappahannock has been destroyed, so the river was a major obstacle to the Army of the Potomac. The town beyond was much smaller than modern Fredericksburg, but its buildings could conceal sharpshooters and observers, compounding the difficulties in crossing the river.

Sumner's command had been the first to reach the area, having arrived with 31,000 men on November 17, followed in the next three days by the rest of the Union army. Burnside had hoped to steal a march on *Lee*, whose nearest troops—*Longstreet's* First Corps—were a long two-days march west of Fredericksburg. Had Sumner been permitted to ford the river above Falmouth, off to your right, as requested, he might have seized Fredericksburg and the heights behind the town without a battle. And had the pontoons that Burnside ordered a week before arrived on time, his entire force could still have crossed with little opposition. But the bridges were late, and when the pontoon train finally arrived on November 24, *Longstreet's* entire corps, some 35,000 strong, had also reached the scene and was digging intrenchments along those heights west of town. *Lee's* second corps, commanded by *Lieutenant General "Stonewall" Jackson,* reached the area toward the end of November and was deployed further down stream to guard other places where the Union army might attempt to cross.

A word should be said of the role of Union artillery emplaced along these hills. As you will note from reading Brig. Gen. Henry J. Hunt's report (pp. 8–10 below), each battery has a specific mission. The job of the 38 guns in battery near this house was to provide tactical support to the men building the pontoon bridges that would span the river slightly upstream from this point. As you face Fredericksburg, look carefully to your right. On the far bank stands a prominent brick house, with dormer windows and a grey slate roof. This house did not exist at the time, but the pontoon bridges were anchored just to the left of the house as you view it.

Originally two batteries were dug in on these premises, but when Confederate sharpshooters firing from houses on the opposite bank made it too hot for Union engineers to continue working on the bridges, three additional batteries were moved into position just north of the Chatham house. If you have an eye for such details you may notice the faint remains of one of these emplacements a short distance from the northeast corner of the house. It looks like a slight terrace today; then it offered welcome shelter to at least one gun crew.

STOP 1, THE LACY HOUSE

Report of Maj. Gen. Ambrose E. Burnside, USA,
Commanding the Army of the Potomac

By this time the enemy had concentrated a large force on the opposite side of the river, so that it became necessary to make arrangements to cross in the face of a vigilant and formidable foe. These arrangements were not completed until about December 10. In the mean time the troops were stationed with a view to accumulating supplies and getting in readiness for the movement. . . .

I determined to make preparations to cross the river at Skinker's Neck, about 14 miles below Fredericksburg, and, if the movements of the enemy favored the crossing at that point, to avail myself of such preparations; otherwise, to adopt such a course as his movements rendered necessary. The ground at this point was favorable for crossing, but our preparations attracted the attention of the enemy, after which he made formidable arrangements to meet us at that place.

The necessary orders . . . had been given for the troops to be in readiness to move, with the requisite amount of ammunition and supplies. Before issuing final orders, I concluded that the enemy would be more surprised by a crossing at or near Fredericksburg, where we were making no preparations, than by crossing at Skinker's Neck, and I determined to make the attempt at the former place. . . . Had it been determined to cross at Skinker's Neck, I should have endeavored . . . to have moved in the direction of Guiney's Station, with a view of interrupting the enemy's communications, and forcing him to fight outside his intrenchments. When this intention was abandoned, in consequence of the heavy concentration of the enemy at or near Skinker's Neck, and it had been decided to cross . . . near the town, I hoped to be able to seize some point on the enemy's line near the Massaponax, and thereby separate his forces on the river below from those occupying the . . . ridge in rear of the town. . . .

It was decided to throw four or five pontoon bridges across the river—two at a point near the Lacy house, opposite the upper part of the town, one near the steamboat landing at the lower part of the town, one about a mile below, and, if there were pontoons sufficient, two at the latter point.

Final orders were now given to the commanders of the three grand divisions to concentrate their troops near the places for the proposed bridges; to the chief engineer, to make arrangements to throw the bridges; to the chief quartermaster, to have the trains of the army in such position as not to impede the movement of the troops and at the same time to be in readiness, in case of success, to follow their separate commands with supplies of subsistence stores, forage, and ammunition; to the chief of artillery, to so post his batteries as to cover the working parties while they were constructing the bridges and the army while crossing. . . .

The right grand division (General Sumner's) was directed to concentrate near the upper and middle bridges ; the left grand division (General Franklin's) near the bridges, below the town; the center grand division (General Hooker) near to and in rear of General Sumner. These arrangements were made with a view to throwing the bridges on the morning of December 11. The enemy held possession of the city of Fredericksburg and the . . . ridge running from a point on the river, just above Falmouth, to the Massaponax, some 4 miles below. This ridge was in rear of the city, forming an angle with the Rappahannock. Between the ridge and the river there is a plain, narrow at the point where Fredericksburg stands, but widening out as it approaches the Massaponax. On the north side of the river the high bluffs gave us good opportunities for placing the batteries, which were to command the town and the plain upon which our troops were to move. . . .

During the night of the 10th the bridge material was taken to the proper points on the river, and soon after 3 o'clock on the morning of the 11th the working parties commenced throwing the bridges, protected by infantry placed under cover of the banks, and by artillery on the bluffs above. One of the lower bridges, for General Franklin's command, was completed by 10.30 a.m. without serious trouble, and afterward a second bridge was constructed at the same point. The upper bridge, near the Lacy House, and the middle bridge, near the steamboat landing, were about two-thirds built at 6 a.m., when the enemy opened upon the working parties with musketry with such severity as to cause them to leave the work. Our artillery was unable to silence this fire, the fog being so dense as to make accurate firing impossible. Frequent attempts were made to continue the work, but to no purpose. About noon the fog cleared away, and we were able, with our artillery, to check the fire of the enemy. [*The War of the Rebellion: A Compilation of the Official Records of the Union and Confederate Armies* (129 vols., Washington, D.C.: Government Printing Office, 1887), vol. XXI (hereafter cited as *O.R.* XXI), pp. 87–89.]

Report of Lieut. Cyrus B. Comstock, USA, Corps of Engineers,
Chief Engineer, Army of the Potomac

The following was the programme. . . . Two bridges to be thrown at upper end of Fredericksburg, one at lower end, and two a mile below, making the distance between the extreme bridges nearly 2 miles. Lieutenant Cross, with Engineer Battalion, to throw the lowest bridge of all. General Woodbury's Volunteer Engineer Brigade to throw the others. Each bridge to be covered by artillery and a regiment of infantry. Heads of bridge trains to arrive at bank of river at 3 a.m.; material to be unloaded and boats in the water by daylight, and bridges to be then finished in two or three hours, if not interrupted by the enemy. . . .

Along the highest ground on the left bank . . . and along the edge of the plateau near the river, one hundred and seventy-nine guns were put in position during the night to cover the crossing. The river being sunk 30 feet below the plateau on its two sides, the bridges were covered from artillery fire; the artillery officers believed that they could at once silence any musketry fire from the town, or from the bank opposite the lower bridges.

The heads of bridge trains arrived on the bank of the river about 3 a.m., as proposed. At the bridge thrown by Lieutenant Cross, the material was unloaded, and then moved by hand about 200 yards to the bank of the river. At the bridge just above, the material was unloaded on the bank of the river, 250 yards above the place of the bridge, and floated down. At 8.15 a.m. this bridge was practicable for infantry, and that of Lieutenant Cross half over, when the parties were fired on by two companies of the enemy, who were, however, soon driven away by the fire of the artillery and infantry covering the bridges. . . .

Meanwhile, at Fredericksburg, nearly all the material had been unloaded (a part on the edge of the river and a part on the plateau above, 100 yards from it), and one bridge at the upper and one at the lower end of town were half way across, when, at 6 a.m., a sharp musketry fire was opened on them from houses and other cover in the city, driving the men from the bridges. Our artillery at once opened on the town, and during the morning several unsuccessful attempts were made to go on with the bridges. There had been a thick haze all the morning, often making distinct vision impossible at distances greater than 400 or 500 yards. This lifted before 3 p.m., rendering effective artillery possible. At that time a heavy fire was concentrated on the houses around the bridge heads, and under its cover men were thrown across in pontoons, the enemy's sharp-shooters captured or driven away, and the bridges completed. . . . If it had not been for the haze this might have been effected in the morning. [*O. R.*, XXI, pp. 167–68.]

Report of Brig. Gen. Henry J. Hunt, USA, Chief of Artillery, Army of the Potomac

In order to control the enemy's movements on the plain; to reply to and silence his batteries along the crest of his ridge; to command the town; to cover and protect the throwing of the bridges and the crossing of the troops, and to protect the left flank of the army from attacks in the direction of the Massaponax River, it was necessary to cover the entire length with artillery, posted in such positions as were favorable for these purposes. The Artillery Reserve had been so much reduced by the assignment of batteries to the cavalry brigades and infantry divisions that all the division artillery, except one battery for each, was withdrawn from the troops and temporarily attached to the reserve, which was arranged in four large divisions.

The right, under command of Lieutenant-Colonel Hays . . . extending from Falmouth dam to a deep, long ravine, about 500 yards below Falmouth, consisted of forty rifled guns, of which six were 20-pounder Parrots, and the remainder light rifled guns.

The right center, under the command of Colonel Tompkins, First Rhode Island Artillery, extended from the ravine to near the point assigned for the middle bridge, and consisted of thirty-eight guns—twenty-four light rifles and fourteen light 12-pounders.

The left center, under command of Col. R. O. Tyler, First Connecticut Artillery, consisting of twenty-seven rifled guns, of which seven were 4½-inch siege guns, eight 20-pounder Parrots, and twelve light rifles, occupied the crest of the high ridge, commencing near the middle bridge, and extending to the wooded ravine near the center of the ridge.

The left, under the command of Capt. G. A. De Russy, Fourth US Artillery, consisting of eight 20-pounder Parrotts and thirty-four 3-inch rifles, occupied the remainder of the crest of this high ridge and the whole of the low ridge, terminating at Pollock's Mill.

The right division was charged with the duty of clearing the hills on the south side of the river in front of them, and their slopes, down as far as the town; to engage the enemy's batteries of position on the crests, and to sweep the plain from below the ford to the hills, so as to clear it of the enemy and thus aid the advance of Sumner's grand division in the assault, which in the original plan of battle was intended to be made on the enemy's extreme left.

The right center was directed to protect the throwing of the bridges and to cover the pontoons and workmen by subduing the fire of the enemy's troops from the houses and cover opposite the points selected; to sweep the streets of all columns of re-enforcements; and to destroy any guns that might be placed in position to bear on the bridges.

The left center commanded the ground between Sumner's left and Franklin's right, from Hazel Run to Deep Run, and was specially directed to prevent the enemy from re-enforcing either of his flanks from the other, except by the circuitous route in rear of his position; to sweep the valley of Hazel Run, and to control the railroad bridge across it.

The left division was directed to cover the ground below the lower bridges; to protect the left flank of the army; to assist in covering the workmen employed in throwing the bridges, and to move its light batteries down the river as occasion required, so as to prevent the enemy crossing the Massaponax River and annoying our left. The left center and left divisions were directed to unite their efforts in keeping clear the plain in front of the lower bridge, and in covering the passage of the troops.

Orders were given for all the batteries, first, to concentrate their fire on such of the enemy's works or guns as should open on our masses as they approached the crossing places; second, to turn their fire upon such bodies of the enemy's troops as should offer to oppose the passage; third, to cover the deployment of the troops when across by checking any advance of the enemy; fourth, after the deployment not to fire over the heads of our own troops, except in case of absolute necessity; and, lastly, to aid their advance, when possible to do so, by sweeping the ground in front of them with their fire. These instructions having been carefully communicated, the batteries of the four divisions were ordered to rendezvous. . . . at points [where] the divisions were met by their commanders, who conducted the batteries to their respective positions. The movement commenced at dusk, and by 11 o'clock all were properly posted, without confusion or any noise by which the enemy could learn that a movement had taken place.

On the morning of the 11th, the construction of the bridges commenced before day. Soon after daylight, the upper and middle bridges being about half constructed, a heavy fire of musketry was opened upon them from the opposite bank, which, after considerable loss, drove the engineer troops from their work at both places, notwithstanding the fire from their infantry supports. The batteries were then opened, and partially silenced the fire of the enemy. As the fog was dense and the batteries at a distance, and those on the bluff could not be used safely on the immediate banks of the river, six light 12-pounder batteries (thirty-six guns) were drawn from the divisions and posted on the banks, four near the upper and two near the middle bridges. . . . In this first cannonade no less than five stock-trails of the 12-pounders were broken by the shock of the firing. They were defective, and, it is almost needless to say, contract work, the contractors being Wood Brothers, of New York. A severe cannonade was now opened upon the cover which protected the enemy's sharpshooters, and after this fire was silenced another attempt was made to throw the bridges, but the enemy's skirmishers soon opened again, and, in addition, a column of infantry moved down the principal street toward the water. Miller's battery drove these back, but their sharpshooters succeeded in stopping the work on the bridges, as it was impossible to open with our artillery so long as the pontoniers were at work and the enemy's cover was proof against our infantry fire.

All the batteries that could be brought to bear were now, by order of General Burnside, turned upon the town, and soon rendered it untenable by any considerable body. Again the fire of the enemy's sharpshooters was beaten down by the artillery; the work of throwing the bridges resumed by men who volunteered for the purpose, but with the same results. A few hundred sharpshooters, scattered among the cellars, in ditches, and behind stone walls, drove them from the bridges.

About 2.30 o'clock I proposed to fill the bateaux, not yet in their places in the bridges, with infantry, to make a dash to the opposite side, and, while the troops should land and attack the enemy in his cover, to row the pontoons to their places and complete the bridges. This plan was adopted. [O.R., XXI, pp. 181–83.]

**Report of Col. Charles H. Tompkins, USA, First Rhode Island
Light Artillery, Commanding Right Center Division, Army
of the Potomac**

In accordance with instructions . . . the batteries were placed in
position on the banks of the Rappahannock, opposite Fredericksburg, during the night of the 10th. . . . At 6 a.m., the 11th instant, the
enemy opened fire upon the engineers engaged in throwing across the
upper pontoon bridge from infantry occupying the houses on the
south bank of the river. In accordance with instructions previously
given, Kinzie's, Graham's, Miller's, and Turnbull's batteries opened a
rapid fire for a few moments; then ceased, to enable the engineers to
continue their work. The enemy's fire preventing the engineers at the
upper and center bridges from remaining at work, the batteries covering both bridges continued to fire at intervals until 8 a.m.

At 9 a.m. Battery I, First U.S. Artillery . . . Battery B, First
Rhode Island Light Artillery . . . and Battery G, First New York . . .
reported to me and were placed on the bluff, to the right of the Lacy
house. . . . The fire of the enemy having increased, all the batteries
under my command opened upon the houses occupied by the rebel
sharpshooters, the 12-pounder batteries using solid shot and a few
shell, and the rifled batteries using percussion shell. As some of the
shells from the 12-pounder guns burst short, thereby endangering our
troops on the banks of the river, orders were given these batteries to
confine themselves to the use of solid shot.

At 10 a.m. ceased firing, to enable the engineers to make another
attempt to finish the bridge. . . .

At 11 a.m., the engineers having again been driven from the
bridges, a rapid fire was opened from all the batteries of my command, which continued for about thirty minutes.

At 12.30 I received orders . . . to open a rapid fire along the whole
line, with the object of burning the town. I continued firing solid shot
and shell until 2.30 p.m., at which time several buildings could be
seen burning.

At 3 p.m. a very rapid fire, of some thirty minutes' duration, was
opened to cover the crossing of the Seventh Michigan Regiment at
the upper and the Eighty-ninth New York Regiment at the center
bridges.

The infantry having driven the enemy from the houses they
occupied, the engineers were enabled to finish the bridges, and our
troops immediately commenced crossing, but were fired upon by the

enemy's batteries on the hills beyond the city. I at once ordered the rifled batteries to reply, firing slowly, and to continue until the enemy's fire ceased.

At 7 p.m. Lieutenants Kirby and Gilliss and Captains Frank and Hazard were ordered to report with their batteries to their division commanders.

At 10 a.m., the 12th instant, the enemy opened fire from their works upon our troops who were crossing at the upper and center bridges. I ordered the rifled batteries to reply slowly, and to continue firing until the enemy ceased, which he did at 10.30 o'clock, but continued to fire at intervals during that day whenever our troops were exposed to view. His fire was replied to by these rifled batteries. . . .

No reliance can be placed upon the Bormann fuse. Many of them burst immediately after leaving the gun. I would suggest that an immediate inspection of all ammunition using this fuse be ordered, that it may be ascertained whether the fault is in the construction of the fuse or in the manner in which it is placed in the projectile. [*O.R.*, XXI, pp. 190–92.]

Report of Brig. Gen. Daniel P. Woodbury, USA, Commanding Engineer Brigade, Army of the Potomac

The lower town bridge and one of the upper ones . . . were about two-thirds built at 6 a.m., when the enemy, availing himself of every possible cover, commenced a strong fire of musketry upon the pontoniers and the infantry supports. . . . Our artillery tried in vain to silence this fire, a dense fog making it impossible to distinguish objects on the opposite shore. The work was resumed several times during the morning, without making much further progress.

About 10 o'clock, I led 80 volunteers from the Eighth Connecticut . . . to the scene of operations, placing one-half of them under cover as a reserve. Before the other half touched the bridge, several of them were shot down, and the remainder refused to work. The fog clearing up soon after noon, our artillery fire upon the opposite banks became very effective, and the fire of the enemy was greatly diminished.

About 3 o'clock, preparations were made for sending over men in pontoons, in accordance with the advice of General Hunt.

After another heavy cannonading, about 120 men of the Seventh Michigan, Hall's brigade, crossed over at the upper bridge in six pontoons, rowed each by three men of the Fiftieth [New York Volunteers], Lieutenant Robbins steering the leading boat to the point indicated. One of the oarsmen in this boat was shot down, and the boat was, for a short time, arrested. A few other casualties occurred while the men were passing over. As soon as they reached the opposite bank, they formed, and gallantly rushed to the buildings occupied by the enemy. . . . Other parties rapidly followed, and the bridges were finished without further opposition. Soon afterward, 100 men of the Eighty-ninth New York crossed at the lower town bridge in four pontoons . . . with crews from the Fifteenth New York. Others followed, and the sharpshooters of the enemy who remained were immediately captured. The bridge was soon afterward finished.

I was greatly mortified in the morning to find that the pontoniers under my command would not continue at work until actually shot down. The officers and some of the men showed a willingness to do so, but the majority seemed to think their task a hopeless one. Perhaps I was unreasonable.

It is generally considered a brave feat to cross a bridge of any length under fire, although the time of danger may not last more than a minute or two. How much more difficult to build a bridge exposed for hours to the same murderous fire, the danger increasing as the bridge is extended.

I found a loop-holed block-house, uninjured by our artillery, directly opposite our upper bridges, and only a few yards from their southern abutment. I also found in the neighborhood a rifle-pit behind a stone wall, some 200 feet long, and cellars enclosed by heavy walls, where the enemy could load and fire in almost perfect safety. There were many other secure shelters. [O.R., XXI, pp. 170–71.]

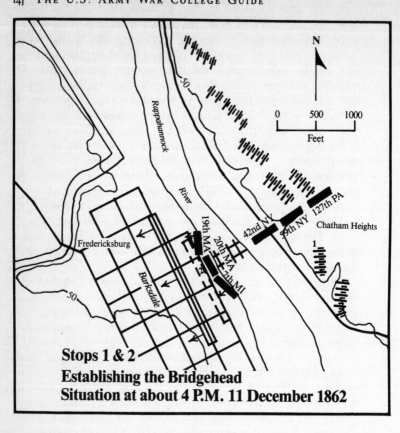

N

0   500   1000
Feet

Rappahannock
River

Fredericksburg

Barksdale

50

50

42nd NY

19th MA
20th MA
7th MI

59th NY   127th PA

Chatham Heights

1

Stops 1 & 2
Establishing the Bridgehead
Situation at about 4 P.M. 11 December 1862

Return to your car. Follow the Park Service signs that direct you back toward the highway. At the STOP sign, TURN LEFT. Drive about 100 yards, then TURN RIGHT ON VIRGINIA ROUTE 3. Cross the bridge and immediately TURN RIGHT ONTO SOPHIA STREET. Drive four blocks to the historical sign on the right. STOP IN FRONT OF THE SIGN.

STOP 2, CROSSING THE RAPPAHANNOCK

You will note from the National Park marker that you are near the point on the river where the pontoons carried the first Union troops into Fredericksburg. Behind you, to your left, on the far side of the street, is a house marked 1312 Sophia Street. This house was here at the time of the battle and it is a reasonably safe bet, given its location, that more than one Confederate sharpshooter fired from its windows.

General Lafayette McLaws' Confederate division was responsible for this sector of Lee's line, and he rotated individual brigades to guard against any attempt to cross the river. On December 11, General Barksdale's Mississippi brigade was on duty when Burnside ordered his army to cross.

The Civil War offers few examples of river crossings under fire or street fighting even in villages: STOP 2 contains rare instances of both.

Report of Col. Norman J. Hall, USA, Seventh Michigan Infantry, commanding Third Brigade, Second Division, Second Army Corps, Army of the Potomac

My command was designated to take the advance of the army, as soon as the bridges should be built. . . . The bridges were not being advanced on account of the deadly fire of the enemy's sharpshooters, posted behind buildings and in cellars and rifle-pits along the opposite bank. Two regiments were deployed (the Seventh Michigan and Nineteenth Massachusetts Volunteers) along the bank of the river to cover the bridge-builders by their fire as skirmishers, but [I] afterward withdrew them, to enable the batteries to fire shell. After some hours of delay, Generals Hunt and Woodbury consulted with me upon the practicability of crossing troops in boats, and storming the strong points occupied by the enemy, so as to protect the heads of the pontoon bridges. . . . It was arranged that, under cover of a heavy artillery fire, the engineers should place boats at intervals along the bank, and provide men to row and steer them.

Lieutenant-Colonel Baxter, commanding Seventh Michigan Volunteers, was informed of the plan, and his regiment volunteered to be crossed and storm the town as proposed. Captain Weymouth, of the Nineteenth Massachusetts, also volunteered to support the Seventh Michigan, if required, crossing in the same way.

The first-named regiment was deployed, and took post along the bank, while the latter lined the river as sharpshooters, together with Captain Plumer's company of sharpshooters (independent), which was ordered to report to me for this object. At a signal, the batteries opened their fire, and continued with great rapidity for over half an hour, the engineer troops failing to perform their part, running away from the boats at the first fire from the enemy and seeking shelter.

No prospect appearing of better conduct, I stated to Colonel Baxter that I saw no hopes of effecting the crossing, unless he could man the oars, place the boats, and push across unassisted. I confess I felt apprehensions of disaster in this attempt, as, without experience in the management of boats, the shore might not be reached promptly, if at all, and the party lost. Colonel Baxter promptly accepted the new conditions, and proceeded immediately to arrange the boats, some of which had to be carried to the water. Lieut. C. B. Comstock, chief engineer . . . directed the embarkation personally. . . . Before the number of boats fixed upon had been loaded, the signal to cease the artillery firing was made, and I thought best to push those now ready across, rather than to wait till all were filled, and to allow the enemy to come out of his concealment from the cannonade.

The boats pushed gallantly across under a sharp fire. While in the boats, 1 man was killed and Lieutenant-Colonel Baxter and several men were wounded. The party, which numbered from 60 to 70 men, formed under the bank and rushed upon the first [Sophia] street, attacked the enemy, and, in the space of a few minutes, 31 prisoners were captured and a secure lodgment effected. Several men were here also wounded, and Lieutenant Emery and 1 man killed. The remainder of the regiment meanwhile crossed, and I directed the Nineteenth Massachusetts to follow and gain ground to the right, while the Seventh was ordered to push to the left. Seeing no preparations for advancing the bridge, which, according to the plan, was to have been under construction when the crossing commenced, I went to the engineer battalion and asked the commanding officer to send down parties at once. He replied that General Woodbury was in command, and was away. I entreated that men should be instantly sent, nevertheless, but could obtain no satisfaction.

The firing in the street had now become general and quite rapid, and as I had been informed that a brigade of the enemy had been seen moving toward the bridge head, I requested General Hunt to reopen fire upon the flanks and in advance of the party which had crossed. I afterward learned from prisoners taken that this brigade of the enemy was *General Barksdale's*. . . . Several prisoners were taken belonging to the Eighth Florida Regiment [*Perry's* Brigade], which was in the city.

All firing upon the bridge had been now silenced, and the bridge was rapidly completed. I reported to General Burnside directly the conduct of the engineer troops. An order for the Twentieth Massachusetts Volunteers to move across the bridge the instant it was down was incorrectly transmitted, so as to cause Acting Major Macy, its commanding officer, to throw it across in boats. This regiment was held in line along the bank to resist any attempts of the enemy to recover this point by an exposed movement, and the Seventh Michigan . . . and the Nineteenth Massachusetts . . . could hold against any advance through buildings.

The moment the bridge was ready, the Forty-second and Fifty-ninth New York Volunteers and the One hundred and twenty-seventh Pennsylvania Volunteers moved across, and the Twentieth Massachusetts was formed in column in the street. The guide, a citizen, was killed at the head of the column. Upon attempting to cross the second [Caroline] street, it became evident that the enemy was in considerable force, and could only be dislodged by desperate fighting. It was fast growing dark, the troops were being crowded near the bridge head in a compact and unmanageable mass, and I was informed that the whole division was to cross to hold the city. It was impracticable, in my opinion, to attempt to relieve the press by throwing troops into the streets, where they could only be shot down, unable to return the fire. To give time to fight the enemy in his own way, I sent urgent requests to the rear to have the column halted on the other side of the river, but was ordered to push ahead. The Seventh and Nineteenth had been brought to a stand, and I ordered Acting Major Macy, commanding the Twentieth Massachusetts, to clear the street [Hawk Street] leading from the bridge at all hazards.

I cannot presume to express all that is due the officers and men of this regiment for the unflinching bravery and splendid discipline shown in the execution of this order. Platoon after platoon was swept away, but the head of the column did not falter. Ninety-seven officers and men were killed or wounded in the space of about 50 yards.

When the edge of the town was reached, the Fifty-Ninth New York was sent to relieve the portion of the Twentieth engaged in the street leading to the left. . . . The positions occupied when the firing was ordered to cease were held till late in the night, when it was found that the enemy had retired from the buildings throughout the town. [*O.R.*, XXI, pp. 282–84.]

Fredericksburg from the east bank of the Rappahannock. (USAMHI)

Report of Lieut. Col. John C. Fiser, CSA, Seventeenth Mississippi Infantry, Barksdale's Brigade, McLaws' Division, First Corps, Army of Northern Virginia.

Being ordered to the city on picket duty, on the 9th instant [I] was ordered to dispose of my regiment so as to guard the river from the ferry to a point about three-quarters of a mile below. I promptly made such disposition as I thought would check the enemy if he attempted to force a passage. . . . The line of pickets consisted of two wings, the right commanded by *Capt. A. R. Govan* and the left by *Capt. A. J. Pulliam.* The reserve I stationed at the markethouse.

About 11 p.m. of the 10th . . . [*Brig. Gen. Barksdale*] ordered me to double my pickets, which was promptly done by sending to the right wing Companies I and K, and to the left Companies H and C, and about 4 a.m. of the 11th instant [he] . . . ordered me with my reserve, consisting of Companies D, E, G, and part of F, to repair at once to the upper ford, as the enemy were rapidly putting in their pontoons preparatory to crossing. I reached the point as soon as possible, and on getting there found the enemy busily working on the bridge, having extended it about 30 feet on the water. . . . I immediately made such disposition of the seven companies as I thought would be most effective. Knowing there were many families occupying the houses on the margin of the river, I deemed it proper to notify all the women and children of their danger and give them time to get from under range of the enemy's guns. This being accomplished, about 5 a.m. I ordered my men to fire on the bridge-builders, which they obeyed promptly and deliberately (and I think with stunning effect), the command being echoed by *Captain Govan* on the right in the same manner and with equal effect, causing the enemy to throw down their implements and quit their work in great confusion, after which they immediately opened a heavy, galling, and concentrated fire of musketry and artillery upon both wings for one hour, and, supposing they had driven us from our position, they again began their work on the bridges; but as soon as we discovered them at work, we renewed the attack and drove them pell-mell from the bridges. They made nine desperate attempts to finish their bridges, but were severely punished and promptly repulsed at every attempt. They used their artillery incessantly with a heavy detachment of sharpshooters for twelve hours, we holding our position firmly the whole time, until about 4.30 p.m., when they increased their artillery and infantry, and, their batteries becoming so numerous and concentrated we could not use our rifles, being deprived of all protection, we were compelled to fall back to Caroline Street, and from there were ordered from town. Having to abandon my position, . . . believing *Captain Govan* still holding the lower bridge, and knowing the enemy to have crossed, I immediately dispatched a courier to notify him to fall back, fearing he would be taken. . . . The casualties in the regiment during the engagement were 116 killed, wounded, and missing. [*O.R.*, XXI, pp. 601–602.]

Report of Capt. A. R. Govan, CSA, Seventeenth Mississippi Infantry, McLaws' Division, First Corps, Army of Northern Virginia

The Florida companies that reported to me on the 11th . . . were ordered into position on my right. The entire command . . . did not constitute 40 men. They were ordered to conform to the movement of the command. The officer in command of said companies failed repeatedly to obey my commands when ordered to fire on the bridge-builders, and so silent was his command that I scarcely knew he was in position. His excuse for not firing was that his position was too much exposed, and firing would draw the fire of artillery. I was informed that the officer was withdrawing his command by 2 o'clock. I passed the order down the line to fall back, which was promptly obeyed. I am convinced that if any were captured it was from inefficiency and from fear of being killed in the retreat. The position was held till sunset. [*O.R.*, XXI, p. 603.]

Report of Col. J. W. Carter, CSA, Thirteenth Mississippi Infantry, Barksdale's Brigade, McLaws' Division, First Corps, Army of Northern Virginia

I was ordered . . . to take position on Caroline Street, await *Lieutenant-Colonel Fiser's* orders, send him re-enforcements whenever he called on me to do so, and, should he be unable to hold his position, then . . . to withdraw my regiment to the market-house. I accordingly took position on Caroline Street, immediately in rear of the position occupied by *Lieutenant-Colonel Fiser,* and opened communication with him, where I remained until about 4 p.m., under a very heavy and destructive [artillery] fire. . . . About 2 p.m. *Lieutenant-Colonel Fiser* asked me for 10 men to act as sharpshooters, which I promptly sent him. About 4 p.m. . . . [he] sent to me for two companies, which I was proceeding with when I met him retiring with his command to the market-house, being unable to hold his position longer. I immediately formed my regiment, and withdrew it to the market-house, when I was ordered . . . to form in the next street (toward the river) and engage the enemy. But before I could do so, I ascertained that the enemy occupied the street on which I was ordered to form, and was advancing. I immediately disposed of my regiment on the street which I then occupied (Princess Anne), so as to command as many streets running at right angles with the river as I possibly could, and engaged the enemy at once, driving him toward the river, after a spirited engagement of two hours. Having fired the last gun at the retreating enemy, I was ordered to withdraw . . . from the town. . . . [O.R., XXI, pp. 600–601.]

Report of Maj. Gen. Lafayette McLaws, CSA, Commanding McLaws' Division, First Corps, Army of Northern Virginia

My division occupied the front of defense from Hazel Run along the ridge of hills to the right and through the point of woods extending into Mr. Alfred Bernard's field, one brigade being in reserve. . . . One brigade was constantly on duty in the city to guard the town and defend the river crossings as far down as a quarter of a mile below Deep Run Creek. Two regiments from *General Anderson's* division picketed the river bank above the town, reporting to the brigadier-general in charge of the brigade on duty in the city. The orders were that two guns should be fired from one of my batteries in a central position, which would be the signal that the enemy were attempting to cross. . . . On that day the brigade of *General Barksdale*, composed of the Mississippi troops, were on duty in the city.

About 2 a.m. on the 11th, *General Barksdale* sent me word that the movements of the enemy indicated they were preparing to lay down their pontoon bridges, and his men were getting into position to defend the crossing. About 4.30 o'clock he notified me that the bridges were being placed, and he would open fire so soon as the working parties came in good range of his rifles. I gave the order, and the signal guns were fired about 5 a.m.

I had been notified . . . the evening previous . . . to have all the batteries harnessed up at daylight on the 11th, and I had given orders that my whole command should be under arms at the same time.

General Barksdale kept his men quiet and concealed until the bridges were so advanced that the working parties were in easy range, when he opened fire with such effect the bridges were abandoned at once. Nine separate and desperate attempts were made to complete the bridges under fire of their sharpshooters and guns on the opposite banks, but every attempt being attended with such severe loss from our men—posted in rifle-pits, in the cellars of the houses along the banks, and from behind whatever offered concealment—that the enemy abandoned their attempts for the time and opened a terrific fire from their numerous batteries. . . . The fire was so severe that the men could not use their rifles, and the different places occupied by them becoming untenable, the troops were withdrawn from the river bank back to Caroline Street at 4.30 p.m. The enemy then crossed in boats, and, completing their bridges, passed over in force and advanced into the town. The Seventeenth Mississippi . . . and 10 sharpshooters from . . . the Thirteenth, and three companies of the Eighteenth Mississippi . . . were all the troops that were actually engaged in defending the crossings in front of the city. More troops were offered, but the positions were such that but the number already there could be employed. As the enemy advanced into the town our troops fell back to Princess Anne Street and as the enemy came up they were driven back, with loss. This street fighting continued until 7 p.m., when I ordered *General Barksdale* to fall back and take position along and behind the stone wall below Marye's Hill, where it was relieved by the brigade of *Brig. Gen. Thomas R. R. Cobb*, and retired to their position—on the right of my line of defense, in the woods of Mr. Bernard.

Lieutenant-Colonel Luse, with . . . the Eighteenth Mississippi, who occupied the river bank below the town, drove back the enemy in their first attempt to cross the river, and kept them in check until about 3.30 p.m. when two regiments (the Sixteenth Georgia . . . and Fifteenth South Carolina) were sent to his support. It was then deemed advisable [to withdraw] . . . the whole force . . . to the river road, where they remained until daylight the next day, when they rejoined their brigades. [*O.R.*, XXI, pp. 578–79.]

Continue on **SOPHIA STREET** to its end and then **TURN LEFT** on **PITT STREET**. Drive two blocks. **TURN LEFT ON PRINCESS ANNE STREET**. Drive ten blocks and **TURN RIGHT** onto **LAFAYETTE BOULEVARD** (Business Route U.S. 1). Drive about 1.3 miles and **TURN LEFT** onto **LEE DRIVE** at the Park Service sign. Drive 0.2 mile and park in the parking lot on the right side of the road at **LEE'S HILL**. Dismount and follow the asphalt trail to the exhibits at *General Lee's* command post at the top of the hill. You may discern trenches and a gun position dug into the hillside on your right as you approach the crest. Position yourself in front of the visitors' shelter where you can get an overview of the field. The area visible from this viewpoint is downstream from Fredericksburg.

STOP 3, LEE'S HILL

You are now facing the battlefield. Across the river is STAFFORD HEIGHTS, which from here blends into the high ground a mile or more beyond and is difficult to identify because of the heavy woods that now cover the former treeless slopes then crowned with Union artillery. Then you would also have seen an observation balloon near the water tower beyond the river—in the vicinity of the Phillips House, where Burnside maintained his headquarters.

The view today, especially in the summer months, is disappointing because of the dense foliage, but in December 1862 Confederate officers standing nearby enjoyed "the grandest panorama of a battlefield ever seen." Although portions of the city and of Marye's Heights were not visible then, Sumner's troops, which came within plain view as they moved out of Fredericksburg, were well within range of rifled field guns—and especially of the 30 pounder Parrott rifle to your right, which could throw a shell over 8,000 yards.

Then it was also possible to observe from here the full sweep of Franklin's Left Grand Division as it advanced majestically against *Jackson's* front, to your right, and it was from here that *Lee*, surveying the movement of the miniature figures on the plain below, mused that "it is well that war is so terrible—we should grow too fond of it."

Throughout the day *Lee* received reports, chatted with his generals, and occasionally gave an order. Even here he was not immune to enemy fire. One Union shell penetrated the parapet at *Lee's* side—perhaps the very one that still shelters the Confederate gun—but failed to explode. The 30 pounder Parrott did explode in firing its 39th round, but although *Lee* and his chief of artillery were standing only ten feet away at the time, none was touched by the flying fragments.

If upon leaving this site you wish to see gun emplacements in a better "state of nature," simply stay on the high ground to the left of the park walk. Within a hundred yards or less you will come upon similar emplacements, protected in front by rifle pits thrown up by *Kershaw's* South Carolinians before they were ordered, the day before the battle, to move from the top of Lee's Hill to the base. [*O.R.*, XXI, p. 595.] From here simply head downhill to rejoin the park walk and return to your car.

Report of General R. E. Lee, CSA, Commanding Army of Northern Virginia

On November 15, [1862] it was known that the enemy was in motion toward the Orange and Alexandria Railroad, and one regiment of infantry, with a battery of light artillery, was sent to reenforce the garrison at Fredericksburg.

On the 17th, it was ascertained that Sumner's corps had marched from Catlett's Station in the direction of Falmouth, and information was also received that on the 15th some Federal gunboats and transports had entered Aquia Creek. This looked as if Fredericksburg was again to be occupied, and *McLaws'* and *Ransom's* divisions, accompanied by *W. H. F. Lee's* brigade of cavalry and *Lane's* battery, were ordered to proceed to that city. To ascertain more fully the movements of the enemy, *General Stuart* was directed to cross the Rappahannock. . . . The information he obtained confirmed the previous reports, and it was clear that the whole Federal Army . . . was moving toward Fredericksburg.

On the morning of the 19th, therefore, the remainder of *Longstreet's* corps was put in motion for that point.

The advance of General Sumner reached Falmouth on the afternoon of the 17th, and attempted to cross the Rappahannock, but was driven back by *Colonel [William B.] Ball* with the Fifteenth Virginia Cavalry, four companies of Mississippi infantry, and *[Capt. J. W.] Lewis'* light battery.

On the 21st, it became apparent that General Burnside was concentrating his whole army on the north side of the Rappahannock. On the same day, General Sumner summoned the corporate authorities of Fredericksburg to surrender the place by 5 p.m., and threatened, in case of refusal, to bombard the city at 9 o'clock next morning. The weather had been tempestuous for two days, and a storm was raging at the time of the summons. It was impossible to prevent the execution of the threat to shell the city as it was completely exposed to the batteries on the Stafford Hills, which were beyond our reach. The city authorities were informed that, while our forces would not use the place for military purposes, its occupation by the enemy would be resisted, and directions were given for the removal of the women and children as rapidly as possible. The threatened bombardment did not take place, but, in view of the imminence of a collision between the two armies, the inhabitants were advised to leave the city, and almost the entire population, without a murmur, abandoned their homes. . . . The citizens of Fredericksburg. . . . cheerfully incurred great hardships and privations, and surrendered their homes and property to destruction rather than yield them into the hands of the enemies of their country.

General Burnside now commenced his preparations to force the passage of the Rappahannock and advance upon Richmond. When his army first began to move toward Fredericksburg, *General Jackson*, in pursuance of instructions, crossed the Blue Ridge [from the Shenandoah Valley] and placed his corps in the vicinity of Orange Court-House, to enable him more promptly to co-operate with *Longstreet*.

About November 26, he was directed to advance toward Fredericksburg, and, as some Federal gunboats had appeared in the river at Port Royal, and it was possible that an attempt might be made to cross in that vicinity, *D. H. Hill's* division was stationed near that place, and the rest of *Jackson's* corps so disposed as to support *Hill* or *Longstreet*, as occasion might require. The fords of the Rappahannock above Fredericksburg were closely guarded by our cavalry, and the brigade of *General W. H. F. Lee* was stationed near Port Royal, to watch the river above and below. . . .

On December 5, *General D. H. Hill*, with some of his field guns, assisted by *Major Pelham*, of *Stuart's* Horse Artillery, attacked the gunboats at Port Royal and caused them to retire. With these exceptions, no important movement took place, but it became evident that the advance of the enemy would not be long delayed. The interval was employed in strengthening our lines, extending from the river about 1½ miles above Fredericksburg along the range of hills in the rear of the city to the Richmond railroad. As these hills were commanded by the opposite heights in possession of the enemy, earthworks were constructed upon their crest at the most eligible positions for artillery. These positions were judiciously chosen and fortified under the direction of *Brigadier-General Pendleton*, chief of artillery;

Colonel Cabell, of *McLaws'* division; *Col. E. P. Alexander,* and *Capt. S. R. Johnston,* of the engineers. To prevent gunboats from ascending the river, a battery, protected by intrenchments, was placed on the bank, about 4 miles below the city, in an excellent position, selected by my aide-de-camp, *Major Talcott.*

The plain of Fredericksburg is so completely commanded by the Stafford Heights that no effectual opposition could be made to the construction of bridges or the passage of the river without exposing our troops to the destructive fire of the numerous batteries of the enemy. At the same time the narrowness of the Rappahannock, its winding course, and deep bed presented opportunities for laying down bridges at points secure from the fire of our artillery. Our position was, therefore, selected with a view to resist the enemy's advance after crossing, and the river was guarded only by a force sufficient to impede his movements until the army could be concentrated. . . .

During the night [of December 11] and the succeeding day the enemy crossed in large numbers at and below the town, secured from material interruption by a dense fog. Our artillery could only be used with effect when the occasional clearing of the mist rendered his columns visible. His batteries on the Stafford Heights fired at intervals upon our position.

Longstreet's corps constituted our left. . . . [*O.R.,* XXI, pp. 550-52.]

Report of Brig. Gen. William N. Pendleton, CSA, Chief of Artillery, Army of Northern Virginia

On Sunday, the 23d, I had arrived with the trains, reported at general headquarters, and located camps, as directed.

The next morning, as requested by the commanding general, I proceeded to the front, for the purpose of observing the dispositions of the enemy and examining the ground, with a view to the best positions for works and batteries. The enemy . . . . had batteries in position, and were in a few places beginning earthworks. On our own line a few hurried works were in progress. *Lane's* battery was already well posted on the heights overhanging the river bend above Falmouth and forming our extreme left. [Artillery] epaulements had been thrown up, but they needed much additional work. *Lewis'* and *Grandy's* batteries, recently called from Richmond . . . were also in position on the lower plateau, about half a mile to the right of *Lane* and nearer the town. These needed for their protection much additional labor. . . .

On the 29th, *Lieutenant Anderson*, of *Ells'* battery near Richmond, reported the arrival of men and horses with two 30-pounder Parrott guns, which . . . the commanding general had ordered up to the lines. Measures were promptly taken to have them tested and to fit them in all respects for service.

December 1, I was diligently engaged in examining again the whole line, with reference to the best positions for these two large guns, facility of ingress and egress being important for them as well as extensive command of the field. The points selected were reported to the commanding general . . . and on his approval the sites were next day pointed out, working parties engaged, clearings commenced, etc. The work on the right and back of Mr. Howison's house was directed by . . . *General Thomas R. R. Cobb*; that on the eminence farther to the left and near the Telegraph Road [Lee's Hill], was staked off and directed by myself. This point, densely wooded when first chosen, became the most important, perhaps, in the entire scene as the position affording the best view of all the field, and, therefore, principally occupied by the commanding general and other chief officers during the battle. . . . Here I remained . . . watching the struggle near and remote, occasionally directing the fire of the large gun, and from time to time receiving instructions from the commanding general concerning movements of batteries and other arrangements. This large Parrott, having been used some hours with terrible effect upon the enemy—especially when, driven back by an intolerable fire from Marye's Hill, they crowded into the deep railroad cut which it enfiladed—burst about the thirty-ninth discharge . . . Although many persons were standing near (among them the commanding general and *Lieutenant General Longstreet* . . .), by a remarkable Providence, the explosion was entirely harmless. Not a single individual received from it so much as a scratch. [*O.R.*, XXI, pp. 563–64. For the sake of consistency and to enhance readability, the First Person in Pendleton's report has been substituted for "the undersigned" whenever appropriate.]

Narrative of Capt. Robert Stiles, CSA, Richmond Howitzers

We were stationed on what was afterwards known as "Lee's Hill," an elevation centrally located between the right and left flanks of our line, and jutting out at quite a commanding height into and above the plain. For these reasons *General Lee* made it, for the most part, his field headquarters during the fight. Portions of the city and of Marye's Heights were not visible, at least not thoroughly so; but every other part of the field was, clear away down, or nearly down, to Hamilton's Crossing. From it we witnessed the break in our lines on the right, where the Federals came in over a piece of marshy ground, supposed to be impassable. . . . The entire attack, from its inception to its unexpected success, was as clearly defined as a movement on a chessboard. . . . [Robert Stiles, *Four Years under Marse Robert* (Washington, 1903), pp. 134–35.]

Return to your car. Continue on LEE DRIVE about 0.5 mile. Park in the parking area on the right side of the road. Dismount and follow the path up to the artillery position. As you approach the battery, note the sign showing the fields of fire for the artillery of the entire Confederate defense.

STOP 4, HOWISON'S HILL

The breastworks that you have seen since the previous stop were constructed shortly before the battle: they are mentioned specifically in after-action reports and were occupied much of the day by troops of *McLaws'* division. This position was never assaulted during the battle of Fredericksburg, but the fact that this sector was fortified enabled *Longstreet* to thin his ranks here in order to reinforce troops defending the stone wall in front of Marye's Heights.

During the *second* battle of Fredericksburg, May 3, 1863, a column of three regiments from Howe's division, Sixth Army Corps, assaulted these works after the other two columns had veered to the right to storm Marye's hill. *Carlton's* battery from *Cabell's* battalion occupied these particular gun pits while *Fraser's* Georgia Battery supported the Confederate line from Lee's hill. Both fired "a very large amount of ammunition of short-range shell and canister" at the Union infantry advancing rapidly across Howison's farm from the crest of the railroad, but once Union forces had seized Marye's hill Confederates on this part of the line were in "imminent danger of being flanked" and the infantry fell back, followed by the two batteries. [*O.R.*, XXV, pp. 599, 842.]

All remnants of trenches and breastworks that you will see from this point until you reach STOP 6, near Hamilton's Crossing, were constructed in the days *after* the battle. The divisions of *Pickett* and *Hood*, which had been stretched dangerously thin before the arrival of *Jackson's* corps enabled *Longstreet* to consolidate his position, utilized existing ditches, fences, rails and road cuts for protection. The ground was frozen, tools for intrenching were scarce, and they scarcely had enough time to improve their position. *Hood's* division had probably been kept busy constructing the military road that ran behind the Confederate lines—a strong defensive measure in itself, since it would enable *Lee* to shift entire divisions back and forth to meet the pressure wherever it was excessive.

Once you cross the intersection after STOP 5, the park road roughly approximates *Hood's* military road.

Report of Lieut. Gen. James Longstreet, CSA, Commanding First Army Corps, Army of Northern Virginia

Upon my arrival at Fredericksburg, on November 19, the troops of this command were assigned to positions as follows, viz: *McLaws'* division upon the heights immediately behind the city and south of the Telegraph Road; *Anderson's* division on *McLaws'* left, and occupying the heights as far as Taylor's Hill, on the Rappahannock; *Pickett's* division on *McLaws'* right, and extending to the rear along the margin of the wood which skirts Deep Run Valley; *Hood's* division near Hamilton's Crossing of the railroad; *Ransom's* division in reserve near my headquarters. Our batteries were assigned positions along the heights by *General Pendleton, Colonels Cabell* and *Alexander*, and *Captain Johnston, Colonel Walton* being absent sick. Pits were made for the protection of the batteries under the supervision of these officers. A portion of *General Pendleton's* reserve artillery was assigned to the heights with *Major-General McLaws'* division. *Colonel Walton's* Washington Artillery occupied the heights at Marye's Hill, and a portion of *Colonel Alexander's* reserve occupied the other portion of *Anderson's* front, extending to the Taylor house, on our left. The brigade batteries that were not assigned to positions on the heights were held in readiness . . . for any . . . service that might be required of them. . . .

Upon the approach of *General Jackson's* army, *Hood's* division was closed in upon the right of *Pickett*, and put in position upon the heights on the opposite side of Deep Run Valley. In addition to the natural strength of the position, ditches, stone fences, and road cuts were found along different portions of the line, and parts of *General McLaws'* line were further strengthened by rifle trenches and abatis. . . . [*O.R.*, XXI, pp. 568–70.]

Report of Maj. Gen. Lafayette McLaws, CSA, Commanding McLaws' Division, First Army Corps, Army of Northern Virginia.

My division occupied the front of defense from Hazel Run along the ridge of hills to the right and through the point of woods extending into Mr. Alfred Bernard's field, one brigade being in reserve. The brigade on the left had an extended rifle-pit at the foot of the main ridge, from the left of the Telegraph Road to a private road near Mr. Howison's barn. The next brigade had rifle-pits along the foot of the hills in front of its position, and others on the crest of the hills. The right brigade constructed rifle-pits and breastworks of logs through the woods, with abatis in front of them. The crests of the hills were occupied by the batteries of *Captain Read*, one 10-pounder Parrott, one 12-pounder howitzer, one 3-inch rifle; *Captain Manly*, three 6-pounders, one 3-inch rifle, two 12-pounder howitzers; *Captain Ells*, one 30-pounder Parrott; *Captain Macon*, two 10-pounder Parrotts and two 6-pounders, *[Capt.] R. L. Cooper*, three 10-pounder Parrotts; *[Capt. Henry H.] Carlton*, two 10-pounder Parrotts; *[Capt. John L.] Eubank*, one 3-inch rifle; *[Capt. E. S.] McCarthy*, two 3-inch rifles; *[Capt. James] Dearing*, one 10-pounder Parrott; *[Capt. H. M.] Ross*, three 10-pounder Parrotts, and, in addition, there was a number of smooth-bore pieces placed along the hills, to be used should the enemy advance near enough for their effectual range. [*O.R.*, XXI, p. 578.]

Col. Henry C. Cabell, Chief of Artillery, *McLaws'* Division, stated that "one of the 30-pounder guns was placed" next to *Read's* battery on Lee's Hill. Both 30-pounders "did good service but exploded during the engagement." (*Ibid.*, p. 587) The breastworks along this portion of the Confederate line were built and initially occupied by *Kershaw's* brigade, which extended along the park drive from the left of Howison's Hill to a point near Howison's Mill on Hazel Run. Throughout the night of December 12 *Kershaw's* men labored on these earthworks and rifle-pits, which they finished and occupied about 8 o'clock on the morning of the battle. A few hours later *Kershaw's* command was ordered to move by the left flank "down the earthworks into the Telegraph road, then down the Telegraph road near the [Howison] mill on [Hazel Run] creek, and then up the newly made road to the top of the hill, just in rear of the cemetery" to support *Cobb's* brigade at the Sunken Road. (*Ibid.*, pp. 580, 588, 595, 597.)

Return to your car. Continue down LEE DRIVE about 0.8 mile. Turn left into the picnic area. Park there, walk to the back of the loop, and then follow the trail back into the woods about 100 feet. You will see artillery epaulements on your right front and a trench on your left front. If you wish, you can follow the trench about 250 feet to another gun position.

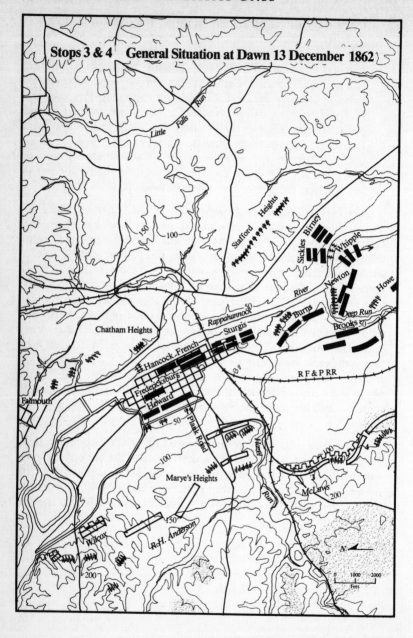

Stops 3 & 4   General Situation at Dawn 13 December 1862

STOP 5, PICKETT'S POSITION

This portion of the Confederate line, which was not fortified at the time of the battle, was occupied by *Maj. Gen. George E. Pickett's* division. Here there was no fighting, for although *Pickett* had been ordered to support *Maj. Gen. John B. Hood's* division, which was to strike the right flank of the Union column moving forward to attack *Jackson's* line "when an opportunity offered," Meade's assault "did not appear to have all the force of a real attack . . . and *General Hood* did not feel authorized to make more than a partial advance." [See STOP 10 for details.]

About 2 a.m., when it became apparent that the attack against the Confederate right had subsided, *Longstreet* directed *Pickett* to send two brigades to the left to reinforce threatened portions of his line. *Kemper's* brigade was placed "in close supporting distance of the crest" of Marye's hill, while *Jenkins'* brigade was ordered to *McLaws* to replace *Kershaw's* brigade, which had advanced to help defend the stone wall at the base of Marye's heights. [*O.R.*, XXI, pp. 570, 580.]

The breastworks that remain beyond the far end of the circle were probably erected during the evening of December 13, for that night *Lee* ordered his troops to construct earthworks at exposed positions. By the morning of December 14 the Confederate commander could claim that his army "is as much stronger for these new entrenchments as if I had received reinforcements of 20,000 men." "We were so well prepared," *Longstreet* recalled "that we became anxious . . . lest General Burnside would not come again." The brigades of *Kemper* and *Jenkins* returned to *Pickett's* front on the night of 14 December, where they joined the rest of the division in taking advantage of "a brilliant aurora" that illuminated the night to further strengthen these earthworks. [General E. P. Alexander, "The Battle of Fredericksburg," *Southern Historical Society Papers*, X (January-December, 1882), p. 461; Douglas Southall Freeman, *R.E. Lee: a Biography* (4 vols., New York: Charles Scribner's Sons, 1936), II, p. 468; James Longstreet, *From Manassas to Appomattox* (Bloomington, Indiana: Indiana University Press, 1960), p. 316.]

In the ensuing weeks Confederate soldiers continued to work "as busy as beavers" along this front all the way from Banks' Ford to Port Royal, a distance of some 20 miles. When *Captain A. S. Pendleton* rode along this line a month or two later, trenches and redoubts were in view everywhere. "The World has never seen such a fortified line," he explained in a letter to his mother. "The trenches are five feet wide and two feet deep, having the earth thrown towards the enemy, making a bank still higher. [W. G. Bean, *Stonewall's Man: Sandie Pendleton* (Chapel Hill: The University of North Carolina Press, 1959) p. 102.]

In these efforts *General Longstreet* appears to have emerged as *the* authority in *Lee's* army on the art of field fortification: at least his counterpart, *'Stonewall' Jackson*, thought enough of his expertise to solicit his views on how best to solve a problem that he faced in fortifying his old position at Fredericksburg, eliciting this response:

Headquarters Army of Northern Virginia
January 18, 1863

Your note of yesterday was received last night. I did not express my idea clearly to you. The problem that you speak of is the one that I was trying to solve. It occurred to me that we might protect our men along your line of rifle trenches from the flank fire of the batteries that the enemy might place on your right, by good traverses for that purpose, with a good traverse on the right flank of each pit. I think the men might be perfectly secure from any fire from that direction, particularly as it seems (from my recollection of the field) that the enemy could not use the battery against our right flank after he began to cross his troops. . . . I did not observe the field with this view when I was on it, and may be mistaken in my idea that the enemy where he attempts to cross would also be under the shells of his battery that he might place on the right flank of your line of rifle trenches. . . .

I am almost convinced that the enemy will not make another effort against our line before spring. The relative condition of the two armies would not warrant any such effort on his part. Our line is stronger now than it was when he advanced before. Even with the two brigades that I have sent off and your two gone, we shall be much stronger, in position, than we were before. He cannot be as strong in numbers, and he must be exceedingly weak in *morale*. I shall send a brigade to the United States Ford tomorrow. With that, strengthened by earthworks, I think that we will be secure against attack.

Very respectfully, your obedient servant

James Longstreet
Lieutenant-General, Commanding.
[*O.R.*, XXI, pp. 1095–96.]

Return to your car. Drive back out to the STOP sign on LEE DRIVE. TURN LEFT. You will now follow LEE DRIVE about 3.2 miles to HAMILTON'S CROSSING. At about 1.1 miles in this drive you will come to a STOP sign. Continue straight ahead on LEE DRIVE. When you reach the gun position at HAMILTON'S CROSSING, park in the parking lot on the right side of the road. Dismount and position yourself near the map and signs behind the guns.

STOP 6, HAMILTON'S CROSSING

This is Hamilton's Crossing, the right of the Confederate line. It was initially occupied by *Hood's* division, and because then "little probability of attack had been foreseen. . . . *Hood* made but two works of preparation. On the edge of the woods, overlooking the railroad, a trench had been dug long enough to hold a brigade and a half; and through the thick wood 500 yards in the rear, a road had been cleared, affording communication behind the general line which occupied the wooded hills." [General E. P. Alexander, *Military Memoirs of a Confederate* (Bloomington: Indiana University Press, 1962), p. 294.]

As you drive back along this road, you may occasionally notice segments of the trace of Hood's military road to your left.

When it became apparent that there would be a battle, *Hood's* division was shifted about a mile to the left and *Lieutenant General T. J. Jackson's* corps moved in. From the appearance of the earthworks overlooking the railroad, this must have been *Hood's* original line. There is no mention in any of the official reports, Union or Confederate, of artillery being dug in on this crest during the battle, and in view of specific orders to keep the guns concealed from Union artillery across the river, it is unlikely that Confederate gunners did much more than move up to *Hood's* breastworks when about to engage. According to *Jackson's* topographical engineer, the day *after* the battle "*Capt. Boswell*, of the Engineers, dug pits on our right for sunken batteries." Artillery elsewhere on this battlefield occupied individual pits or epaulements: here it would seem that *Boswell's* engineers were able to adapt *Hood's* trenches to their needs. [Archie P. McDonald, ed., *Make me a Map of the Valley: The Civil War Journal of Stonewall Jackson's Topographer* (Dallas: Southern Methodist University Press, 1973), p. 101.]

Report of Lieut. Gen. Thomas J. Jackson, CSA, Commanding
Second Army Corps, Army of Northern Virginia

In pursuance to orders, *Maj. Gen. A. P. Hill* moved his division at dawn on the morning of the 12th from his encampment, near Yerby's, and relieved *Major-General Hood*, then posted near Hamilton's Crossing. At the same time *Brigadier-General [William B.] Taliaferro*, then in command of *Jackson's* division, moved from his encampment above Guiney's Depot, and took position in rear of *Maj. Gen. A. P. Hill.*

Early on the morning of the 13th, *Ewell's* division, under command of *Brig. Gen. J. A. Early*, and *Maj. Gen. D. H. Hill*, with his division, arrived, after a severe night's march, from their respective encampments in the vicinity of Buckner's Neck and Port Royal, the troops of *Maj. Gen. D. H. Hill* being from 15 to 18 miles distant from the point to which they were ordered.

On the morning of that day the troops were arranged as follows: *Maj. Gen. A. P. Hill* occupied the front line, formed of two regiments of *Field's* brigade, commanded by *Colonel Brockenbrough*, and the brigades of *Archer, Lane,* and *Pender* (posted from right to left in the order named), his right resting on the road leading from Hamilton's Crossing to the Port Royal road, and his left extending to within a short distance of Deep Run. These troops were partially concealed by the wood, near the edge of which they were posted. The remainder of *Brockenbrough's* command . . . was immediately in rear of *Walker's* batteries, and acting as a support to them. Of the other two brigades, *Gregg's* and *Thomas',* of the same division, the first was in rear of the interval between *Archer* and *Lane*, and the second in rear of the interval between *Lane* and *Pender.* The divisions under *Generals Early* and *Taliaferro* formed the second line, *Early* being on the right. The division of *Maj. Gen. D. H. Hill*, which was still farther in rear, constituted the reserve.

Upon the eminence immediately to the right, *Lieutenant-Colonel [R.L.] Walker (Maj. Gen. A. P. Hill's* chief of artillery) had in position fourteen guns, composed of the batteries of *Pegram* and *McIntosh*, with sections from the batteries of *Crenshaw, Latham,* and *Johnson.* . . . On the left of the line, and near the Bernard cabins, were posted twenty-one guns, of the batteries of *Captains Davidson, Raine, Caskie,* and *Braxton*, all under the immediate direction of *Captain Davidson.* To the right and some 200 yards in front of these, and beyond the railroad, were posted twelve guns, from the batteries of *Captains Carpenter, Wooding,* and *Braxton*, under the direction of *Captain*

Brockenbrough, General Taliaferro's chief of artillery. . . . On my left was *Major-General Hood*, of *Longstreet's* corps, and on my right and front the cavalry, under command of *Major-General [J.E.B.] Stuart*, with a battery near the Port Royal road, under the direction of *Major [John] Pelham*, of the *Stuart* Horse Artillery, aided in the course of the day by sections of the batteries of *Captain Poague . . . Capts. David Watson, B. H. Smith, Jr., [A.W.] Garber, [Willis, J.] Dance*, and the Louisiana Guards, of my corps, thrown into position so as to cross their fire with the guns of *Lieutenant-Colonel Walker*, and designed to check the advance of the enemy in that direction.

About 10 o'clock, as the fog disappeared, the lines of the enemy, arranged in order of battle, were distinctly visible in the plain between us and the river, covering my front and extending far to the left toward Fredericksburg. The force in front of me I supposed to number about 55,000. *Pelham*, with part of the *Stuart* Horse Artillery, was soon engaged with the artillery of the enemy, and a brisk and animated contest was kept up for about an hour. Soon after *Pelham*, in obedience to orders, had withdrawn from his position on the Port Royal road, the enemy directed his artillery on the heights, held by *Lieutenant-Colonel Walker*, and upon the wood generally occupied by our troops, evidently with a view of causing us to disclose whatever troops or artillery were there. Not eliciting any response, the enemy was seemingly satisfied that he would experience but little resistance to an effort to obtain possession of this hill.

Accordingly, about 11 o'clock, he advanced by the flank parallel to the Port Royal road nearly to the road running from thence to Hamilton's Crossing, now unimpeded in his march, as *Pelham* was withdrawn. Facing to the front, he advanced in line of battle across the plain, straight upon the position occupied by *Walker*. His batteries reserved their fire until the enemy's lines came within less than 800 yards, when the fourteen guns opened, pouring such a storm of shot and shell into his ranks as to cause him first to halt, then to waver, and at last seek shelter by flight.

About 1 o'clock, the main attack was made by heavy and rapid discharges of artillery. Under the protection of this warm and well-directed fire, his infantry in heavy force advanced, seeking the partial protection of a piece of wood extending beyond the railroad.

The woods mentioned by *Jackson* can still be seen to your left, across the railroad tracks and beyond the large stone pyramid, which was erected about 30 years after the battle to mark the general area where Meade's Union division broke through the gap in *Jackson's* first line.

The batteries on the right played on their ranks with destructive effect. The advancing force was visibly staggered by our rapid and well-directed artillery, but, soon recovering from the shock, the Federal troops . . . continued to press forward. Advancing within point-blank range of our infantry, and thus exposed to the murderous fire of musketry and artillery, the struggle became fierce and sanguinary.

They continued, however, still to press forward, and before *General A. P. Hill* closed the interval which he had left between *Archer* and *Lane,* it was penetrated, and the enemy, pressing forward in overwhelming numbers through that interval, turned *Lane's* right and *Archer's* left. Thus attacked in front and rear, the Fourteenth Tennessee and Nineteenth Georgia, of *Archer's* brigade, and the entire brigade of *Lane* fell back, but not until after a brave and obstinate resistance. Notwithstanding the perilous situation in which *Archer's* brigade was placed, his right, changing front, continued to struggle with undaunted firmness, materially checking the advance of the enemy until re-enforcements came to its support. The brigade of *General Thomas* . . . moved gallantly forward, and, joined by the Seventh and part of the Eighteenth North Carolina, of *Lane's* brigade, gallantly drove back a Federal column which had broken through *Lane's* line. [*O.R.,* XXI, pp. 630–32.]

Report of Col. S. Crutchfield, CSA, Chief of Artillery, Second Army Corps, Army of Northern Virginia

The heights on the right of our line were held by fourteen guns of the batteries of *Maj. Gen. A. P. Hill's* division, under *Lieut. Col. R. L. Walker.* . . . The position was a commanding one and afforded admirable advantages against a direct assault from infantry; but, what was more important, so controlled the ground in front as to force the enemy to open a heavy cannonade upon it in hopes of silencing these batteries before they could move any considerable mass of their infantry down the plain, as would be necessary should they endeavor to turn our right. On the other hand, it was liable to the disadvantages always attaching to a fixed position, that it must receive a concentrated fire from many points, added to which the formation of the ground at the top of the hill was such as not to afford much protection to men and hardly any to horses. It was, of course, a position of great importance, and it being specially necessary that its batteries should be able to open an effective fire upon the enemy's infantry in the plain below should they endeavor to move down the river to threaten or turn our right, I directed *Lieutenant Colonel Walker* to keep his guns concealed as well as he could, and not to allow himself to be drawn into an artillery duel, but, disregarding the fire of the enemy's batteries, to reserve his own for their infantry when it should come within effective range. . . .

The enemy, after furiously cannonading *Lieutenant-Colonel Walker's* position till they imagined his batteries crippled, advanced their infantry. One body moved toward the point of woods in our center, and the other, with its front parallel to the road from Hamilton's Crossing, to the river road. When distant about 800 yards, *Lieutenant-Colonel Walker's* batteries opened upon them with great effect, and at the same time fifteen guns . . . were thrown into position into the plain to our right, so as to cross their fire with that of the guns of *Lieutenant-Colonel Walker*, being specifically designed to check the advance of the enemy toward the road from Hamilton's Crossing to the river road. These pieces were under the immediate command of *Major Pelham*, and were admirably managed and bravely fought, and perfectly accomplished their object. All these batteries did not go in at once, but were added as the weight of the enemy's fire seemed to require it. . . .

I beg . . . to call your special attention to the valuable and gallant services of *Lieutenant-Colonel Walker* and *Major Pelham*. The position in which *Colonel Walker* was placed was peculiarly trying, from his being required to endure for a long time a very heavy fire without replying to it. [*O.R.*, XXI, pp. 636–39.]

Report of Lieut. Col. R. L. Walker, CSA, Commanding Artillery, A. P. Hill's Division, Second Army Corps, Army of Northern Virginia

The batteries of *Captains McIntosh* and *Pegram*, with a section of the batteries of *Captains Latham, Johnson*, and *Crenshaw* . . . numbering altogether fourteen guns, had position on the heights near the railroad, supported by the brigades of *Brigadier General Field*, (*Colonel Brockenbrough* commanding) and *Brigadier-General Archer*. *Captains Braxton* . . . and *Davidson*, with five and four guns, respectively, took position on the left wing of the Light Division [*A. P. Hill*], in the plain just to the right of Deep Run Creek, and were supported by the brigades of *Brigadier Generals Pender* and *Lane*.

About 10 a.m. the enemy began a desultory fire from several batteries, as if feeling our position. Their fire, about 11 a.m., became hot and well directed, causing us some loss in men and horses. *Captain McIntosh*, commanding his own guns and the sections of *Captains Latham* and *Johnson*, and *Captain Pegram*, commanding his own guns and the section of *Crenshaw*, were directed to withhold their fire until there should be an infantry demonstration.

The enemy, weary of suspense, about 12 a.m. formed a front to attack the heights. Their advance, made by a division, apparently, was speedily broken and driven back by *Captains McIntosh's* and *Pegram's* murderous fire, the enemy opening upon them meanwhile very destructively with at least twenty-five guns. This attempt having failed, the enemy concentrated in mass, and, in enormous forces, moved forward rapidly, protected by a fearful fire from all their guns, toward the point of woods in the plain in defiance of our guns, which were served rapidly and with great havoc upon their dense ranks. In advancing . . . they suffered heavy loss from the fire of our guns. While the attention of our guns was devoted to their infantry, their artillery caused us heavy loss, but, as soon as engaged by our guns, their shot flew wide, though in weight of metal they much exceeded us.

At 3.30 p.m., *Captains McIntosh* and *Pegram* becoming short of men and ammunition, and having one gun disabled, a caisson and limber exploded, they were relieved by the corps of *Colonel Brown*, except one section of *Captain Pegram's* battery, which remained till nightfall. . . . The guns upon both flanks were served with the coolness of a parade, though exposed to a fire which seemed to fill the air with destruction. [*O.R.*, XXI, pp. 649–50]

Return to your car. Exit the parking lot to retrace your route on LEE DRIVE. After you have driven 0.2 mile, pull out and park on the right side of the road near "A Southern Memorial." Dismount and walk forward along the shoulder of LEE DRIVE about 250 feet to the point where an old road intersects from the right. Follow that old road to the railroad right of way, then turn left and walk along the edge of the woods (well away from the railroad tracks) for about 600 feet until you are opposite a woodline on the far side of the tracks. As you face that woodline, there is a shallow ditch about 40 yards behind you that may be a trace of the Confederate position.

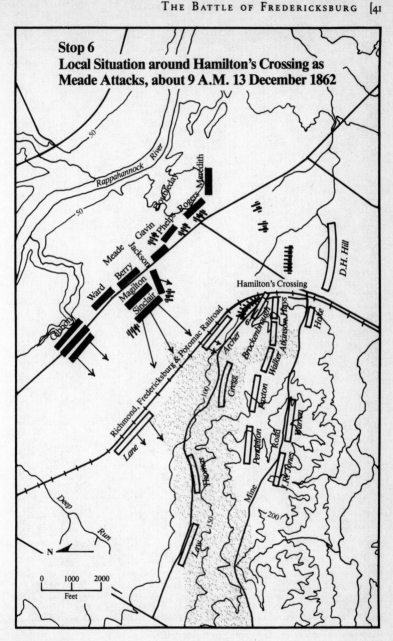

Stop 6
Local Situation around Hamilton's Crossing as Meade Attacks, about 9 A.M. 13 December 1862

Stone wall at the foot of Marye's Heights (USAMHI)

STOP 7A, THE MEADE MONUMENT

Report of Maj. Gen. Ambrose P. Hill, CSA, Commanding A.P. Hill's Division, Second Army Corps, Army of Northern Virginia

I was directed by *General R. E. Lee* . . . to move my division at dawn on the 12th, and relieve *Major-General Hood.* In obedience to this order I put my troops in position, my front line consisting of two regiments of *Brockenbrough's* brigade, the brigades of *Generals Archer, Lane,* and *Pender,* my extreme right resting upon the road leading from Hamilton's Crossing to the Port Royal road, and my left to within a short distance of Deep Creek. Upon the hill crowning the right of my line, *Lieut. Col. R. Lindsay Walker,* my chief of artillery, had in position, under his own immediate direction, fourteen rifle and Napoleon guns. . . . The batteries of *Captains Davidson* and *Braxton* . . . were placed to cover my left, about 200 yards in front of *Pender's* brigade.

My line of battle as thus formed was fully 1½ miles in extent, the division of *Major-General Hood* being on my left. *Lane's* brigade was some 150 yards in advance of my general line, the timber, in the skirt of which was posted his brigade, jutting out into the low grounds some distance from the main body. Along the military road—a new road running in rear of my front line from right to left, cut by *Major-General Hood*—were posted my reserves, consisting of the remainder of *Brockenbrough's* brigade . . . as a support to *Walker's* batteries, *Gregg's* brigade crossing the interval between *Archer* and *Lane,* and *Thomas'* brigade the interval between *Lane* and *Pender.* The division remained as thus posted during Friday and Friday night, undisturbed except by the shelling from the enemy's guns.

On Saturday morning, *Lieutenant-General Jackson* directed that *Braxton's* battery and two batteries from *Brigadier-General Taliaferro's* division be placed in advance of the railroad, and *General Lane* was directed to support them. . . .

About 10 o'clock Saturday morning, the lifting of the fog discovered to us the lines of the enemy drawn out in battle array on the low grounds between us and the river, covering the whole of my front and extending far to the left toward Fredericksburg. They were deployed in three lines, with heavy reserves, behind the Port Royal Road. Soon their lines, accompanied by ten full batteries (six on their left and four on the right) moved forward to the attack. They had advanced but a short distance when, *Stuart's* Horse Artillery opening on them from the Port Royal road and enfilading their lines, the advance was halted, and four of the batteries gave their attention for an hour or more to *Major Pelham*. As soon as *Pelham* ceased his fire, all their batteries, right and left, opened a terrific fire upon the positions occupied by my batteries and shelled the woods promiscuously. There being no reply from any of our batteries, and being unable to elicit any discoveries from this sharp practice, continued for an hour or more, the advance was again sounded, and, preceded by clouds of skirmishers, they right gallantly essayed another attempt.

To cover this advance their batteries were now served with redoubled activity; and now, the mass of infantry being within point-blank range, the roar was deepened and made deadly to the enemy as shell and canister from our long-silent but now madly aroused batteries plowed through their ranks. The enemy, however, continued to advance, and the three batteries . . . posted in advance of the railroad were compelled to retire. [*O.R.*, XXI, pp. 645–46.]

MEADE'S ASSAULT

Report of Maj. Gen. Ambrose E. Burnside, USA, Commanding Army of the Potomac, Continued.

During . . . the 12th, Sumner's and Franklin's commands crossed over and took position on the south bank, and General Hooker's grand division was held in readiness to support either the right or left, or to press the enemy in case the other command succeeded in moving him.

The line, as now established, was as follows: The Second Corps held the center and right of the town; the Ninth Corps was on the left of the Second Corps, and connected with General Franklin's right, at Deep Run, the whole of this force being nearly parallel to the river; the Sixth Corps was formed on the left of the Ninth Corps, nearly parallel with the old Richmond road, and the First Corps on the left of the Sixth, nearly at right angles with it, its left resting on the river.

The plain below the town is interrupted by hedges and ditches to a considerable extent, which gives good covering to an enemy, making it difficult to maneuver upon. The old Richmond road . . . runs from the town in a line nearly parallel with the river, to a point near the Massaponax, where it turns to the south, and passes near the right of the crest, or ridge, which runs in rear of the town, and was then occupied by the enemy in force. In order to pass down this road it was necessary to occupy the extreme right of this crest, which was designated on the map then in use by the army as "Hamilton's."

By the night of the 12th the troops were all in position, and I visited the different commands with a view to determining as to future movements. The delay in laying the bridges had rendered some change in the plan of attack necessary, and the orders already issued were to be superseded by new ones. [*O.R.*, XXI, pp. 89–90.]

I felt satisfied that . . . if we could divide their forces by piercing their lines at one or two points, separating their left from their right, then a vigorous attack with the whole army would succeed in breaking their army in pieces. The enemy had cut a road along in the rear of the line of heights where we made our attack, by means of which they connected the two wings of their army, and avoided a long detour around through a bad country. I obtained from a colored man from the other side of the town information in regard to this new road, which proved to be correct. I wanted to obtain possession of that new road, and that was my reasons [*sic*] for making an attack on the extreme left. I did not intend to make the attack on the right until that position had been taken, which I supposed would stagger the

Pontoon Bridge across the Rappahannock from the photo by A. Gardner May 1863. (NPS)

enemy, . . . and then I proposed to make a direct attack on their front, and drive them out of their works. . . . Their works are not strong works, but they occupy very strong positions. . . . I felt . . . that we would have a more decisive engagement here, and that if we succeeded in defeating the enemy here, we could break up the whole of their army here, which . . . is now the most desirable thing, not even second to the taking of Richmond. . . . [U.S. Congress, Joint Committee on the Conduct of the War, *Report* (Washington: Government Printing Office, 1863), Part 1, pp. 652–54.]

It was after midnight when I returned from visiting the different commands, and before daylight of the 13th I prepared the following orders:

Maj. Gen. E.V. Sumner, Commanding Right Grand Division . . .

The general commanding directs that you extend the left of your command to Deep Run, connecting with General Franklin, extending your right as far as your judgment may dictate. He also directs that you push a column of a division or more along the Plank and Telegraph Roads, with a view to seizing the heights in the rear of the town. . . . Great care should be taken to prevent a collision of our own forces during the fog. The watchword for the day will be "Scott." The column for a movement up the Telegraph and Plank Roads . . . will not move till the general commanding communicates with you.

Maj. Gen. Joseph Hooker, Commanding Center [Grand] Division . . .

The general commanding directs that you place General Butterfield's corps and Whipple's division in position to cross, at a moment's notice, at the three upper bridges, in support of the other troops over the river, and the two remaining divisions of General Stoneman's corps in readiness to cross at the lower ford, in support of General Franklin. The general commanding will meet you at headquarters very soon.

Major-General Franklin, Commanding Left Grand Division . . .

The general commanding directs that you keep your whole command in position for a rapid movement down the old Richmond road, and you will send out at once a division at least to pass below Smithfield, to seize, if possible, the height near Captain Hamilton's, on this side of the Massaponax, taking care to keep it well supported and its line of retreat open. He has ordered another column of a division or more to be moved from General Sumner's command up the Plank Road to its intersection with the Telegraph Road, where they will divide, with a view to seizing the heights on both of these roads. Holding these two heights, with the heights near

Captain Hamilton's, will, he hopes, compel the enemy to evacuate the whole ridge between these points. He makes these moves by columns distant from each other, with a view of avoiding the possibility of a collision of our own forces, which might occur in a general movement during a fog. Two of General Hooker's divisions are in your rear, at the bridges, and will remain there as supports. Copies of instructions given to Generals Sumner and Hooker will be forwarded to you . . . very soon. You will keep your whole command in readiness to move at once, as soon as the fog lifts. The watch-word, which, if possible, should be given to every company, will be "Scott." . . .

The forces now under command of General Franklin consisted of about 60,000 men. . . . General Sumner had about 27,000. . . . General Hooker's command was about 26,000 strong. . . .

The object of this order [to General Franklin] is clear. It was necessary to seize this height in order to enable the remainder of his forces to move down the old Richmond Road, with a view of getting in rear of the enemy's line on the crest. He was ordered to seize these heights, if possible, and to do it at once. . . . The movements were not intended to be simultaneous; in fact, I did not intend to move General Sumner until I learned that Franklin was about to gain the heights near Hamilton's, which I then supposed he was entirely able to do. [*O.R.*, XXI, pp. 71, 89–90.]

Report of Maj. Gen. William B. Franklin, USA, Commanding Left Grand Division, Army of the Potomac

The ground upon which the troops were disposed is, in general, a plain. It is cultivated and much cut up by hedges and ditches. The old Richmond Road traverses the plain from right to left, about 1 mile from the river and nearly parallel to it. This road is bordered on both sides by an earthen parapet and ditch, and is an exceedingly strong feature in the defense of the ground, had the enemy chosen to hold it. . . . The plain is bordered by a range of high hills in front, which stretches from Fredericksburg to the Massaponax . . . In front of and nearly parallel to the old Richmond Road, and about 500 or 600 yards from it, at the foot of the range of hills, is the railroad. . . . The enemy had artillery on the hills and in the valley of Deep Creek, in the wood near Reynolds' right, and on the Massaponax, so that the whole field was surrounded by it, except the right flank. His infantry appeared in all directions around the position. In front of Reynolds' right the forest extends to the old Richmond Road. . . . The railroad traverses the forest . . . I thought . . . that General Reynolds' force of three divisions would be sufficient to carry out the spirit of the order, the words of it being "You will send out at once a division at least . . . taking care to keep it well supported and its line of retreat open." [*O.R.*, pp. 449–50.]

Report of Maj. Gen. John Reynolds, USA, Commanding First Army Corps, Left Grand Division, Army of the Potomac

I received . . . the orders of the General-in-Chief for the attack on the right of the enemy's position, and immediately directed General Meade to form his division for the attack, informing him that I would support him on the right with Gibbon's division and cover his left with Doubleday's. . . . I directed General Meade to put his column directly for the nearest point of wood, and, having gained the crest, to extend his attack along it to the extreme point of the heights, where most of the enemy's artillery was posted. As the column crossed the Bowling Green [Old Richmond] Road the artillery of his division was ordered into position on the rise of the ground between this road and the railroad; Cooper's and Ransom's batteries, to the front, soon joined by Amsden's, to oppose those of the enemy on the crest, while Simpson's had to be thrown to the left, to oppose that on the Bowling Green Road, which was taking the column in flank. Hall's battery was at the same time thrown to the front, on the left of Gibbon's division, which was advancing in line on Meade's right. The artillery combat here raged furiously for some time, until that of the enemy was silenced, when all of our batteries were directed to shell the wood where his infantry was supposed to be posted. This was continued some half hour, when the column of Meade, advancing in fine order and with gallant determination, was directed into the point of wood which extended this side of the railroad, with instructions, when they carried the crest and the road which ran along it in their front, to move the First Brigade along the road, the Second Brigade to advance and hold the road, while the Third moved across the open field, to support the First in carrying the extreme point of the ridge. At this time I sent orders to General Gibbon to advance, in connection with General Meade, and carry the wood in his front. The advance was made under the fire of the enemy's batteries on his right and front, to which Gibbon's batteries replied. . . .

Meade's division successfully carried the wood in front, crossed the railroad, charged up the slope of the hill, and gained the road and edge of the wood, driving the enemy from his strong positions in the ditches and railroad cut, capturing the flags of two regiments and sending about 200 prisoners to the rear. At the same time Gibbon's division had crossed the railroad and entered the wood, driving back the first line of the enemy and capturing a number of prisoners; but, from the dense character of the wood, the connection between his division and Meade's was broken. The infantry combat was here kept up with great spirit for a short time, when Meade's column was vigorously assailed by the enemy's masked force, and, after a severe contest, forced back. Two regiments of Berry's brigade, Birney's division, arrived about this time, and were immediately thrown into the wood on Gibbon's left, to the support of the line, but they too were soon overpowered, and the whole line retired from the wood, Meade's in some confusion, and, after an ineffectual effort by General Meade and myself to rally them under the enemy's fire, that of the artillery having resumed almost its original intensity, I directed General Meade to reform his division across the Bowling Green road, and ordered the remainder of Berry's brigade . . . to the support of the batteries. . . . General Gibbon's division was assailed in turn in the same manner, and compelled to retire from the wood soon after Meade's. General Gibbon having been wounded just before entering the wood and obliged to leave the field, his division fell back in good order . . . to its original position. . . . [*O.R.*, XXI, pp. 453–54.]

Report of Maj. Gen. George G. Meade, USA, Commanding Third Division, First Army Corps, Left Grand Division, Army of the Potomac

The enemy occupied the wooded heights, the line of railroad, and the wood in front. Owing to the wood, nothing could be seen of them, while all our movements on the cleared ground were exposed to their view. Immediately on receiving orders, the division was moved forward across the Smithfield ravine, advancing down the river some 700 or 800 yards, when it turned sharp to the right and crossed the Bowling Green Road. . . . Some time was consumed in removing the hedge fences on this road, and bridging the drains on each side for the passage of the artillery.

Between 9 and 10 o'clock the column of attack was formed as follows: the First Brigade in line of battle on the crest of the hollow, and facing the railroad, with the Sixth Regiment deployed as skirmishers; the Second Brigade in rear of the First 300 paces; the Third Brigade by the flank, its right flank being a few rods to the rear of the first Brigade, having the Ninth Regiment deployed on its flank as skirmishers and flankers, and the batteries between the First and Second Brigades. This disposition had scarcely been made when the enemy opened a brisk fire from a battery posted on the Bowling Green Road, the shot from which took the command from the left and rear.

Apprehending an attack from this quarter, the Third Brigade was faced to the left, thus forming, with the First, two sides of a square. Simpson's battery was advanced to the front and left of the Third Brigade, and Cooper's and Ransom's batteries moved to a knoll on the left of the First Brigade. These batteries immediately opened on the enemy's battery, and, in conjunction with some of General Doubleday's batteries in our rear, on the other side of the Bowling Green Road, after twenty minutes' firing, silenced and compelled the withdrawal of the guns. During this artillery duel the enemy advanced a body of sharpshooters along the Bowling Green Road, and under cover of the hedges and trees on the roadside. General Jackson promptly sent out two companies of marksmen from his brigade, who drove the enemy back. No further demonstration on our left and rear being made, the advance was again determined on.

Previous to pushing forward infantry, the batteries were directed to shell the heights and the wood in front. . . . During this operation, by the orders of the general commanding the First Corps, the Third Brigade changed front and formed in line of battle on the left of the First Brigade, its left extending very nearly opposite to the end of the ridge to be attacked. The formation was barely executed before the enemy opened a sharp fire from a battery posted on the heights to our extreme left. Cooper's, Amsden's, and Ransom's batteries were immediately turned on it, and after about thirty minutes' rapid firing the enemy abandoned the guns, having had two of his limbers or caissons blown up, the explosions from which were plainly visible.

As soon as the enemy's guns were silenced, the line of infantry was ordered to attack. The First Brigade, on the right, advanced several hundred yards over cleared ground, driving the enemy's skirmishers before them, till they reached the woods . . . in front of the railroad, which they entered, driving the enemy out of them to the railroad, where they were found strongly posted in ditches and behind temporary defenses. The brigade drove them . . . up the heights in their front, though, owing to a heavy fire being received on their right flank, they obliqued over to that side, but continued forcing the enemy back till they had crossed the crest of the hill; crossed a main road which runs along the crest, and reached open ground on the other side, where they were assailed by a severe fire from a large force in their front, and, at the same time, the enemy opened a battery which completely enfiladed them from the right flank. After holding their ground for some time, no support arriving, they were compelled to fall back to the railroad.

The Second Brigade, which advanced in rear of the First, after reaching the railroad, was assailed with so severe a fire on their right flank that the Fourth Regiment halted and formed, faced to the right, to repel this attack. The other regiments, in passing through the woods, being assailed from the left, inclined in that direction and ascended the heights, the Third going up as the One hundred and twenty-first of the brigade was retiring. The Third continued to advance and reached nearly the same point as the First Brigade, but was compelled to withdraw for the same reason. The Seventh engaged the enemy to the left, capturing many prisoners and a stand of colors, driving them from their rifle-pits and temporary defenses, and continuing the pursuit till, encountering the enemy's reinforcements, they were in turn driven back.

The Third Brigade had not advanced over 100 yards, when the battery on the height on its left was remanned, and poured a destructive fire into its ranks. Perceiving this, I dispatched my aide-de-camp, Lieutenant Dehon, with orders for General Jackson to move by the right flank till he could clear the open ground in front of the battery, and then, ascending the height through the woods, swing around to the left and take the battery. Unfortunately Lieutenant Dehon fell just as he reached General Jackson, and a short time afterward the latter officer was killed. The regiments, however, did partially execute the movement by obliquing to the right, and advancing across the railroad, a portion ascending the heights in their front. The loss of their commander, and the severity of the fire from both artillery and infantry . . . compelled them to withdraw when those on their right withdrew. . . .

The attack was for a time perfectly successful. The enemy was driven from the railroad, his rifle-pits, and breastworks, for over half a mile. Over 300 prisoners were taken and several standards, when the advancing line encountered the heavy re-enforcements of the enemy, who, recovering from the effects of the assault and perceiving both our flanks unprotected, poured in such a destructive fire from all three directions as to compel the line to fall back, which was executed without confusion. Perceiving the danger of the too great penetration of my line, without support, I dispatched several staff officers both to General Gibbon's command and General Birney's (whose division had replaced mine at the batteries from whence we advanced), urging an advance to my support, the one on my right, the other on my left. A brigade of Birney's advanced to our relief just as my men were withdrawn from the wood, and Gibbon's division advanced into the wood on our right in time to assist materially in the safe withdrawal of my broken line.

An unsuccessful effort was made to reform the division in the hollow in front of the batteries. Failing in this, the command was reformed beyond the Bowling Green Road and marched to the ground occupied the night before, where it was held in reserve till the night of the 15th, when we recrossed the river. . . .

When I report that 4,500 men is a liberal estimate of the strength of the division taken into action, this large loss [175 killed, 1,241 wounded and 437 captured or missing], being 40 per cent., will fully bear me out in the expression of my satisfaction at the good conduct of both officers and men. . . . With one brigade commander killed, another wounded, nearly half their number *hors du combat*, with regiments separated from brigades, and companies from regiments, and all the confusion and disorder incidental to the advance of an extended line through wood and other obstructions, assailed by a heavy fire, not only of infantry but of artillery—not only in front but on both flanks—the best troops would be justified in withdrawing without loss of honor. [*O.R.*, XXI, pp. 140, 510–13.]

Return to your car.

STOP 7B, ARCHER'S DEFENSE

Report of Brig. Gen. James J. Archer, CSA, Commanding Fifth (Archer's) Brigade, A.P. Hill's Division, Second Army Corps, Army of Northern Virginia

On arriving from sick leave Saturday morning, I found my brigade posted in the edge of a wood before [opposite] Bernard's house, overlooking the plain through which the railroad and Bowling Green turnpike pass, the former at a distance from my front of about 250 yards, the latter of about three-quarters of a mile, my left resting where the wood extends forward to the front to a point beyond the railroad. *General Lane's* brigade was on my left, with an interval of about 600 yards between us, while (as I was informed) *General Gregg's* brigade was immediately behind the interval close enough to prevent my being flanked. On my right I found *Lieutenant-Colonel Walker* with fifteen pieces of light artillery, supported by *Colonel Brockenbrough's* brigade.

As the fog cleared away the enemy was seen advancing from the Bowling Green Road, and a little after 9 a.m. several batteries were brought forward and placed in position about 1,000 yards from us, which were fired on by some of our batteries far off to the right, and with which they carried on a brisk exchange of shots for about an hour, occasionally throwing shell into the wood where I was posted. About 10.30 they turned all their guns on our position, and after thirty or forty minutes' severe shelling their lines of infantry formed and advanced rapidly to the attack.

When they had arrived near enough, I perceived them massing in front of and entering the point of wood . . . projecting on my left beyond the railroad, and immediately sent my ordnance officer . . . to warn *General Gregg* that it was time for him to move forward into the interval between *Lane's* and my brigade to prevent my being flanked. Shortly after, fearing that *General Gregg* might be too late, I drew out the right battalion (Fifth Alabama) and ordered it to the left. When the enemy in my front arrived near the railroad, my brigade opened a rapid and destructive fire upon them, which soon checked their career and forced them to retire and take shelter in the railroad track, from which they kept up a desultory fire upon our line.

In the mean time the columns which had entered the point of wood on my left succeeded in passing round my flank, and attacked the Nineteenth Georgia and Fourteenth Tennessee in rear and flank. These regiments were compelled to retire, leaving about 160 prisoners in the enemy's hands. The greater part of the Seventh Tennessee, also seeing the regiments on their left give way and hearing the cry that the enemy was in their rear, left the trenches in disorder. The First Tennessee, together with . . . a portion . . . of the Seventh Tennessee, held its ground gallantly, and after its ammunition was exhausted, charged under *Lieutenant-Colonel George* (*Colonel Turney* having been severely wounded early in the action) across the railroad track with *Colonel Hoke's* brigade, of *Early's* division, and returned to its original position when the charge was over. The Fifth Alabama Battalion, which I had sent from the right to aid in opposing the enemy on the left, discharged their duty faithfully, first under *Major Van de Graaff*, and, after he was wounded, under *Captain Stewart*.

After sending *Lieutenant Lemmon*, I also sent my aide-de-camp . . . to explain the urgency of the case to *General Gregg*, and to bring down another brigade in support of my front, which, although not then pressed in front, had nearly exhausted its ammunition. *Generals Gregg's* and *Lawton's* brigade and the Fifth Alabama Battalion drove back the enemy who had passed my flank, and *Colonel Hoke*, in command of *Trimble's* brigade, came down to the edge of the wood (my original position) which I still maintained with the right of my brigade, but with empty rifles and cartridge-boxes. The whole line then charged over the field beyond the railroad. When it returned to the edge of the wood, I drew back my troops about 30 yards, re-formed my brigade, and remained in support of the front line—*Hoke's* brigade—which had relieved me in the trenches. . . .

The attack along my whole front was gallantly and successfully repelled by my brigade. No enemy ever arrived within 50 yards of my front; and even after my left was broken by the attack in rear and flank, the enemy in front had been so sharply repulsed that he did not venture to come again. [*O.R.*, XXI, pp. 656–57].

Report of Col. John F. Goodner, CSA, Seventh Tennessee Infantry, Archer's Brigade, A. P. Hill's Division, Second Army Corps, Army of Northern Virginia

In the fight near Fredericksburg . . . my regiment . . . was situated in the center of the brigade and posted in a ditch along an old fence row. The enemy advanced in front of us through an open field, and when they came near enough for us to fire with effect, we did so. By this time the firing was general all along our line, and it was so galling on the enemy that it caused them to oblique rather to . . . our left and bear into a skirt of woodland that projected into the field. We continued a left-oblique fire upon them until the most of them had passed by the left of our line, and were pouring in a galling fire from our left, raking it to the right. I saw the two regiments on my left give way, which exposed the left of my regiment to the whole force of the enemy engaged at that place. We had been loading and firing very rapidly for some time, and were about out of ammunition. Some of the men had still two or three rounds, but the most of them were entirely out. Consequently, under these circumstances, being opposed by vastly superior numbers, and out of ammunition, the left and a portion of the right of the regiment gave way, not until, however, the enemy had come up and demanded a surrender. Five of the men on the extreme left were captured, and the balance made their escape by a hasty retreat a short distance to the rear, where they were supplied with ammunition, and returned again immediately to the front lines ready to renew the conflict. I did not observe any misconduct in my regiment. . . . [*O.R.*, XXI, p. 660.]

Report of Lieut. Col. James W. Lockert, CSA, Fourteenth Tennessee Infantry, Archer's Brigade, A.P. Hill's Division, Second Army Corps, Army of Northern Virginia

About noon the enemy's batteries in front of our position opened a terrific fire of shot and shell upon us, which was kept up at intervals until about 2 p.m., when three dense columns of infantry commenced to advance upon our position through a large open field in front. We, having taken shelter in a ditch, remained quiet until the enemy's front line was within 200 yards of our own. The Nineteenth Georgia Regiment, on our left, and the Seventh Tennessee, on our right, commenced firing upon them. I then ordered firing to commence in my own. The firing along the line of your brigade now became general, and had great effect upon the Federal lines, killing and wounding a large number of men and officers and confusing others. The fighting with small-arms had only lasted about ten minutes, when the enemy directly in front of our position took shelter in the railroad cut. We then directed our fire to the left-oblique on a column that was advancing under shelter of the timber there and in front whenever a good shot could be had. In about ten minutes more

I noticed that the Nineteenth Georgia Regiment was giving way, but supposed that their supply of ammunition, like ours, had been exhausted.

In a few moments, however, *Lieutenant Hutcheson*, of Company C, came up from the left and informed me that the enemy had gained our rear. I determined still to hold our position, and did so until I saw the Yankee line advancing through the small pines on our left. I then ordered my regiment to retreat. We fell back in disorder to the open field in our rear, reformed the few men left, got a supply of ammunition, and returned to our original position, the enemy having been driven back by other troops.

The officers and men during the entire engagement showed great courage and coolness. In fact, I did not see an act of cowardice, and never saw shots better aimed or more effective. [*O.R.*, XXI, p. 661. The 14th Tennessee lost 59 killed or wounded, the greatest number in Archer's brigade. *Ibid.*, p. 560.]

Report of Col. J. M. Brockenbrough, CSA, Commanding First (Field's) Brigade, A. P. Hill's Division, Second Army Corps, Army of Northern Virginia

Stationed upon the extreme right of our division, we remained in this position until the concentrated forces of the enemy passed through a gap in and reached the rear of our lines. There being no enemy in our immediate front, and re-enforcements being called for, I withdrew my command from its first position and hurried as rapidly as possible to the point indicated.

We moved up by the left flank, and so urgent and repeated were the calls for re-enforcements that my two leading regiments . . . the only regiments actively engaged, advanced in a run, separated themselves from the brigade, passed well to the left, and encountered the enemy in rear of our front lines about midway between *Generals Archer* and *Lane*. Firing one volley into their left flank and charging them with a yell, they fled precipitately to the shelter of the railroad cut. Here they rallied and made a short stand, but being joined by a Georgia brigade (*Lawton's*, I believe), we made a second charge, which drove them from the railroad. Here the men were ordered to halt, but such was their impetuosity that much the larger portion of these two regiments advanced to the position which had been occupied by two of the enemy's batteries, which they found deserted. Being unsupported, they were, of course, compelled to retreat, which was done, under the most galling fire of grape, canister, and minie balls.

The fact that only two regiments were actively engaged was accidental and unavoidable. The woods through which we passed being dense and filled with troops, the rapid run of the leading regiments soon separated them from the brigade, and while they passed well around to the left, the remainder of the brigade only marched by direct line to *General Archer's* left, who was said to have been flanked. Driving the enemy from the woods was a task of short duration, and the troops engaged were completely successful in driving back the enemy before the remaining regiments (a few minutes behind them) could come to their assistance. During the fight several of the enemy's mounted officers were shot down, and the colors of one regiment were seen to fall four times. . . .

The valor and daring of the men was unprecedented. . . . Our loss was considerable, being about 20 per cent. of the troops actively engaged. [*O.R.*, XXI, pp. 650–51.]

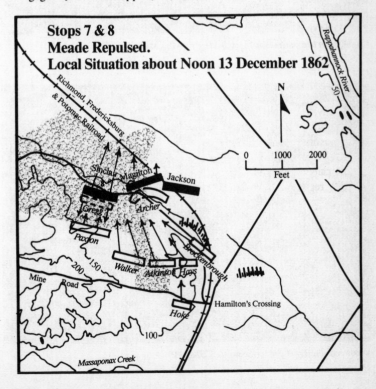

Stops 7 & 8
Meade Repulsed.
Local Situation about Noon 13 December 1862

Confederate earthworks on Marye's Heights (USAMHI)

Wounded soldiers at Fredericksburg. (USAMHI)

Drive about 0.3 miles on **LEE DRIVE**. Pull off to the right in front of the sign.

STOP 8, JACKSON'S COUNTER-ATTACK

You are now in the area where *Gregg's* South Carolina brigade was struck by Meade's column of attack. This portion of the Confederate line was not strengthened by earthworks until after the battle.

Report of Maj. Gen. Ambrose P. Hill, CSA, Commanding A. P. Hill's Division, Second Army Corps, Army of Northern Virginia

The attack directly in front of *Archer* and of *Walker's* guns had been gallantly repulsed, the enemy finding what shelter they could along the railroad. Concentrating their columns of attack, the enemy now made a bold effort, and pushing onward turned *Lane's* right. . . .

In the mean time the main column of attack had wedged in to the right and rear of *Lane,* encountered *Archer's* left, and, attacked in flank and rear, the Fourteenth Tennessee and Nineteenth Georgia were compelled to give back. *General Archer,* observing the threatening condition of affairs on his left, very promptly detached the Fifth Alabama Battalion, holding his line with the brave First Tennessee . . . and this movement, rapidly executed and assisted by two regiments of *Brockenbrough's* . . . was attended with signal success.

The advancing columns of the enemy had also encountered an obstacle in the military road which they little expected. *Gregg's* brigade of South Carolinians stood in the way. Taken somewhat by surprise, *Orr's* Rifles was thrown into confusion, mistaking the advancing enemy for our own troops falling back. It was at this moment that *Brig. Gen. Maxcy Gregg,* himself fearful of harming our friends, fell in front of the Rifles, mortally wounded. . . . One company of the Rifles . . . and the four remaining regiments . . . stood firm as on parade. *Colonel Hamilton,* now in command of the brigade, threw back the right wing of his regiment and opened a destructive fire. The Twelfth [South Carolina] faced about, and the Thirteenth and Fourteenth [South Carolina], under the direction of *Colonel McGowan,* faced by the rear rank, changed front forward, and stood prepared to resist any attempt to sweep down my rear.

The combat was short, sharp, and decisive. The rattling musketry and charging yell of the Fifth Alabama Battalion, the Forty-seventh Virginia, and Twenty-second Virginia Battalion, the withering fire from *Hamilton's* regiment right in their faces, was more than Yankee firmness could stand. In addition to this, that gallant old warrior, *General Early*, to whom I had sent, requesting that he would move down to my support, came crashing through the woods at the double-quick. The enemy, completely broken, fled in confusion. The two regiments of *Brockenbrough's* brigade, *Archer*, with the First Tennessee and Fifth Alabama Battalion, and *Early's* troops, chased them across the railroad and back to their reserves. In this backward movement of theirs, my artillery again inflicted heavy loss upon them. . . .

I cannot close this report without calling . . . attention . . . to the admirable manner in which the troops of this division behaved under that most trying of all things to the soldier, viz., inaction under a heavy fire of artillery. The absence of all straggling was remarkable. . . . The conscripts showed themselves desirous of being thought worthy comrades of our veteran soldiers. In this . . . my thanks are eminently due to the brigade commanders for their hearty co-operation—the coolness and skill with which they have handled their troops. . . . The chief surgeon of the division, *(Dr. Powell)*, by his system and order and untiring personal attention, secured more comfort to the wounded than has been usual. By 10 o'clock the next day his hospital had been cleared of all those who could be moved, and, with their wounds dressed, they were on their way to Richmond.

The loss in the Light Division is 231 killed, 1,474 wounded, [and] 417 missing: total 2,122. [According to the Medical Director, Army of Northern Virginia, Hill's division lost 211 killed and 1,408 wounded.] [*O.R.*, XXI, pp. 646–48, 560.]

Report of Col. D. H. Hamilton, CSA, First South Carolina Infantry, Commanding Second (Gregg's) Brigade, A. P. Hill's Division, Second Army Corps, Army of Northern Virginia

So soon as I was informed that I was in command of *General Gregg's* brigade, I mounted a horse standing near and rode down the lines, informing the commanders of the regiments that I was in command of the brigade, and cautioning the soldiers of the brigade to remain quiet and steady under the severe fire of shell which was falling along the line which we occupied, and I am pleased to say that their courage and steadiness were of the highest character. The brigade, except my own regiment . . . and *Orr's* rifle regiment, was not engaged with the enemy, as they retired under the fire from my own regiment, no doubt accelerated by their finding themselves at the mercy of the Second Brigade, which had faced about, and in an advance a few yards beyond their entire flank would have been exposed to a severe and raking fire. [*O.R.*, XXI, pp. 651–52]

Narrative of Capt. J. F. J. Caldwell, CSA, First Regiment South Carolina Volunteers, Gregg's Brigade, A. P. Hill's Division, Second Army Corps, Army of Northern Virginia

The second line was on the Military road, parallel with the first, and consisted of the remaining two regiments of *Brockenborough's* [sic] brigade, supporting the artillery on the right; *Gregg's* brigade crossing the interval between *Archer* and *Lane; Thomas's* brigade crossing the interval between *Lane* and *Pender,* and joining with *Gregg.* The second line was just at the foot of the hills, and concealed from the enemy by a thick forest. . . . The enemy. . . . driving in our skirmishers like a flock of birds . . . pushed upon our first line of battle. . . . Those . . . who were not immediately next either *Lane's* or *Archer's* brigades, bore forward, through the woods, towards the second line. *Gen. Gregg,* informed of a line of our troops before him, had taken every precaution to prevent this brigade's firing into our friends—a thing too often done in our woods-fights. He had, therefore, made known to the regiments, that we were only the second line, and had caused arms to be stacked, while the brigade lay down under such cover from the enemy's artillery as the trees afforded. The order of the regiments, from right to left, was as follows: *Orr's* Rifles, First, Twelfth, Thirteenth, Fourteenth.

Unfortunately, *Gen. Gregg* was not aware of the interval between *Lane's* and *Archer's* brigades . . . directly in his front. We could not see the first line, of course. Soon after the break through . . . the right of our brigade, especially *Orr's* regiment of Rifles, became persuaded of the approach of the enemy through the woods. Had not the enemy been as ignorant of our position as we of theirs, this knowledge might have come in time to give us an easy victory. But they, never dreaming of an obstacle, blundered on rapidly, until, all at once, they fell upon the Rifle regiment . . . and immediately opened [fire].

These sprang to their arms to oppose them. But *Gen. Gregg,* who was rather deaf, not being able to see the true state of affairs, and anxious to prevent firing into the first line of our troops, (who must, in reason, fall back over us before the enemy could reach us,) rode rapidly to the right and ordered the men to quit the stacks and refrain from firing. . . . He rode in front of the line, and used every effort to stop them.

By this time the Federal line was right upon the Rifles, and before one could scarcely reason, much less act, they precipitated themselves upon the stacks of arms. Then ensued a scramble and hand-to-hand fight. . . . The Rifle regiment was, as a body, broken, slaughtered and swept from the field. *Gen. Gregg* was . . . riding, in full uniform, in front of the regiment. The enemy fired upon him, and he fell, mortally wounded through the spine. . . . The left company of the Rifles . . . and such men as could be rallied from the rout, closed upon the First regiment, which, with the other three regiments . . . stood their ground. . . . *Col. Hamilton* . . . being the senior colonel of the brigade . . . now took command. . . . He swung the right of the First regiment around and back, so as to front the enemy as they pressed the flank, and opened fire on them. The Twelfth regiment faced about, the Thirteenth and Fourteenth, under *Col. McGowan*, wheeled so as to form at right angles with their former line and thus front the enemy moving down from the right. Never did soldiers behave with more coolness and intrepidity.

The fire between the First regiment and the enemy was, in some places, at an interval of only a few paces. Almost every shot told. But we were not left alone. Two regiments of *Brockenborough's [sic]* brigade, and two brigades, under *Gen. Early,* pushed into the fray, the regiments of *Brockenborough [sic]* doing special execution among the Federals. Such an onslaught soon broke the latter. They fought a space, then swayed back, and finally fled, in complete disorder, pursued by *Early's* cheering line. The chase only ended when the survivors . . . reached their reserve at the railroad. . . .

The brigade [lost] . . . 366. Our force was about fifteen hundred men. The proportion of killed to wounded in this battle will help to correct a very common error, in the army as well as out of it, viz., that shell-wounds are more fatal than those from small arms. The large majority of wounds were from shell . . . and the deaths were less than one to eight. Moreover the two regiments (the First and the Rifles) which did almost exclusively the small-arm fighting, lost more than one in six of the wounded. [J. F. J. Caldwell, *History of a Brigade of South Carolinians, known first as "Gregg's" and subsequently as "McGowan's Brigade"* (Philadelphia: King and Baird, 1866), pp. 57–62.]

Report of Brig. Gen. Jubal A. Early, CSA, Commanding Ewell's Division, Second Army Corps, Army of Northern Virginia

Having . . . marched the division, on the night of the 12th . . . to the vicinity of Hamilton's Crossing . . . and bivouacked for the night, early next morning, in accordance with . . . orders, I moved to the crossing and posted the division nearly at right angles with the railroad, along the dirt road which here crosses the railroad, with my right resting on the latter, so as to support the right of *Maj. Gen. A. P. Hill's* division. . . . *Hays'* brigade was placed on the right, with *Trimble's* brigade, under command of *Col. R. F. Hoke* . . . immediately in rear of it. To the left of *Hays* was *Lawton's* brigade, under command of *Col. E. N. Atkinson* . . . and to the left of the latter was my own brigade, under command of *Col. J. A. Walker.* . . . The batteries of the division . . . were . . . parked under cover in the rear until wanted.

As the division moved into position, the artillery fire commenced from the enemy's batteries, though not at first directed toward the place occupied by the division. After a short interval, however, shell began to fall in the vicinity, and for two or three hours the division was exposed to quite a severe cannonade. . . .

A little after noon, the infantry fire having commenced in front, and becoming quite animated, a messenger from *Brigadier-General Archer* . . . came to the rear, stating that *General Archer* was pressed and wished re-enforcements. Just at this moment I received an order from the lieutenant-general commanding the corps, through one of his staff officers, to hold my division in readiness to move to the right of the railroad, as the enemy was making a demonstration in that direction. This caused me to hesitate a moment about sending a brigade forward, but I directed *Colonel Atkinson* to get ready to advance with his brigade, and the order had hardly been given before an officer of artillery came galloping to the rear with the information that an interval (an awful gulf, as he designated it) had been left in our front line . . . through which the enemy were penetrating with a heavy column, thus endangering *Archer's* brigade and all our batteries on the right. I immediately ordered *Colonel Atkinson* to move forward with his brigade (*Lawton's*), as I was informed the interval was in front of it. . . .

The brigade, with the exception of . . . the Thirteenth Georgia, moved forward in fine style, and in a few minutes encountered the enemy in the woods on the hill immediately in rear of a point at which the railroad passes through a small neck of swampy woods . . . thus greatly endangering our right, as in a few minutes *Archer's* and *Field's* brigades, with our batteries on the right, would have been surrounded, and the enemy have obtained a lodgment from which it would have been difficult to drive him.

Lawton's brigade, without hesitating, at once dashed upon the enemy with the cheering peculiar to the Confederate soldier (and which is never mistaken for the studied hurrahs of the Yankees) and drove the column opposed to it down the hill, across the railroad, and out into the open plain, advancing so far and with such ardor as to cause one of the enemy's batteries to be abandoned. This brigade, however, was compelled to fall back . . . by the approach of a large column on its right flank, which proved to be Birney's division of Stoneman's corps. . . .

In a very few moments after ordering the advance of *Lawton's* brigade, I also ordered *Colonel Walker* forward with my own brigade, as I was informed *Lawton's* brigade would not cover the interval in the line. This order was executed in double-quick time, and *Walker* encountered the enemy in the woods to the left of . . . *Lawton's* brigade. . . . This column . . . having turned *General Lane's* right flank . . . was quickly driven out of the woods by *Walker* across the railroad and into the plain beyond; but perceiving still another column [Gibbon's division] crossing the railroad to his left and entering the woods, he withdrew the brigade back to the railroad and took position on it, detaching at the same time the Thirteenth Virginia . . . to attack the last named column of the enemy on the flank. About the same time *General Thomas*, of *General A. P. Hill's* division, with his brigade, attacked this column in front, and under the two fires it was driven back with considerable slaughter.

As soon as *Lawton's* and my own brigades were ordered forward, I directed *Colonel Hoke* to move with his brigade *(Trimble's)* to the left of *Hays'*, on the same line; but he had hardly got into position before I received information that *Archer's* brigade was giving way, and I ordered *Hoke* to advance to his support, obliquing to the right. This was done in gallant style, and *Hoke* found the enemy in possession of the trench (which had been occupied by *General Archer's* brigade) on the crest of the hill and in the woods in rear of it. *Hoke* attacked the enemy vigorously and drove him from the woods and trench to the railroad in front, in which there were reserves. He followed up his attack, and drove the enemy from the railroad . . . some distance in front, capturing a considerable number of prisoners and . . . several hundred stand of arms. He advanced his brigade to a fence some distance in front of the railroad, but perceiving his danger of being flanked by the enemy, who had brought up large, fresh columns, I sent an order to him to fall back to the original line, which . . . he anticipated by retiring in good order, leaving two regiments and a battalion in the railroad, and occupying the trench on the crest of the hill with the two other regiments. . . .

The . . . three brigades . . . engaged three separate bodies of the enemy. They were, however, moved forward in rapid succession . . . and were, in fact, all engaged at the same time. . . . The railroad makes a circle in passing from the right of our position around to the left, so that *Lawton's* brigade in passing to the front with *Walker's* and *Hoke's*, respectively, on the left and right of it, was thrown into the apex of an angle, and having the start of them both, it was necessarily thrown farther forward than either of the others when it crossed the railroad and advanced into the plain. This exposed its flanks, and hence . . . this brigade was compelled to fall back. . . .

About sundown . . . I saw *General D. H. Hill's* division moving to the front, and was informed by one of his brigadier-generals that the whole line was ordered to advance, and that his division was ordered to follow. This was the first intimation I had of it. . . . In a few moments, however, *Lieutenant Morrison*, aide-de-camp, rode up and informed me that *General Jackson's* orders were that I should hold myself in readiness to advance. . . . I gave the order to *Colonel Hoke* and *General Hays* accordingly, and . . . *Colonel Hoke* advanced with a part of his command to the railroad. . . . The enemy immediately opened a terrible artillery fire, and it becoming quite dark, our own artillery was withdrawn and the movement countermanded. [*O.R.*, XXI, pp. 663–66.]

Report of Major D. B. Bridgford, C.S.A., Chief Provost-Marshal, Jackson's Corps, Army of Northern Virginia

December 12, moved at dawn . . . to Hamilton's Crossing, where I placed a guard, for the purpose of arresting all stragglers. Also placed a guard, consisting of cavalry and infantry, along the whole line of the corps and in rear of the line of battle about half a mile, with instructions to arrest all men without proper passes on author-ized business for their commands, to be brought to the guard placed on the railroad; there my surgeon was stationed to examine all men claiming to be sick without proper passes from their brigade or regimental surgeons. Numbers, however, were really sick and totally unfit for duty; they were without passes. When a sufficient number were collected together, I sent them under charge of cavalry to be delivered to the first major general whose command was going into the fight, to place them in front and most exposed portion of his command. I am happy to state the number arrested and sent forward were comparatively few in consideration of the size of the army.

During the 13th and 14th, the number sent in under guard was only 526. Numbers were turned back, owing to their not having proper passes to return to the rear to cook, etc.

I am most happy to state I had no occasion to carry into effect the order to shoot all stragglers who refused to go forward, or, if caught a second time, upon the evidence of two witnesses to shoot them. Had I occasion to carry it into effect, it certainly should have been executed to the very letter. [*O.R.*, XXI, p. 641.]

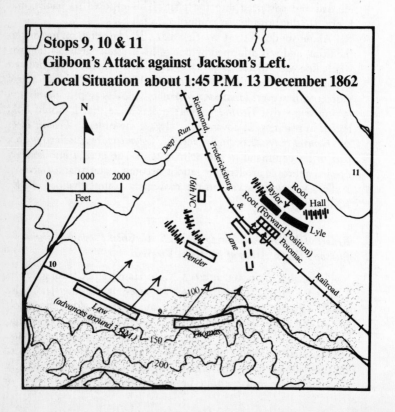

Stops 9, 10 & 11
Gibbon's Attack against Jackson's Left.
Local Situation about 1:45 P.M. 13 December 1862

Continue on LEE DRIVE about 0.9 mile. Pull off to the right at the sign.

STOP 9, JACKSON'S LEFT

The following action did not occur here but along the railroad, about 0.6 mile to your right. The intervening woods contain several lines of breastworks, all of which were constructed after the battle. Nothing is left of Bernard's Cabins but the remnants of a well, but the site is easily identified in a field approximately 0.4 mile to the right. A short distance behind you is a trace of an old road that leads into the area, but it is easy to lose one's bearings and there are often wet spots in the woods. The tree lines in this portion of the battlefield appear to be much like they were at the time of the battle.

Report of Lieut. Gen. Thomas J. Jackson, CSA, Commanding Second Army Corps, Army of Northern Virginia

On the extreme left, the day did not pass without some incidents worthy of notice. Early in the day the enemy opened upon the left with sixteen guns, afterward increased to twenty-four. The officers in command obeyed their orders, and, reserving their fire, the enemy advanced his skirmishers in heavy line upon the points occupied by the commands of *Captains Davidson* and *Brockenbrough*. They were soon driven off by canister; but the position of these batteries being thus disclosed to the enemy, a heavy artillery fire was directed upon them, which was replied to with animation and spirit. The ammunition of *Captain Raine's* battery proving defective, it was withdrawn, and *Captain Latimer*, acting chief of artillery of *Ewell's* division, was ordered to take a position still farther to the front and left. These last pieces were admirably served, and, though suffering severely from skirmishers and sharpshooters, drove them back, and by the accuracy and rapidity of their fire inflicted a severe loss upon the enemy.

As the Federal infantry pressed forward upon our front, it was deemed advisable to withdraw the batteries of *Captain Brockenbrough* placed in advance of the railroad, before the enemy should seize the point of woods to their right and rear, which they a short time afterward penetrated, the withdrawal of the batteries being covered by *Lieutenant-Colonel Hill*, of the Seventh North Carolina. The brigade of *General Pender* was immediately in rear of the batteries of *Captains*

Davidson and *Latimer,* and was without any protection from the enemy's artillery; and thus, notwithstanding the efficacy of the batteries acting in conjunction with *Major Cole,* of the Twenty-second North Carolina, in dispersing the cloud of skirmishers and sharpshooters that hung all day upon that part of the line, that brigade received much of the fire that was directed at these guns, and suffered severely. *General Pender* was himself wounded. The Sixteenth North Carolina . . . which had been thrown out as a support to *Latimer's* battery, became warmly engaged with a brigade of the enemy, which had advanced up Deep Run under cover, and, acting with two other North Carolina regiments of *Law's* brigade, *Hood's* division, drove them back. [*O.R.,* XXI, pp. 633–34.]

Report of Maj. Gen. Ambrose P. Hill, CSA, Commanding A. P. Hill's Division, Second Army Corps, Army of Northern Virginia

Lane's brigade was the first to encounter the masses of the enemy, who, recoiling somewhat from his direct front, shifted their main attack to his right, endeavoring to penetrate through the interval between *Archer* and himself. . . . Concentrating their columns of attack, the enemy now made a bold effort, and pushing onward turned *Lane's* right, although obstinately resisted by the Twenty-eighth and Thirty-seventh North Carolina Regiments. *Colonel Barbour,* of the Thirty-seventh, finding his right turned, changed front with his three right companies and poured in a destructive fire. These two regiments continued to fight until their ammunition was exhausted, and were then quietly and steadily retired from the field, refilling their boxes and rejoining their brigade. The three remaining regiments of *Lane's* brigade (Seventh, Eighteenth, and Thirty-third North Carolina) steadily continued to battle against overwhelming numbers, and the attack was checked by well-directed volleys from the Thirty-third Regiment. . . . *General Thomas,* responding to the call of *General Lane,* rapidly threw forward his brigade of Georgians by the flank, and, deploying by successive formations, squarely met the enemy, charged them, and, joined by the Seventh and part of the Eighteenth North Carolina, drove them back, with tremendous loss, to their original position. [*O.R.,* XXI, p. 646]

Report of Brig. Gen. James H. Lane, CSA, Commanding Lane's Brigade, A. P. Hill's Division, Second Army Corps, Army of Northern Virginia

At 6.30 o'clock on the morning of the 12th, we left our bivouac and took the position assigned us on the railroad, my right being about 250 yards to the left of the small piece of woods beyond the track, and my left resting on a dirt road which crosses the railroad near the point where it makes a bend. Several batteries were to my left and rear [at Bernard's cabins] and *General Pender* some distance farther back, my left nearly covering his right. When I had made this disposition of my command, I rode to the right of *General Archer's* brigade, which was posted in the woods some 400 yards from the railroad, and informed *Colonel Turney*, who was at that time commanding, that there was an open space between us of about 600 yards. I also informed *General Gregg* of this opening, his command, which was to have been my support, being on the military road opposite this opening and some 500 or 600 yards from the railroad. I subsequently met *General A. P. Hill* and spoke to him of our relative positions.

Nothing of interest occured on Friday and Friday night [December 12].

Saturday morning I ordered the Seventh and Eighteenth Regiments beyond the railroad, to support three batteries which had been placed on a hill immediately in their front. *Lieutenant-Colonel Hill* at once approached the captain of one of these batteries, told him he would ensure its safety against any attempt on the part of the enemy to capture it, and that he must let him know when he wished him to move to the front. As soon as the fog lifted, heavy skirmishing commenced along my whole line, and the enemy were seen advancing. Our skirmishers, with the exception of *Captain Turner's* company, on the left, fell back. The batteries just alluded to then opened with telling effect and checked their advance. During this firing *Captain Turner* withdrew his company, as his men were suffering, and rejoined his regiment. Several pieces of artillery, after firing a few rounds, hurried from the field, saying they were choked. On intimation from one of the captains of the batteries, *Lieutenant-Colonel Hill* promptly moved his regiment to the crest of the hill in front of the artillery, and delivered a volley at the sharpshooters, who were in range, the artillery all limbering up and driving to the rear. The Seventh and Eighteenth both suffered from the enemy's artillery fire, and at times from their sharpshooters.

About two hours later the enemy advanced in strong force across the open field to the right of my front. *Colonel Barbour,* his regiment being on the right, informed me, through *Adjutant Oates,* of the advance, and wished to know what he must do should he be flanked. On being ordered to hold his position as long as possible, he deflected his three right companies, and formed them to the rear, at right angles to the track. I at once sent my courier, *Mr. Shepperd,* to inform *General A. P. Hill* that the enemy were advancing in force upon the opening, *Captain Hawks* having been previously sent to apprise him that their skirmishers were in front of the same. Eight regiments were seen to pass to my right, and another to move by the right flank by file left, between the small body of woods and the fence beyond the track. This last regiment then faced by the rear rank, and opened fire upon my right. The three right companies of the Thirty-seventh became hotly engaged, and *General Gregg's* command was soon after encountered on the military road.

Although our right was turned by such a large force, our position was deemed too important to be given up without a blow, and nobly did both officers and men await the approach of another large force along our entire front [Gibbon's division]. As this force was concealed from the Thirty-third, Eighteenth, and Seventh Regiments by the hill about 40 yards beyond the track, they were cautioned to reserve their fire. The Twenty-eighth and Thirty-seventh, however, had open, level ground in their front, and when the enemy had gotten within 150 yards of our line they opened a terrific and deadly fire upon them, repulsing their first and second lines and checking the third. These two regiments were subjected not only to a direct, but to right and left oblique fires, that portion of the enemy's force behind the hill nearest the Twenty-eighth firing upon them.

As soon as the right of my command became engaged with such an overwhelming force, I dispatched *Captain Hawks* to *General Gregg* for re-inforcements, with instructions, if he was unable to send them, to apply to *General Thomas,* or anybody else whom he might see in command of troops, for assistance. My whole command held their ground until the Twenty-eighth and Thirty-seventh had fired away not only their own ammunition, but that of their own dead and wounded, which in some cases was handed to them by their officers.

When these regiments had ceased firing, the enemy, in column doubled on the center, bore down in mass from behind the hill upon the left of the Twenty-eighth and right of the Thirty-third, and the power of numbers forced them entirely across the railroad. The

Twenty-eighth and Thirty-seventh, being flanked right and left, fell back in an orderly manner, and were resupplied with ammunition. A well-directed volley from the Thirty-third checked the enemy for a time, and *Colonel Avery* ordered a charge, but, being unsupported on his right, he countermanded the order and withdrew his regiment into the woods, about 75 yards from the railroad. The Eighteenth Regiment then fell back about 100 yards, the right companies firing into the foe until he reached the woods in the pursuit. The Seventh, being on the left, fell back about 50 yards in perfect order.

During the greater part of the engagement the enemy's artillery played upon the woods in our rear. While awaiting re-enforcements, I sent my aide, *Lieutenant Lane*, to the left to tell *Lieutenant Colonel Hill*, if he could possibly be spared, to come to the assistance of my right, as it was heavily pressed. The right, however, was forced to fall back before the order could be delivered. *General Thomas* came to my assistance, but too late to save my line. He encountered the enemy in the edge of the woods, drove them back, and, with the Eighteenth and Seventh Regiments of my brigade on his left, chased them to their first position. The Thirty-third, in accordance with orders, held the position in the woods to which it had fallen back until I could move up the Twenty-eighth and Thirty-seventh, when all again resumed their positions on the railroad.

That night the whole brigade was aligned on the track, and skirmishers thrown forward preparatory to a general advance. After this order was countermanded, my command rested on their arms until morning, when, having already been on duty upward of forty-eight hours, there was heavy skirmishing along my whole front. . . . We formed a portion of the second line on Monday, and, as we occupied an exposed position, the men soon constructed a very good temporary breastwork of logs, bush, and dirt, behind which they rested until . . . it was ascertained that the enemy had all recrossed the Rappahannock.

The men of the Twenty-eighth and Thirty-seventh "fought like brave men, long and well," while those of the other regiments calmly held their positions under a heavy artillery fire, one of the most trying positions in which soldiers can be placed. I cannot refrain making special allusion to our conscripts, many of whom were under fire for the first time. They proved themselves worthy accessions to a brigade which has borne itself well in all the battles of the last eight months. . . . Our ambulance corps was very efficient, and removed our wounded rapidly. Our loss . . . was . . . 535. [*O.R.*, XXI, pp. 653–56.]

The 'hill' mentioned in *Lane's* report is in fact a gentle rise a short distance beyond the railroad about where it makes its slight bend to the east. If one were to walk parallel to the tracks from Stop 7 A, it is the first slight—but significant—rise, "about 40 yards" to the right of the tracks after passing the point of woods east of the railroad.

Report of Col. S. Crutchfield, CSA, Chief of Artillery, Second Army Corps, Army of Northern Virginia

On the left of our line were posted twenty-one guns as follows: just at Bernard's cabins and to their left nine guns (consisting of six rifles, two Napoleons, and one 6-pounder). . . . Some 200 yards in front of these, to their right and beyond the railroad, were placed twelve guns (consisting of six rifles, three Napoleons, and three 6-pounders). . . .

From the first it was evident that the enemy's attack might be expected upon our center, where the heights on our right descended to a level with the plain, and a point of woods running out into the field offered them early and good shelter, or that they would endeavor to turn our right. A considerable artillery force was held ready to meet this latter contingency by moving out and taking positions in the fields to our right, so as to cross its fire with the batteries of *Lieutenant-Colonel Walker.* The center of the line was our weakest part, since *Lieutenant-Colonel Walker's* guns could not oblique their fire to the left sufficiently to hope to prevent the enemy seizing the point of woods. . . . The batteries near Bernard's cabins more directly controlled this point, but only by a quite oblique fire to the right; so that there were some 800 or 1000 yards of our front near the center undefended by a direct artillery fire to the front. I examined the ground carefully in the woods behind this point, in hopes of being able to establish batteries of howitzers, which, by canister fire, might soon check the enemy's infantry in their advance through the woods. But I found the ground unfavorable, being intersected by a deep ravine and the undergrowth so thick as to require more time to clear it away than we had before the action began.

The instructions given to *Captains Brockenbrough* and *Davidson* [commanding the batteries on the left of *Jackson's* line] were to reserve their fire for the enemy's infantry at close range, and not to engage his batteries unless he advanced them to the support of his infantry, and then they were to concentrate their fire on the advancing battery, and not to fall back from their position so long as our infantry supported them. The enemy opened the attack by the fire of some twenty-five or thirty guns directed upon *Lieutenant-Colonel Walker's* position, and from about sixteen guns (afterward increased to twenty-four) upon our batteries at and near Bernard's cabins. The officers in charge of these batteries obeyed their orders, and the enemy's fire not being replied to, he advanced his skirmishers in heavy line upon the points occupied by the commands of *Captains Brockenbrough* and *Davidson*. These were soon driven off by canister, and the exact positions of our batteries being thus disclosed to the enemy, he directed a heavy artillery fire upon them, and advanced one of his batteries near a chimney in the center of the plain. This fire was replied to by our batteries, and soon two of the enemy's batteries were withdrawn and their places supplied by others of longer range.

About this time two of our rifled guns belonging to *Captains Wooding's* and *Caskie's* batteries were disabled by their axles breaking from the recoil of the gun, and had to be withdrawn. All this time the enemy's sharpshooters annoyed us greatly, working around to the right of *Captain Brockenbrough's* position whenever driven from his front, and pertinaciously readvancing whenever they could under the shelter of their artillery fire. Though they were once or twice repelled by canister when advancing imprudently, they were so well protected by the accidents of the ground, and so feebly opposed by our own sharpshooters, that they could not be entirely dislodged, and caused heavy loss in our batteries, both among men and horses. *Captain Brockenbrough* was wounded . . . and *Captain Wooding* badly shot while acting as gunner to one of his pieces.

Being badly supported by the infantry in their rear, after severe losses in officers, men, and horses, the batteries of *Captain Brockenbrough's* command were withdrawn, or they would have been lost so soon as the enemy seized the point of woods to their right and rear, as they did. The ammunition in *Captain Raine's* battery . . . was so defective (from the bad fuses, I think), that none of their shells bursting, it was withdrawn and its place supplied by the Chesapeake Artillery, of three guns . . . while a section of *Captain Latimer's* battery, under his own charge, was sent still farther to the front and left. These latter pieces were excellently managed, and though losing heavily from the enemy's sharpshooters, drove back their lines with canister, and caused them great loss by an uncommonly accurate and rapid shell-fire, as they were driven back by *General Law's* brigade in their attempted advance. . . .

The loss in horses, and the nature of the ground, together with the position of the enemy's batteries, and their number, effectively prevented any advance of our batteries as their infantry fell back, and before fresh batteries could get in, their line was reformed near the river road and it was nearly night.

I cannot close this report without calling your attention to the great defect in the ammunition we used, by which few of our shells burst. My own observation entirely confirmed the numerous complaints made to me from the batteries. Much, if not most, of this difficulty is, I am satisfied, justly attributable to the fuses. [*O.R.*, XXI, pp. 636–39]

Report of Brig. Gen. William B. Taliaferro, CSA, Commanding Jackson's Division, Second Army Corps, Army of Northern Virginia

On the morning of the 12th, I marched from Guiney's Station to Hamilton's Crossing, at which place I found the division of *Maj. Gen. A. P. Hill* posted in order of battle from the crossing, on the right, to Bernard's quarters, on the left. I took position on the railroad to his right, but was subsequently ordered to move my command to the rear of the left of his line. I posted *Paxton's* and *Starke's* brigades in rear of *Gregg's* and *Thomas'*, of *Hill's* division, and held *Taliaferro's* and *Jones'* brigades in reserve. . . . *General Early's* line connected with mine on the right. My artillery was held at the crossing on the Mine Road, to the left of the division. I reported to *General A. P. Hill* my dispositions in his rear, and informed him that I had ordered the brigade and battery commanders to recognize any demands for support, if pressing, without the intervention of immediate superiors.

Early on the morning of the 13th, the batteries of *Captain Wooding* and *Carpenter* . . . were posted in the field across the railroad, to the right of *Bernard's* quarters, and the *Lee* battery . . . and two pieces of *Lusk's* battery on the hill to the left. The other pieces of these batteries operated on the extreme right.

The enemy advanced about 9 o'clock, when our batteries opened a destructive fire upon them, causing them to waver and break, but they again advanced, concentrating so heavy a fire of artillery upon the position that it became necessary to retire the batteries behind the railroad, in rear of the quarters, after two hours' action. The infantry of the division during this time were subjected to the shells of the enemy, but advanced to the military road, to be in easy support of

General Hill's line, with perfect steadiness and enthusiasm. *General Paxton*, finding that our troops were giving back to the right of *Gregg's* brigade, and the enemy advancing beyond the front line through a gap which fronted a boggy wood, supposed to be inaccessible to the enemy, moved his brigade to the right and engaged, with two of his regiments, the enemy who had penetrated to the military road but who were retiring by the time he reached that point. He then pushed forward to the front and occupied for the rest of the day the front line at that place. The other brigades were held in position in rear of the military road until the morning of the 14th. . . . [*O.R.*, XXI, pp. 675–76.]

Report of Lieut. Gen. Thomas J. Jackson, CSA, Commanding Second Army Corps, Army of Northern Virginia, Continued.

Repulsed on the right, left, and center, the enemy soon after reformed his lines, and gave some indications of a purpose to renew the attack. I waited some time to receive it; but he making no forward movement, I determined, if prudent, to do so myself. The artillery of the enemy was so judiciously posted as to make an advance of our troops across the plain very hazardous; yet it was so promising of good results, if successfully executed, as to induce me to make preparations for the attempt. In order to guard against disaster, the infantry was to be preceded by artillery, and the movement postponed until late in the evening, so that, if compelled to retire, it would be under the cover of night. Owing to unexpected delays, the movement could not be gotten ready until late in the evening. The first gun had hardly moved forward from the wood 100 yards when the enemy's artillery reopened, and so completely swept our front as to satisfy me that the proposed movement should be abandoned. [*O.R.*, XXI, p. 634.]

Continue on LEE DRIVE about 0.6 mile. Pull out to the right at the signs just short of the STOP sign.

Fredericksburg, a present-day view of Bernard's Cabin site looking northwest toward the railroad tracks across the ground over which the Confederates counterattacked. (HWN)

Today's view of the swampy ground in front of Gregg's position where Meade's attack suceeded. (HWN)

STOP 10, HOOD'S OPPORTUNITY

From this position *Hood* sent *Law's* brigade forward, across the field to your right, to support *Latimer's* battery, guarding *A. P. Hill's* left flank, when it was threatened by Torbert's brigade from the Union Sixth Army Corps. At first glance it does not seem to be a strong position, but remember that any Union attack here would involve advancing across this field into a *cul-de-sac*, exposed to Confederate artillery fire from both flanks. From *Longstreet's* official report it would appear that *Hood* was expected to attack the lines of Meade and Gibbon in flank "and take the attacking forces in reverse."

According to the following narratives, this is not exactly what happened. In his memoirs *Longstreet* recalled that "at the first moment of the break on *Jackson's* lines *Pickett* rode to *Hood* and urged that the opportunity anticipated was at hand, but *Hood* failed to see it in time for effective work." *Longstreet* did not stress the point in his official report because, he later explained, as *Hood* "was high in favor with the authorities, it did not seem prudent to attempt to push the matter." [James Longstreet, *From Manassas to Appomattox* (Bloomington: Indiana University Press, 1960), pp. 307, 309, 317.]

Report of Lieut. Gen. James Longstreet, CSA, Commanding First Army Corps, Army of Northern Virginia

Early on the morning of the 13th I rode to the right of my position (*Hood's* division). The dense fog in the early twilight concealed the enemy from view, but his commands "Forward, guide center, march!" were distinctly heard at different points near my right. From the direction of the sound and the position of his troops the day before, I concluded that his attack would be upon *General Jackson* at some point beyond my right. I therefore rode back to a point near the center of my forces, giving notice to *General Hood* that the enemy would attack *General Jackson* beyond his right; that he should watch carefully the movements, and when an opportunity offered he should move forward and attack the enemy's flank. Similar instructions were given to *General Pickett*, with orders to co-operate with *General Hood*. The attack was made as had been anticipated. It did not appear to have all the force of a real attack, however, and *General Hood* did not feel authorized to make more than a partial advance. When he did move out, he drove the enemy back in handsome style. [*O.R.*, XXI, p. 570.]

Report of Maj. Gen. John B. Hood, CSA, Commanding Hood's Division, First Army Corps, Army of Northern Virginia

In obedience to instructions from the lieutenant-general commanding, on hearing the signal guns about 2 o'clock on the morning of December 11, I immediately formed my command and moved into position along the crest of hills stretching from Dr. Reynolds' house to near the railroad crossing, and occupied the Bowling Green road with a heavy line of skirmishers. Soon afterward I pushed forward about 100 riflemen to harass the enemy in his efforts to throw a bridge across the Rappahannock River at the mouth of Deep Run. . . . The enemy commenced crossing infantry and artillery at dark, and continued doing so throughout the night, at the same time deploying to their left to and below Mr. Arthur Bernard's house, thereby indicating his intention to attack our right. During the night I withdrew the force from the Bowling Green Road. . . .

About 10 o'clock on the morning of the 12th, I was relieved by *General A. P. Hill's* division, and, in obedience to orders . . . relieved *General Pickett* on my left. Discovering a body of the enemy's cavalry deployed along the railroad, I detached two companies from *Toombs'* and one company from *Law's* brigades, and without loss on our side drove them off. . . . About dark, *General Pickett* reoccupied his original position, and, in compliance with instructions . . . I moved my command back to my original position, with orders to co-operate with *A. P. Hill* or any other troops of *General T. J. Jackson's* corps.

On the 13th, during the engagement on the right of our line, a considerable force of the enemy defiled from the right bank of Deep Run, and, forming line of battle, advanced, driving our skirmishers from and occupying the railroad. Two of *Brigadier-General Law's* regiments, the Fifty-seventh . . . and Fifty-fourth North Carolina . . . were thrown forward, the Fifty-seventh leading, and in a gallant style drove the enemy from the position he had gained, following him up to within 300 yards of the Bowling Green Road, and punishing him severely. These regiments, with the Fourth Alabama (*Law's* brigade) in support, held the railroad until dark, when they were relieved by other troops from my command, who retained possession of it until the enemy recrossed the river. . . .

As usual, *Brigadier-General Law* was conspicuous upon the field, acting with great gallantry, and had his horse killed under him while personally directing the movements of his brigade. It is with much pleasure that I call your attention to the gallant bearing of both the officers and men of the Fifty-seventh North Carolina . . . in their charge on a superior force of the enemy posted in the strong position he had gained. Equal praise is due the Fifty-fourth North Carolina . . . for their display of discipline in changing front under fire to cover the left flank of the Fifty-seventh from the fire of a force of the enemy occupying Deep Run below the railroad, to which they became exposed in consequence of their pursuit of the force they had dislodged. [*O.R.*, XXI, pp. 621–22.]

Report of Brig. Gen. E. M. Law, CSA, Commanding Law's Brigade, Hood's Division, First Army Corps, Army of Northern Virginia

On the plateau directly in front of the position occupied by my brigade, and about 500 yards distant, the skirt of timber bordering on Deep Run from its confluence with the Rappahannock abruptly terminates. From this point to the river the channel of the run becomes gradually wider and deeper, its general direction being almost perpendicular to our own line and that of the enemy on the Bowling Green Road. I received orders during the morning from *Major-General Hood* . . . to render assistance to *Maj. Gen. A. P. Hill's* troops, in the event it should be required, and was ordered by *General Hill* to support *Brigadier-General Pender*, who held the left of the first line to my front and right.

At 3 o'clock in the afternoon, a force of the enemy defiled from the wood on Deep Run, and, forming into line of battle, advanced upon *Latimer's* battery, which was posted in the plateau on *General Pender's* left and supported by one of his regiments. Perceiving this attack, I moved my brigade forward to the edge of the timber, in rear of the battery. Detaching the Fifty-seventh and Fifty-fourth North Carolina Regiments, I advanced with them to attack the enemy, who had now gained the line of railroad which crosses the plateau directly in front of the battery and about 200 yards from it. The enemy was promptly driven from the railroad by the Fifty-seventh North Carolina, which was in advance, and the regiment continued to move steadily forward to within 300 yards of the Bowling Green Road, driving his infantry before it. During the action a body of the enemy opened fire from the wood bordering the run, upon the left of the advancing line. This was promptly checked by a fire from the left of the Fifty-seventh and from the Fifty-fourth, which changed front obliquely to the left in order to face the wood.

In the meantime the Fourth Alabama had been brought forward in front of the battery as a support. Having accomplished my purpose of driving the enemy from the vicinity of the battery, I ordered the two regiments in advance to retire and take position on the railroad, which they held until after dark, when they were relieved by the Sixth North Carolina. [*O.R.*, XXI, pp. 623–24.]

Report of Capt. Latimer, CSA, Acting Chief of Artillery, Ewell's [Early's] Division, Second Army Corps, Army of Northern Virginia

Early on the morning of the 13th, I was ordered by *General Early* to take command of the batteries of the division . . . and I immediately reported to *Colonel Crutchfield*, chief of artillery, Second Corps, for instructions. He ordered me to park the batteries in a sheltered spot behind a range of hills about half a mile behind our line of battle, and there await orders. He shortly after returned and directed me to take my own battery, under command of *Lieutenant Tanner*, and *Captain Brown's* . . . to the relief of some batteries occupying a position near the extreme left of the line formed by the Second Corps, and to report to *Brigadier-General Pender*, whose brigade then occupied this position. Only five guns were required, and by direction of *General Pender* I relieved five of the guns at that point by the two rifles belonging to my battery and the three rifles composing *Captain Brown's*.

The position on which these guns were posted was not a very advantageous one, but the best that could be selected. It was a small rising in an open field, with a wood to the right, in which a portion of *General A. P. Hill's* division was posted, and on the left was a ditch and bank running parallel with the railroad, behind which a portion of *General Hood's* division was posted. In front, at the distance of about a mile, were four of the enemy's batteries, with lines of skirmishers considerably advanced in front. . . . We were exposed to quite a heavy fire from these batteries, but gained the position without loss.

My orders were to fire only at infantry unless the batteries advanced, which orders I obeyed, firing only once at them, and then only to cover the advance of *General Law's* brigade . . . late in the day. I was kept constantly engaged at this point from 11 a.m. (when I gained it) until night, repelling repeated advances of the enemy by the use of canister. I relieved these batteries that night. . . . [*O.R.*, XXI, 668–69.]

Report of Brig. Gen. W. D. Pender, CSA, Commanding Pender's Brigade, A. P. Hill's Division, Second Army Corps, Army of Northern Virginia

When the enemy advanced on the right, they opened a most tremendous fire of artillery upon the batteries in my front, playing upon them from the front and right from at least four batteries. This fire was most destructive to my men. At about this time a heavy line of skirmishers advanced to within range of *Captain Davidson's* battery and kept up a hot fire upon him. . . . These skirmishers became so annoying that additional companies had to be thrown out. . . . *Colonel McElroy*, with . . . the Sixteenth North Carolina, had been placed early in the morning near the railroad cut, and in front of the left battery, which . . . consisted of some rifle pieces under *Captain Latimer*—as brave a soldier as I ever saw—to support it. He was here much exposed, being far in advance of the general line, with his left totally unprotected, but with the ravine of Deep Run to cover the movement of the enemy on his left. After the heat of the action on the right, the enemy advanced a brigade up Deep Run, throwing one regiment somewhat in advance, which so sheltered itself behind the trees as to get near enough to take an officer and 15 men of the Sixteenth prisoners, who were protecting the left flank of their regiment. This left the regiment to be raked by a fire down the railroad track. The colonel drew his regiment back to the ditch near, and here held his ground until *General Law* sent forward two regiments to his assistance. These three then charged the enemy, driving them from the railroad cut and across the field to within a short distance of their batteries. Owing to a great many of *Colonel McElroy's* men not having cartridge boxes, they got out of ammunition, but, getting into the ditch and dividing there, they maintained their ground. [*O.R.*, XXI, pp. 661–62.]

Report of Col. A. T. A. Torbert, USA, Commanding First Brigade, First Division, Sixth Army Corps, Center Grand Division, Army of the Potomac

At daylight on the 12th, the brigade started to cross the river. On reaching the south bank it was formed in two lines, in rear of the division; first line, Fifteenth and Twenty-third [New Jersey] Regiments, deployed; second line, First, Second, Third, and Fourth [New Jersey] Regiments, in line of masses 100 yards in rear.

About 1 o'clock the brigade advanced across a beautiful plain to support the second line of the division, during which time the enemy shelled them, but without effect. They were then put in a deep ravine to shelter them from the enemy's fire, where they lay on their arms all night. . . .

On the morning of the 13th, I relieved the pickets of the division by the Fifteenth Regiment, and supported them by the balance of the brigade.

About 3 p.m. General Brooks, commanding division, ordered me to advance one regiment, supported by another, and drive the enemy from and hold their position, posted in a railroad cut and behind the embankment, just where the railroad crossed a deep ravine, and on the extreme left of my picket line. At the same time two regiments of the Third Brigade were placed under my orders. I immediately ordered Colonel Hatch, with the Fourth Regiment New Jersey Volunteers (about 300 rifles), to advance and take the position . . . at the same time directing the left of my picket line, with its reserve, under Major Brown, Fifteenth Regiment, to advance with them.

These troops advanced in a handsome manner under a severe fire, and then charged the enemy's position, led by their gallant leader . . . driving them from it with great loss, capturing about 25 prisoners of a Georgia and North Carolina regiment. The enemy being in a stronger force than was supposed, I at once ordered the Twenty-third Regiment New Jersey Volunteers . . . and the two regiments of the Third Brigade to advance and support the Fourth and Fifteenth. Six companies of the Twenty-third were soon engaged. At this time I received orders to halt the balance of my supports and fall back from the railroad, and hold it with pickets only, if possible, for fear that a general engagement might be brought on. The enemy seeing my small force at the railroad, and that retiring, charged with a whole brigade to the railroad. My men fell back and the pickets held their original line. . . .

In this affair I regret to mention the loss of 1 officer and 16 enlisted men killed; 5 officers and 90 enlisted men wounded, and 50 enlisted men missing in action. Many of the missing were wounded and taken prisoners. . . . I am pleased to speak in the highest terms of the conduct of the Twenty-Third Regiment New Jersey Volunteers, being a nine-months' regiment, and the first time they were under fire. Their Colonel (Ryerson), formerly of the Second Regiment New Jersey Volunteers, who was badly wounded at Gaines' Mill, was to be seen in the thickest of the fight (mounted), cheering on his men. [O.R., XXI, pp. 527–28.]

Turn RIGHT at the STOP sign. Drive 1.6 miles on LANS-DOWNE ROAD to a STOP sign at a "T" intersection. Turn RIGHT on U.S. 17 and drive about 1.15 miles to a crushed rock turnout on the right. Pull over and stop there.

STOP 11, GIBBON'S ATTACK

Gibbon's leading brigade crossed the Bowling Green Road here, moved forward through the field to your right, and lay down under cover of the slight elevation easily identified by the large weathered barn and the white house to its right, about 0.3 mile from your location. Gibbon's two other brigades followed and took shelter in a shallow depression a hundred feet or so to the rear. Hall's Maine battery was posted about where the barn stands today.

Because the point of woods through which Meade advanced extended only a few hundred yards *east* of the railroad at the time of the battle, Hall's battery was visible and well within the range of *Walker's* Confederate guns near at STOP 6.

Gibbon's attack was directed against *Lane's* Confederate brigade, posted behind the railroad embankment and in the woods that you see a quarter of a mile or more beyond the weathered barn. The events described by *Law* (Stop 10) took place in the distant field to the right of the barn and white house.

Report of Maj. Gen. William B. Franklin, USA, Commanding Left Grand Division, Army of the Potomac

A 8.30 o'clock General Meade's division moved forward. . . . It was met by a severe fire of artillery . . . [which] was answered by the artillery of Reynolds' corps, which, in the course of two hours or more, silenced the enemy's batteries . . . and Meade's division immediately afterward moved on to the attack. . . . Meade passed into the wood, carried it, crossed the railroad, and gained the crest of the hill. . . .

At the same time Gibbon's division advanced, crossed the railroad, entered the wood, and took some prisoners, driving back the first line of the enemy; but the wood was so dense that the connection between Meade's and his line could not be kept up. In consequence . . . Meade's line, which was vigorously attacked by a large column of fresh troops . . . was repulsed, leaving the wood at a walk, but not in order. . . . Gibbon's division was also repulsed shortly afterward. Just as Meade was repulsed, two regiments of Berry's brigade, Birney's division, Stoneman's corps, which had just arrived, were thrown into the wood on Gibbon's left. They also were soon driven out. While Meade's division was getting rallied, the remainder of Birney's division came up and drove the enemy from the front of the wood, where he had appeared in strong force. This division, with the aid of the artillery, soon drove the enemy back to shelter, and he did not again appear. It also materially aided in saving Hall's battery, then seriously threatened. Gibbon's division then fell back in good order . . . and was relieved by General Sickles' division, of Stoneman's corps. . . . [*O.R.*, XXI, p. 450]

Report of Brig. Gen. John Gibbon, USA, Commanding Second Division, First Army Corps, Left Grand Division, Army of the Potomac

On the morning of the 13th, the Second Division occupied the right of the First Corps, and was immediately on the left of the Sixth Corps, and in rear of the Bowling Green Road. At 9 a.m. an advance was ordered by General Reynolds, when I directed Taylor's brigade, preceded by skirmishers, to cross the road and the open field between us and the wood occupied by the enemy. On reaching half way across this field, the men were directed to lie down, under cover of a slight elevation, which protected them from the fire in front, but not from a heavy cross-fire of artillery, which the division remained under the whole of the morning. Lyle's brigade was moved forward to within supporting distance of Taylor's and Root's, in close column of regiments, was formed in rear of the left and in support of Hall's Maine battery, which, under a heavy artillery fire, came into action on the left of Lyle's brigade.

In this position the division remained, waiting for orders, until about 12 o'clock, at which time, the fog having somewhat lifted, the enemy opened with a number of guns from an eminence in front of Meade's division. The fire of Hall's battery was joined to that of Meade's batteries, and, after a heavy cannonading, several of the enemy's ammunition boxes were blown up and the guns silenced.

Immediately after, seeing Meade's men advancing to assault the enemy's position, I ordered Taylor's brigade forward. A severe fire was at once opened upon it by the enemy, posted behind the railroad embankment and in the wood. The left of Taylor's line was subjected to the heaviest fire, and was thrown into confusion. Lyle's brigade was now ordered up in support, and took post on the left of Taylor's right wing . . . which still held its position. Thompson's Pennsylvania battery was also ordered up to the right of the line to aid in the attack. Lyle's brigade soon fell into confusion, and most of it retired in disorder. The gallant Twelfth Massachusetts . . . however, held its ground.

Finding we were making but little impression on the enemy's position, sheltered as he was, I ordered up Root's brigade and directed it to take the position with the bayonet. The charge was gallantly made, and the brigade, being joined by the Twelfth Massachusetts and the remnants of some other regiments, took and held the embankment for some time, capturing 180 prisoners. Our forces on the right did not advance. I had exhausted my last man in capturing the position. Meade's men were retiring on the left, and without the speedy arrival of re-enforcements the position would have to be abandoned, as the enemy was pushing forward his.

About 2.30 o'clock, after directing the fire of Hall's battery upon a force of the enemy which issued from the wood on the left of my line, I was wounded and left the field. . . .

I desire to call special attention to the . . . gallantry and steadiness under fire of the . . . Sixteenth Maine. . . . [which], although for the first time under fire, gave an example of gallantry and steadiness worthy of the imitation of some of the older regiments. Hall's battery was under the severest fire, and was served with its usual efficiency and gallantry.

The loss in the division was 1,249 killed, wounded, and missing. . . . [O.R., XXI, pp. 480–81.]

Report of Col. Adrian R. Root, USA, Commanding First Brigade, Second Division, First Army Corps, Left Grand Division, Army of the Potomac

At 10 o'clock . . . pursuant to orders . . . I moved the brigade to the left about 400 yards, and then, changing direction to the right, advanced to the front, across a deep, wooded ravine and over an adjacent elevation of ground, to the Bowling Green turnpike. In effecting this movement the brigade was exposed to a severe fire of shell from the enemy's batteries, planted upon the wooded heights to the front, and, in order to avoid this fire, I made a considerable detour to the left, and succeeded in reaching the position assigned me with the loss of but 3 men wounded. I then deployed the One hundred and seventh Regiment Pennsylvania Volunteers . . . and the One hundred and fifth Regiment New York Volunteers . . . in two parallel lines in a plowed field between the turnpike and the heights to the front, supporting Hall's battery and the left of the first and second lines of the division. I deployed the Sixteenth . . . Maine, . . . the Ninety-fourth . . . New York, . . . and the One hundred and fourth New York . . . in three parallel lines to the right and rear of Hall's battery. The men were ordered to lie down, and for several hours the brigade remained without loss under a severe and constant fire from the enemy's batteries.

At 1.30 p.m. the brigades of . . . the first and second lines of the division advanced in succession to the front and opened a fire of musketry upon the enemy's position in the wood skirting the base of the heights.

At 1.45 p.m. I received an order from General Gibbon in person to charge to the front with my brigade, storm the enemy's breast-work, and occupy his position. I at once deployed the One hundred and seventh Pennsylvania . . . the One hundred and fifth New York . . . and the Sixteenth Maine . . . in line of battle, at double quick, to the right of Hall's battery, and strengthened this line by deploying the Ninety-fourth New York . . . and One hundred and fourth New York Volunteers . . . in its rear in two parallel lines, with intervals of 15 paces. Having unslung knapsacks and fixed bayonets, the brigade advanced to the front under a severe fire of . . . artillery and musketry, moving steadily across the plowed field and passing through the broken lines of the Second and Third Brigades, which, with the exception of the Twelfth Massachusetts, . . . Second Brigade, and the Eighty-eighth Pennsylvania . . . and Ninety-seventh New York, . . . Third Brigade, were retiring to the rear in confusion. On approaching the wood the enemy's position was first fully developed to my brigade, and consisted of the embankment and ditches of the Richmond railway, the approaches being rendered extremely difficult by several parallel ditches, or rifle-pits, and its rear protected by thick wood, sheltering infantry supports.

As the brigade arrived upon the ground previously occupied by the Second and Third Brigades, the fire of the enemy became so incessant and galling, and so many of my men fell killed or wounded, that the front line of the brigade slackened its pace, and the men, without orders, commenced firing. A halt seemed imminent, and a halt in the face of the terrific fire to which the brigade was exposed would have been death; or, worse, a disastrous repulse.

At this moment Brigadier-General Taylor came up in person, and rendered me timely assistance in encouraging the brigade to advance, and Colonel Bates, Twelfth Massachusetts Volunteers, whose ammunition had been exhausted, promptly complied with my request that his regiment might unite with my brigade in a bayonet charge. By the strenuous exertions of the regimental commanders and other officers, the firing was nearly discontinued. The brigade resumed its advance, and as the men recognized the enemy their movement increased in rapidity until, with a shout and a run, the brigade leaped the ditches, charged across the railway, and occupied the wood beyond, driving the enemy from their position, killing a number with the bayonet, and capturing upward of 200 prisoners. These prisoners belonged principally to the Thirty-third North Carolina . . . [*Lane's* brigade], including its lieutenant-colonel and several line officers, and were at once sent to the rear under a small guard. In charging over the railway, the brigade had necessarily become somewhat broken, especially as the Ninety-fourth and One hundred and fourth New York Volunteers had, in their eagerness to engage the enemy, broken through the first line of the brigade.

Leaving my aides . . . and the regimental commanders to reform the lines, I rode rapidly to General Gibbon, reported the success of the charge, and asked for further instructions. General Gibbon directed me to go on. On returning to the wood, I found that the enemy had rallied in superior force, and were vigorously pressing the front and flank of my brigade. I again rode to General Gibbon and requested support, to enable me to retain my position, and was informed that re-enforcements would shortly arrive. I applied also to Colonel Lyle, commanding the Second Brigade, and entreated him to return with his men to the assistance of my brigade, but could not persuade him to do so. While urging detached parties of men back to the wood, I was informed that General Gibbon had been wounded and had left the field. General Taylor, of the Third Brigade, being the next senior officer, I reported to him the situation of the brigade, and was directed to withdraw it from the wood whenever its safety demanded it. Returning to the railway, I found that the enemy, in an attempt to turn the flanks of my brigade, were emerging from the wood in defiance of the shells with which Hall's battery, to the left and rear, and Thompson's battery, to the right and rear, were endeavoring to protect my flanks. . . . The position, which, with supporting brigade, would have been perfectly tenable, was, by the absence of any infantry support whatever, rendered simply murderous to my command. . . .

With real pain . . . I gave the order . . . to fall back. The officers and men received it with surprise and grief, and retired so reluctantly that the enemy was enabled to close upon the rear of the brigade and inflict a loss exceeding that incurred during the charge itself. As the brigade retired, most of the wounded were brought from the wood and field. . . . Arriving at the Bowling Green turnpike, I halted the brigade, faced it about, and reformed it in line of battle, and deployed the Ninety-fourth . . . New York . . . as skirmishers 40 yards to the front. . . .

The loss of the brigade. . . . Officers killed, 2; wounded, 26; missing, 4; total, 32. Enlisted men killed, 50; wounded, 343; missing, 53; total, 446. Aggregate, 478.

I wish to acknowledge my obligations to Colonel Bates, Twelfth Massachusetts Volunteers, for his prompt and generous response to my request for his co-operation. He promptly united his regiment with my brigade and charged upon the enemy's position with fixed bayonets and empty cartridge-boxes. [*O.R.*, XXI, pp. 486–89.]

Report of Capt. James A. Hall, USA, Second Maine Battery, Second Division, First Corps, Left Grand Division, Army of the Potomac

The battery was ordered into position by Colonel Wainwright, at 9 a.m., in the corn-field on the south of the Plank Road, and on the left of General Gibbon's division, to support its left flank. A battery of the enemy at the time was playing upon us, and did us considerable harm for a short time; but, as we opened upon them with shell, they soon ceased firing, or turned their fire in another direction. This battery was 1,600 yards diagonally on our right flank. As there was considerable smoke, it was difficult to tell the effect of our shots upon them. As the heavy mist which hung over the field cleared away, I found I was exposed to a cross-fire from a battery of the enemy, 700 yards directly on our left flank, which opened with a rapid and well-directed fire of solid shot which was very galling. After firing for some thirty minutes I was ordered to cease, by order of General Reynolds, as we were firing over our line of infantry.

We did not open upon the battery on our left flank, there being a mass of our own troops intervening; besides, there were other batteries farther to our left which opened upon it and soon caused it to change position.

By order of General Gibbon, I sent my caissons back across the road, under cover; not, however, until a limber chest . . . had been blown up. The guns were kept in position, firing only occasionally into the woods, until 2 p.m., when we commenced shelling the woods in front of us where our infantry were about to advance, and also fired some 60 rounds at the battery [*Walker's* guns at Stop 6] which was playing upon General Meade's left flank as his division advanced. This battery of the enemy opened with ten guns, which were engaged by some forty from our lines, making it difficult to tell the effect of any one of our batteries, but the enemy's guns were soon silenced, and three of their caissons blown up. This battery was 1,300 yards diagonally on our left flank.

When General Gibbon's line went forward, he ordered the battery to advance, posting it within 200 yards of the woods, into which he directed a rapid fire of shell, continuing it until General Gibbon's division fell back, retiring some distance to my rear.

I now discovered a body of the enemy advancing from the woods, in front of my left, and opened upon them with case shot and canister at 200 yards distance. . . . This last fire was very effectual, cutting down men and colors. My last round of ammunition being fired, I was obliged to retire, and, in limbering to the rear, five horses were shot from my left gun, and I was obliged to leave it upon the field for a time, as I had only horses enough to get the others away. As soon as I had got from under fire of the enemy's musketry, I halted my guns, taking four horses from one of them, and with 6 men I returned to my abandoned piece and dragged it safely off the field. My horses had become so reduced, I could only move with three pieces. . . .

My casualties . . . were 2 men killed, 14 wounded; also 25 horses killed and 6 wounded. Eleven hundred rounds of ammunition were expended. [*O.R.*, XXI, pp. 483–84.]

Welford's Mill on Hazel Run. Telegraph Road in the foreground and Marye's Heights in the background. (USAMHI)

ARTILLERY SUPPORT

Report of Brig. Gen. Henry J. Hunt, USA, Chief of Artillery, Army of the Potomac

Franklin's attack on the left was made by his grand division, Smith's and Reynolds' corps, re-enforced by Birney's and Sickles' divisions, of Stoneman's corps, and the deployment of the attack enabled him to bring all his division artillery into action.

The right of the troops connected with Getty's division between Deep and Hazel Runs. On the right of Deep Run was placed Williston's battery (six 12-pounders). On the left, Ayres' . . . Butler's, McCartney's, Clark's, and Snow's batteries . . . were in line parallel to and in front of the Bowling Green Road, forming a large battery of twenty-eight guns, to protect the flank of the attack. In rear of Williston's battery was posted Hexamer's six 10-pounders.

This development of artillery was rendered necessary, first, to keep clear the spur on our right, from which our advancing line could be enfiladed; second, to prevent the enemy striking at our bridges and cutting our communication with them, and, third, to clear the hill in front of our line of battle, should the enemy attempt to prevent our deployment. This line of artillery was prolonged to the left by Hall's, Ransom's and Cooper's batteries, the last of which extended to the road which runs perpendicular to our front, and strikes the river at Smithfield. Our troops occupied this road, thus forming a crotchet at Cooper's position. On the prolongation of the Bowling Green Road, at its intersection with another cross-road, the enemy had placed a battery [Pelham] which could enfilade our left batteries.

About 9 a.m. the enemy's whole line opened on our front and left, and Simpson's battery (four 12-pounders) changed front to fire to the left, on the guns . . . on the Bowling Green Road . . . enfilading our line. He was assisted in this duty by Wolcott's battery (six 3-inch guns), stationed at Smithfield, where our extreme left struck the river. From this position the enemy's battery was taken obliquely, one of their guns dismounted, and the rest driven off. The enemy also opened fire from his advanced position on the spur near Hazel Run [Latimer's position]. Martin's, Butler's, and McCartney's batteries immediately changed front, by order of Captain Ayres, chief of artillery, Sixth Corps, and, assisted by Hexamer's battery, already in position, entirely subdued the enemy's fire by 12 m. and drove him from his position with the loss of a part of a battery, left disabled on the field. Amsden's battery now joined from the north side of the river, and was posted near Ransom's.

About 2 p.m. our guns opened all along the front, to clear the woods for an infantry assault by Meade's and Gibbon's divisions. . . . The enemy replied with his artillery, but was silenced on the right by the dismounting of one of his guns and the blowing up of two of his caissons. On the left the enemy replied by his batteries in our front, and also from six or eight guns to the front and left of his former enfilading position on the Bowling Green Road. Wolcott's battery of five guns (one having been disabled by the enemy's shot) was brought up to the Bowling Green Road and posted about half way between Simpson's battery and the enemy's former enfilading position. Three batteries (Gerrish's, Stewart's, and Reynolds', numbering in all fourteen guns) were placed in position at the point formerly occupied by the enemy. The batteries all opened, and in half an hour silenced those of the enemy, after blowing up four of his caissons.

Our line had been steadily extending toward the left. This was safely done under protection of De Russy's batteries, on the north side of the Rappahannock River, which he moved up and down the river, and so maneuvered as to defeat all the demonstrations of the enemy against our left flank. One of his batteries (Taft's) was so placed as to sweep the valley of the Massaponax for about 1½ miles from its mouth, and so command its bridges that the enemy were unable to communicate across the creek, except by the head of it, and were thus prevented from extending toward the river on our left. As our line extended to the left, the openings were filled by Birney's and Sickles' divisions, which brought Randolph's, Turnbull's, and Seeley's batteries in position, giving a total force of sixty-seven guns on this front.

The assault of our infantry having been repulsed, they were closely followed by the enemy, who were driven back by the canister fire of Randolph's, Ransom's, Cooper's, Turnbull's, and Amsden's batteries, and charged by Robinson's brigade, which was acting as their support. Hall's Maine battery . . . was especially exposed to the attack of the enemy, and was ordered to retire. . . .

About sunset the enemy opened again for a short time, and there was some artillery fire on both sides until dark. The batteries . . . on the north side of the river opened fire upon the enemy whenever they could do so without damage to our own troops. . . .

The chiefs of artillery of corps whose batteries were engaged . . .

performed these duties with their accustomed skill and gallantry. . . . The artillery seems to have been managed by them with judgment. The expenditure of ammunition was notably reduced when compared with the effect produced and former experience; and in all cases where the material was endangered, or from reduction in the number of men and horses exposed to danger, proper measures were adopted to secure them. Not a gun nor a carriage was lost; repairs of damages were effected promptly, and the batteries were placed in as effective condition as circumstances would permit.

The supply of artillery ammunition from the division trains was uncertain, and, until those trains are placed under the exclusive control of the chiefs of artillery, reliance cannot . . . be placed upon them. The ammunition train of the Artillery Reserve, however, as has always been the case . . . supplied all deficiencies. All artillery and . . . infantry ammunition should be transported in caissons, under the direction of properly organized companies. In this way only can supplies under all circumstances, on the field of battle as elsewhere, be certainly provided when wanted.

Attention has been called in the course of these reports . . . to the absolute necessity of keeping up, especially in the light 12-pounder batteries, the number of men required for their efficient service. This should never be less than 150 for a six-gun battery. The service of guns on the field requires a great amount of physical power. Under all circumstances the work is exceedingly exhausting, and when the number of men is much reduced it becomes too great for endurance. Details of 20 and 30 men in several cases had to be furnished from the infantry. The men furnished were necessarily unacquainted with the duties and worked to disadvantage, while their service in the positions for which they had been trained were lost. . . . It is . . . affecting all batteries throughout the army, and can only be adequately provided for by some general regulations, rigidly enforced. . . . A special recruiting service for the artillery of each State, with one or more depot batteries for their instruction and to which sick and wounded men can be sent, with perhaps authority to enlist for volunteer batteries in the field, from the regiments of their own State, a limited number of men, as now permitted for regular batteries, would do much to relieve the service of the evils it suffers from this cause. [*O.R.*, XXI, pp. 185–89.]

Journal of Colonel Charles S. Wainwright, USA, Chief of Artillery, First Army Corps, Left Grand Division, Army of the Potomac

December 21. Have just finished my detailed report to General Hunt, a copy of which I will send to General Reynolds, for I mean so far as possible to do all that lies in my power to look upon Hunt as my actual commander, and the artillery as simply attached for service to the corps. The report gave me an excellent opportunity to show some of the bad workings of the present artillery system, especially in that the corps chief of artillery has no control over the extra ammunition. I might have gone farther and shown what blunders General Doubleday made, and some on Gibbon's part too. Meade, when [Capt. R. R.] Ransom [commanding artillery, Third Division] went to him for orders, told him to go to me, that he had nothing to do with the artillery. If our division chiefs of artillery had more rank, and it was distinctly understood that they held their positions because they were supposed to be particularly well acquainted with their own arm of the service, so that the division commander would rely on their judgment and take their advice, it would be different. But as it is they do little more than look after their own battery, and do not dare to state their objections to anything their division commander may order. I might too have enlarged on the fact that the batteries of all the divisions were posted with the First [Division] on Sunday and Monday [December 14–15], and that on Saturday the firing of the First Division batteries had but little to do with the movement of that division. [Allan Nevins, ed., *A Diary of Battle: the Personal Journals of Colonel Charles S. Wainwright 1861–1863* (New York: Harcourt, Brace and World, Inc., 1962), pp. 148–49.]

When traffic allows, turn around, reversing your route on U.S. 17. Drive 2.5 miles to CHARLES STREET and turn LEFT, following Truck Route 17 north into Fredericksburg. At the traffic light just beyond the railroad underpass, turn left on Business Route 1 (LAFAYETTE AVENUE) and follow it 0.5 mile to the VISITOR CENTER. Turn right just short of the VISITOR CENTER, and park in the parking area behind the building.

Walk to the front of the VISITOR CENTER and then follow the walk up the hill through the gate into the National Cemetery. Continue to the top of the hill, then follow the path to the left to the vicinity of the sign and the cannon.

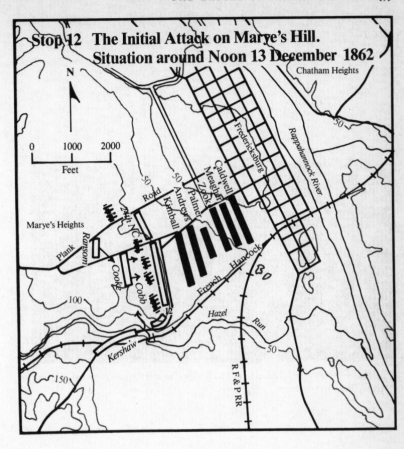

Stop 12   The Initial Attack on Marye's Hill.
Situation around Noon 13 December 1862

A postwar view of Fredericksburg from Marye's Heights and the new National Cemetery. (USAMHI)

STOP 12A, MARYE'S HILL

Report of Lieut. Gen. James Longstreet, CSA, Commanding First Army Corps, Army of Northern Virginia

The enemy held quiet possession of the Stafford Heights until 3 o'clock on the morning of the 11th, when our signal guns gave notice of his approach. The troops, being at their different camp-grounds, were formed immediately and marched to their positions along the line. *Ransom's* division was ordered to take a sheltered position in easy supporting distance of the batteries on Marye Hill. . . . Soon after dark, *General McLaws* ordered *Barksdale's* brigade to retire [from Fredericksburg, where it had "engaged the enemy at the river"]. . . . His brigade was then relieved by that of *Brig. Gen. T. R. R. Cobb*, which was placed by *General McLaws* along the Telegraph Road, in front of the Marye house (a stone fence and cut along this road gave good protection against infantry). When *Cobb's* brigade got into position, *Ransom's* division was withdrawn and placed in reserve. During the night the enemy finished his bridges and began to throw his troops across.

His movements early on the 12th seemed to be directly against our right, but when the fog lifted columns were seen opposite Fredericksburg, the head of them then crossing at the bridges. . . . *Ransom's* division was moved back to the Marye Hill. *Featherston's* brigade, of *Anderson's* division (previously occupying this hill) was closed in upon the other brigades of *Anderson*. The entire day was occupied by the enemy in throwing his forces across the river and in deploying his columns. Our batteries were opened upon the masses of infantry whenever they were in certain range. Our fire invariably drew that of the enemy's batteries on the opposite heights, and they generally kept up the fire long after our batteries had ceased. . . .

About 11 a.m. [on the 13th] I sent orders for the batteries to play upon the streets and bridges beyond the city, by way of diversion in favor of our right. The batteries had hardly opened when the enemy's infantry began to move out toward my line. Our pickets in front of the Marye house were soon driven in, and the enemy began to deploy his forces in front of that point. Our artillery, being in position, opened fire as soon as the masses became dense enough to warrant it. This fire was very destructive and demoralizing in its effects, and frequently made gaps in the enemy's ranks that could be seen at the distance of a mile. [*O.R.*, XXI, pp. 569–70.]

Report of Col. J. B. Walton, CSA, Commanding Battalion, Washington Artillery, First Army Corps Artillery, Army of Northern Virginia

At 12.30 p.m. the enemy was observed in force moving down upon our position through the streets of the town. Everything being in readiness, fire was immediately opened from all my batteries, at once halting and breaking his first advance. Again they emerged in greater force and apparently with much steadiness. Gaining the crest of an elevated piece of ground in our front, he opened upon our position a galling fire of musketry and of artillery from the hills beyond. The brigade of *General Cobb* in front of my batteries then opened fire and the battle became general all along our line. Again and again did their heavy masses come forth from the town, only to be mowed down and scattered in confusion as each time they formed and advanced. Three times their colors were leveled by the unerring aim of the gunners.

At 2 p.m. a portion of *General Ransom's* division (supporting column) moved steadily across the plateau in my rear. Halting but an instant on the crest of the hill, they delivered a volley, then plunged with a cheer into the road below and in front of us, already occupied by *Cobb's* troops. The sharpshooters of the enemy, under cover of a cut in front and the slope of the hill, kept up a galling fire upon our works, causing many of my gallant men to fall . . . at their posts. . . . Five several times did heavy masses of the enemy's infantry, supported by light batteries which had been placed in position on the field, advance from the cover of the town and the scattered houses, only to meet the fate of those who had preceded them. They fell by thousands under the judicious, steady, and unerring fire of my guns, encouraged and aided by the gallant conduct of the brave troops in the road in front of us.

At 5 p.m., after having been engaged four hours and a half against overwhelming odds . . . I was compelled to relinquish the post of honor to *Woolfolk's* and *Moody's* batteries, *Alexander's* battalion, having one gun disabled, and having exhausted all the canister, shell, and case shot, and nearly every round of solid shot in the chests. More could not be supplied in position in time, the train being several miles distant. [*O.R.*, XXI, p. 574.]

Report of Lieut. Col. E. P. Alexander, CSA, Commanding Battalion, Reserve Artillery, First Army Corps, Army of Northern Virginia

At 3.40 p.m. . . . . I received an order to relieve the Washington Artillery on Marye's Hill, their ammunition being nearly exhausted. I at once hastened there with *Captain Woolfolk's* battery, *Captain Moody's* 12-pounder guns, and two guns of *Captain Jordan's* battery, and occupied the pits under a heavy fire, which caused three-fourths of my entire loss while galloping up. The enemy were already within 300 yards, and seeing the Washington Artillery leave after so protracted and gallant a defense, cheered and pressed on heavily, aided by three batteries which opened from the edge of the town and their line of heavy guns on the opposite bank. Disregarding the latter, we poured a rapid and murderous fire on the former and their advancing infantry, under which — and the accurate aim of our veteran infantry beneath us — they were soon driven to shelter behind the houses of the town. About dark the remaining section of *Captain Jordan's* battery was brought up, one gun replacing a damaged gun of *Captain Maurin's* in a pit left of the Plank Road, and the other remaining near, under the control of *General Ransom*, for any emergency. About 7 p.m. the enemy, said to have been Sykes' division of regulars, again advanced under cover of darkness until opened on by our infantry below. My guns opened with canister and case shot at the flashes of their muskets, and this their last repulse was said to have been the bloodiest. . . .

On the 14th, we fired but few shots, and only at bodies of the enemy's infantry, being compelled to economize ammunition. . . . [That] night . . . *Captain Parker* discovered a position enfilading the canal valley in front of the town, and two pits were constructed at it, which I occupied before day with *Moody's* 12-pounder guns. When the fog lifted, the reserves of the enemy's pickets could be seen lying flat on their faces in the valley — in the language of General Burnside, "holding the first ridge." A few well-directed shots . . . soon . . . broke this hold, and all who could not find fresh shelter fled in confusion to the city, under the fire of our sharpshooters and several guns immediately in their rear. This, with a single shot in the brick tannery, broke up entirely the annoying fire of sharpshooters, under which we suffered considerably the day before, and for the rest of the day we worked openly in our pits, and fired at all bodies of infantry appearing in town, unannoyed. [*O.R.*, XXI, p. 576.]

Report of Brig. Gen. Robert Ransom, Jr., CSA, Commanding Ransom's Division, First Army Corps, Army of Northern Virginia

On the morning of [the 11th] . . . the division took position about 600 yards in rear of our batteries, which were upon Marye's and Willis' Hills, and at the time occupied by the Washington Artillery. About noon it was withdrawn to the Telegraph Road, a little in rear of where *General Longstreet* had his headquarters during the day. At 9 p.m. it retook the position of the morning, *Cooke's* brigade being advanced to within 200 yards of our batteries, and the Twenty-fourth North Carolina Volunteers, of my brigade, was placed in a ditch on the left and in the prolongation of *Cobb's* brigade, which occupied the Telegraph Road in front of Marye's and Willis' Hills. The left of the Twenty-fourth rested on the Plank Road. My batteries remained in rear of the division.

On the 12th, there was no change, except the placing of three long-range guns from *Cooper's* battery near Howison's house, on the right of the Telegraph Road. During these two days occasional shells from the enemy's guns burst among and near the troops, but there were few or no injuries.

About 11.30 a.m. on the 13th, large numbers of skirmishers were thrown out from the town by the enemy, and it soon became evident that an effort would be made to take our batteries which I was supporting. *Cooke's* brigade was ordered to occupy the crest of Marye's and Willis' Hills, which was done in fine style. By this time the enemy backed his skirmishers with a compact line and advanced toward the hills, but the Washington Artillery and a well-directed fire from *Cobb's* and *Cooke's* brigades drove them quickly back to their shelter in the town. But a few minutes elapsed before another line was formed by the enemy, he all the while keeping up a brisk fire with sharpshooters. This line advanced with the utmost determination, and some few of them got within 50 yards of our line, but the whole were forced to retire in wild confusion before the telling fire of our small-arms at such short range.

During this attack two of *Cooke's* regiments, being badly exposed (for there were then no rifle-pits on the hills) were thrown into the road with *Cobb's* brigade. For some few minutes there was a cessation of fire, but we were not kept long in expectancy. The enemy now seemed determined to reach our position, and formed apparently a triple line. Observing this movement . . . I brought up the three regiments of my brigade to within 100 yards of the crest of the hills, and pushed forward the Twenty-fifth North Carolina Volunteers to the crest. The enemy, almost massed, moved to the charge heroically, and met the withering fire of our artillery and small-arms with wonderful staunchness. On they came to within less than 150 paces of our line, but nothing could live before the sheet of lead that was hurled at them from this distance. They momentarily wavered, broke, and rushed headlong from the field. A few, however, more resolute than the rest, lingered under cover of some fences and houses, and annoyed us with a scattering but well-directed fire. The Twenty-fifth North Carolina Volunteers reached the crest of the hill just in time to pour into the enemy a few volleys at most deadly range, and then took position shoulder to shoulder with *Cobb's* and *Cooke's* men in the road. During this attack the gallant *Brigadier-General Cobb* was mortally wounded, and almost at the same instant *Brigadier-General Cooke* was wounded and taken from the field. *Colonel Hall,* Forty-sixth North Carolina Volunteers, succeeded to the command of his brigade.

Nothing daunted by the fearful punishment he had received, the enemy brought out fresh and increased numbers of troops. Fearing lest he might by mere force of numbers pass over our line, I determined to resist him with every man at my disposal, and started in person to place the remaining two regiments of my brigade. Just at this instant *Brigadier-General Kershaw* dashed on horseback at the head of one of his regiments up the new road, leading from the Telegraph Road and near the mill, and led it into the fight immediately at Marye's house. A second regiment from his brigade followed and took position in rear of and near the grave-yard on Willis' Hill and remained there. I now advanced my regiments, and placed one a few yards in rear of Marye's house and the other on its right and a little more retired.

With his increased numbers the enemy moved forward. Our men held their fire till it would be fatally effective. Meantime our artillery was spreading fearful havoc among the enemy's ranks. Still he advanced and received the destructive fire of our line. Even more resolute than before, he seemed determined madly to press on, but his efforts could avail nothing. At length, broken and seemingly dismayed, the whole mass turned and fled to the very center of the town.

At this time I sent my adjutant-general to the road to ascertain the condition of the troops and the amount of ammunition on hand. His report was truly gratifying, representing the men in highest spirits and an abundance of ammunition. I had ordered *Cobb's* brigade supplied from my wagons.

The afternoon was now nearly spent, and it appeared that the enemy would not again renew his attempts to carry our position. Again, however, an effort, more feeble than those which had preceded, was made to push his troops over the bodies of the . . . slain. The sun was down, and darkness was fast hiding the enemy from view, and it was reasonable to suppose there would be no further movements, at least toward the point we held; but the frequent and determined assaults he had made would not permit me to despise either his courage or his hardihood; and thinking that as a last alternative he might resort to the bayonet, under cover of darkness, I massed my little command, so as to meet such an attack with all the power we were capable of exerting. Instead, however, of a charge with the bayonet, just after dark he opened a tremendous fire of small-arms and at short range upon my whole line. This last desperate and murderous attack met the same fate which had befallen those which preceded, and his hosts were sent, actually howling, back to their beaten comrades in the town.

A short time before the last attack, *Brigadier-General Kemper* had reported to me with his brigade. With two of his regiments I relieved the Twenty-fourth North Carolina Volunteers, which had been in the ditch two days, and placed the others in close supporting distance of the crest of the hill. During the whole time the enemy's artillery had not ceased to play upon us, but our batteries took no notice of it, reserving their fire and using it against his infantry as it would form and advance with extraordinary effect. Thus ended the fighting in front of Fredericksburg. [*O.R.*, XXI, pp. 625–26.]

Retrace your route to the Sunken Road. Follow the marked walking tour that parallels that road to a point just beyond stop six in that tour. This should put you near the campaign signs at the junction of **KIRKLAND STREET.** You may want to cross the Sunken Road to the area where trenches that sheltered the 24th North Carolina still show behind the stone wall, and you may also want to walk down **KIRKLAND** to the first traffic light to get an impression of the ground over which the Union attackers tried to move.

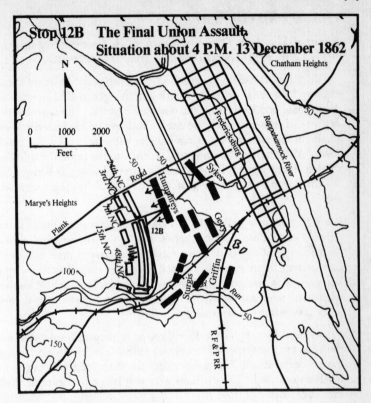

Stop 12B   The Final Union Assault, Situation about 4 P.M. 13 December 1862

STOP 12B, THE STONE WALL

Narrative of Lieut. General James Longstreet, Commanding First Army Corps, Army of Northern Virginia

The stone wall was not thought before the battle a very important element. We assumed that the formidable advance would be made against the troops of *McLaws's* division at Lee's Hill, to turn the position at the sunken road, dislodge my force stationed there, then to occupy the sunken road, and afterwards ascend to the plateau upon which the Marye mansion stands; that this would bring their forces under cross and direct fire of all our batteries—short- and long-range guns—in such concentration as to beat them back in bad disorder. [Longstreet, *From Manassas to Appomattox* (Bloomington: Indiana University Press, 1960), pp. 316–17.]

THE SECOND CORPS ATTACKS

Report of Maj. Gen. Darius N. Couch, USA, Commanding Second Army Corps, Right Grand Division, Army of the Potomac

In rear of the town the ground is a broken plain, traversed about midway by a canal or ditch, running from right to left. Across this plain, some 600 yards from the outer edge of town, commences the first rise of hills on which the enemy had erected his batteries. Two roads cut the plain nearly at right angles with the canal . . . a plank road, [William Street] leading to Culpeper, to the right; the other to the left, the Telegraph Road [Hanover Street] leading to Richmond.

At 8.15 on the morning of the 13th, the following order was received:

You will . . . form a column of a division for the purpose of pushing in the direction of the Plank and Telegraph Roads, for the purpose of seizing the heights in rear of the town. This column will advance in three lines, with such intervals as you may judge proper, this movement to be covered by a heavy line of skirmishers in front and on both flanks. You will hold another division in readiness to advance in support of this movement, to be formed in the same manner as the leading division. . . .

General French was at once directed to prepare his division for the advance, and General Hancock to follow with his division in the same order of attack. The distance between the successive lines was to be about 200 yards. The divisions were sent into action as came their turn in the order of march.

At 9.50 a.m. General French reported that he had made his dispositions, and General Sumner was signaled that all was ready. The fog that covered the town . . . commenced lifting. French commenced his movement by throwing out a strong body of skirmishers, under command of Col. J. S. Mason, Fourth Ohio. The division moved out of the city by two parallel streets, running into the Plank and Telegraph Roads, and at 12.10 p.m. became engaged. General Kimball's brigade was in front. . . . followed in succession by the brigades of Col. J. W. Andrews . . . and Colonel Palmer. . . .

The troops debouched from the town by two streets leading into the Plank and Telegraph Roads. The ditch or canal . . . was impassable, except at the bridges. A little beyond it the ground rises, forming a cover, behind which the troops were able to deploy. The rise or crest is about half way between the outer edge of the city and the foot of the heights which were to be carried. The intermediate ground was obstructed here and there by houses and garden fences. This plain was swept by the converging artillery and musketry fire of the enemy.

Over it Mason went with his skirmishers, followed by Kimball and the balance of French's division, working nearly up to the stone wall at the foot of the heights, behind which the enemy sought shelter. To support his advance, General French had . . . Arnold's battery. . . . Hancock followed with his division . . . and, pressing on, came up with the advance of French, and, joining it, pushed on with determination. At this moment (1 p.m.) I ordered Hancock and French to carry the enemy's works by storm. [*O.R.*, XXI, pp. 222–23.]

Report of Brig. Gen. Nathan Kimball, USA, Commanding First Brigade, Third Division, Second Army Corps, Right Grand Division, Army of the Potomac

At a few minutes before 12 o'clock, I moved my brigade, which had already been formed on Caroline Street . . . by the right flank, out Princess Anne Street; crossed the open space near the depot buildings and the canal bridge near there; filed to the right and formed line of battle under cover of the low bluff on which my skirmishers had deployed, my right resting on Hanover Street, and my left on the so-called Telegraph Road.

From the time my column came in sight at the depot buildings all these movements were executed under a most murderous fire from the enemy's artillery, several shells bursting in the ranks and destroying a company at a time. Yet all the regiments . . . moved steadily forward without confusion, those in the rear quickly closing up the gaps left by their fallen comrades. . . . As soon as my line came in sight on the top of the small hill, under cover of which it was formed, it was met by a deadly fire from the enemy's batteries in front and on each flank, but in the face of this it moved steadily forward with fixed bayonets, and without firing a gun, over rough and muddy ground, through fences and all other obstacles, until, reaching the enemy's rifle-pits, it was met by his infantry, posted behind stone walls and earthworks, and in cover of a small ravine, in superior numbers, and by a fire so fierce as to compel it to halt and open fire. . . .

The right of my line then occupied a small village at the forks of the Hanover Road, and my left rested at the Telegraph Road. A fourth of my command had fallen while crossing the plain, and those left with me were exhausted by the fatigue of clearing away fences and marching so far at double-quick over rough and muddy ground;

and they were exposed to a most murderous fire of grape and musketry. The support had not then come up from under cover of the bluff. My command held its ground, but could advance no farther. [*O.R.*, XXI, p. 290.]

Report of Brig. Gen. Winfield S. Hancock, USA, Commanding First Division, Second Corps, Right Grand Division, Army of the Potomac

My division followed that of General French, without intervals, so long as we moved by the flank. The difficulty of the movement consisted in the fact that we had to march for a considerable distance by the flank through the streets of the town, all the time under a heavy fire, before we were enabled to deploy; and then, owing to obstacles—among them a mill-race—it was impossible to deploy except by marching the whole length of each brigade in a line parallel to the enemy's works after we had crossed the mill-race by the bridge.

The troops then advanced, each brigade in succession, under a most murderous fire of artillery and musketry, the artillery fire reaching the troops in a destructive manner in the town even before they had commenced the movement. The distance . . . before reaching the enemy's works was probably 1,700 yards, [and] it took an unusually long time . . . as the planking of one of the bridges was found to be partly taken up, requiring the men to cross on the stringers.

Colonel Zook's brigade was the first in order. . . . It advanced to the attack with spirit, passing the point at which the preceding troops had arrived, and being joined as it passed by the brave regiments of Kimball's brigade and some other regiments of French's division. It failed, however, to take the stone wall . . . although our dead were left within 25 paces of it. These troops still held their line of battle in front of the enemy and within close musketry range.

The Irish Brigade next advanced to the assault. . . . with the same results. Caldwell's brigade was next ordered into action, and, although it behaved with the utmost valor, failed to carry the enemy's position. All the troops then formed one line of battle, extending from a point a little distance to the right of Hanover Street, in a line nearly parallel to the enemy, with the left thrown back, the extreme left extending about the front of two regiments to the left of the railroad culvert. This line was held during the entire day . . . until it was relieved, some of the regiments not coming off the field until 10 o'clock the following morning. . . . hours after the troops had exhausted their ammunition. . . . Shortly after the last of my brigades came into action, it appeared as if the crest of the enemy's hill might have been taken had there been other troops at hand, for the enemy were at that time running from their rifle-pits and works on the crest directly in front of our right. But by the time Howard's troops were ready to attack, the enemy had repaired this, and making a strong attack at the same time toward our left, it became necessary that a portion of that division should be detached toward that flank. After this hour it appeared to me, although reports were occasionally received that we were gaining ground, . . . that our object having failed, the only thing to be done was to maintain our front line by constantly supporting it until darkness covered the scene.

At one time, about 3 p.m., the enemy essayed an attack in column down Hanover Street, and advanced within 150 yards of our front line. The leader being killed, the column was dispersed. . . .

It seemed that the defenses of the enemy were too powerful to be taken by an assault of infantry. One serious difficulty . . . was in the nature of the obstacles . . . and the fact that a number of substantial fences intervened, which were required to be pulled down before the troops could continue their advance. Each of these fences destroyed the unity of at least one brigade . . . for all these operations were conducted under a terrific fire. . . .

Out of 5,006 men . . . the loss was 2,013. . . . The Fifth New Hampshire. . . . numbered 23 commissioned officers and 280 enlisted men when it went into action; 17 officers and 165 men were killed and wounded. This regiment had five commanders during the action, the first four having been killed or wounded. [O.R., XXI, pp. 227–29.]

Report of Brig. Gen. Oliver O. Howard, USA, Commanding Second Division, Second Army Corps, Right Grand Division, Army of the Potomac

At about 12.55 p.m. I was ordered to move to the right of Hancock and attack the works there, debouching on the right of the Plank Road, where I had already located a company of sharpshooters . . . to pick off the enemy's cannoneers within range. This order was immediately countermanded by General Couch, and I was sent to support General Hancock. My command was moved out, Colonel Owen's brigade in front. He was ordered . . . to cross the bridge over the mill-race, which is just outside of the town, moving on Hanover Street by the flank, left in front. As soon as he reached a plowed field on the left of the road, he was to deploy and move forward in line of battle.

This he did in fine style. He moved, without breaking his line, to the vicinity of a small brick house, where he halted because, unsupported and fearing he should lose ground, [he] caused the men to lie down. He was now within 100 yards of the enemy's first line. I sent him word to hold what he had got, and to push forward the first opportunity, and not to fire except when he had something to fire at. Colonel Hall, meanwhile, following Colonel Owen by the flank, was ordered by General Couch, both directly and through me, to deploy to the right of Hanover Street, which he did. He made several bold attempts to storm the enemy's rifle-pits, but the concentrated fire of artillery and infantry was too much to carry men through. [O.R., XXI, p. 263.]

KERSHAW'S DEFENSE

Report of Brig. Gen. Joseph B. Kershaw, CSA, Commanding Kershaw's Brigade, McLaws' Division, First Army Corps, Army of Northern Virginia

About 1 o'clock . . . I was directed to send two regiments into the city to the support of *General Cobb*, then engaged with part of his brigade at the foot of Marye's Hill, and having called for re-enforcements. I sent forward at once *Col. John D. Kennedy* with his own (Second) regiment and the Eighth . . . South Carolina. . . . Within a few minutes after, I was directed to take my entire command to the same point and assume command there. I had just moved when I was informed that *General Cobb* was wounded, and was directed by *Major-General McLaws* to hasten forward in person immediately and take command. Leaving my staff to conduct the troops, I proceeded as rapidly as possible to the scene of action, reaching the position at Stevens' house [immediately south of the Ennis House, which still stands] at the moment that *Colonel Kennedy* arrived with the Second and Eighth Regiments, and just in time to meet a fresh assault of the enemy.

The position was excellent. Marye's Hill, covered with our batteries . . . falls off abruptly toward Fredericksburg to a stone wall, which forms a terrace on the side of the hill and the outer margin of the Telegraph Road, which winds along the foot of the hill. The road is about some 25 feet wide, and is faced by a stone wall about 4 feet high on the city side. The road having been cut out of the side of the hill, in many places this last wall is not visible above the surface of the ground. The ground falls off rapidly to almost a level surface, which extends about 150 yards, then, with another abrupt fall of a few feet, to another plain which extends some 200 yards, and then falls off abruptly into a wide ravine, which extends along the whole front of the city and discharges into Hazel Run. I found, on my arrival, that *Cobb's* brigade . . . occupied our entire front, and my troops could only get into position by doubling on them. This was accordingly done, and the formation along most of the line during the engagement was consequently four deep. As an evidence of the coolness of the command . . . notwithstanding that their fire was the most rapid and continuous I have ever witnessed, not a man was injured by the fire of his comrades.

The first attack being repelled at 2:45 p.m., the Third Regiment . . . and Seventh . . . came into position on the hill at Marye's house, with *Colonel De Saussure's* Fifteenth . . . South Carolina . . . in reserve, and under cover of the cemetery. *James'* Third South Carolina battalion . . . I left in position at Howison's Mill, to protect our right from any advance of the enemy up Hazel Run.

While the Third and Seventh Regiments were getting into position, another fierce attack was sustained, and those regiments, especially the former, suffered severely. . . . In the mean time line after line of the enemy deployed in the ravine, and advanced to the attack at intervals of not more than fifteen minutes until about 4.30 o'clock, when there was a lull of about a half hour, during which a mass of artillery was placed in position in front of the town and opened upon our position. At this time I brought up *Colonel De Saussure's* regiment. Our batteries on the hill were silent, having exhausted their ammunition, and the Washington Artillery were relieved by a part of *Colonel Alexander's* battalion. Under cover of this artillery fire, the most formidable column of attack was formed, which, about 5 o'clock, emerged from the ravine, and, no longer impeded by our artillery, impetuously assailed our whole front. From this time until after 6 o'clock the attack was continuous, and the fire on both sides terrific. Some few, chiefly officers, got within 30 yards of our lines, but in every instance their columns were shattered by the time they got within 100 paces. The firing gradually subsided, and by 7 o'clock our pickets were established within 30 yards of those of the enemy.

Our chief loss after getting into position in the road was from the fire of sharpshooters, who occupied some buildings on my left flank in the early part of the engagement, and were only silenced by

Captain Wallace, of the Second regiment, directing a continuous fire of one company upon the buildings. *General Cobb*, I learn, was killed by a shot from that quarter. The regiments on the hill suffered most, as they were less perfectly covered. . . .

That night we materially strengthened the position, and I more perfectly organized and arranged my command. [*O.R.*, XXI, pp. 588–90.]

Report of Lieut. Col. Elbert Bland, CSA, Seventh South Carolina Infantry, Kershaw's Brigade, McLaws' Division, First Army Corps, Army of Northern Virginia

I moved by the left flank in rear of the Third South Carolina Regiment down the Telegraph Road for 150 yards, then filed to the left across Hazel Run, up the bluff in rear of *Colonel Walton's* battery to the hill in rear of Marye's house, where I met *Lieutenant Doby*, of *General Kershaw's* staff, who ordered me to form the regiment in rear of *Colonel Nance's* Third South Carolina which was on the left and upon a line with the Marye house. Immediately after I formed line the Fifteenth South Carolina filed in my rear. At this point I lost several officers and men, wounded by fragments of shell. . . .

In about three-quarters of an hour I was called upon by the commanding officer of the Fifteenth North Carolina [*Cooke's* brigade, *Ransom's* division] to re-enforce him. I at once moved by the right flank into his position, which was to the right and in front of the Marye house, my three left companies being in front of the house. The position was a good one, with the crest of the hill just in our front, at which point it descended rapidly toward the enemy. About 70 yards below and in front of us was the Telegraph Road, with a stone wall . . . on the enemy's side, behind which rested three regiments of *Cobb's* brigade and the Second and Eighth South Carolina . . . [which had] just re-enforced them. The knoll in my front rendered it impossible for us to injure our friends, but placed us in fine range of the enemy. We would load and advance to fire, then drop back to reload. My right flank was exposed by a slight depression in the hill to an oblique fire from the enemy, which was taken advantage of; hence the greater loss in the right wing. We continued in the engagement until night, when the final charge was made and the enemy repulsed. [*O.R.*, XXI, p. 597.]

THE NINTH CORPS RENEWS THE ASSAULT

Report of Brig. Gen. Orlando B. Willcox, USA, Commanding Ninth Army Corps, Right Grand Division, Army of the Potomac

I was ordered by Major-General Sumner to extend my left over Hazel Run to Deep Run, and to form the corps in three lines, with batteries in suitable positions, connecting on the right with the Second Corps and on the left with General Franklin. . . . Accordingly, Brig. Gen. S. D. Sturgis' division was placed nearest to Couch's corps, Burns' division nearest to Franklin's . . . between Deep and Hazel Runs, and Getty's division between Sturgis' and Burns'. Each division was in two lines. . . .

About noon . . . I directed the Second Division to support General Couch's attack, then about to begin. General Sturgis promptly got his troops in readiness, and selected a point near a brick-kiln for Dickenson's horse artillery. A portion of Hooker's grand division had now crossed the river, and was in the rear of Couch's troops.

Stone wall at the foot of Marye's Heights which was carried by the 6th Maine Infantry. Confederate dead in the trenches shortly after the conflict. (USAMHI)

As soon as Couch's left began to break, General Sturgis advanced four regiments of Ferrero's brigade. . . . General Ferrero succeeded in checking the advance of the enemy on the left of the Second Corps, and drove him back to his . . . stone wall and rifle-pits. . . . Ferrero's brigade now encountered the full weight of the enemy's metal, and Nagle's brigade was ordered to its support. . . . All these troops behaved well and marched under a heavy fire across the broken plain, pressed up to the field at the foot of the enemy's sloping crest, and maintained every inch of their ground with great obstinacy until after nightfall, but the position could not be carried. . . .

Meantime General Whipple [commanding Third Division, Third Corps, Center Grand Division] sent me Carroll's brigade . . . which, together with some brigades of General Griffin's division, also sent to co-operate . . . gallantly pushed up to the support of General Sturgis' left, under a heavy fire, gaining also a certain point, but beyond this nothing could live. . . .

It must be borne in mind that all the troops formed under fire. It was impossible to clear the shelter of the town otherwise than by marching each regiment by a flank to the open ground, and even this could not be done without confusion. Thus forming in two brigade lines, Getty's division marched gallantly over the broken field, crossed the railroad cutting, then an old canal ditch and some marshy ground, under an artillery fire which increased every moment, until he nearly reached the enemy's works in front, when a line of musketry opened, and his first brigade was forced back under a severe front and enfilading storm. [*O.R.*, XXI, pp. 311–12.]

Report of Brig. Gen. Andrew A. Humphreys, USA, Commanding Third Division, Fifth Army Corps, Center Grand Division, Army of the Potomac

My division (about 4,500 strong) being massed in the vicinity of the Phillips house, received orders at 2.30 in the afternoon to cross the river and enter Fredericksburg. . . . I had not as yet seen any part of the ground . . . and the necessity was so urgent that I could not take time to examine it. At my request an officer of General Hancock's staff . . . accompanied me to the ground, first to a ravine crossing the Telegraph Road, where the troops could form under partial cover; then to the high ground above on which, some 200 yards in advance, were the troops I was to support, slightly sheltered by a small rise in the ground. One hundred and fifty yards in advance of them was a heavy stone wall . . . strengthened by a trench. . . . heavily lined with the enemy's infantry.

The Second brigade was quickly formed under my direction by Colonel Allabach. . . . It moved rapidly and gallantly up to General Couch's troops, under the artillery and musketry fire of the enemy. The nature of the enemy's line of defense could not be clearly perceived . . . until I reached our line. The troops I was to support, as well as those on their left (I could not see those on their right from the interruption of the line by a road and the thick smoke) were sheltering themselves by lying on the ground. This example Colonel Allabach's brigade immediately followed, in spite of an effort to prevent it, and opened a fire upon the enemy. A part only of his men were able to reach the front rank, owing to the numbers already occupying the ground.

The continued presence of the troops I was to support or relieve proved a serious obstacle to my success. As soon as I ascertained the nature of the enemy's position, I was satisfied that our fire could have but little effect . . . and that the only mode of attacking him successfully was with the bayonet. This I resolved to do, although my command was composed of troops that entered the service in August. With great difficulty their firing was arrested, chiefly by the exertions of myself and staff, and Colonel Allabach. . . . While this was being done, I sent a staff officer to General Tyler with instructions to bring his command to the left of the road in the ravine, and prepare it to support or take the place of Allabach's brigade. . . . The charge was then made, but the deadly fire of musketry and artillery broke it after an advance of 50 yards. . . .

The greater part of my staff were now on foot, having had their horses killed or disabled. . . . Mounting the horse of my special orderly . . . I rode to General Tyler's brigade to conduct it to the enemy, and while doing so received three successive orders from General Butterfield [commanding Fifth Army Corps] to charge the enemy's line, the last order being accompanied by the message that both General Burnside and General Hooker demanded that the crest should be taken before night.

It was already growing dusky. General Tyler's brigade was not yet entirely formed, and was impeded in doing so by a battery of six guns, whose limbers occupied a part of his ground, and whose fire would have rendered it impossible for him to advance. With great difficulty I brought this battery to cease firing. Then, riding along the two lines, I directed them not to fire; that it was useless; that the bayonet alone was the weapon to fight with here. Anticipating, too, the serious obstacle they would meet with in the masses of men lying under the little shelter afforded by the natural embankment in front . . . who could not be got out of the way, I directed them to disregard these men entirely and to pass over them. I ordered the officers to the front, and, with a hurrah, the brigade, led by General Tyler and myself, advanced gallantly over the ground under the heaviest fire yet opened, which poured upon it from the moment it rose from the ravine.

As the brigade reached the masses of men . . . every effort was made by [them] . . . to prevent our advance. They called to our men not to go forward, and some attempted to prevent by force their doing so. The effect upon my command was what I apprehended—the line was somewhat disordered, and, in part, forced to form into a column, but still [it] advanced rapidly. The fire of the enemy's musketry and artillery . . . now became still hotter. The stone wall was a sheet of flame that enveloped the head and flanks of the column. Officers and men were falling rapidly, and the head of the column was at length brought to a stand when close up to the wall.

Up to this time not a shot had been fired by the column, but now some firing began. It lasted but a minute when, in spite of all our efforts, the column turned and began to retire slowly. . . . The united efforts of General Tyler, myself, our staffs, and the other officers could not arrest the retiring mass. My efforts were the less effective since I was again dismounted, my second horse having been killed under me. The only one of my staff now mounted was Lieutenant Humphreys, whose horse had been three times wounded. All the rest had their horses either killed or disabled except one officer, who had been sent off with orders.

Directing General Tyler to reform his brigade under cover of the ravine, I returned to the portion of Allabach's brigade still holding, with the other troops, the line of natural embankment. . . . Our loss in both brigades was heavy, exceeding 1,000 in killed and wounded. . . . The greater part of the loss occurred during the brief time they were charging and retiring, which scarcely occupied more than ten or fifteen minutes for each brigade. . . .

I cannot refrain from expressing the opinion that one of the greatest obstacles to my success was the mass of troops lying on our front line. They ought to have been withdrawn before mine advanced. The troops on their right and left would have prevented the enemy from advancing. Finding them lying there, the men of Allabach's brigade, who had never before been in battle, instinctively followed their example. Besides, they disordered my lines and were greatly in the way when I wished to bring the brigade to a charge. When General Tyler's brigade advanced, they, together with some of my own men of Allabach's brigade, not only impeded its progress but converted it . . . into a massive column too large to be managed properly.

As soon as the troops were placed in the new positions they were directed to occupy, parties were sent out to bring in the wounded and dead, and the division ambulances and stretcher-bearers were dispatched upon the same errand. The latter, however, had scarcely any stretchers, the repeated requisitions for the same never having been filled. They were obliged to use shutters. The wounded were nearly all brought in before daylight. . . . I ordered out burying parties on the following night. . . . [O.R., XXI, pp. 430–33.]

Narrative of James Pratt, USA, Thirty-fifth Massachusetts Infantry, Second Brigade, Second Division, Ninth Army Corps, Right Grand Division, Army of the Potomac

About noon we were ordered onto the field of battle. We were under a scorching fire till after dark. . . . We lay under the brow of the hill in the mud. . . . The shells came so near me that the mud filled my ears. . . . It was horrid to put men in the position that they were on . . . the 13th. We had to march over a plain to meet them. They were in trenches, the same as if they were behind Mr. Henry's Mill and we had to march double quick across our pasture to the side of the hill and they behind the hill. You see they had a better chance than we. We would lay down and load, get up and fire. Most all that was killed, was killed coming across the plain with their big guns pouring into us. . . . We do not blame Captain Pratt here. He was in front of the battle. He did go on, but "Come on boys", Colonel [Major] Wilde says, "Go in there, damn you." I heard him. He lost his arm and we do not care. He had no business to carry us in there.

After dark we marched to the city, what we could find of the regiment, about 25 of us, and slept in a small house. The next morning went to the river and found the rest of the regiment. We lay there all day. Sunday night our Brigade went on pickets to the Battlefield, close to the rebel battery. We lay there from Sunday night till Monday night, 24 hours. We were not allowed to get up all that time, if we did they would pop at us. . . . We lay low. After dark we were relieved.

That battle did no good at all. Great many lives were lost and for nothing, but I think they have got about enough of the rebs. We shall have to give up to them, the sooner the better. I suppose folks say there, "Why don't they go on with the war?" Tell them to come out here and try it. [James Pratt to Charlotte Pratt, December 16, 19, 1862. James Pratt Papers. U.S. Army Military History Institute, Carlisle Barracks, Pa.]

In repeated assaults against Marye's heights, the Second Corps suffered 4,114 casualties, most of them in the divisions of French and Hancock. The Ninth Corps lost 1,330; Carroll's brigade from Whipple's division, Third Corps, lost 118, or nearly 20 percent, and the Fifth Corps added another 2,175 to the list of casualties. Nearly 8,000 men, most of them killed or wounded, paid the price for Burnside's order to move "directly to the front, with a view to taking the heights that command the Plank and the Telegraph Road." In the attacks in this sector over 27,000 Union infantry were thrown against defending forces of about 6,000 muskets and 20 guns. The infantry in the Telegraph Road fired about 55 rounds per man, while the supporting guns on Marye's hill expended about 2400 rounds from eleven gun pits. The Confederates lost 1,589 men here: "along the rest of *Longstreet's* line . . . hostilities were limited to distant sharpshooting and artillery practice, except in *General Hood's* front . . ." [General E. P. Alexander, *Military Memoirs of a Confederate* (Bloomington: Indiana University Press, 1962), p. 313; "The Battle of Fredericksburg," *Southern Historical Society Papers*, X (December 1882), pp. 457, 464.]

In the battle of Fredericksburg the Confederates lost 5,322 men to 12,553 Union casualties. About 10% were killed. About 5% of the Union casualties were caused by shell and 14% by roundshot—"a much larger proportion than is usually due to artillery fire." [Lieut.-Col. G. F. R. Henderson, *The Campaign of Fredericksburg: a Tactical Study for Officers* (London: Gale and Polden, Ltd., n.d.), p. 142.]

AFTERMATH

Report of General Robert E. Lee, CSA, Commanding Army of Northern Virginia

During the night our lines were strengthened by the construction of earthworks at exposed points, and preparations made to receive the enemy next day. The 14th, however, passed without a renewal of the attack. The enemy's batteries on both sides of the river played upon our lines at intervals, our own firing but little. The sharpshooters on each side skirmished occasionally along the front. On the 15th, the enemy still retained his position, apparently ready for battle, but the day passed as the preceding.

The attack on the 13th had been so easily repulsed, and by so small a part of our army, that it was not supposed the enemy would limit his efforts to an attempt which, in view of the magnitude of his preparations and the extent of his force, seemed to be comparatively insignificant. Believing, therefore, that he would attack us, it was not deemed expedient to lose the advantages of our position and expose the troops to the fire of his inaccessible batteries beyond the river by advancing against him; but we were necessarily ignorant of the extent to which he had suffered, and only became aware of it when, on the morning of the 16th, it was discovered that he had availed himself of the darkness of night and the prevalence of a violent storm of wind and rain to recross the river. The town was immediately reoccupied and our position on the river bank resumed. . . .

The troops displayed . . . in a high degree the spirit and courage that distinguished them throughout the campaign, while the calmness and steadiness with which orders were obeyed and maneuvers executed in the midst of battle evinced the discipline of a veteran army.

The artillery rendered efficient service on every part of the field, and greatly assisted in the defeat of the enemy. The batteries were exposed to an unusually heavy fire of artillery and infantry, which officers and men sustained with a coolness and courage worthy of the highest praise. Those on our right, being without defensive works, suffered more severely. . . .

To the vigilance, boldness, and energy of *General Stuart* and his cavalry is chiefly due the early and valuable information of the movements of the enemy. His reconnaissances frequently extended within the Federal lines, resulting in skirmishes and engagements in which the cavalry was greatly distinguished. In the battle . . . the cavalry effectually guarded our right, annoying the enemy and embarrassing his movements by hanging on his flank and attacking when opportunity occurred. The nature of the ground and the relative positions of armies prevented them from doing more.

To *Generals Longstreet* and *Jackson* great praise is due for the disposition and management of their respective corps. Their quick perception enabled them to discover the projected assaults upon their positions, and their ready skill to devise the best means to resist them. Besides their services in the field . . . I am also indebted to them for valuable counsel, both as regards the general operations of the army and the execution of the particular measures adopted. [*O.R.*, XXI, pp. 555–56.]

Report of Maj. Gen. Ambrose E. Burnside, USA, Commanding Army of the Potomac

Our forces had been repulsed at all points, and it was necessary to look upon the day's work as a failure. It is not pleasant to dwell upon these results, even at this distance of time. . . .

From the night of the 13th until the night of the 15th, our men held their positions. Something was done in the way of intrenching, and some angry skirmishing and annoying artillery firing was indulged in the meantime. . . . On the night of the 15th, I decided to remove the army to the north side of the river. . . . [*O.R.*, XXI, p. 95].

Burnside to Maj. Gen. H. W. Halleck, General in Chief,
December 17, 1862

How near we came to accomplishing our object future reports will show. But for the fog and unexpected and unavoidable delay in building the bridges, which gave the enemy twenty-four more hours to concentrate his forces in his strong positions, we would almost certainly have succeeded; in which case the battle would have been . . . far more decisive than if we had crossed at the places first selected. As it was, we came very near success. . . .

For the failure in the attack I am responsible, as the extreme gallantry, courage, and endurance shown by [the men] . . . was never excelled, and would have carried the points had it been possible.

To the families and friends of the dead I can only offer my heartfelt sympathy. . . . Our killed amounted to 1,152; our wounded, about 9,000; our prisoners, about 700, which have been paroled and exchanged for about the same number taken by us. The wounded were all removed to this side of the river before the evacuation and are being well cared for, and the dead were all buried under a flag of truce. The surgeon reports a much larger proportion than usual of slight wounds, 1,630 only being treated in hospitals. [*O.R.*, XXI, pp. 66–67.]

Burnside made several attempts to retrieve the situation. On December 26 he ordered the army to be ready to move on short notice, this time to cross the river seven miles below the city. The cavalry had already commenced movement and orders were about to be issued to all units when Burnside received a telegram from President Lincoln forbidding a general movement without first informing him. Two of his most senior officers—Major Generals W. B. Franklin and William F. Smith—had confided to the President that the army was not in condition to move.

Three weeks later Burnside endeavored to outflank the Confederate defenses along the Rappahannock by crossing the upper Rappahannock at fords above Falmouth, but the entire country was "an ocean of mud" and he soon had to abandon what officially—and also derisively—became known as the "Mud March." On January 25, 1863, Burnside was relieved.

He was replaced by Major General Joseph Hooker, an experienced corps commander with a well-deserved reputation throughout the army as an aggressive leader in combat, and in Washington circles for his talent for intrigue. "What I ask of you is military success," Lincoln explained when he appointed Hooker to the command.

I much fear that the spirit which you have aided to infuse into the army, of criticising their commander and withholding confidence from him, will now turn upon you. . . . Neither you nor Napoleon, . . . could get any good out of an army while such a spirit prevails. . . . Beware of rashness, but with energy and sleepless vigilance go forward and give us victories. [*O.R.*, XXV, Part 2, p. 4.]

In the weeks that followed, Hooker made many far-reaching changes. He abolished the "Grand Divisions" that Burnside had introduced and created corps badges to be worn by officers and men to indicate the units to which they belonged. He established the corps as a unit for the organization of artillery, although in the process he stripped Hunt of all tactical functions and reduced him pretty much to his original, purely administrative usefulness. He consolidated all of his cavalry into one corps under Major-General George P. Stoneman—another overdue change—but he offset the benefit of this new organization by sending Stoneman with the bulk of his cavalry on a fruitless raid deep behind enemy lines. During the coming operations at Chancellorsville, Hooker had available only a single brigade of cavalry under the command of Brig. Gen. A. Pleasonton, and even this was fragmented in order to perform reconnaissance duties for the separate columns.

Hooker also substituted pack-mules for army wagons on an extensive scale—an innovation that would cause difficulties in resupply at critical situations—reorganized the inspector-general's department to provide inspectors for his combat arms as well as for each brigade, and he significantly improved the soldiers' fare, even to the point of seeing that tobacco was issued regularly and that on occasion even an issue of whiskey was available. He made sure that clothing would be inspected and furnished of better quality. He also overhauled his intelligence service. [John Bigelow, Jr., *The Campaign of Chancellorsville: A Strategic and Tactical Study* New Haven: Yale University Press, 1910), pp. 40–49. Details of the intelligence services are treated in the Appendix.]

The problem Hooker faced is best described by his topographical engineer.

THE PROBLEM

Report of Brig. Gen. Gouverneur K. Warren, USA, Chief of Topographical Engineers, Army of the Potomac

At the time the operations . . . began, the enemy occupied in strong force the heights south of the Rappahannock River, from Skinker's Neck to Banks' Ford, having continuous lines of infantry parapets throughout (a distance of about 20 miles), his troops being so disposed as to be readily concentrated on any threatened point. Interspersed along these lines of intrenchments were battery epaulements advantageously located for sweeping the hill slopes and bottom lands, on which our troops would have to march to the assault, and which effectually protected the enemy's artillery from our own. Abatis, formed of fallen timber, and impassable swamps in places, still further strengthened his lines and reduced the number of assailable points. The crests of the main hills, where the enemy had prepared to receive us, were from three-quarters to 1½ miles from the margin of the river, but this margin was strongly guarded by men sheltered behind rifle-pits, which . . . were made quite formidable at every available crossing-place. In fact, every little rise of ground that could shelter the enemy and enable him to check our advance was intrenched and prepared for us.

To gain the immediate banks opposite the center of the enemy's line, however, was practicable in several places where the high ground on our side approached the river and enabled our artillery to command it; but the prospect of . . . gaining a footing on the heights, exposed as our troops would be for long distances to concentrated artillery fire, and finally to meet fresh infantry behind parapets fully prepared, seemed hopeless. Previous experience in attempting it under General Burnside, when the enemy's preparations were far less complete, had made this a conviction in the mind of every private in the ranks.

To turn the enemy's *right* flank [south of Skinker's Neck], and cross the river so as to gain the heights below his intrenchments, required a secret move of pontoon-trains and artillery for more than 20 miles, over a broken and wooded country, with clayey soils, which, in the conditions of the roads at that time, was impossible. The difficulty of constructing practicable roads toward King George Court House [about 3 miles cross-country east of Skinker's Neck] was great. The side streams running into the Rappahannock and those running into the Potomac interlaced each other at their sources, so as to quite destroy the continuity of the main dividing ridge, and on every road presented transverse ravines with steep hills and oozing springs, which our wheels soon mixed with the clay, and turned literally to streams of mud. . . .

General Lee's spy system was so perfect that the move could not have been kept from him, and it is not saying too much that he could have extended his intrenchments down the river as fast as we could have built practicable roads. Add to this the rapidly increasing width of the river, which our pontoons could not span, and which required 1,000 feet of bridging at the first available point below Skinker's Neck, and the impracticability of this flank movement is obvious.

On the enemy's *left*, even the crossing of the river was a matter of the greatest difficulty. Above Beck's Island, about 2½ miles above Fredericksburg, the high bluffs on each side close in upon the river, having a height above it of perhaps 150 feet, with slopes generally well wooded, very steep, and deeply cut by side ravines. Favorable conditions of approach to the river from either side first present themselves about 6 miles by the road we had to take above Fredericksburg, at . . . Banks' Ford, not then fordable. . . . A place of such importance was guarded by the enemy with the utmost care. . . .

The next point on the enemy's left which offered a practicable approach to the stream was at the United States Mine Ford, not then fordable, about 7 miles by the road above Banks' Ford. The intermediate space along the river was so difficult in its approaches to the water on either side that any work of ours to make them practicable would have given time to the enemy to fortify the opposite side, so as to render the attempt abortive. At the approaches to the United States Mine Ford, too, the enemy had created long lines of infantry parapets, with battery epaulements, and an ample force was encamped near to occupy them.

The junction of the Rapidan occurring just above the United States Mine Ford, involved the passage of that stream, also, in any attempt to turn the enemy's left by going farther up the river. The passages of two streams, not fordable, and having a width of 200 to 300 feet, at such a long distance from our base by a flank movement, with heavy pontoon and artillery trains, in the presence of an enemy who was also supposed to be supplied with pontoons by which he could cross in our rear, over roads almost impassable and through interminable forests, seemed so unlikely that the enemy gave himself no concern about it. . . . Indeed, he was at the time rebuilding the Germanna bridge. . . . [*O.R.*, XXV, Part 1, pp. 194–96.]

THE OPERATIONAL PLAN

Testimony of Maj. Gen. Joseph Hooker, USA,
Commanding Army of the Potomac

My object in moving the cavalry was to cut the enemy's communications with his base, and when this was done, to cross the infantry below Fredericksburg and attack him or pursue, as occasion might require. . . .

The cavalry left on the 13th, and after marching two days succeeded in throwing one division across the river, above Rappahannock station, but they were obliged to return, by swimming their horses, from the sudden rise in the river. The second day out it commenced storming, and the river was so much swollen as to render its passage impossible. . . . As the river continued impassable until the 27th, the movement was suspended until that time. . . .

But as the season was now more advanced, and the roads firmer, with a prospect that the rainy season had ended, I concluded to change my plan and strike for the whole rebel army instead of forcing it back on its line of retreat, which was as much as I could hope to accomplish in executing my first design.

As modified, the problem was to throw a sufficient infantry force to cross at Kelly's Ford, descend the Rappahannock, and knock away the enemy's forces holding the United States and Banks' Fords by attacking them in rear, and as soon as these fords were opened to reenforce the marching column sufficiently for them to continue the march upon the flank of the rebel army until his whole force was routed, and, if successful, his retreat intercepted. Simultaneous with this movement on the right, the left were to cross the Rappahannock below Fredericksburg and threaten the enemy in that quarter, including his depot of supplies, to prevent his despatching an overwhelming force to his left.

In pursuance of this plan the following instructions were given. . . . [U.S. Congress, Joint Committee on the Conduct of the War, *Report* (Washington: Government Printing Office, 1865), I, p. 115–16. Cited hereafter as 1865 *Report.*]

Commanding Officer, Cavalry Corps, April 22, 1863

After you break through the enemy's advanced lines [south of the Rappahannock], you will find no force in the direction of Richmond, that city itself being without a sufficient force to keep out your own command, should you advance on it. This, however, is not expected. Major-General Keyes has a command at Gloucester Point, and also at Fort Magruder [Williamsburg]. Wise is in his front with a small force.

After crossing the Rapidan, the major-general suggests that you sub-divide your command, and let them take different routes, and have some point of meeting on your line of general operations. These detachments can . . . inflict a vast deal of mischief, and at the same time bewilder the enemy as to the course and intentions of the main body. . . . These should move without artillery, and, if necessary to strike a railroad or effect a surprise, make long marches at night. . . . You must move quickly. . . . [*O.R.*, XXV, Part 2, p. 244.]

Commanding Officers, Eleventh and Twelfth Corps, April 26, 1863

The Eleventh and Twelfth Corps, in the order named, will begin their march at sunrise tomorrow morning, the former to encamp as near Kelly's Ford as practicable, without discovering itself to the enemy, and the latter as nearly in its rear as circumstances will permit. They will be established in their camps on or before 4 p.m. on . . . the 28th . . . Corps commanders will be held responsible that the men are kept in camp and do not go to the river. Each corps will march with one battery and two ambulances to [a] division and the pack train of small ammunition. If necessary, a small number of wagons can accompany the column to the camp with forage for animals. The balance of the trains will be parked in the vicinity of Banks' Ford, off the road and convenient to crossing the river at that point, the ammunition wagons and ambulances being in readiness to take the lead in the train. No extra guards for this part of the train will be required. Corps commanders can leave behind such men of those whose term of service is about to expire as they think proper, with such instructions for the safety of the camps and preservation of the public property as they may deem necessary. All property not removed with the troops must be turned in to the quartermaster. Corps commanders will consider so much of the above as relates to the destination of their commands as strictly confidential. [O.R., XXV, Part 2, pp. 255–56.]

Commanding Officer, Fifth Corps, April 27, 1863

Your corps is to march tomorrow, so as to reach the vicinity of Kelly's Ford by Tuesday at 4 p.m. The corps of Generals Slocum and Howard take the same direction (and will be on the same route, probably) from Hartwood. The provisions, as to rations, in former circular (eight days'), will be complied with. The trains will be left in the vicinity of Stoneman's Switch. . . . Further details . . . will be sent you early tomorrow morning. Two ambulances and one battery only will accompany each division, with the pack train of small-arm ammunition. A few wagons only to accompany the column, sufficient to carry forage for the animals. The destination of your command will be strictly confidential. General Couch [commanding Second Army Corps] has been directed to send a regiment to Banks' Ford to relieve your regiment there. [O.R., XXV, Part 2, p. 262.]

Commanding Officer, Second Corps, April 27, 1863

The major general commanding directs that you move at sunrise tomorrow morning two divisions of your corps, to encamp as near as practicable to Banks' Ford without exposing your camps to the view of the enemy; that one brigade and one battery of one of these two divisions take position at United States Ford; the movement to be made quietly. . . . The division left in camp should be the one whose camps are most exposed to the view of the enemy. All of the artillery attached to the two divisions moving up the river must move with them, and be ready to be thrown into position to cover the passage of the river and to drive the enemy from his defenses thrown up opposite that point. . . .

No effort is to be made to lay the bridges at Banks' Ford until the night of the 29th, but . . . they [must] be held in readiness to be thrown across the instant the enemy may leave or be driven from the opposite side. . . . The positions, etc. of the artillery at Banks' Ford, to cover the crossing, has been intrusted to General Hunt, chief of artillery. . . . You will establish the most rigid and strict guard along the river bank, to prevent any crossing or information, and to arrest any and all citizens within the lines if deemed necessary. [*O.R.*, XXV, Part 2, pp. 266–67.]

Major General Sedgwick, Commanding Sixth Army Corps, April 27, 1863

The major-general commanding directs that the Sixth Corps, Major General Sedgwick, First Corps, Major General Reynolds, and Third Corps, Major General Sickles, put themselves in position to cross the river as follows: Sixth Corps at Franklin's Crossing, First Corps at the crossing below at Pollock's Mill Creek, and the Third Corps as a support to cross at either point. These movements to be made so that the respective corps are in position—the First and Sixth on or before 3.30 a.m. of the 29th, and the Third Corps on or before 4.30. . . . The ambulances and trains to be parked in the rear, and concealed behind the range of hills visible to the enemy, and ready to move when desired. . . .

The bridges, two at each crossing, to be laid complete before 3.30 of the 29th, under the supervision of General Benham. . . . Any troops needed to assist the Engineer Brigade in the performance of this duty will be furnished to General Benham, under the direction of General Sedgwick. General Sedgwick . . . will be charged with the command of the three corps . . . and will make a demonstration in full force . . . upon the enemy's defenses, with a view of securing the Telegraph Road. In the event of the enemy detaching any considerable part of his force against the troops operating at the west of Fredericksburg, he will attack and carry their works at all hazards, and establish his force on the Telegraph Road, cutting off all communication by the enemy in order to prevent their turning his position on that road. In case the enemy should fall back on Richmond, he will pursue them with the utmost vigor, fighting them whenever and wherever he can come up with them. [*O.R.*, XXV, Part 2, p. 268.]

Major General Slocum, Commanding Eleventh and Twelfth Corps, April 28, 1863

So long as the Eleventh and Twelfth Corps are operating on the same line, you will exercise the command of both. The general directs that the Eleventh Corps cross . . . the river tonight, and that the Twelfth Corps commence crossing at daylight tomorrow . . . with all possible rapidity, and both corps march by the most direct route, without delay, and seize the bridge . . . and the ford at Germanna Mills. . . . Major General Meade [Fifth Army Corps] will move on almost a parallel line at the same time, and will be in easy communication with you. He will cross at Ely's Ford. If his passage should be disputed, as you will probably be able to learn from the firing . . . dispatch a corps along the south bank of the Rapidan, to knock away the enemy, to enable him to cross, and when the Fifth Corps is across . . . push on with both of your corps to Chancellorsville, at which point the three corps will come together, and which you will command by virtue of your seniority.

The enemy have a brigade holding the United States Ford, which they will abandon as soon as they hear of your approach. This will open the United States Ford to us, when bridges will at once be thrown across the river, and will afford you a direct communication with headquarters. Telegraphic communication is established from that point.

If your cavalry is well advanced from Chancellorsville, you will be able to ascertain whether or not the enemy is detaching forces from behind Fredericksburg to resist your advance. If not in any considerable force. . . . you will endeavor to advance at all hazards, securing a position on the Plank Road and uncovering Banks' Ford, which is also defended by a brigade of the rebel infantry and a battery. If the enemy should be greatly re-enforced, you will then select a strong position and compel him to attack you on your ground. You will have nearly 40,000 men, which is more than he can spare to send against you. [O.R., XXV, Part 2, pp. 273–74.]

Major General Couch, United States Ford, April 30, 1863

You are directed to cross as speedily as practicable with your infantry, artillery, ammunition wagons, and a few wagons for forage, and two ambulances to a division. You will have the bridge laid without delay as soon as the enemy leaves. Don't let a small force keep you back. Establish rapid communication with the telegraph at Banks' Ford and with Meade and Slocum, as the telegraph from Banks' to United States Ford works so slow. You will move to support Slocum. Be careful that no trains cross at United States Ford until further orders, as they will only be in the way. . . . In moving in support of Slocum, move toward the heaviest firing in the event of his advance being disputed. [*O.R.*, XXV, Part 2, pp. 304–5.]

On Marye's Heights 3 May 1863. Confederate caisson wagon and eight horses destroyed by explosion of a shell. Brig. Gen. Herman Haupt is pictured leaning on a stump. (USAMHI)

THE BATTLE

OF

CHANCELLORSVILLE

Directions for the Chancellorsville portion of this Guide begin at the Fredericksburg National Battlefield Visitor Center. National Park Service signs will direct you to that site if you have not completed the Fredericksburg portion of the battlefield tour and wish to begin with the Chancellorsville battle.

When you leave the parking lot at the Visitor Center, TURN LEFT on LAFAYETTE BOULEVARD (U.S. Business Route 1). Drive about 0.7 mile and TURN LEFT on CAROLINE STREET. Drive approximately 2.2 miles. You will drive through Fredericksburg, pass Old Mill Park and drive along the Rappahannock. CAROLINE STREET BECOMES RIVERSIDE DRIVE during the course of this drive and then ends at FALL HILL AVENUE. TURN RIGHT. Drive slightly more than 0.3 mile to the point where the road crosses the canal. Park on either side of the bridge. Dismount and position yourself under the powerline on the side of the canal away from the river. Walk away from the road along the powerline right of way about 150 yards. You will see a small trail coming down the hillside from the right just before you reach the second pair of powerline poles. Climb that trail about 40 yards and you will find trenches to your left and right.

George E. Chancellor's house on the Plank Road near Wilderness Church. This building served as General Howard's headquarters and a hospital.* (USAMHI)
*Also known as Dowdall's Tavern or the Melzi Chancellor House.

STOP 1, WILCOX'S MANEUVERS

These earthworks were constructed by men of *Brig. Gen. Cadmus Wilcox's* brigade in the days preceding the battle of Fredericksburg. Most maps place *Wilcox's* brigade north of FALL HILL AVENUE, but his official report specifies that his left rested on the River "150 yards to the left of Dr. Taylor's house," and his line "then extended to the right across the road on the right of Dr. Taylor's leading into the town, and thence along the base of the hill." Because the position was enfiladed by Union batteries "near a mile above Falmouth," the officers who laid out this portion of the line resorted to this innovative zigzag configuration, more typical of World War I than the Civil War, to minimize casualties.

Perhaps they were also reflecting an expensive lesson learned from their previous battle, for these troops had been exposed to deadly enfilade fire in the Bloody Lane at Antietam.

One rarely finds remnants such as these on any Civil War battlefield. *Wilcox* estimated that his troops were bombarded by no less than fifty guns. "More artillery appeared to be used on this day than I had ever known before. Frequently during the continuance of the battle I counted as many as fifty shots per minute."

His brigade lost but 1 killed and 8 wounded, "none by the musket." To *Wilcox* it seemed to be "almost incredible that the loss should have been so inconsiderable." [*O.R.*, XXI, pp. 612–13.]

In the Chancellorsville campaign, as you shortly will see, *Wilcox* owed more to the legs of his men than to these impressive earthworks.

Report of Brig. Gen. Cadmus M. Wilcox, CSA, Commanding Brigade, McLaws' Division, First Army Corps, Army of Northern Virginia

On the 29th . . . orders were received to be ready to move at a moment's notice, it being known that the enemy were advancing in heavy force from the direction of Chancellorsville.

The following day artillery was heard at intervals in that vicinity, and on . . . the 1st the brigade moved under orders up the Plank Road, and soon came within hearing of musketry. Arriving at the intersection of the Plank Road and the old turnpike, the command followed the latter, and it was not long till they came under a distant artillery fire, our troops being at the time engaged skirmishing with the enemy, [Sykes' division, Stop 5] about 1 mile off. Having reported to *General McLaws*, commanding on this road, the brigade was ordered to the right on the Mine Road, and a battery was directed to be posted with the view of engaging one of the enemy's, then sweeping with its fire the old turnpike. . . . The enemy, however, ceasing to fire, the brigade was formed in line on the right of *General Perry's* brigade. . . . This brought my command to occupy in part a line of rifle-pits running from Banks' Ford to within a few hundred yards of the Mine Road.

At 6.30 p.m. orders were received to advance to the front. This forward movement was continued, though with much difficulty, owing to the densely thick forest, till the darkness of the night rendered it impracticable to go farther. The command was halted near Duerson's Mills, on Mott's Run, three-fourths of a mile from the Rappahannock, and, having established pickets in our front and on our flanks, the command bivouacked for the night. Two companies were ordered out on patrol, with the view of ascertaining whether or not the enemy occupied the River Road near Decker's house, and, if not, to communicate with our pickets, left near Banks' Ford. The enemy were found not to occupy the River Road. The companies, returning, captured 3 Federal soldiers, making their way, so they stated, to the United States Ford.

At 10 p.m. orders were received to return to the old turnpike, and halt for the remainder of the night . . . near the advanced troops on that road. This point was reached near 2.30 a.m., and soon after orders came to return to Banks' Ford, and to hold it at all hazards, it being reported that the enemy were in force there and threatened to cross. The ford was reached at daylight; the command had thus been on the march the entire night.

The 2nd . . . the brigade remained near Banks' Ford. Large bodies of the enemy's infantry and artillery were seen moving up on the opposite side of the river [Reynolds' I Corps]. Artillery was also heard in the direction of Chancellorsville. Strong pickets were kept up during the night near the ford.

Having visited my line of pickets on the morning of the 3d . . . I found that the enemy had reduced very much (apparently) his force. The sentinels on post had their haversacks on, a thing unusual. This induced me to believe that much of the force from Banks' Ford had been sent to Chancellorsville, and, having been ordered the day before by the commanding general to leave a small force to watch the ford if in my judgment I was satisfied that the enemy did not intend to cross, and then move up the Plank Road, reporting the fact to him, I relieved my pickets, being convinced . . . that the enemy had removed most of his forces from Banks's Ford and did not intend crossing there. Leaving only about 50 men and two pieces of artillery to guard Banks' Ford, my command was being formed to march to Chancellorsville, when one of my pickets (infantry) came running from the canal in front of Dr. Taylor's to report . . . that the enemy were advancing up the [River] road between the canal and the river. Hurrying rapidly to the canal, I saw the enemy advancing on the direct road from Fredericksburg, three regiments being seen, the leading one not more than 1,000 yards distant. Gathering in my pickets along the canal and at the dam above Taylor's—in all less than 20 men—they were deployed as skirmishers on the crest of the hill in front of Dr. Taylor's, and near the canal. Two rifled pieces of *Huger's* battery, already prepared to move to Chancellorsville, were ordered into position in the battery across the road from Taylor's. While these dispositions were being made, our infantry were seen taking position in the rifle-pits near Stansbury's house. . . .

The enemy . . . halted in the road upon the display of our skirmishers. . . . The enemy being so easily checked by the display of such a small force on our side, I was induced to believe that it was only a demonstration to keep us near Fredericksburg and prevent re-enforcements from going to Chancellorsville. Seeing a group of officers near Stansbury's house, I rode to them, and met *Generals Barksdale* and *Hays*. The former informed me that the enemy were in considerable force in and below Fredericksburg (this was the first intimation I had of the fact), and expressed some anxiety as to his right flank, and said that he should have re-enforcements. I now determined not to move my command . . . until I knew definitely the intention of the enemy, and ordered them in the ravine opposite Dr. Taylor's, where they would be near and yet out of sight. I now rode to the vicinity of the Marye house to . . . confer with *General Barksdale*. While near the house, I saw great numbers of the enemy in Fredericksburg, and . . . I returned to my command without seeing *General Barksdale*. . . .

I had been with my command but a few minutes when one of *General Barksdale's* staff reported to me that the general was hard pressed and wanted me to send him a regiment. I instantly ordered the Tenth Alabama to move in the direction of the Marye house, and rode rapidly in that direction myself, and when in the open field and high ground between Stansbury's and the Plank Road, saw *Hays'* brigade moving over in the direction of the Plank Road. This I supposed to be for the support of *General Barksdale*, but upon inquiry from one of *Hays'* regiments [I] learned that the enemy had taken

Marye's Hill and a portion of two of *Barksdale's* regiments, and that *Hays'* brigade was falling back to the Telegraph Road. Soon a courier from *General Barksdale* confirmed this report . . . with a suggestion . . . that I also had better fall back to the Telegraph Road. On the left of the Plank Road the ground in rear of Marye's Hill is higher, and overlooks and commands well that hill. Believing that my own and *Hays'* brigade could form in line . . . along the crest of the hills . . . and contest the field at least for a time . . . I asked *General Hays* not to cross the Plank Road, but to remain with me. This he declined doing, having been ordered to fall back to the Telegraph Road, and was soon out of sight. . . .

Finding myself alone on the left of the Plank Road, with the enemy in full view on the crests of the first range of hills in rear of Fredericksburg, and with three times my own force clearly seen and in line, I felt it a duty to delay the enemy as much as possible in his advance, and to endeavor to check him . . . should he move forward. . . . With this view, I formed my brigade promptly in line along the crests of the hills running near Stansbury's house, at right angles to the Plank Road. Two rifled pieces . . . were placed in position to the rear of the left of my line, and two slightly in front of my right. . . . Skirmishers were thrown forward, covering my entire front. . . . [The] artillery . . . opened fire upon the enemy's lines, some 800 or 900 yards to the front. This held the enemy in check for some time.

At length they deployed skirmishers . . . and began to advance. This was slow, and, delayed by frequent halts, they seemed reluctant to advance. The enemy now brought a six-gun battery to the front on the left of the Plank Road . . . and opened with a fire of shells upon my line. The enemy's skirmishers now advanced and engaged ours—not nearer, however, than 350 or 400 yards, their solid lines remaining some distance behind. . . . The enemy's battery having fired for some time, both the skirmishers and lines in rear advanced. They had also moved by a flank across the Plank Road. . . . The artillery was now directed to withdraw; then the skirmishers joined their regiments, and all moved to the rear on the River Road, half a mile in rear of Dr. Taylor's, where they were halted. . . .

From this slight affair . . . I felt confident, if forced to retire along the Plank Road, that I could do so without precipitancy, and that ample time could be given for re-enforcements to reach us from Chancellorsville; and, moreover, I believed that, should the enemy pursue, he could be attacked in rear by *General Early*, re-enforced by

General Hays and *Barksdale*. I now directed *Major Collins*, [15th] Virginia Cavalry, who was with me with some 40 or 50 men, to move over to the Plank Road . . . and, dismounting a part of his men in rear of a thicket of pine, to deploy them to the right and left of the road as skirmishers. The command then moved on to the . . . Salem Church, on the Plank Road. The enemy followed . . . and halted when the skirmishers of *Major Collins* were seen. . . .

Having examined the ground near the toll-gate, I determined to make a short stand there. My brigade was then moved back in line from Salem Church, and halted in rear of the gate. Two rifled pieces were placed in the road, and we waited the approach of the enemy. They were soon heard to fire on *Major Collins'* skirmishers, who retired after a short skirmish, and at length appeared in lines preceded by skirmishers. *Major Collins'* men now retired to the rear, and skirmishers were deployed from the regiments to their front. Our artillery opened fire upon the enemy's advancing lines. This caused a halt, and a slight fire ensued between the skirmishers. The enemy now brought up artillery, and began a brisk shelling of our lines. At this time *Major Goggin*, assistant adjutant-general to *General McLaws*, reported to me that *General McLaws* had sent three brigades to my support, and that they would soon arrive. These brigades were directed to be halted in rear of the church and out of view of the enemy. . . . At Salem Church line of battle was formed, crossing the road at right angles. [*O.R.*, XXV, Part 1, pp. 854–57.]

Modern soldiers will recognize that *Wilcox* in his delaying operations did everything prescribed in current army doctrine. It almost appears that *FM 100-5* describes *Wilcox's* movements from these trenches to Salem Church.

A commander who is delaying may defend initially. He may shift to the delay only after the enemy has concentrated overwhelming combat power against his initial positions. He can then gain time by occupying succeeding battle positions and conducting short counter-attacks until he runs out of space. . . . A commander's orders may require him to delay the enemy forward of a certain line until a certain time. To do so, he would have to accept a decisive engage-

Todays view of Banks' Ford on the Rappahannock. (HWN)

ment. Cavalry units train and organize especially for delaying operations. When available, they should execute the delay. . . .

A delaying force must—
- Maintain contact with the enemy to avoid being
  outmaneuvered.
- Cause the enemy to plan and conduct successive attacks.
- Preserve its freedom to maneuver.
- Maintain operational coherence.
- Preserve the force.

A delaying force can—
- Harass, exhaust, weaken, and delay enemy forces.
- Expose or discover enemy weaknesses.
- Avoid undesirable combat.
- Gain time for the remainder of the force.
- Conform to movements of other friendly troops or shorten
  lines of communications.
- Cover the deployment, movement, retirement, or retreat of
  friendly units.

[Department of the Army, *Field Manual 100-5* (Washington, D.C.
1982), pp. 12–2. The commander's requirements in the delay are discussed
in greater detail in the new FM 100-5 (Washington, D.C., 1986). See pp.
154–157.]

Return to your car. Resume driving in the same direction on FALL HILL ROAD for 2.0 miles. TURN RIGHT on RIVER ROAD. At 0.7 mile on your right there is a turnout where the road nears the river. Park there and dismount to get a better view of the ford and the high bluffs on both sides of the river.

STOP 2, BANKS' FORD

This picturesque scene is Banks' Ford, the first place above Fredericksburg where roads or trails penetrated the high bluffs and wooded slopes that lined both sides of the river to permit bodies of troops, horses and wagons to cross. According to a *Military Dictionary* published in 1861,

> In examining and reporting upon a ford, the main points to be considered are the firmness and regularity of the bottom, its length, width, and direction; the depth, . . . the rapidity of the current, the facilities of access, security from attack, and the means of rendering it impassable. . . . The *depth* of fords for cavalry should not be more than 4 feet 4 inches, and for infantry 3 feet 3 inches. . . . Should the stream be very rapid, however, depths much less than these could not be considered fordable, particularly if the bottom is uneven. . . . Fords are generally to be found above or below a bend, and often lie in lines diagonally across the river; small gravel forms the best bottom; and rock, on the contrary, the most dangerous, unless perfectly regular and not slippery. . . . The approaches should also be levelled, and where the soil is soft, rendered firm by covering them with fascines, etc., so that the troops may advance with a broad front, and rapidly mount the further bank.
>
> Colonel H. L. Scott, *Military Dictionary*
> (New York: D. Van Nostrand, 1861), pp. 309–10.

The road that provided access to the north bank of the river exists today only as a footpath: it left the high ground about 0.6 mile northwest of this point and descended to the river directly opposite your location. The *Hotchkiss* Map shows two additional roads approaching the river from both sides at Scott's Ford, about half a mile downstream. In many accounts these names are confused, but it was at Scott's Ford, and not here, that two pontoon bridges were laid to permit Sedgwick's Sixth Corps to recross the river. Impressive remnants of Confederate earthworks guarding both fords remain, and on the high ground across from Stop 2 can be found remnants of works constructed by Couch's Union Second Corps on the night of April 28, and formidable artillery epaulements used later to cover Sedgwick's withdrawal.

Lee first became interested in Banks' Ford when Burnside, hoping to cross here to turn the Fredericksburg position, began his Mud March on January 20. "Our positions at Banks' and United States Mine Fords were strengthened and reinforced," he reported on January 29, "these being the points apparently threatened." [*O.R.*, XXI, p. 755.]

By the time the first elements of Couch's Second Corps reached the heights above Banks' Ford on the morning of April 28, the Confederate works that guarded these fords were truly formidable.

Report of Brig. Gen. Gouverneur K. Warren, USA, Chief of Topographical Engineers, Army of the Potomac

A place of such importance was guarded by the enemy with the utmost care. His earth parapets, placed so as to sweep with musketry every crossing-place and practicable slope, were in three lines from the water's edge to the summit of the slope, and traversed so as to quite protect the defenders from our artillery fire. . . . At Banks' Ford, moreover, two of these lines were so close to each other that both could in places bring their fire upon a party crossing the river, the rising slope permitting the rear line to shoot over that in front. The obstacles here were so great to our forcing a passage that the enemy forbore to plant a redoubt on the summit of the hill, thus, as it were, inviting us to try it. A large force constantly near the place rendered a surprise impossible, and, in addition, the bend in the river was such that though Fredericksburg was but 3 miles distant over a good plank road for the enemy, it was 6 miles for us through a forest. [*O.R.*, XXV, Part 1, pp. 195–96.]

On April 28 the telegraph line was completed from Union headquarters camp to Banks' Ford.

By April 29 Couch had completed the road through the woods to United States Ford and marched his troops to that point, where his working parties completed a pontoon bridge by late afternoon. On that same day a Union observation balloon was moved to the high ground opposite your location. By May 1, Aeronaut E. S. Allen, from *Balloon Eagle* hovering 800–1000 feet in the air, was submitting frequent and explicit reports of Confederate movements and locations as *Lee* moved out from his Fredericksburg lines to meet the threat in his rear.

By daylight on May 2, *Wilcox's* Confederate brigade had returned to Banks' Ford with orders "to hold it at all hazards," but as we have seen, when *Wilcox* observed Union sentinels across the river wearing haversacks

(Couch's two divisions having already moved on to United States Ford), he felt free to react to news that Sedgwick's troops were advancing against the lightly held position behind Fredericksburg by returning rapidly to his old intrenched position above the canal. (Stop 1).

Modern army doctrine defines a position that "will have an extraordinary impact" upon a commander's mission as "decisive terrain," since the success of his concept of operations "depends upon seizing or retaining it." Given Hooker's operational plan, Banks' Ford must be considered "decisive terrain," for as long as *Lee* controlled this position, Hooker must advance and fight on two fronts, while *Lee* was free to concentrate against one while fighting a holding action against the other. Hooker recognized, of course, the advantage of uncovering Banks' Ford, but neither his dispositions here nor his instructions to subordinate commanders indicate that this was a high priority. He assumed that *Lee* would abandon this position once the Union columns had converged upon Chancellorsville, and he instructed the Engineer Brigade to take up one of Sedgwick's bridges at Fredericksburg and have it in position to be laid at Banks' Ford "before daylight" on May 1. [*FM 100-5: Operations* (1982), p. 3–4. This term is not defined in the 1986 manual.; *O.R.*, XXV, Pt. 2, pp. 306–8.]

This of course did not occur, which meant that *Lee* was able to operate on interior lines against Hooker at Chancellorsville and Sedgwick at Salem Church.

It is a difficult problem for the historian to describe two battles simultaneously; it becomes impossible when the problem is to be at two places at the same time. Since it is easier to turn pages than to shuttle back and forth between Fredericksburg and Chancellorsville, the tour will be devoted to the operations around Chancellorsville on May 1–3; we shall leave *Wilcox* at Salem Church and return to his battle with Sedgwick after *Lee* has neutralized Hooker at Chancellorsville.

We must keep in mind, however, that during the three days that *Lee* maneuvered and fought at Chancellorsville, Sedgwick was expected to apply pressure at Fredericksburg. He had crossed the Rappahannock on April 29–30 with his own Sixth Corps and one division of Reynolds' First Corps. On May 1 he was instructed "to make a demonstration in force . . . to let it be as severe as possible without being an attack, [and] to assume a threatening attitude." Most of these orders were issued by Maj. Gen. Daniel Butterfield, Hooker's Chief of Staff, who had remained at the headquarters camp near Falmouth to facilitate communications and coordinate movements of the two wings. On May 2 Reynolds' corps was withdrawn from Sedgwick's command to rejoin Hooker near Chancellorsville. That night Sedgwick was ordered to move in the direction of

Chancellorsville, and "to attack and destroy any force on the road" between Fredericksburg and the forces with Hooker. [*O.R.*, XXV, Part 1, p. 558.]

Sedgwick's forces carried the Confederate works at Fredericksburg by assault late on the morning of May 3—about the same time that *Lee's* troops were bringing the battle at Chancellorsville to a victorious climax. As *Early's* division along with *Barksdale's* brigade fell back along the Telegraph Road two miles to the south, Sedgwick advanced cautiously to the west, astride the Plank Road, to link up with Hooker. As we have seen, *Wilcox* effectively delayed this movement while *Lee* rushed reinforcements to join him at Salem Church. There, on the afternoon of May 3, Sedgwick's lead division under Brooks was checked by five brigades from the divisions of *McLaws* and *Anderson.* The following day, after additional reinforcements had reached the area from Chancellorsville and *Early* and *Barksdale* had rejoined the fight, Sedgwick withdrew to a bridgehead covering these fords. Some of the rifle pits mentioned in the following *Report* still exist along the southern slope of the hill to your right.

Report of Brig. Gen. Henry J. Hunt, USA, Chief of Artillery, Army of the Potomac

On April 27, in pursuance of your instructions, I made a reconnaissance of the enemy's position at Banks' Ford, and determined upon the number and position of the guns to be placed there to enfilade the enemy's rifle-pits; to crush the fire of his work on the hill overlooking the river; to cover the throwing of the bridges at that ford; and to protect the crossing of the troops. The necessary instructions to supervise this work, to place the batteries, to prepare cover for those that were exposed, and to take command there in case of my absence, were given to Maj. A. Doull, inspector of artillery on my staff, who executed them with his customary energy, taking with him two batteries of position [four 4½ inch guns and four 20-pounders] . . . from the Artillery Reserve. The 20-pounder battery under Lieutenant Blucher . . . was placed in a very exposed position, but with the labor of his men he constructed good cover for them. The remaining batteries required for this position were drawn from the Second, Eleventh, and Twelfth Corps. . . .

May 1 Soon after General Sykes became engaged. . . . at 1.30 p.m. I received verbal instructions from you to return to headquarters camp, near Falmouth, collect the disposable artillery, move it to Banks' Ford, and to prevent any attempt of the enemy to cross at that point. . . . From the telegraph station at the United States Ford I sent a message to Major-General Butterfield, chief of staff, requesting him to send to Banks' Ford the disposable batteries near the headquarters camp, and proceeded myself to reconnoiter the ford and select positions for them. In conformity with my request for infantry, the remainder of General Owen's brigade, a portion of which was on duty at the ford, under the orders of General Benham, reported to me that night. . . . No demonstrations were made by the enemy.

On the afternoon of the 3d, he abandoned his rifle-pits opposite us, Major-General Sedgwick having carried the heights above Fredericksburg, and being then on the advance along the Chancellorsville road. I sent Major Doull across (swimming his horse) to communicate with General Sedgwick. . . . In the meantime General Benham laid the bridges and I crossed to inspect the different works of the enemy. The firing . . . growing into the sounds of a battle, I immediately returned to the north side of the river in order to send support to Sedgwick. On reaching the bridge, I found Brigadier General Owen crossing and directed him to connect with Sedgwick's right, so as to keep up communication with the bridges. . . . About this time I received a dispatch . . . directing me to report immediately to you at Chancellorsville. . . . [O.R., XXV, Part 1, pp. 246–49.]

Report of Maj. Gen. John Sedgwick, USA, Commanding Sixth Army Corps, Army of the Potomac

I received a dispatch from the major-general commanding, informing me that he had contracted his lines; that I must look well to the safety of my corps, preserve my communications with Fredericksburg and Banks' Ford, and suggesting that I fall back upon the former place or recross, in preference, at Banks' Ford, where I could more readily communicate with the main body. To fall back upon Fredericksburg was out of the question. To adopt the other alternative, except under cover of night, was equally so, for the enemy still maintained his position on Salem Heights and was threatening my flank and rear from the direction of Fredericksburg. . . . Subsequent dispatches directed me to hold a position on the right bank of the river until the following morning. . . .

As soon as it was dark, Newton's and Brooks' divisions, with the light brigade, fell rapidly back upon Banks' Ford, and took position on the heights in that neighborhood and in the rifle-pits. When these movements were completed, Howe . . . at once abandoned his posi-

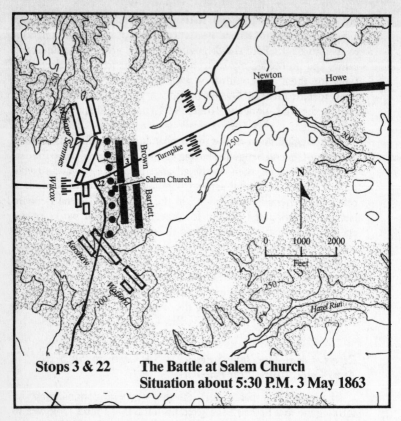

**Stops 3 & 22   The Battle at Salem Church
                    Situation about 5:30 P.M. 3 May 1863**

tion and moved to the river, taking position on Newton's right.

On Tuesday, the 5th, at 2 a.m., I received the order . . . to withdraw from my position, cross the river, take up the bridge, and cover the ford. The order was immediately executed, the enemy meanwhile shelling the bridges from commanding positions above us, on the river. When the last of the column was on the bridge, I received a dispatch from the commanding general countermanding the order to withdraw. My command was on the left bank . . . [and] could not recross before daylight, and must do it then . . . in face of the enemy, whose batteries completely commanded the bridges. I accordingly went into camp in the vicinity of the ford, sending an adequate force to guard the river and watch the ford. [*O.R.*, XXV, pp. 560–61.]

House where Stonewall Jackson died. (USAMHI)

Major-General John Sedgwick and his staff. (MIL)

Return to your car. TURN AROUND and go back up RIVER ROAD toward Fredericksburg. At the "T" intersection, turn right at the STOP sign. Drive about 0.9 mile to the traffic light on VIRGINIA HIGHWAY 3. TURN RIGHT. Drive about 0.5 mile to the monument on the right side of the road, marked with a brown historical marker sign. Pull off into the small parking lot, being careful to avoid on-coming traffic on Route 694 as you enter the parking area in front of the monument to the 15th Regiment, New Jersey Volunteers.

STOP 3, ENGAGEMENT AT SALEM HEIGHTS

Although the tour follows *Lee* to Chancellorsville, this is a good occasion to view the battle of Salem Church (May 3) from the Union perspective. You will visit the old Salem Church, which is preserved by the National Park Service, and read the relevant Confederate *Reports* on the final stop of the tour as you return to Fredericksburg.

Report of Maj. Gen. John Sedgwick, USA, Commanding Sixth Army Corps, Army of the Potomac

[May 2] That night at 11 o'clock I received an order . . . directing me to cross the Rappahannock at Fredericksburg immediately upon receipt of the order, and move in the direction of Chancellorsville until I connected with the major-general commanding; to attack and destroy any force on the road, and be in the vicinity of the general at daylight.

I had been informed repeatedly by Major-General Butterfield, chief of staff, that the force in front of me was very small, and the whole tenor of his many dispatches would have created the impression that the enemy had abandoned my front and retired from the city and its defenses had there not been more tangible evidence . . . that the chief of staff was misinformed.

The order to cross at Fredericksburg found me with my entire command on the south side of the river, ready to pursue by the Bowling Green Road. To recross for the purpose of crossing again at Fredericksburg, where no bridges had been laid, would have occupied until long after daylight. I commenced, therefore, to move by the flank in the direction of Fredericksburg, on the Bowling Green Road. . . . A sharp skirmish commenced as the head of the column moved from the immediate vicinity of the bridges, and continued all the way to the town, the enemy falling slowly back. . . .

When the head of the column entered the town, four regiments from Wheaton's and Shaler's brigades were sent forward against the rifle-pits, and advanced within 20 yards of the enemy's works, when they received a sudden and destructive fire. An immediate assault was made, but repulsed by the fire of the rifle-pits and batteries on the heights. It was evident that the enemy's line of works was occupied in considerable force. . . . It was now daylight, and batteries were placed in position to shell the enemy until the troops could be formed for another attack. . . . Nothing remained but to carry the works by direct assault.

Two storming columns were formed . . . [and] a line of battle [about 4700 men from Newton's and Burnham's divisions]. . . . The columns moved on the Plank Road and to the right of it directly up the heights. The line of battle advanced on the double-quick to the left of the Plank Road against the rifle-pits, neither halting nor firing a shot until they had driven the enemy from their lower line of works. In the meantime the storming columns had pressed forward to the crest, and carried the works in the rear of the rifle-pits, capturing the guns and many prisoners. These movements were gallantly executed under a most destructive fire.

In the meantime Howe [commanding Second Division] advanced rapidly on the left of Hazel Run in three columns of assault, and forced the enemy from the crest in front, capturing five guns. The entire corps was at once put in motion and moved in pursuit. Considerable resistance was made on the next series of heights, but the position was carried without halting. A section of horse artillery on our right occupied every successive crest upon our line of march, and much annoyed our advance.

At Salem Chapel the enemy were re-enforced by a brigade from Banks' Ford *[Wilcox]* and by troops in the direction of Chancellorsville, and made a determined resistance. Brooks' division formed rapidly across the road and Newton's upon his right, and advanced upon the woods, which were strongly held by the enemy. After a sharp and prolonged contest, we gained the heights, but were met by fresh troops pouring in upon the flank of the advanced portion of the line. For a short time the crest was held by our troops with obstinate resistance, but at length the line was forced slowly back through the woods. The advance of the enemy is checked by the splendid firing of our batteries. . . . Wheaton still holds his position on the right, gallantly fighting. On the left the troops are rapidly reformed, and, after a short interval, again advance upon the woods. The enemy is once more forced back in much confusion on our right, but steadily resisting on the left.

This was the condition of things when night put an end to the battle. [*O.R.*, XXV, Part 1, pp. 558–60.]

Report of Col. Charles H. Tomkins, USA, Chief of Artillery, Sixth Army Corps, Army of the Potomac

From [Marye's Heights] to Salem Heights, the advance of the corps was annoyed by a section of horse artillery, the only guns not captured . . . in the assault, which took position upon every available point and opened upon our troops, firing until driven off by the fire of the batteries . . . which were with the advance, and the near approach of the infantry, which continued steadily to advance.

At Salem Heights the enemy were found to be in force. Brooks' division, which had come up and taken the advance, moved forward to the assault on the left of the Plank Road, and Newton's division upon the right. Williston's, Rigby's, and Hexamer's batteries were placed in position near the toll-gate, where a slight rise in the ground afforded good cover for the limbers and caissons. . . . From the batteries to the wood, which begin at the foot of the heights, was about 500 yards of open ground. The infantry moved steadily across this ground, charged the wood, and, after a severe contest, reached the crest, held it for a few moments, and then, being greatly outnumbered, was forced to retire. It came out of the wood, many of the regiments in great confusion, closely followed by the enemy.

Already had the batteries opened fire over the heads of the retiring troops, firing slowly at first, and, as the enemy attempted to follow our troops out of the wood, rapidly, Williston using canister. The enemy were checked and driven back by this fire. The infantry reformed behind the batteries, advanced, entering the wood, and held the position until darkness ended the conflict. [*O.R.*, XXV, Part 1, p. 564.]

Report of Brig. Gen. William T. H. Brooks, USA, Commanding First Division, Sixth Army Corps, Army of the Potomac

After the heights in rear of Fredericksburg were carried, the division left its position, and proceeded on the Plank Road toward Chancellorsville . . . After passing the remainder of the corps, and when about . . . 3 miles out on the Plank Road, a small cavalry force of the enemy, with two or three pieces of artillery, was discovered on the road. A line of skirmishers was thrown quickly to the front . . . and the Jersey brigade deployed, with one regiment on the left of the road and the others, excepting the Fifteenth New Jersey Volunteers, which was then in the rear, on the right. At this point several discharges were fired by the enemy . . . artillery. . . . Captain Rigby's battery was then put in position, and the enemy retired after a few rounds.

The different lines were then advanced. The enemy, firing at one or two different points without effect, finally disappeared in a belt of timber which crosses the road and is immediately in front of Salem Church. In and in rear of this timber the enemy was in strong force and position. . . .

At 5.30 p.m. the action became general. The Second brigade . . . with the Second and Twenty-third New Jersey Volunteers, of the First Brigade, on the left of the road, and the First, Third, and Fifteenth New Jersey . . . of the First Brigade, with the Ninety-fifth and One hundred and nineteenth Pennsylvania . . . of the Third Brigade, on the right of the road, advanced against the enemy.

Immediately upon entering the dense growth of shrubs and trees which concealed the enemy, our troops were met by a heavy and incessant fire of musketry; yet our lines advanced until they had reached the crest of the hill in the outer skirts of the wood when, . . . being attacked by fresh and superior numbers of the enemy, our forces were finally compelled to withdraw.

The lines were re-established near the batteries of Rigby, Parsons, and Williston, now posted on a crest overlooking the ground . . . across which the enemy attempted to follow our retiring line; but this was soon stopped by the artillery and the reenforcements from Newton's division, posted on our right.

In this brief but sanguinary conflict this division lost nearly 1,500 men and officers. [*O.R.*, XXV, Part 1, pp. 567–68.]

Report of Col. Henry W. Brown, USA, Commanding
First Brigade, First Division, Sixth Army Corps,
Army of the Potomac

We were . . . in the advance, and I formed my brigade; six companies of the Second . . . as skirmishers on either side of the road, The First and Third [New Jersey] . . . on the right of the road, in line of battle, and the Twenty-third . . . on the left, at about 200 yards in rear of the line of skirmishers, and so moved about half a mile, when we were met by a fire of shell from a battery in position on the crest of a hill at about 300 yards distant. Our skirmishers still advanced gallantly, and by their fire drove the enemy to a precipitate retreat, our batteries, which had now come into position, contributing to this result. Our advance continued about 1½ miles farther, the enemy still retreating and fighting, using their batteries at every advantageous point. . . .

When we arrived at this point we found the enemy in strong position, and also that he had received re-enforcements. I here received orders to send in a regiment to clear some woods on my right flank, and, as the advance seemed to be checked, I went with the Third Regiment . . . which I ordered on this duty. . . .

The regiment advanced gallantly, but was met by an overwhelming fire from the enemy, concealed in some trenches and behind a fence, to which it replied with vigor. The Fifteenth Regiment had now come up, and I directed it to advance to the support of the Third. . . . It came into its position in beautiful order, and I cannot speak too highly of the manner in which this regiment was fought by its gallant commander, Colonel Penrose. He relieved the Third, almost worn out by its long march and fight, and held the enemy in check, who, having had fresh troops come up, were preparing to attack both in front and on our right flank. After a few minutes' rest, and having reformed his regiment, slightly disordered by the march through the thick wood and undergrowth, in line of battle, Major Stickney gallantly led . . . the Third in again to the support of the Fifteenth, and so we held them until about 6.30. [*O.R.*, XXV, Part 1, pp. 570–71.]

Report of Brig. Gen. Joseph J. Bartlett, USA, Commanding Second Brigade, First Division, Sixth Army Corps, Army of the Potomac

The column moved on, the New Jersey Brigade forming in two lines on the right of the road and my brigade a few minutes afterward making the same disposition on the left. . . . Our skirmishers pressed those of the enemy steadily back, while the batteries of our division drove the three pieces which were used upon us from successive positions until we arrived in front of a dense thicket, crossing the road at right angles and partially concealing the heights of Salem Church. Here our skirmish line was checked. . . . The dispositions for the attack were rapidly made. . . .

The woods were thick with harsh, unyielding undergrowth, with little large timber. It afforded no protection to our troops from the showers of bullets which were rapidly thinning my ranks, but retarded their advance so much that nothing but the most unflinching bravery could make them withstand their fearful loss while overcoming so many natural obstacles. Under all these disadvantages I reached and held the crest until two fresh lines were hurled upon my exhausted troops, which forced them back through the woods and upon our second line, in rear of which I reformed my brigade and rested until morning.

My loss in this attack was 580 officers and men out of four regiments numbering less than 1500. . . . Nothing could surpass the gallantry with which my troops threw themselves against the enemy's well-selected position. . . . It was the first time they were ever repulsed. . . . it was the first time they had ever retired in the face of an enemy. . . . Col. Emory Upton, commanding the One hundred and twenty-first New York Volunteers . . . led his regiment into action in a masterly and fearless manner, and maintained the unequal con-

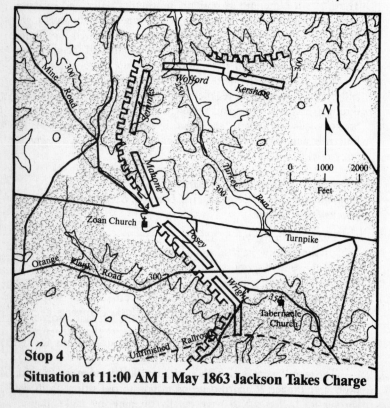

Stop 4

Situation at 11:00 AM 1 May 1863 Jackson Takes Charge

test to the last with unflinching nerve and marked ability, and his regiment, although it was their first battle, have won for themselves the proud title of soldiers. [*O.R.*, XXV, Part 1, pp. 581–83.]

Continue in the same direction on ROUTE 3 for about 2.5 miles. As you approach the intersection with State Road 620, you will notice the ZOAN BAPTIST CHURCH across the highway on your left. Pull off the highway on the right by the historical marker for SPOTSWOOD'S FURNACE just short of the intersection.

STOP 4, LEE REACTS

General Robert E. Lee to Lieutenant General Thomas J. Jackson, April 23, 1863

From the account given me by *Lieutenant Colonel Smith* of the Engineers, who was at Port Royal yesterday, of the enemy's operations there the day and night previous, that his present purpose is to draw our troops in that direction, while he attempts a passage elsewhere. I would not then send down more troops than are actually necessary. I will notify *General McLaws* and *Anderson* to be on the alert for I think that if a real attempt is made to cross the river it will be above Fredericksburg. [Clifford Dowdey, ed., *Wartime Papers of R. E. Lee* (Boston: Little, Brown and Company, 1961), p. 438.]

General Lee to President Jefferson Davis, April 29, 1863

The enemy crossed the Rappahannock [below Fredericksburg] today in large numbers, and have taken position under the bank of the river, under cover of their heavy guns on the opposite side. . . . Tonight he will probably get over the remainder of his forces.

Besides the force which was reported by *General Stuart* to have crossed on the pontoon bridges laid below Kelly's Ford, I have learned this evening by couriers from Germanna and Ely's Fords that the enemy's cavalry crossed the Rapidan at those points about 2 p.m. today. I could not learn their strength, but infantry was said to have crossed with the cavalry at the former point.

Their intention, I presume, is to turn our left, and probably to get into our rear. Our scattered condition favors their operations. I hope if any reinforcements can be sent they may be forwarded immediately. The bridges over the [North and South] Annas ought to be guarded, if possible. [*O.R.*, XXV, Part 2, pp. 756–57.]

*General Lee to Maj. Gen. Lafayette McLaws, Commanding
Division, First Army Corps, Army of Northern Virginia,
April 29, 1863 — 6.30 p.m.*

As arranged today, I wish you to draw your troops out of Fredericksburg, leaving your sharpshooters, and take a position in the rifle-pits, so as to maintain the heights back of the town, as in December. Extend your right to Deep Run, and the troops not necessary on the front hold in reserve to throw where they may be required.

You should have all your men in position by daylight in the morning, with rations for the day.

Caution your officers to be vigilant and energetic; repair your line of defense when you may find it necessary, and pay every attention to the comfort of your men and the support of your horses.

Communicate to *General Jackson* and *General Anderson* all movements of the enemy effecting them, and, if they ask for re-enforcements, furnish what you can. I have just heard that the enemy's cavalry, accompanied by infantry, had crossed at Germanna Ford (the Rapidan).

P.S. I have just heard that a regiment of cavalry crossed at Ely's Ford. We may be obliged to change our position in consequence of the enemy's having come in between us and *General Stuart.* Make your preparatory arrangements tonight to secure all your property. Leave no more sharpshooters on the river and in Fredericksburg than are absolutely necessary, so as to have as strong a force as possible to strengthen our left. [*O.R.,* XXV, Part 2, p. 759.]

*Lee to Maj. Gen. R. H. Anderson, CSA, Commanding Division,
First Army Corps, Army of Northern Virginia,
April 29, 1863. 6.45 P.M.*

I have just heard that a portion of the enemy's cavalry, accompanied by infantry, crossed the Rapidan at Germanna Ford about 1 o'clock. Draw in your brigade at United States Ford, and throw your left back so as to cover the road leading from Chancellorsville down the river, taking the strongest line you can, and holding it to the best advantage. I wish you to go forward yourself and attend to this matter.

Let me know where communications will reach you, and inform me of the condition of things. . . . [*O.R.,* XXV, Part 2, p. 759.]

Lee to Anderson, **April 30, 1863**

I have received your note of this morning. . . . I hope you have been able to select a good line and fortify it strongly. At what point will your right rest? Will it include *Wilcox's* position [near Banks' Ford], and can you draw him on the line?

Set all your spades to work as vigorously as possible. I hope to send you additional troops if I can learn in time; so hold your position firmly, and prepare your line for them. Send me word this evening what additional guns you will require. . . . Keep two days' rations cooked that the men can carry on their persons, and give orders that everything be prepared to pack your trains and to move off at any moment when ordered. All your baggage, camp equipage, including your headquarters, etc., must be immediately reduced in order to accomplish this. . . . [*O.R.*, XXV, Part 2, p. 761.]

SPECIAL ORDERS NO. 121.   Hdqrs. Army of
      April 30, 1863.   Northern Virginia.

I. *Major-General McLaws* will designate a brigade of his division to hold the lines in rear of Fredericksburg, the commander of which will report to the major-general left in charge *[Early]*. With the rest of his division, *General McLaws* will move as soon as possible to re-enforce *General Anderson* at the Tabernacle Church, on the Plank Road to Orange Court House.

II. *General Jackson* will designate a division to hold the lines in front of the enemy [at Fredericksburg] on Pratt's and Bernard's farms. . . . With the remainder of his corps, *General Jackson*, at daylight tomorrow morning, will proceed to Tabernacle Church, and make arrangements to repulse the enemy.

III. The troops will be provided with two days' cooked provisions. The trains of all the divisions will be packed with all their equipage, and move to the rear under the direction of the chief quartermaster of the army. The reserve ammunition trains will be under the charge of the chief of ordnance. The regimental ordnance wagons, ambulances, and medical wagons will accompany the troops.

IV. The chief of artillery will superintend the service of the batteries in position on the lines and will take charge of those not required to operate with the troops. [*O.R.*, XXV, Part 2, p. 762.]

Report of General Robert E. Lee, Commanding Army of Northern Virginia.

No demonstration was made opposite any other part of our lines at Fredericksburg, and the strength of the force that had crossed and its apparent indisposition to attack indicated that the principal effort of the enemy would be made in some other quarter. This impression was confirmed by intelligence received from *General Stuart*. . . .

On the night of the 29th, *General Anderson* was directed to proceed toward Chancellorsville, and dispose *Wright's* brigade and the troops from the Bark Mill Ford to cover these roads. Arriving at Chancellorsville about midnight, he found the commands of *Generals Mahone* and *Posey* already there, having been withdrawn from the Bark Mill [United States] Ford, with the exception of a small guard.

Learning that the enemy had crossed the Rapidan, and were approaching in strong force, *General Anderson* retired early on the morning of the 30th to the intersection of the Mine and Plank Roads, near Tabernacle Church, and began to intrench himself. . . . *General Stuart* marched by Todd's Tavern toward Spotsylvania Court House, to put himself in communication with the main body of the army. . . .

The enemy in our front near Fredericksburg continued inactive, and it was now apparent that the main attack would be made upon our flank and rear. It was, therefore, determined to leave sufficient troops to hold our lines, and with the main body of the army to give battle to the approaching column. *Early's* division, of *Jackson's* corps, and *Barksdale's* brigade, of *McLaws'* division, with part of the Reserve Artillery . . . were intrusted with the defense of our position at Fredericksburg, and, at midnight on the 30th, *General McLaws* marched with the rest of his command toward Chancellorsville. *General Jackson* followed at dawn next morning with the remaining divisions of his corps. He reached the position occupied by *General Anderson* at 8 a.m. and immediately began preparations to advance. [*O.R.*, XXV, Part 1, pp. 796–7.]

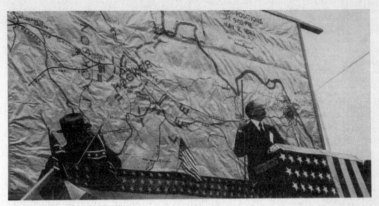

Douglas Southall Freeman speaking about the campaign at the Chancellorsville Anniversary Battle Celebration in May 1935. Photo courtesy National Park Service.

ZOAN CHURCH

Here, on this ridge overlooking the intersection of the Orange Turnpike and the Old Mine or Mountain Road that in 1863 led to U.S. Ford, *Lee* ordered *Anderson* "to select a good line and fortify it strongly." According to Douglas Southall Freeman, the distinguished biographer of the Confederate commander, "these orders were of historical importance. It was the first time, in open operations, that *Lee* had ordered the construction of field fortifications." [Douglas Southall Freeman, *R. E. Lee: a Biography* (4 vols., New York: Charles Scribner's Sons, 1936), II, p. 514.]

The intrenched line extended along this ridge to the north for about three-fourths of a mile and then veered off well to the east, in the direction of Banks' Ford. South of the Turnpike the line followed the high ground southeast to the vicinity of Tabernacle Church, where it commanded the Orange Plank Road. This position therefore blocked the three main roads by which Hooker's columns could advance from Chancellorsville. Remnants of the old earthworks reveal how the art of field fortification had progressed since *McLaws* threw up his breastworks at Lee's Hill in December.

Here *Wilcox* heard the battle in progress between Sykes' division and troops under *Anderson* and *McLaws* on May 1. Ordered to advance to "the front," his weary brigade moved out on the Old Mine Road to the right for about half a mile and then turned right on a road to Duerson Mill. When he was recalled he returned to this point to rest briefly before being ordered to march to Banks' Ford. [See STOP 1 for text.]

Report of Maj. Gen. Richard H. Anderson, CSA, Commanding Division, First Army Corps, Army of Northern Virginia

Upon arriving at the intersection of the Old Mine and Plank Roads, I met *Col. W. P. Smith*, chief engineer Army of Northern Virginia, and *Captain Johnston*, of the Engineer Corps, who had been sent by the commanding general to examine the position and establish a line of intrenchments. The work of intrenching was commenced immediately after the line had been selected, and was continued with great diligence and activity throughout that day [April 30], the night following, and the early part of the next morning. During the day there were occasional skirmishes with the enemy's cavalry, who had followed from Chancellorsville. In the afternoon *Colonel Owen*, commanding Third Regiment Virginia Cavalry, joined me with his regiment, and threw out pickets to the front and upon each flank.

A little before sunrise on May 1, *Major-General McLaws*, having come up with his division, strengthened the force immediately in front, and secured our right flank by occupying the trenches along Mott's Run. At 8 a.m. *Lieutenant General Jackson* arrived. By his orders the work on the trenches was discontinued, and the troops were put in readiness for an advance, *Wilcox's* and *Perry's* brigades, which had been left above Fredericksburg, being at the same time ordered to join their division. [*O.R.*, XXV, Part 1, p. 850.]

Report of Maj. Gen. Lafayette McLaws, CSA, Commanding Division, First Army Corps, Army of Northern Virginia

On May 1, at 12.30 at night, the brigades of *Generals Kershaw, Semmes*, and *Wofford* were put in march up the Plank Road . . . and by 6 o'clock in the morning were in position behind the rifle-pits about Smith's Hill, and extending to the right and left, joining *General Anderson's* command on the left, to defend the approaches from the United States Ford and from the direction of Chancellorsville.

About 11 a.m. *General Jackson*, who had arrived with his forces and assumed command, directed me to advance along the Turnpike Road, having *Mahone's* brigade, of *Anderson's* division, in advance. I collected my own division as rapidly as possible from the rifle-pits, each brigade as it was relieved falling in rear of the others as they advanced in the march. [*O.R.*, XXV, Part 1, pp. 824–25]

By-road diverging from the Plank Road just east of the Union Line. Lieut. Gen. Thomas J "Stonewall" Jackson went up this road to the Plank Road on which he was shot. (USAMHI)

Continue in the same direction on Route 3 for about 2.3 miles. Move into the LEFT LANE as you near the end of that distance, when you see a sign notifying you that you are 2 miles from the Chancellorsville Visitor Center, and TURN LEFT onto McLAWS DRIVE. A few hundred feet after you have entered that drive you will find a place to pull off to the right. Park there, walk back to the median of Route 3 and then walk back toward Fredericksburg along the median about 200 feet so that you get a clear view of the landscape rolling eastward.

STOP 5, THE BATTLE BEGINS

As you look to the east, you are standing about a mile behind Sykes' line of battle as it moved forward across these fields to the left to engage the Confederate divisions of *McLaws* and *Anderson*. Most of the fighting took place north of the highway. While Sykes endeavored to halt the Confederate advance on the TURNPIKE, *Jackson's* corps was moving along the PLANK ROAD against Slocum's Twelfth Corps. The TURNPIKE and the PLANK ROAD occasionally converge on this battlefield, and these segments usually are referred to as the Plank Road in *Reports*.

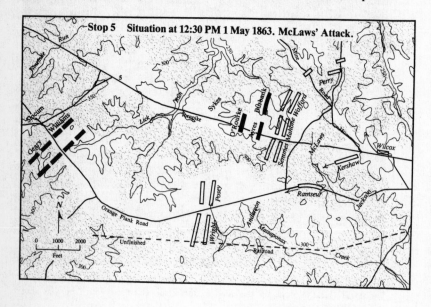

Stop 5   Situation at 12:30 PM 1 May 1863. McLaws' Attack.

Report of Maj. Gen. Lafayette McLaws, CSA, Commanding Division, First Army Corps, Army of Northern Virginia

After proceeding but a short distance, the skirmishers became engaged. The main column, advancing slowly until the enemy appeared in force, was deployed, and the line of battle formed across the Turnpike Road, *Semmes'* brigade on the left and those of *Mahone, Wofford,* and *Perry,* of *Anderson's* division, in the order here named to the right, extending so as to cover the Mine Road, *Jordan's* battery on the main turnpike. Our skirmishers were driven in. Fire was opened on our lines from a battery 400 or 500 yards in front, and, after skirmishing to the right and left, the main assault was made on the left *(Semmes)* by Sykes' Regulars, but they were repulsed at every attempt.

Before the first assault, I sent word to *General Jackson,* by my aide-de-camp, that the enemy were in force in my immediate front, and were advancing, and that a large force could be seen along the heights about 1 mile or more to the rear, and that the country was favorable for a flank attack from his side. After the first assault, I received answer from *General Jackson* to hold my position, and that he would advance, or was advancing, his artillery, and if that did not answer he would endeavor to gain the rear of the enemy. *General Kershaw* coming up, his brigade was placed in support of *General Semmes,* extending beyond his left. The cavalry reported that the enemy were advancing along the Mine Road, *General Wilcox's* brigade was ordered and took position (guided by *Captain Johnston,* of *General Lee's* staff) to protect my right, taking artillery with him. *General Jackson's* artillery and his advance, in conjunction with the failure of the attack on my front, forced the enemy to retire, when, by *General Jackson's* order, my whole line advanced. . . . The order to advance was received at 4 p.m. My line halted at dark, and bivouacked along the heights just beyond the point where the Mine Run crosses the turnpike. [*O.R.,* XXV, Part 1, p. 825.]

Report of Brig. Gen. Paul J. Semmes, CSA, Commanding Brigade, McLaws' Division, First Army Corps, Army of Northern Virginia

At about 12 m. Friday, May 1, this brigade (with others) was ordered forward in pursuit. Having advanced more than a mile, the enemy's skirmishers were discovered. The brigade was then immediately formed into line, under a scattering fire from the enemy's infantry and artillery . . . and advanced a short distance, and halted in the edge of a wood overlooking open fields, in which the enemy was formed; being supported by *Kershaw* on my left and *Mahone* on my right, *Mahone's* left resting on the road.

Soon the enemy's line of infantry was pushed forward. When within easy range, the order was given to commence firing. The enemy, after a sharp contest, retired a short distance and took shelter under a crest, from which position he continued the fight, advancing once more only to be again promptly repulsed. His cavalry essayed a charge on *[Jordan's]* battery, posted in the road, and was driven back in disorder. After the fight had continued some little time, a strong line of skirmishers from the Tenth Georgia was thrown far forward, to the left of the Fifty-first Georgia, who, by an enfilading fire, contributed materially to the repulse of the enemy's lines.

It has been since ascertained that the United States Regulars, under Sykes, were here encountered. They were finally and handsomely driven from the field after a sharp contest of perhaps three-fourths of an hour, in which this brigade was the chief participant, the Fifty-first Georgia Volunteers receiving and repelling the main attack, and sustaining more loss than the balance of the brigade. . . . [*O.R.*, XXV, Part 1, pp. 833–34.]

Report of Maj. Gen. George G. Meade, USA, Commanding Fifth Army Corps, Army of the Potomac

[On May 1], under the orders of the major-general commanding, the corps was put *en route* to take a position to uncover Banks' Ford, the left resting on the river, the right extending on the Plank Road. For this purpose, Sykes' division was ordered to advance on the . . . turnpike until after crossing Mott's Run, when he was to move to the left, deploy, and open communication with Griffin on his left and Slocum on his right, and, when all were in position to advance simultaneously against the enemy, supposed to be in position from the Plank Road to the river. Griffin was ordered to move down the River . . . Road until in the presence of the enemy, when he was to deploy, his left resting on the river and his right extending toward Sykes. Humphreys was ordered to follow Griffin, to be held in reserve to re-enforce Griffin or Sykes as the exigencies might require.

These movements were commenced about 11 a.m. Sykes moved out on the old pike, and, after proceeding over a mile, met the enemy's skirmishers. He immediately deployed, and, after a spirited engagement, drove the enemy for a considerable distance.

Finding the enemy in force and making dispositions to outflank him on both flanks, without any communication either on the right or left with a supporting force, General Sykes reported the condition of affairs to the major-general commanding the army, and by him was ordered to withdraw. This he did in good order, returning to Chancellorsville.

In the meantime the column of Griffin and Humphreys proceeded on the River Road, and had reached Decker's house, within view of Banks' Ford, without any opposition from the enemy, when the order of recall was received, and the column returned to Chancellorsville.

Being directed to occupy a line from Chancellorsville to the river, General Humphreys' division was immediately sent to occupy the extreme left of this line, on the river bank, and directed to hold the approach to the United States Ford by the . . . River Road, in force. General Griffin was halted on his return march, owing to the advance of the enemy on the withdrawal of Sykes. Griffin formed on the left of Hancock [Second Army Corps], who had come up to relieve Sykes.

About 6 p.m. the enemy advanced on Sykes, who had just returned to camp, who formed line immediately, and repulsed him handsomely.

In this position the troops bivouacked for the night, but before daylight Griffin and Sykes were withdrawn and took up a position on the Mineral Spring Road. . . . The next day . . . was occupied in strengthening this position by the construction of rifle pits, abatis, etc. [O.R., XXV, Part 1, p. 507]

Report of Brig. Gen. Gouverneur K. Warren, USA, Chief Engineer, Army of the Potomac

On the morning of May 1, I went out 3 miles on the turnpike to Fredericksburg to reconnoiter. . . . The country along the road for the first mile is wooded on both sides, and was generally so to the left of it (except some cleared fields) nearly to the river. . . . To the right of the road it was rather more open, and in places the clearing extended across from the road to the Plank Road. . . . I found the Eighth Pennsylvania cavalry picketing the road for 3 miles and to within sight of the enemy's breastwork thrown across the road [at Zoan Church], which was as far as I could go. . . .

On my return to headquarters, about 10 a.m., I found that an advance had been ordered. The First and Third Divisions of the Fifth Corps were to take the road along the river toward Banks' Ford; the Second Division of the Fifth Corps, the turnpike, to be followed by a portion of the Second Corps, and the Twelfth Corps to move out on the Plank Road toward Fredericksburg. This was a movement to take up a line of battle about 2½ miles in front, preparatory to a simultaneous advance along the line at 2 p.m.

I went back over the route I had examined, which was that given to the Second Division . . . under General Sykes. On gaining the ridge, about 1¼ miles from Chancellorsville, we found the enemy advancing and driving back our cavalry. This small force resisted handsomely, riding up and firing almost in the faces of the Eleventh Virginia Infantry, which formed the enemy's advance. General Sykes moved forward at double-quick time, attacked the enemy vigorously, and drove him back with loss till he had gained the position assigned him. This he obtained about 12 o'clock. No sound yet reached us indicating that any of our column had encountered the advance of the enemy.

In General Sykes' front the enemy deployed to the right and left, in line far outreaching the whole of ours, and I have never seen the steadiness of our troops more tried and proved. Captain Weed brought his battery into the front line on the ridge where it could operate against the enemy, and was able to reply to him within musket-range, and used his guns with great effect. When the division had all been deployed to extend the line of battle, the lack of numbers compelled a regiment to be deployed as skirmishers. No connection, however, could even thus be made with our own troops [Twelfth Corps] on the right, and my aide . . . in attempting to communicate with the presumed position of General Slocum, ran against the enemy's skirmishers, from which he fortunately escaped, though many shots were fired after him. A similar effort by one of General Sykes' aides was foiled in the same way. General Sykes bravely resolved to hold the position assigned him which his command had so gallantly won from the enemy, and I set out with all possible speed to report the condition to the commanding general.

From information received since the advance began, the [commanding] general decided to countermand it, and receive the enemy in the line occupied the night before. Unfortunately, this line had been taken up . . . by tired troops toward the close of the day and without much prospect of fighting a pitched battle upon it. It was a bad line, and had several commanding positions in its front for the enemy to occupy. It was, perhaps, the best that could be designated for such a sudden change of programme in the face of the enemy.

I carried to General Sykes the order to fall back, and he then withdrew his command in perfect order, bringing off his wounded, with the exception of a few who were cut off in the extreme right of his extended skirmish line. All the other columns withdrew to the vicinity of Chancellorsville without having engaged the enemy. The enemy advanced cautiously till he came upon our new lines, and made some feeble demonstrations, easily repulsed, and the day closed without any real trial of strength. During the evening the Third Corps joined us at Chancellorsville.

Two general plans of operations were now considered. One was to choose a position and intrench; the other, to choose our point of attack and advance with our whole force of five corps upon it. The saving of our men and the advantages of resuming the offensive after a tactical repulse favored the one; the increased *elan* of our men and the choice of our point of attack the other. I was in favor of advancing, and urged it with more zeal than convincing argument. I thought, with our position and numbers, to beat the enemy's right wing. This could be done by advancing in force on the two main roads toward Fredericksburg, each being in good supporting distance, at the same time throwing a heavy force on the enemy's right flank by the River Road. If this attack found the enemy in extended line across our front, or in motion toward our right flank, it would have secured the defeat of his right wing and consequently the retreat of the whole. The advantage of the initiative in a wooded country like this, obscuring all movements, was incalculable. . . .

The general's original determination to await the attack had in it also the design to contract our line and throw back the right to a better position, our left being secure. On the assurance of the commander on the right that they were abundantly able to hold their position against any force the nature of the ground would enable the enemy to bring against them, and because they thought to fall back would have some of the demoralizing influences of a retreat, it was decided to make no changes in the [right wing under Slocum], but to strengthen it with breastwork and abatis. The sound of the ax broke the stillness of the night along the lines of both armies. . . .

A proper understanding of the country . . . will help to relieve the Americans from the charge . . . of want of generalship in handling troops in battle—battles that had to be fought out hand to hand in forests, where artillery and cavalry could play no part; where the troops could not be seen by those controlling their movements;

where the echoes and reverberations of sound from tree to tree were enough to appall the strongest hearts engaged, and yet the noise would often scarcely be heard beyond the immediate scene of strife. Thus the generals on either side, shut out from sight or from hearing, had to trust to the unyielding bravery of their men till couriers from the different parts of the field, often extending for miles, brought word which way the conflict was resulting before sending the needed support. We should not wonder that such battles often terminated from the mutual exhaustion of both contending forces. . . . [*O.R.*, XXV, Part 1, pp. 193, 198–99.]

Return to your car. The trench lines you will see to your left as you drive forward are part of McLaws' position after his successful attack. You can read the material for this stop where you are currently parked or at any spot ahead of your car in the next few hundred yards where you get a good view through the trees and underbrush to your right.

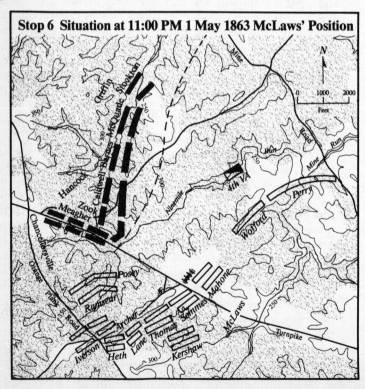

Stop 6 Situation at 11:00 PM 1 May 1863 McLaws' Position

STOP 6, McLAWS' POSITION

Report of Brig. Gen. Paul J. Semmes, CSA, Commanding Brigade, McLaws' Division, First Army Corps, Army of Northern Virginia

After the repulse of the enemy, pursuit was again ordered. The road, the woods, and fields on either side over which the enemy retired were strewn with knapsacks, blankets, overcoats, and many other valuable articles. After continuing the pursuit for over 2 miles, the enemy's skirmishers were again encountered, covering what afterward proved to be his strongly intrenched position at Chancellorsville. Here, in pursuance of orders from *Major-General McLaws*, the brigade again took position in line of battle, as before, with its right resting on the turnpike and left on *Kershaw*, *Mahone's* left still resting on the road, and bivouacked for the night, throwing out a strong line of skirmishers to the front and flanks.

Saturday morning [May 2] came, and with it desultory skirmishing, sometimes growing quite sharp, which continued throughout the day, from which the brigade suffered some slight loss. . . . During the day the brigade, by order of *Major-General McLaws*, was moved farther to the left. . . . The orders of the major-general were then to engage the enemy with a strong line of skirmishers, well supported, so as to occupy his attention while *Lieutenant-General Jackson's* corps was attaining his rear by making the circuit of Chancellorsville. [*O.R.*, XXV, Part 1, p. 834.]

Report of Maj. Gen. Lafayette McLaws, CSA, Commanding Division, First Army Corps, Army of Northern Virginia

My line halted at dark, and bivouacked along the heights. . . . The next morning (the 2d), my line of battle was reformed along the heights in the same order as before, excepting that *General Wilcox* had been ordered during the night previous to return to Banks' Ford and hold that position, it having been reported that the enemy were moving down the River Road, and, besides, were making demonstrations to cross the river at that ford.

Two batteries were placed on the heights [to the right of the Turnpike] between *Generals Semmes* and *Wofford*. A strong line of skirmishers was advanced, and were constantly engaged with those of the enemy, *General Kershaw's* brigade held in reserve. I received orders from *General Lee* to hold my position, as *General Jackson* would operate to the left and rear. Not long after, I was directed to replace *General Posey's* brigade [*Anderson's* division], on my left, by one from my command and *General Kershaw* moved to that position on the left of *General Semmes*. Following this order, I was directed to send the brigades of *Generals Mahone* and *Perry* to the left, and close in my command so as to connect with *General Anderson's* right, holding my right at the turnpike, but constantly pressing to the left, so as to be in communication with *General Anderson;* to do which, as the country was broken and densely wooded and the direction constantly changing, I ordered the two brigades on the left (*Kershaw* and *Semmes*) to advance by battalion from the left, so as to form a broken line, but still covering the front and forming the connection. The batteries opened whenever the masses of the enemy on the hills in my front offered an opportunity, and with marked results.

My orders were to hold my position; not to engage seriously, but to press strongly so soon as it was discovered that *General Jackson* had attacked. It was not until late in the evening that it was known *General Jackson* had commenced his assault, when I ordered an advance along the whole line to engage with the skirmishers, which were largely re-enforced, and to threaten, but not attack seriously; in doing which *General Wofford* became so seriously engaged that I directed him to withdraw, which was done in good order, his men in good spirits after driving the enemy to their intrenchments.

As *General Jackson* advanced, the enemy massed in front of the batteries on my line, which opened on them with excellent effect. This continued until darkness prevented any further efforts in my front. [*O.R.*, XXV, Part 1, pp. 825–26.]

The Union troops opposite this position belonged to Hancock's division, Second Army Corps.

THE BATTLE OF CHANCELLORSVILLE [167

Report of Brig. Gen. John C. Caldwell, USA, Commanding First Brigade, Second Division, Second Army Corps, Army of the Potomac

[May 1] I formed my brigade in line of battle in the open field near Chancellorsville. . . . My troops lay down and the artillery fired over them. . . . After the enemy was repulsed my line was again changed, and I formed a line of battle on the left of the road. . . . It was now nearly dark, and we worked all the evening cutting an abatis. About dark the enemy shelled our line, but without doing any harm.

About 3 o'clock on the morning of the 2d, I received from General Hancock the order to fall back to a line that had been previously designated, near Chancellorsville. Here I found the rest of my brigade established in line. . . . We immediately set to work digging intrenchments and constructing an abatis, and before noon had a line of great strength. . . .

Colonel [Nelson A.] Miles . . . was placed by General Hancock in command of the picket line of the division, which consisted of six companies of the One hundred and forty-eighth Pennsylvania Volunteers, the Fifty-seventh New York, two companies of the Fifty-second New York Volunteers, and four companies of the Second Delaware, supported by the Eleventh Massachusetts Volunteers. . . . With this force Colonel Miles skirmished all day long with the enemy, and at 3 p.m. repulsed, with signal loss, a determined attack of the enemy, made in two columns on each side of the road. I do not doubt that this repulse of the enemy, which kept them from our main lines, was due principally to the skill and gallantry of Colonel Miles, who, with a single line of skirmishers, deployed at 3 paces, repelled a determined attack of the enemy made in column, a feat rarely paralleled.

We lay in our intrenchments, under a heavy artillery fire, on the morning of the 2d and the morning of the 3d, the men behaving with the greatest coolness. . . .

I greatly regret to report that Colonel Miles was severely, if not mortally, wounded . . . while handling the picket line with masterly ability. I have had occasion heretofore to mention the distinguished conduct of Colonel Miles in every battle in which the brigade has been engaged. His merits as a military man seem to me of the very highest order. I know of no terms of praise too exaggerated to characterize his masterly ability. If ever a soldier earned promotion, Colonel

Miles has done so. Providence should spare his life, and I earnestly recommend that he be promoted and intrusted with a command commensurate with his abilities. ['Providence' did so: General Miles was the last Commanding General of the U.S. Army, 1895–1905.] [O.R., Part 1, pp. 318–21.]

The slight breastworks that you see to your left as you continue on *McLaws Drive* were constructed on the night of May 1 by the 8,500 men of *McLaws'* division. Obviously they constituted a much more formidable obstacle before the logs rotted away and the ditch behind them was filled by dirt washed down by rains for over a century. There is no trace of the entanglement of felled trees, or *abatis,* in front of the breastworks, which usually brought any attacking line to a halt while the thick woods made it extremely difficult for the enemy to use his artillery.

Continue down McLAWS DRIVE until you come to a STOP sign (about o.6 mile from your stopping place when you left Route 3). Drive straight through the intersection, crossing the Orange Plank Road, and park near the signs on the right side of the road.

STOP 7, SLOCUM'S ADVANCE

Report of Brig. Gen. Alpheus S. Williams, USA, Commanding First Division, Twelfth Army Corps, Army of the Potomac

On the . . . morning, May 1, I . . . was ordered by the major-general commanding the corps to proceed down the Plank Road toward Fredericksburg, sweeping the woods and fields on the left, and connecting with Geary's division on the right of the road. I formed Knipe's and Ruger's brigades, with two regiments, each deployed in line of battle, and the Second Brigade (Ross') following the center in double column, as a reserve.

Notwithstanding the density of the underbrush and evergreen thickets, the division moved rapidly to the front, driving before them the pickets of the enemy. During the most of our advance we were under artillery fire, which, however, inflicted no injury. I had crossed some open fields, perhaps 2 miles in advance of Chancellorsville, to a point where the first sight was obtained of the enemy's intrenchments and rifle-pits, and had halted Knipe's brigade to establish my line and put the reserve brigade in position. My skirmishers were sharply

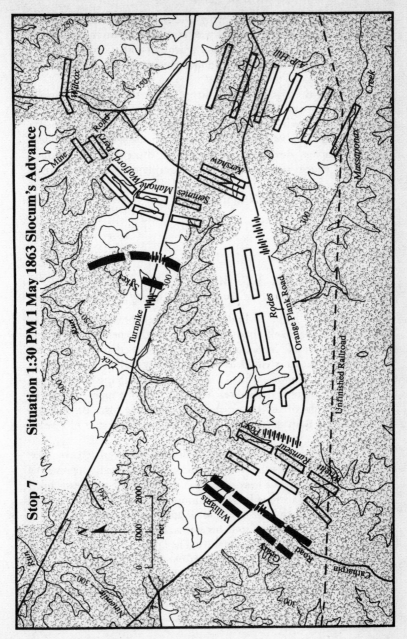

Stop 7   Situation 1:30 PM 1 May 1863 Slocum's Advance

engaged with those of the enemy, and the troops seemed never so eager to engage, when an order was received to return to my original position, which was done in good order and without loss. Two or 3 men were killed and 7 or 8 wounded among my skirmishers in the advance.

During the night we strengthened and extended our barricades and rifle-pits, and connected the line with the Plank Road near an unfinished church, west of Chancellorsville. The enemy opened a battery from our left front, which was soon silenced by the artillery under Captain Best, chief of artillery of the corps. The enemy's pickets, which attempted to crowd our lines, were also driven back. . . . [*O.R.*, XXV, Part 1, p. 677–78. Slocum lists "only 10 killed and wounded" for the Twelfth Corps on May 1. *Ibid.*, p. 670.]

Report of Brig. Gen. A. R. Wright, CSA, Commanding Brigade, Anderson's Division, First Army Corps, Army of Northern Virginia

At about noon on Friday, May 1, I was ordered to move my brigade up the Plank Road, and, feeling for the enemy, to drive him before me, should he be found. Having proceeded about 1 mile, my skirmishers became engaged with the enemy's advance, who began very soon to give way, while I pressed forward with the main body of my command until, having reached within 1½ or 2 miles of Chancellorsville, I discovered the enemy in considerable force occupying a position on both sides of the Plank Road, along the skirt of a heavy forest, with a large clearing in his front.

At this point, by command of *Lieutenant-General Jackson, Alexander's* battalion of artillery was placed in position, and, supported by my brigade, opened a heavy fire upon the enemy's line. Meanwhile I threw forward a strong body of skirmishers from the Third Georgia Regiment on both sides of the road, and, pushing them well to the front, those on the right soon became actively engaged with a considerable body of the enemy's infantry. The firing continuing very heavy on my right, I ordered *Captain Jones'* company, Second Georgia Battalion, to the support of Company H, Third Georgia Regiment, then on the right. In a very few minutes the enemy began to give way, and *Captain Jones* continued to press them for some distance through the dense wood. [*O.R.*, XXV, Part 1, pp. 865–66.]

THE FLANKING MOVEMENT

In this clearing, in the shadow of the pines, *Lee* met with *Jackson* late on the afternoon of May 1. The Union lines, *Jackson* informed him, were fortified and protected by thick woods and plenty of artillery. A frontal attack was out of the question. Earlier *Lee* himself had reconnoitered the ground near the Union left flank, hoping to find some way to get around Hooker's lines and cut off his army from its line of retreat across U.S. Ford, but there the terrain was against him. Meade's corps had not yet dug in, but it was present in force along the Mineral Springs Road after being ordered back from its advanced positions along the River Road and astride the Turnpike, and it occupied forbidding ridges with a deep gorge along most of the front. Meade's left extended to the banks of the Rappahannock and throughout May 2 his troops labored to strengthen this line by constructing rifle-pits, abatis, and artillery epaulements. [*O.R.*, XXV, Part 1, p. 507.]

Narrative of Brig. Gen. Fitzbugh Lee, CSA, Commanding Brigade, Stuart's Cavalry Division, Army of Northern Virginia

Time was an important element; for near Fredericksburg, in his rear, was Sedgwick, largely outnumbering the Confederate force in his front under *Early*. . . .

Returning at night, he found *Jackson*, and asked him if he knew of any place to attack. *Jackson* said, "No." *Lee* said, "Then we must get around on the Federal right." *Jackson* said he had been inquiring about roads by the [Catharine] furnace. *Stuart* came up then, and said he would go down to the furnace and see what he could learn about roads. He soon returned with Rev. D. B. T. Lacy, who said "a circuit could be made around by Wilderness tavern"; and a young man living in the country, and then in the cavalry, was sent for to act as guide. . . .

At sunset they took their seats on a log on the . . . north side of the Plank Road, and a little distance in the woods. *Colonel Marshall*, the . . . aide-de-camp of *General Lee*, was the only other person present, having been ordered to come to the spot for the purpose of writing a letter to *Mr. Davis*, dictated by *General Lee*. *Marshall* sat on the end of a fallen tree, within three feet of the two generals, and heard every word that passed between them, and this is what he tells me *Lee* and *Jackson* talked about on that eventful night.

Jackson spoke to *General Lee* about what he had seen and heard during the advance, and commented upon the promptness with which the enemy had appeared to abandon his movement towards Fredericksburg when opposed, and the ease with which he had been driven back to Chancellorsville, and concluded by expressing the opinion very decidedly . . . that the enemy would recross the Rappahannock before morning. He said, in substance, 'By tomorrow morning there will not be any of them this side of the river.'

General Lee expressed the hope that *General Jackson's* expectations might be realized, but said 'he did not look for such a result; that he did not believe the enemy would abandon his attempt so easily,' and expressed his conviction that the main body of General Hooker's army was in his front, and that the real move was to be made from this direction, and not from Fredericksburg. On this point there was a great difference of opinion among our higher officers, and *General Lee* was the only one who seemed to have the absolute conviction that the real movement of the Federal army was the one he was then meeting. In this belief he never wavered from the first. After telling *General Jackson* that he hoped his opinion might be proved to be correct, *General Lee* added: 'But, General, we must get ready to attack the enemy, if we should find him here to-morrow, and you must make all arrangements to move around his right flank.

General Lee then took up the map, and pointed out to *Jackson* the general direction of his route by the Furnace and Brock roads. Some conversation took place as to the importance of endeavoring to conceal the movement . . . *and as to the existence of roads further to the enemy's right, by which General Jackson might pass so as not to be exposed to observation or attack.* The general line of *Jackson's* route was pointed out, and the necessity of celerity and secrecy was enjoined upon him. The conversation was a lengthy one, and at the conclusion of it *General Lee* said to *Jackson* 'that before he moved in the morning, if he should have any doubt as to whether the enemy was still in position, he could send a couple of guns to a spot close by, and open fire on the enemy's position, which would speedily settle the question.' From the spot referred to, two of our guns had to be withdrawn that afternoon, as the infantry were suffering from the fire they were drawing from the enemy. *General Jackson* then withdrew, and *General Lee* dictated . . . a long letter to *President Davis*, giving him fully the situation. . . .

In a little pine thicket close by the scene of this conference, *General Lee* and staff bivouacked that night. During the evening, reports reached him from *Early* that all was quiet along the Rappahannock. *Wilcox* was ordered back to Banks' Ford, in consequence of other rumors. *Lee's* orders had been issued, his plans digested—his trusty lieutenants were to carry them out; the Chieftain slept. . . .

The morning of May the 2d . . . broke clear. *General Lee* emerged from the little thicket and stood on its edge at sunrise, erect and soldierly, to see *Jackson's* troops file by. They had bivouacked on his right, and were now commencing the flank movement. About half an hour after sunrise *Jackson* himself came riding along. When opposite to *General Lee* he drew rein and the two conversed for a few minutes. *Jackson* then started forward. . . . His face was a little flushed, *Colonel Marshall* says, as it was turned back towards *General Lee,* who nodded approval to what he had said. ["Chancellorsville—Address of General Fitzhugh Lee before the Virginia Division, A.N.V. Association, October 29th, 1879," *Southern Historical Society Papers,* VII (Richmond, Va: 1879), pp. 566–70. Emphasis added.]

What *Lee* proposed was to send *Jackson's* entire corps—about 28,000 men—on a flanking movement, retaining only the divisions of *Anderson* and *McLaws*—perhaps 15,000 men—to hold off Hooker's vastly superior force until *Jackson* could mount his attack. Both men must have been well aware that if Hooker were to shove even a single corps forward into the widening gap between them, it could mean disaster. The risk was enormous.

We will never know the details of the conversation *Lee* had with *Jackson* while the two plotted their move, but the following letters written by *Lee* after the war—one to *Stonewall Jackson's* widow and the other to the editor of *Southern Review*—makes it clear that it was his plan—and his responsibility.

Robert E. Lee to Mrs. T. J. Jackson, January 25, 1866

I am misrepresented at . . . Chancellorsville in proposing an attack in front, the first evening of our arrival. On the contrary I decided against it and stated to *General Jackson,* we must attack on our left as soon as practicable, and the necessary movements of the troops began immediately. In consequence of a report received about that time from *General Fitz Lee* describing the position of the Federal army and the roads which he held with his cavalry leading to its rear, *General Jackson* after some enquiry concerning the roads leading to the Furnace, undertook to throw his command entirely on Hooker's rear, which he accomplished with equal skill and boldness; the rest of the army being moved to the left flank to connect with him as he advanced.

Robert E. Lee to Dr. A. T. Blesdoe, October 28, 1867

In reply to your enquiry . . . I have not read the article on Chancellorsville . . . nor have I read any of the books published on either side since the termination of hostilities. I have as yet felt no desire to revive any recollections of those events, and have been satisfied with the knowledge I possessed of what transpired. I have, however, learned from others that the various authors [R. L. Dabney] of the *Life [and Campaigns of Lieut. Gen. Thomas J.] Jackson* award to him the credit of the success gained by the Army of Northern Virginia when he was present, and describe the movements of his corps or command as independent of the general plan of operations and undertaken at his own suggestion and on his own responsibility.

I have the greatest reluctance to do anything that might be considered detracting from his well-deserved fame, for . . . no one was more convinced of his worth or more highly appreciated him than myself; yet your knowledge of military affairs, if you have none of the events [facts] themselves, will teach you that this could not have been so. Every movement of an army must be well considered and properly ordered, and everyone who knew *General Jackson* must know that he was too good a soldier to violate this fundamental principle. In the operations round Chancellorsville I overtook *General Jackson,* who had been placed in command of the advance, as the skirmishers of the approaching armies met, advanced with the troops to the Federal line of defences, and was on the field until their whole army recrossed the Rappahannock. There is no question as to who was responsible for the operations of the Confederates, or to whom any failure would have been charged. [Major General Sir Frederick Maurice, ed., *An aide-de-camp of Lee* (Boston: Little, Brown and Company, 1927), pp. 164–66.]

Continue to drive in the same direction. McLaws' Drive has now become Furnace Road. After driving a bit more than 0.9 mile from STOP 7 you will come to a sign on your right for HAZEL GROVE. Stop there.

STOP 8, HAZEL GROVE OVERLOOK

From here the road descends into the valley of Scott's Run, about half a mile ahead. To your right you will see that trees have been cut away in a swath to make visible in the distance several large buildings with prominent roofs. These stand near a place called Hazel Grove, which was to be key terrain to both armies on May 2 and 3.

Jackson's troops had only been marching an hour when they were spotted, as they passed this point, by Union observers in the tops of high trees near Hazel Grove, 1¼ miles to the northwest. Several hours later a section of artillery (2 guns) posted at Hazel Grove opened fire, causing some confusion to the Confederate ranks as they passed this point. The trains following *Jackson's* infantry turned abruptly to the left and followed a more concealed route behind this exposed high ground. The distance from Hazel Grove to this point is about 2,000 yards, well within effective range for rifled field guns.

Three weeks earlier, almost as if it were in anticipation of this occasion, Jackson had issued General Orders governing the movement of his corps on the march.

An 1880's view looking south through the Vista from The Turnpike toward Hazel Grove. (NPS)

GENERAL ORDERS   HDQRS. SECOND CORPS,
    No. 26   ARMY OF N.VA.
                                      April 13, 1863

Each division will move precisely at the time indicated in the order of march, and if a division or brigade is not ready to move at that time, the next will proceed and take its place, even if a division should be separated thereby.

On the march, the troops are to have a rest of ten minutes each hour. The rate of march is not to exceed 1 mile in twenty-five minutes, unless otherwise specially ordered. The time of each division commander will be taken from that of the corps commander. When the troops are halted for the purpose of resting, arms will be stacked and ranks broken, and in no case during the march will the troops be allowed to break ranks without previously stacking arms.

When any part of a battery or train is disabled on a march, the officer in charge must have it removed immediately from the road, so that no part of the command be impeded upon its march.

Batteries or trains must not stop in the line of march to water; when any part of a battery or train, from any cause, loses its place in the column, it must not pass any part of the column in regaining its place.

Company commanders will march at the rear of their respective companies; officers must be habitually occupied in seeing that orders are strictly enforced; a day's march should be with them a day of labor; as much vigilance is required on the march as in camp.

Each division commander will, as soon as he arrives at his camping-ground, have the company rolls called and guard details marched to the front of the regiment before breaking ranks, and immediately afterward establish his chain of sentinels, and post his pickets so as to secure the safety of his command, and will soon thereafter report to these headquarters the disposition made for the security of his camp.

Division commanders will see that all orders respecting their divisions are carried out strictly; each division commander before leaving an encampment will have all damages occasioned by his command settled for by payment or covered by proper certificates.

All ambulances in the same brigade will be . . . parked together, and habitually kept together, not being separated unless the exigencies of the service require, and on marches follow in rear of their respective brigades.

Ample details will be made for taking care of the wounded; those thus selected will wear the prescribed badge; *and no other person belonging to the army will be permitted to take part in this important trust.* [Emphasis added.]

Any one leaving his appropriate duty, under pretext of taking care of the wounded, will be promptly arrested, and as soon as charges can be made out, they will be forwarded.

By command of *Lieutenant-General Jackson* [*O.R.*, XXV, Part 2, pp. 719–20.]

As *Jackson's* column passed, *Anderson's* division extended to the left to occupy this position and erect defenses, and when, toward midday, Union troops from Sickles' Third Army Corps "appeared in some force at the Furnace," *Anderson* sent *Posey's* brigade to dislodge them.

Report of Brig. Gen. Carnot Posey, CSA, Commanding Brigade, Anderson's Division, First Army Corps, Army of Northern Virginia

Saturday, May 2, about 10 a.m., my command moved down the Furnace Road, and formed a line of battle with three regiments (the Forty-eighth [Mississippi] being left behind as skirmishers) . . . on each side of the road, about 500 yards from the furnace. Here my skirmishers were hotly engaged with the enemy during the whole day and part of the night, the enemy being in heavy force in my front, and made frequent efforts to advance, without success. On every occasion my line of skirmishers drove them back in confusion. [*O.R.*, XXV, Part 1, p. 871.]

As Union strength in the area increased, *Anderson* was forced to send *Wright's* brigade to support *Posey*, and to slide *Mahone's* brigade to the left to occupy the position just vacated by *Wright*.

Continue to drive in the same direction for about 0.4 mile. Bear left at the "Y"-shaped intersection and stop in the parking lot on the left just beyond the intersection and across from the ruins of Catharine Furnace. Dismount and cross the road to the vicinity of the maps and signs.

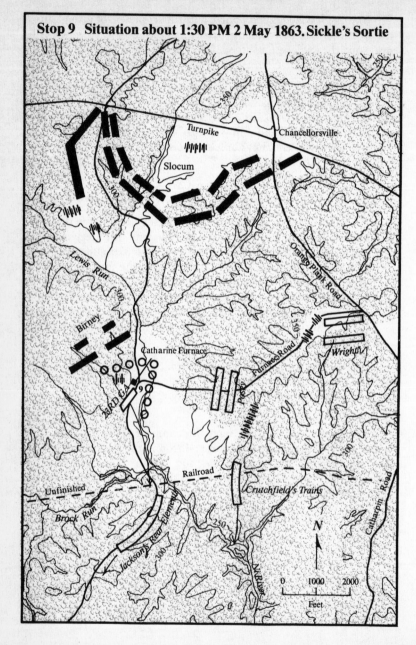

Stop 9   Situation about 1:30 PM 2 May 1863. Sickle's Sortie

STOP 9, CATHARINE FURNACE

These ruins are all that remain of the buildings that once comprised the iron furnace known as "Welford's" or "Catharine" Furnace. At the time of the battle the proprietor, Colonel Wellford (the spelling had changed since the family first came to America during the Revolution) lived nearby, his Fredericksburg home having been destroyed by Burnside's artillery the previous December, and it was Wellford who revealed the existence of the route that would take *Jackson's* column through the wilderness to the Brock Road.

On the evening of May 1, *Fitz Lee's* brigade of *Stuart's* cavalry division, which had fallen back from the Upper Rappahannock as the Union Eleventh and Twelfth corps advanced, was in this area protecting the Confederate left flank when *Wright's* infantry brigade—which had used the unfinished railroad as a 'covered way,' from the Plank Road—reached the Furnace about 6 p.m. Here he found *Stuart*, who informed him "that the enemy in considerable force were occupying the thick woods to the north, in the direction of Chancellorsville." Quickly *Wright* deployed two regiments and moved forward to drive back the scouts and pickets of a brigade from the first division, Twelfth Corps, that had just moved into position at Hazel Grove. *Wright* called upon *Stuart* for artillery support and *Major R. F. Beckham*, commanding *Stuart's* horse artillery, sent forward four guns "with a view of driving back a line of the enemy's infantry from the heights, about 1,200 yards in our front." This in turn caused eight Union guns in position on the 'heights' at Fairview to enter the engagement, and after being pounded for about forty-five minutes *Wright* ordered *Beckham* to withdraw his pieces to the Furnace. "I do not think that men have been often under a hotter fire than that," *Beckham* recalled in his official report. At dark *Wright* was ordered to fall back and rejoin the rest of the division near the Plank Road. His losses were minimal. [*O.R.*, XXV, Part 1, pp. 866, 1049.]

As *Jackson's* column marched by, the Twenty-third Georgia was detached from the leading division, by order of *Jackson*, "with instructions to guard the flank of the column . . . against a surprise, and to call, if necessary, upon any officer whose command was passing for re-enforcements." [*Ibid.*, p. 975.]

Report of Col. Emory F. Best, CSA, Twenty-third Georgia Infantry, Colquitt's Brigade, D. H. Hill's Division [commanded at Chancellorsville by Rodes], Second Army Corps, Army of Northern Virginia

In compliance with orders received from *Brigadier-General Rodes*, commanding division . . . I remained with my regiment at the furnace . . . for the protection of troops, and to give notice of any advance of the enemy at that point, with authority from *General Jackson* to order any troops to my support if attacked. While the troops were passing, no demonstration was made by the enemy, except the shelling of the woods through which the troops passed from a hill about 200 yards from my vedettes, and about 600 or 700 yards distant from the furnace. On account of the exposure of my flanks, it became necessary to deploy three companies as skirmishers besides the company covering the front of my main body, to give notice of any movement on my right and to fill a vacant space between my left and what was named to me as the Block [sic] Road. My main body was thus reduced to five companies.

About 1 p.m. my vedettes were driven in, closely followed by the enemy's skirmishers. At the same time I discovered that the enemy were moving to my right, and would attack me with a front of at least one brigade. Before I could make any preparation to place a force in his front at that point, my skirmishers became warmly engaged. I had engaged the enemy but a short time when my vedettes on the right reported that the enemy were about to pass my right flank. I immediately ordered the regiment to fall back, and moved to the right, to place myself in his front near the road. At the same time I ordered two pieces of artillery, which were then passing, to move in position on the hill above the furnace, without caissons, and placed about 40 men in the road to check the advance upon the train. As soon as the artillery moved off, I ordered the regiment to retire, and formed them in the railroad cut to the left of the road, having previously established a line of skirmishers to protect their retreat from that point. The regiment was brought from that line with a very slight loss of prisoners.

By this time the train was virtually saved, as far as I have been able to learn. No part . . . was lost except a caisson, where the horses were wounded and the tongue broken. The time between the first fire of skirmishers and when the regiment left the furnace was about forty-five minutes.

After forming in the railroad cut, I received orders from *General Archer* [*A. P. Hill's* division], who had arrived and taken command, to hold my position until he ordered me to leave. I sent word to *General Archer* that I could hold my position if my flanks were protected, especially my left. About thirty minutes afterward, during which time there was a spirited duel between a battery of *Colonel Brown's* regiment and the enemy's battery on Furnace Hill, *General Archer* withdrew his skirmishers from my left. He then sent me orders to move out quickly, but I did not receive the order . . . until the enemy had taken the railroad on my left and nearly surrounded me. I ordered the regiment to fall back, but it was too late to bring out the regiment, except those that escaped after the enemy closed upon us. . . .

My loss in prisoners was 26 officers and 250 enlisted men. . . . My colors were saved. . . . I feel satisfied that every effort was made to save the train and extricate the command. . . . [*O.R.*, XXV, Part 1, pp. 979–80.]

The Union forces involved in the fighting at Catharine Furnace came from Sickles' Third Army Corps, which had crossed the United States Ford early on the morning of May 1, and late in the afternoon had arrived to take up position "parallel to the Plank Road at Chancellorsville." At daylight the next morning Sickles moved Birney's division forward to occupy a line between the Twelfth and the Eleventh corps, "thereby relieving portions of the troops of each . . . corps and enabling them to strengthen materially their lines," and at the same time he sent two regiments, accompanied by a detachment of Berdan's Sharpshooters, through Hancock's lines to probe *McLaws'* position.

Report of Maj. Gen. Daniel E. Sickles, USA, Commanding Third Army Corps, Army of the Potomac

My attention was now withdrawn from Chancellorsville, where [the divisions of] Berry and Whipple remained in reserve, by several reports in quick succession from General Birney, that a column of the enemy was moving along his front toward our right. This column I found on going to the spot to be within easy range of Clark's battery (about 1,600 yards), and Clark so effectually annoyed the enemy by his excellent practice that the infantry sought cover in the woods or some other road more to the south, while the artillery and trains hurried past in great confusion, vainly endeavoring to escape our well-directed and destructive fire.

This continuous column—infantry, artillery, trains, and ambulances—was observed for three hours moving apparently in a southerly direction toward Orange Court-House, on the Orange and Alexandria Railroad, or Louisa Court-House, on the Virginia Central. The movement indicated a retreat on Gordonsville or an attack upon our right flank—perhaps both, for if the attack failed the retreat could be continued. The unbroken mass of forest on our right favored the concealment of the enemy's real design. I hastened to report these movements through staff officers to the general-in-chief, and communicated the substance of them in the same manner to Major-General Howard, on my right, and also to Major General Slocum, inviting their co-operation in case the general-in-chief should authorize me to follow up the enemy and attack his columns.

At noon I received orders to advance cautiously toward the road followed by the enemy, and harass the movement as much as possible. Immediately ordering Birney to push forward over Scott's Run and gain the heights in the Wilderness, I brought up two battalions of sharpshooters under Colonel Berdan, to be deployed as skirmishers and as flankers, so as to get all possible knowledge of the enemy's movement and of the approaches to his line of march. At the same time I communicated again with Major-Generals Slocum and Howard, and was assured of their prompt co-operation.

Two bridges having been rapidly thrown over Scott's Run, Birney's division, the Twentieth Indiana leading, pressed forward briskly, meeting considerable opposition from skirmishers thrown out by *McLaws'* division [in reality this was the Twenty-third Georgia, from *Rodes'* division] . . . which was found in position to cover the enemy's movement. I then directed Whipple to come up within supporting distance. Reaching the iron foundry, about a mile from his first position, Birney's advance was checked by a 12-pounder battery of the enemy, which, at short range from Welford's house, near the road, poured in a destructive fire. [*O.R.*, XXV, Pt. 1, p. 386.]

Report of Brig. Gen. David B. Birney, USA, Commanding First Division, Third Army Corps, Army of the Potomac

At 12 m. . . . I received orders . . . to follow the enemy, pierce the column, and gain possession of the road over which it was passing. Colonel Berdan reported to me at the same time with his sharpshooters. The Twentieth Indiana . . . entered the woods and ascended the hill, driving the skirmishers of the enemy before them. We quickly bridged Scott's Run with rails, and, crossing Berdan's Sharp-shooters, ordered Colonel Berdan to advance rapidly toward the road at the point we had reached with our artillery [Stop 8], which was to the left. Hayman's brigade was ordered to follow and attack the enemy, if found between the point of entrance and the road. . . . The firing increasing, I sent for Graham's brigade, to keep my connections complete, and then sent for Ward's brigade as we advanced, crossing all over the small creek, which was some 5 feet deep, with high banks.

We met with no serious opposition until reaching the forge, which was occupied by a company. Berdan's Sharpshooters, with great skill, captured this company. The enemy now opened on me with a battery placed near Welford's house, near the road that I intended to take. I sent back for Turnbull's battery, which, after an exciting artillery duel, drove off the enemy. The fire upon my left flank from musketry was galling, and at this point I received orders from Major-General Sickles to wait for the advance of General Whipple's division and a brigade from the Twelfth Corps, on my left. I rode to the rear and pointed out to General Whipple the position to be taken by him on my left. On my return to the front, Brigadier-General Barlow, commanding a brigade of the Eleventh Corps, reported to me that he was on my right, and had completed the connection between it and his corps. I now sent forward the Twentieth Indiana and Fifth Michigan to support the sharpshooters, and ordered them to advance toward the road. The movement was quite successful, as the capture of some 180 prisoners was almost immediately made by the party.

At about 6.30 p.m. I received orders from Capt. Alexander Moore, of Major-General Hooker's staff, to advance rapidly, which I did, taking the road, and placing Randolph's battery, which I had ordered up, in position, poured a well-directed fire on the retreating column of the enemy. In this advance Hayman's brigade led, followed by Graham's and Ward's, General Ward keeping open the communication to the forge. Sending out scouts, I found the enemy in some force on three sides, and, disposing my troops to meet attack from any direction, I was preparing to bivouac when I was informed by Lieutenant-Colonel Hart, assistant adjutant-general, who had gallantly reached me, that our right, occupied by the Eleventh Corps, had given way in entire disorder, and Major-General Sickles ordered my immediate return. [*O.R.*, XXV, Part 1, pp. 408–9.]

Report of Col. Hiram Berdan, USA, First U.S. Sharpshooters, Commanding Third Brigade, Third Division, Third Army Corps, Army of the Potomac

I received general instructions from General Birney, which were to skirmish through the woods, keeping in the direction of a smoke which was rising from the woods on the southeast of our position. I deployed my First Regiment in the woods, using the Second Regiment as a reserve, and ordered them to advance and drive the rebels from the woods.

My skirmishers soon engaged the enemy's skirmishers, consisting of a portion of the Twenty-third Georgia, and drove them steadily from the woods, where they rallied at a large building, apparently used as a foundry. I then advanced my right and left, with flankers from the Second Regiment, and kept up so accurate and rapid a fire that the enemy dared not leave the cover of the building. I then ordered my men to cease firing, and called upon the rebels to surrender, upon which they came in, after throwing down their arms and showing a white rag.

The support of their skirmishers, with those who were able to escape, fell back along the road and rallied in a lane, covering in their retreat a wagon train which was visible moving down the road. After sending the prisoners to the rear, I caused my left to gradually advance, keeping the attention of the enemy by desultory firing while I rapidly pushed forward my right in the woods until I had outflanked them and opened fire. They then attempted to come out of the railroad cut, in which they had taken shelter, and to retreat to the rear, but on meeting our fire they returned again to their cover, and very soon threw down their arms and surrendered. The whole number of prisoners taken was 365, including 19 officers. . . . Our loss was trifling.

Four regiments of infantry were brought up to our support, and I established a line of pickets along the road as far as I thought it safe to do so. About sunset we were ordered to withdraw, which we did, bringing all of our men who had not been killed. The guns, which were Springfield muskets, we were compelled to destroy. The whole affair was very successful, and had we been promptly supported, I am confident we could have taken the battery and a portion of the enemy's train. At night we bivouacked with our division, and on Sunday morning I was relieved from duty with General Birney and reported to General Whipple. [O.R., XXV, Part 1, p. 502.]

Before you return to your car you may enjoy a short walk along a remnant of the old road that *General Jackson's* column actually used. If so, follow the narrow unmarked trail that begins next to the post-and-rail fence at the north end of the Furnace site. That trail will take you to the top of the hill, where you can turn left to follow the trace of the old road for about 200 yards as it inclines back toward the modern Park Service road. Then, as the old road curves back to the right, you can leave it and turn to the left on the modern road to return to your car.

Continue driving the same direction on **FURNACE ROAD**. After about 0.6 mile you will come to the railroad cut mentioned in the reports you have just read. It is clearly marked by a sign, and you may wish to pause there before continuing on the path of *General Jackson's* flank march. The road climbs to the right after crossing the railroad cut, and you pass a field on your right. This is the vicinity of the Wellford house, where Confederate artillery engaged the Union guns pushed forward onto the hill next to the furnace. After you have driven about 2.9 miles from Stop 9 you will come to a **STOP** sign on **BROCK ROAD**. Pull off to the right there. You need not dismount.

Catharine Furnace today. (HWN)

STOP 10, THE BROCK ROAD

The march of the Second Army Corps through the Wilderness was protected by *Fitz Lee's* brigade of cavalry, which cleared *Jackson's* way "in turning the enemy's right flank" and covered "the movement of this corps, masking it on its right flank" and "driving off the enemy's cavalry whenever it appeared." The previous evening, *Captain Breathed* of the *Stuart* Horse Artillery, who was accompanying *Fitz Lee's* brigade, had a brush with an infantry regiment from Howard's Eleventh Army Corps when he opened fire on the Union lines from the vicinity of the Carpenter farm, about two miles north of this spot. Maj. Gen. Carl Schurz, commanding Howard's Third Division, immediately ordered a regiment of infantry forward "to capture or drive away those pieces," and after "a short but lively skirmish" *Breathed's* guns withdrew.

This insignificant affair, in which only a few Union troops were wounded, may have led *Fitz Lee* to assume that his cavalry was in the immediate vicinity of the Union right flank, for here, at the intersection with the Brock Road, *Jackson* turned his column to the left—*away* from the position of Howard's Eleventh Corps. It may be recalled that in the conversation between *Jackson* and *Lee* the previous evening there was mention of the importance of concealing the movement from the enemy *"and as to the existence of roads further to the enemy's right"* by which *Jackson's* column might pass "so as not to be exposed to observation or attack." Obviously *Jackson* moved to the left and then again to his right in order to conceal his march.

Few historians, however, have raised the question: "On the evening of May 1, where did *Lee* and *Jackson* believe that the Union right flank rested?" Subsequent events indicate that the Confederate commanders assumed that the Plank Road would take *Jackson* to some point beyond the Union right flank; but the ultimate success of *Jackson's* attack has perhaps obscured the need to ask the question.

Fifty years ago Major Porter, a student at the Army War College, while preparing his presentation for the Chancellorsville portion of the annual Field Exercise, or Staff Ride, over Civil War battlefields, endeavored to get inside the skin of *Lee* and *Jackson* as they analysed the situation and made their decision.

Major Ray E. Porter, Infantry, speaking at Talley's Farm.

Just where *Jackson* had expected to find Hooker's right is not recorded. Many writers have assumed the road junction [of the Plank Road and the Turnpike]. It is my opinion that *Lee* and *Jackson* had estimated the Federal right to rest about Carpenter's Farm, more than a mile due south of this point. You will recall that *Lee* was seeking to cut Hooker's communications with the United States Ford which would require the placing of a force in rear of the Federal army. On Friday *Wright* had been driven back from Hazel Grove. The only recorded contact between *Fitzhugh Lee's* cavalry and the enemy, except with scattered pickets, is his repulse south of Carpenter's Farm.

Jackson was expected to *turn*, not merely assault the hostile right. We know that he expected to accomplish his mission via the Orange Plank Road, which would have brought him directly against a position at the road junction. . . . He took the longer and more difficult farm road west of the Brock Road, because the Brock Road at points is visible from Carpenter's. When he saw Hooker's men about Talley he wrote Lee, "The enemy has made a stand at Chancellor's (Dowdall's Tavern), two miles west of Chancellorsville," indicating his belief that they had recently retired from about Carpenter's.

All of these facts support my supposition that Lee and Jackson estimated the Federal line to extend from south of Chancellorsville, through Hazel Grove, to Carpenter's Farm. [Major Charles S. Kilburn, Major Ward H. Maris, Major Ray E. Porter, "The Chancellorsville Campaign," Conduct of War Course, Army War College, 1936–37. United States Army Military History Institute, Carlisle Barracks, Pa.]

YOU WILL NOW TURN LEFT, as *Jackson* did, and follow the Brock Road, modern day Route No. 613, for precisely three-tenths of a mile. There you will come to a dirt road with a National Park marker indicating JACKSON'S FLANK MARCH.

TURN RIGHT onto the dirt road. Continue along the Jackson Trail until you reach the next intersection with a hard-surfaced road. This will be the Brock Road again. This detour enabled *Jackson* to avoid detection from enemy troops that might have remained in the vicinity of the Carpenter Farm.

The breastworks that you see lining the left side of the road played no part in this battle. These were erected by Winfield Hancock's Second Army Corps, Army of the Potomac, during the first day of the battle of the Wilderness, almost exactly one year later. The second Corps had marched through Chancellorsville en route to this position and had bivouacked on the same ground it held during the battle of Chancellorsville.

When you come to the intersection with the ORANGE PLANK ROAD, about 1.2 miles on the BROCK ROAD (3.7 miles from STOP 10), TURN LEFT and immediately TURN LEFT AGAIN into the small roadside parking area with historical markers for the battle of the Wilderness. This is a safe haven from traffic while you read.

STOP 11A, JACKSON DISCOVERS THE UNION FLANK

Narrative of Brig. Gen. Fitz. Lee, CSA, Commanding Second Brigade, Stuart's Cavalry Division, Army of Northern Virginia

Jackson was marching on. My cavalry was well in his front. Upon reaching the Plank Road, some five miles west of Chancellorsville, my command was halted, and while waiting for *Jackson* to come up, I made a personal reconnaissance to locate the Federal right for *Jackson's* attack. With one staff officer, I rode across and beyond the Plank Road, in the direction of the Old Turnpike, pursuing a path through the woods, momentarily expecting to find evidence of the enemy's presence. Seeing a wooded hill in the distance, I determined, if possible, to get upon its top, as it promised a view of the adjacent country. Cautiously I ascended its side, reaching the open spot upon its summit without molestation. What a sight presented itself before me! Below, and but a few hundred yards distant, ran the Federal line of battle. I was in rear of Howard's right. There were the line of defence, with abatis in front, and long lines of stacked arms in rear. Two cannon were visible on the part of the line seen. The soldiers were in groups in the rear, laughing, chatting, smoking . . . while feeling safe and comfortable, awaiting orders. In rear of them were other parties driving up and butchering beeves. . . . So impressed was I with my discovery, that I rode rapidly back to the point on the Plank Road where I had left my cavalry, and back down the road *Jackson* was moving, until I met "Stonewall" himself. "General," said I,

if you will ride with me, halting your column here, out of sight, I will show you the enemy's right, and you will perceive the great advantage of attacking down the Old Turnpike instead of the Plank Road, the enemy's lines being taken in reverse. Bring only one courier, as you will be in view from the top of the hill.

Jackson assented, and I rapidly conducted him to the point of observation. ["Chancellorsville," *Southern Historical Society Papers*, VII, pp. 571–72.]

If your schedule is tight, you can read the material for STOP 11B here and proceed directly to STOP 12. However, you will get a far better impression of the importance of *Fitz Lee's* discovery and *Jackson's* decision if you take the short detour to STOP 11B.

To reach STOP 11B, cross the **BROCK ROAD** on the **ORANGE PLANK ROAD** (Route 621). Drive about 1.4 miles on the **ORANGE PLANK ROAD** until you come to a Park Service sign on the left side of the road. Pull off to the side and stop there. *Fitz Lee* describes the view from the top of the hill immediately to your left.

Lieut. Gen. Thomas J. "Stonewall" Jackson (USAHMI)

STOP 11B, JACKSON'S RESPONSE TO THE DISCOVERY

Narrative of Brig. Gen. Fitz. Lee, CSA, Commanding Second Brigade, Stuart's Cavalry Division, Army of Northern Virginia

I only knew *Jackson* slightly. I watched him closely as he gazed upon Howard's troops. It was then about 2 p.m. His eyes burned with a brilliant glow, lighting up a sad face. His expression was one of intense interest, his face was colored slightly with the paint of approaching battle, and radiant at the success of his flank movement. Was he happy at the prospect of the "delightful excitement"—terms, *[Lieutenant-General] Dick Taylor* says, he used to express his pleasure at being under fire? To the remarks made to him while the unconscious line of blue was pointed out, he did not reply once during the five minutes he was on the hill, and yet his lips were moving. From what I have read and heard of Jackson since that day, I know now what he was doing then. Oh! "beware of rashness," General Hooker. *Stonewall* is praying in full view and in rear of your right flank!

While talking to the Great God of Battles, how could he hear what a poor cavalryman was saying. "Tell *General Rodes*," said he, suddenly whirling his horse towards the courier, "to move across the Old Plank Road; halt when he gets to the Old Turnpike, and I will join him there." One more look upon the Federal lines, and then he rode rapidly down the hill, his arms flapping to the motion of his horse, over whose head it seemed, good rider as he was, he would certainly go. I expected to be told I had made a valuable personal reconnoissance—saving the lives of many soldiers. . . . Perhaps I might have been a little chagrined at *Jackson's* silence. . . .

While *Jackson's* column was moving to the Old Turnpike, my cavalry, supported by the Stonewall brigade under *[Brig. Gen. E. F.] Paxton*, moved a short distance down the Plank Road to mask the movement. ["Chancellorsville," *Southern Historical Society Papers*, VII, pp. 572–73.]

Jackson to Lee,   Near 3 P.M., May 2d, 1863

General:

The enemy has made a stand at Chancellor's [Melzi Chancellor's house, known also as Dowdall's Tavern], which is about two miles from Chancellorsville. I hope as soon as practicable to attack.

I trust that an ever kind Providence will bless us with great success.

The leading division is up and the next two appear to be well closed.

T. J. J.

[Capt. James Power Smith, Assistant Adjutant-General, Second Army Corps, "Stonewall Jackson's Last Battle," *Battles and Leaders of the Civil War* (4 vols., New York: The Century Co., 1884), III, 206.]
This is the last communication that *Lee* received from *Jackson.*
The following account of an early Army War College Staff Ride to Chancellorsville may be of interest here. Lieut. Gen. Hunter Liggett, who attended the Army War College in 1909–10 and then stayed on as a director for the next three years and finally as president in 1913–14, recalls visiting this spot with the class.

On May 1 the War College class was divided into sections and each section assigned to an intensive study of some Virginia, Maryland or Pennsylvania campaign of the Civil War. Papers detailing every movement of troops on both sides were prepared to be read later on the battleground. Then about June 1, the whole class took to the saddle for staff rides over these battlefields. A detachment of negro cavalry from Fort Myer . . . took care of the horses, served as orderlies and manned the wagon train which carried our food, camp equipment, and personal baggage.

Fredericksburg was the first stop. First reviewing the general nature and purposes of the fight, class and faculty then would follow the course of the battle from point to point. This done, the students were set the problem of what the course of the battle would have been under the changed conditions of modern warfare. . . .

On one staff ride, Colonel Faison, a member of the class, suggested that the distinguished Confederate cavalry leader, *General Munford,* was living at Charlottesville, and that it would be mutually

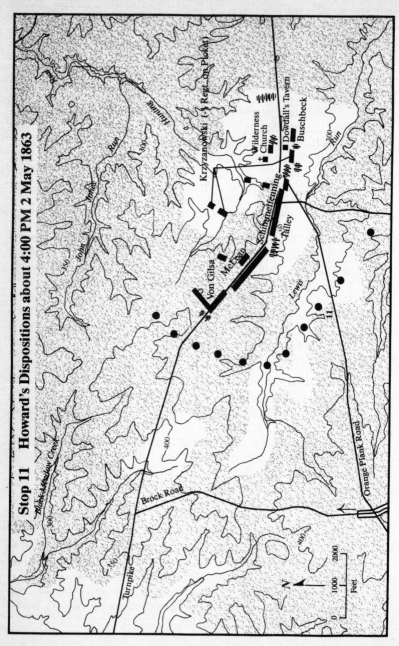

Stop 11   Howard's Dispositions about 4:00 PM 2 May 1863

interesting if the veteran should accompany us. *General Munford* accepted our invitation eagerly and joined us at Fredericksburg.

At Chancellorsville he had been with *Fitzhugh Lee*, whose cavalry brigade had covered *Jackson's* march against the right flank of Hooker's army. There he led me to a little hill in the angle of the Brock and the Plank Roads and showed me where *Jackson*, whose army was moving up the Brock Road, had ridden to the crest of the hill and looked directly down along the length of Howard's lines not 500 yards away. The Northern troops had stacked their arms and were smoking and lounging while the cooks butchered cattle and prepared the evening meal. *Jackson* ordered *Munford* and the courier to remain under cover, but he himself stood for five minutes studying the Union positions without being observed. Turning to his courier he ordered him to go back and instruct *General Rodes*, commanding the advance of *Jackson's* column, to continue up the Brock Road to the turnpike, where he would join him. *Jackson* did join *Rodes* there and turned his column down the turnpike. Where he would have attacked Howard's corps obliquely, but for his discovery, he now struck the Union forces in reverse as well as in the flank, and routed them.

Howard's corps, of course, should have seized the hill as an elementary precaution, commanding the two roads as it did. Had they used the observation it offered they would have seen *Jackson* coming. It was an inexplicable case of negligence, for Howard was a good soldier. [Hunter Liggett, *A.E.F.: Ten Years Ago in France* (New York: Dodd, Mead and Company, 1928), pp. 293–95.]

Continue to drive in the same direction. About 0.6 mile from STOP 11B a power line right-of-way crosses the road, giving you a better view of the landform to your left. Beyond the power line is a road junction where you can **TURN AROUND** and return to the intersection at STOP 11A. After stopping at the STOP sign, **TURN RIGHT** on **BROCK ROAD** (Route 613).

Continue driving north on the **BROCK ROAD** for 1.5 miles, to the intersection with **ROUTE 3**. At the STOP sign, **TURN RIGHT** onto **ROUTE 3** and drive about 1.3 miles, moving into the left lane near the end of that distance. **TURN LEFT**, cross the median and the west-bound traffic and drive into the cemetery. Drive one-quarter of the way around the circular drive, so that you are near the top of the hill with Route 3 behind you. Pull over and stop.

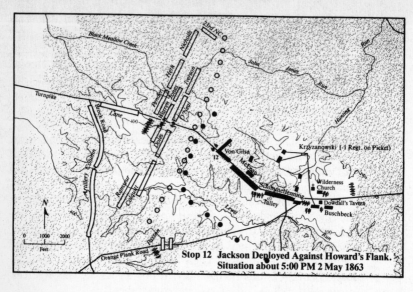

Stop 12   Jackson Deployed Against Howard's Flank. Situation about 5:00 PM 2 May 1863

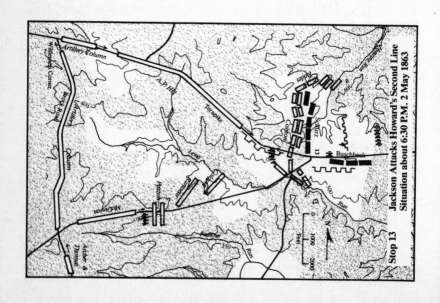

Stop 13   Jackson Attacks Howard's Second Line. Situation about 6:30 P.M. 2 May 1863

eastward, facing south-southeast. He had three regiments of General Schimmelfennig's brigade deployed and two regiments in reserve. He had also two regiments of Colonel Krzyzanowski's brigade in the front line and two regiments in reserve. On the proper front, General Steinwehr, commanding Second Division, had two regiments deployed and two in reserve—all of Colonel Buschbeck's brigade.

On the morning of May 2, General Birney [Third Army Corps] had relieved a portion of General Steinwehr's division from the front line, viz, General Barlow's brigade. This I placed in position for a general reserve of the corps. The artillery was disposed as follows: Two pieces near General Deven's (First Division) right, enfilading Old Turnpike; the rest of Dieckmann's battery on the left of General Devens, covering approaches along the Plank Road. Four guns of Wiedrich's battery were placed near Steinwehr's right, and two guns near his left, covering approaches from the front. Dilger's battery was posted near the intersection of the Turnpike and the Plank Road. Three batteries were in reserve, and so placed to be used on any of the approaches. Our front was covered with rifle-pits and abatis. . . .

Early Saturday morning, General Hooker visited my corps and rode along my front lines. At one point a regiment was not deployed and at another a gap in the woods was not filled. The correction was immediately made and the position strengthened. The front was covered by a good line of skirmishers. . . .

[During the day] . . . the same general made frequent reconnaissances. Infantry scouts and cavalry patrols were constantly pushed out on every road. The unvarying report was, "the enemy is crossing the Plank Road and moving toward Culpeper."

At 4 p.m. I was directed to send a brigade to the support of General Sickles [near Catharine Furnace]. I immediately took General Barlow's brigade by a short route to General Sickles' right, some 2½ miles from the Plank Road to the front.

At about 6 p.m. I was at my headquarters, at Dowdall's Tavern, when the attack commenced. I sent my chief of staff to the front when firing was heard. General Schurz, who was with me, left at once to take command of his line. [*O.R.*, XXV, Part 1, pp. 628–30.]

JACKSON'S ATTACK

Report of Brig. Gen. R. E. Rodes, CSA, Commanding D. H. Hill's Division, Second Army Corps, Army of Northern Virginia

At 5.15 p.m. the word was given to move forward, the line of sharpshooters being about 400 yards in advance. In consequence of the dense mass of undergrowth, and orders not having been promptly given to the skirmishers of *Rodes'* brigade, some little delay was caused when the main line reached the skirmishers' line. This latter was put in motion again by my order, and soon after the Alabama brigade *[Col. E. A. O'Neal]* encountered the fire of the enemy. At once the line of battle rushed forward with a yell, and *Doles* at this moment debouched from the woods and encountered a force of the enemy and a battery of two guns intrenched. Detaching two regiments to flank the position, he charged without halting, sweeping everything before him, and, pressing on to Talley's, gallantly carried the works there, and captured five guns by a similar flank movement of a portion of his command. So complete was the success of the whole maneuver, and such was the surprise of the enemy, that scarcely any organized resistance was met with after the first volley was fired. They fled in the wildest confusion, leaving the field strewn with arms, accouterments, clothing, caissons, and fieldpieces in every direction. The larger portion of his force, as well as intrenchments, were drawn up at right angles to our line, and, being thus taken in the flank and rear, they did not wait for the attack. [O.R., XXV, Part 1, p. 941.]

Report of Capt. M. F. Bonham, CSA, Third Alabama Infantry, Rodes' [Alabama] Brigade, D. H. Hill's Division, Second Army Corps, Army of Northern Virginia

At 6 p.m. we advanced, the right of the Third resting on the road. We advanced with order and regularity through the woods half a mile; encountered the enemy's first line behind a breastwork of fallen timber, which was broken and routed without our movement being a moment checked. The firing of my command was executed in excellent order, the front line firing and loading as they marched on, while the rear came to the front, fired and loaded as the march continued. Leaping over the breastworks [your present location] we swept onward and over a line of intrenchments, routing the enemy, capturing one cannon and two caissons, and, through a hot fire of shell, grape, canister, and musketry, moved forward to a second and stronger line of intrenchments, which were speedily occupied, the enemy retiring in disorder after a few rounds. At this point we captured two cannon and one stand of colors. Here, after having driven the enemy 1½ miles without a moment's check, darkness prevented farther pursuit.

The regiment was soon collected and casualties ascertained to be slight. Officers and men, veterans of two years and new recruits, behaved with the greatest gallantry throughout the charge. [*O.R.*, XXV, Part 1, p. 956.]

Report of Brig. Gen. George Doles, CSA, Commanding Brigade, D. H. Hill's Division, Second Army Corps, Army of Northern Virginia

At 5 p.m. the order was given to advance against the enemy. The brigade moved as rapidly as possible through a very thick wood, and skirmishers were immediately engaged by those of the enemy. Our forces, marching rapidly forward, assisted in driving in the enemy's sharpshooters, when we were subjected to a very heavy musketry fire, with grape, canister, and shell. The command was ordered to attack the enemy in his intrenched position, drive him from it, and take his batteries.

The order was promptly obeyed. The Fourth and Forty-fourth Georgia assaulted his position in front; the Twenty-first Georgia was ordered to move toward the left and flank him, so as to enfilade his intrenchments; the Twelfth Georgia was ordered forward and to the right, to attack a force of the enemy on the right. After a resistance of about ten minutes, we drove him from his positions on the left and carried his battery of two guns, caissons, and horses. The movement of the Twelfth Georgia on the right was successful. The order to forward was given, when the command moved forward at the double-quick to assault the enemy, who had taken up a strong position on the crest of a hill in the open field. He was soon driven from this position, the command pursuing him.

He made a stubborn resistance from behind a wattling fence, on a hill covered thickly with pine. The whole command moved gallantly against this position. . . . Here we captured one gun. . . . We pursued his retreating forces about 300 yards over an open field, receiving a very severe fire from musketry and a battery of four pieces on the crest of the hill that commanded the field below. His infantry was in large force, and well protected by rifle-pits and intrenchments. The command was ordered to take the intrenchments and the battery, which was done after a resistance of about twenty minutes. The enemy fled in utter confusion, leaving his battery of four pieces, his wounded, and many prisoners. [O.R., XXV, Part 1, pp. 966–67.]

Report of Col. John T. Mercer, CSA, Twenty-first Georgia Infantry, Doles' Brigade, D. H. Hill's Division, Second Army Corps, Army of Northern Virginia

At 5 p.m. the brigade advanced in line of battle, with the Fourth the battalion of direction. Having marched in this order for half a mile through oak timber, we came upon an open field, when we were fired upon from a battery and with musketry posted on an eminence on our left and front [your present position]. Owing to the position of the enemy, it became necessary for the brigade to change direction to the left, which was done at a run. The Twenty-first Georgia flanked the position on their left, while the Fourth and Forty-fourth Georgia advanced upon their front, and the enemy fled. Still advancing at the run, the colors . . . in advance of the line were planted upon a captured piece of field artillery. Halting for a moment in a covered position to reform the line, we continued to advance at double-quick through a strip of pine bushes, over a cleared field, and up to an intrenched position. [Stop 14]. [O.R., XXV, Part 1, p. 971.]

Report of Brig. Gen. Charles Devens, Jr., USA, Commanding First Division, Eleventh Army Corps, Army of the Potomac

During the night of the 1st, rifle-pits were constructed along the front of the Second Brigade under the direction of Major Hoffmann, chief engineer of the Eleventh Army Corps. A picket line was thrown out at a distance of from half a mile to a mile, and stretching well around, covering our right flank, the pickets on Brock's road still remaining in position. . . . I had now in reserve the Seventy-fifth and Twenty-fifth Ohio.

During the forenoon of May 2, the line was visited and the dispositions for defense carefully inspected by the major-general commanding the army, accompanied by the major-general commanding the Eleventh Corps. Some slight alterations suggested by General Howard were immediately adopted.

About 11 a.m. a large moving column, in which could plainly be distinguished infantry, artillery, cavalry, and wagons, was seen moving rapidly from a point to the left of our position toward our right, with the evident intention of either passing around our right or of retreating. Of this fact the major-general commanding the corps was immediately apprised by me, but he had already become aware of it.

Shortly after, skirmishing took place along the line of my Second Brigade, caused by some rebel cavalry, indicating the vicinity of the enemy's pickets. Soon after, 2 men, who stated that they had been sent out from another portion of the line as scouts, were brought in by my pickets, reporting that the enemy were moving in great force upon our right flank. They were immediately sent . . . to corps headquarters, under charge of a trusty sergeant, with orders that after reporting to General Howard they should at once proceed to the headquarters of the major-general commanding the army.

Several reconnaissances, made by a small body of cavalry placed at my disposition, discovered early in the afternoon bodies of the enemy's cavalry moving upon our right. One of these portions . . . was fired upon, and the fact immediately reported . . . to the major-general commanding the corps. Colonel von Gilsa's skirmishers were, between 3 and 4 o'clock in the afternoon, attacked by the skirmishers of the enemy, with the evident intention of feeling our position. After this, Colonel von Gilsa's skirmishers were pushed farther to the front, and the major-general commanding the corps again rode down the line. After his return, a company of cavalry was sent me for the purpose of making further examination of the woods, which examination, though not thoroughly made, was still sufficient to show that the enemy's cavalry were deployed along the front of my First Brigade, accompanied by some pieces of horse artillery. I directed the captain commanding the cavalry to return and report at corps headquarters.

At about 6.30 p.m. the enemy were reported as advancing in great force upon our right flank. This report was immediately telegraphed to headquarters, and I proceeded at once, under a heavy fire of shell, with my staff from my headquarters, at the left of the line, to the position of Colonel von Gilsa. The enemy were moving down in line embracing the right and left of the Turnpike, with the intention of attacking at the same time our front and rear.

Desirous of protecting as much as possible the line of Colonel von Gilsa, I ordered the Seventy-fifth Ohio . . . to support him on the right. The Twenty-fifth Ohio, the only other regiment of my reserve, was at once ordered to deploy in rear of the line of Colonel von Gilsa for its support, facing to the west.

As it has been suggested that the First Division was to some extent surprised, I deem it my duty to say that in riding down the entire line I found no officers or men out of their assigned positions, but all prepared to meet the attack. The line of skirmishers along the front of both brigades behaved with great resolution, keeping the enemy back as long as they could be expected to resist so fierce an attack by so overwhelming a force; in fact, they emerged from the woods at the right of the Second Brigade at the same time with the attacking force.

From the great extent of the enemy's line, as soon as it came in contact with ours, we were completely outflanked on the right, and the fire began to be felt in the rear of the Second Brigade, while the skirmishers of the enemy were finding their way to the rear of and firing on the First Brigade, commanded by Colonel von Gilsa. I had at this time a full view of . . . the enemy's line. . . . The formation . . . as well as could be seen in the smoke and confusion of the battle . . . was that of a line of regiments in double column, closed in mass . . . numbering from 25,000 to 30,000 men.

In the position the division was to receive such attack in so large force . . . it was rapidly forced back. . . . A change of front at this time by the Second Brigade would have been impracticable under so severe a fire, and, even were it otherwise, I should have considered it unwise, as pivoting upon either flank would have separated the two brigades or else cut me off from General Schurz on my left, and in nowise have saved me from being outflanked. . . .

Notwithstanding the necessary confusion in which the division was forced to relinquish its first position (no order to retreat having been given), I think that a second line might have been formed within the lines of General Schurz had his division been able to maintain its position. The retreat of my own, however, must . . . have added to the difficulties. . . .

Of about 4,000 men reported that day for duty, the names of at least 1,600 have been forwarded to corps headquarters as killed, wounded and missing [later revised to list 61 dead, 477 wounded, and 432 missing]. [*O.R.*, XXV, Part 1, pp. 633–35.]

Report of Col. Leopold von Gilsa, USA, Commanding First Brigade, First Division, Eleventh Army Corps, Army of the Potomac

The First Brigade had the following position: Two regiments in line of battle along the road from Chancellorsville to Gordonsville, front toward the Plank Road, connecting on the left with the Second Brigade . . . and two regiments in a right angle to the above line, also in line of battle. The whole brigade was about 1,400 men strong, and I foresaw, having no reserve at all, that I would be obliged to leave that position in case of an attack by strong forces of the enemy. All representations . . . to the division commander to send me reserves were unfruitful, except that the Seventy-fifth Ohio was located near my left wing. This was in part division reserve.

The cavalry returned from the front of my line, and reported no enemy at all in front. A quarter of an hour later, a patrol of the Forty-fifth New York Regiment reported masses of the enemy in an open field opposite my line. I reported this fact at once to the division commander, and at the same moment my skirmishers were driven in by overwhelming forces of the enemy. The whole line was at once engaged furiously, and my brigade stood coolly and bravely, fired three times, and stood still after they had outflanked me already on my right.

The enemy attacked now from the front and rear, and then, of course, my brave boys were obliged to fall back, the Fifty-fourth New York and the right wing of the One hundred and fifty-third Pennsylvania forcing their way back through the enemy's skirmishers in their rear. I had no regiment to cover my right flank, and no reserves to drive back the enemy with the bayonet. Retreating, I expected surely to rally my brigade behind our second line, formed by the Third Division, but I did not find the second line; it was abandoned before we reached it.

I am obliged to express my thanks to the men of my brigade, with very few exceptions, for the bravery and coolness which they have shown in repulsing three attacks, and they retreated only after being attacked in front and from the rear at the same time; but I am also compelled to blame most of my line officers that they did not or could not rally their companies half a mile or a mile more back . . . and I hope that in the next engagement every officer and man . . . will try to redeem this unsoldierlike conduct. On the same evening, nearly the whole brigade was rallied near General Hooker's headquarters. . . . [O.R., XXV, Part 1, p. 636.]

*Report of Maj. Jeremiah Williams, USA, Twenty-fifth Ohio
Infantry, Second Brigade, First Division, Eleventh Army Corps,
Army of the Potomac*

Our formation at the commencement of the engagement . . . was
in double column, about 100 paces in rear of the center of the left
wing of the three regiments which were in line of battle, the direction
of our column being parallel with their line.

The attack was made by the enemy with suddenness and great
fury upon the right flank of our brigade. The enemy's balls were
already reaching our regiment when we commenced forming our line
of battle. We had first to change direction at right angles, and, while
deploying, the enemy had gained to within 200 paces, and was driving back through our lines the troops that were in advance of our
new front.

The deployment was made under great difficulties. Fleeing men
dashed through our lines, while the enemy's musketry and grape and
canister killed and disabled many of our men before the formation
was completed. It was, however, successfully accomplished . . . and
the line was nearly as good as if no enemy had been present.

The enemy was now within 150 paces, in very heavy column,
and steadily advancing. The regiment opened fire with a coolness and
deliberation highly commendable, in view of the general confusion
with which it was surrounded. Our right wing rested among some
scrubby bushes and saplings, while the left was in comparatively open
ground. The fire of the enemy as they approached was murderous,
and almost whole platoons of ours were falling; but our men stood
firmly. The enemy's left flank extended far beyond our right, and was
being rapidly pushed farther. There was now of our forces none but
broken and retreating troops within 600 yards of our line, every other
regiment in our part of the field having broken and retreated, and the
enemy were nearer our next line of breastworks than we were.

The men had fired here an average of 5 to 6 rounds when the
enemy had approached to within 30 paces of our left wing, and
perhaps 50 on our right wing, and was rushing upon us with redoubled speed and overwhelming numbers, when the order was given
to about face.

We had in line of battle 333 men and 16 commissioned officers, of
whom 5 officers (including the colonel) and over 130 men . . . were
killed and wounded at this point. Two companies were on picket, and
escaped with 1 man wounded and 1 officer and 7 men missing.

The line of our retreat was through a dense thicket, from which the men emerged much shattered. A large portion of them were rallied at the breastworks near General Howard's headquarters [Stop 14]. . . . None of the missing have been seen since the . . . battle. [*O.R.*, XXV, Part 1, pp. 640–41.]

Return to ROUTE 3. CROSS THE MEDIAN and TURN LEFT. Drive about 1.3 miles. At about 1 mile you will see the WILDERNESS CHURCH on your left. Move into the left lane, and REVERSE DIRECTION with a LEFT TURN at the next crossover, turning LEFT again on westbound ROUTE 3 to return 0.25 mile to the Wilderness Church. TURN RIGHT into the church parking lot and position yourself so that you can look back toward STOP 12.

Wilderness Church photographed in 1884. (USAMHI)

STOP 13, WILDERNESS CHURCH: HOWARD'S SECOND LINE

Report of Maj. Gen. Carl Schurz, USA, Commanding Third Division, Eleventh Army Corps, Army of the Potomac

To change the front of the regiments deployed in line on the Old Turnpike Road was extremely difficult. . . . They were hemmed in between a variety of obstacles in front and dense pine brush in their rear. . . . The officers had hardly had time to give a command when almost the whole of General McLean's brigade, mixed up with a number of Colonel von Gilsa's men, came rushing down the road from General Devens' headquarters in wild confusion, and, worse than that, the battery of the First Division broke in upon my right at a full run. This confused mass of guns, caissons, horses, and men broke lengthwise through the ranks of my regiments deployed in line on the road. While this was going on, several men of the Seventy-fourth Pennsylvania, which formed my extreme right, were shot from behind, the enemy having already penetrated into the woods immediately in the rear of our original position. . . . Under such circumstances it was an utter impossibility to establish a front at that point. The whole line deployed on the old turnpike, facing south, was rolled up and swept away in a moment. If the regiments had remained as they were at first formed, in column on the open field, it would have been easy to give them a correct front by a simple wheeling, and the turmoil on the road would not have disturbed them. As it was, the Seventy-fourth Pennsylvania and the Sixty-first Ohio Regiments, which I had counted among the best I had . . . could do nothing but endeavor to rally behind the second line.

This second line . . . had changed front, and was formed behind a rise of ground between the [Wilderness] Church grove and the woods from which the enemy was expected, but every evolution was attended with the greatest difficulty, as the scattered men of the First Division were continually breaking through our ranks.

In my extreme right, where the Twenty-sixth Wisconsin and the Fifty-eighth New York stood, things wore a similar aspect. A short time after the attack had commenced, a large number of men of the First Brigade [von Gilsa], First Division [Devens], came running back through the woods, the enemy following closely on their heels. Captain Braun, commanding the Fifty-eighth New York, fell from his horse, mortally wounded, immediately after having deployed his regiment. The enemy was, however, received at that point with great firmness. The Fifty-eighth New York, a very small regiment, exposed to a flanking fire from the left, where the enemy broke through, and severely pressed in front, was pushed back after a struggle of several minutes. The Twenty-sixth Wisconsin, flanked on both sides and exposed to a terrible fire in front, maintained the unequal contest for a considerable time. This young regiment, alone and unsupported, firmly held the ground where I had placed it for about twenty minutes; nor did it fall back until I ordered it to do so.

There is hardly an officer in the Twenty-sixth Wisconsin who has not at least received a bullet through his clothes. Had it not been for the praiseworthy firmness of these men the enemy would have obtained possession of the woods opposite without resistance, taken the north and south rifle-pit [STOP 14] from the rear, and appeared on the Plank Road between Dowdall's Tavern and Chancellorsville before the artillery could have been withdrawn. The order to fall back to the border of the woods behind was given to Colonel Krzyzanowski in consequence of the following circumstances:

The tide of fugitives had hardly subsided a little on our left when the enemy's columns, preceded by a thick cloud of skirmishers, presented themselves on and to the right and left of the old turnpike. My regiments had hardly had time to change their position and to wheel into the new front. . . . They had just formed behind the little rise of ground in front of the church grove when the enemy's columns issued from the woods.

The enemy's front of attack, as we saw it, extended considerably beyond our extreme right. His regiments were formed apparently in column by division, the skirmishers throwing themselves into the intervals whenever their advance was checked. The enemy was formed at least three, perhaps four, lines of columns deep, the intervals between lines being very short, the whole presenting a heavy, solid mass.

It was observed by Captain Dilger that several [Confederate] regiments marched from Talley's farm by the right flank down to the Plank Road and the low ground south of it, so as to envelop our left. The Seventy-fifth Pennsylvania, which was on picket, was thus taken in the rear, and in its dispersed condition found itself . . . obliged to fall back, its line of skirmishers . . . facing south, being driven in from the flank or captured. . . .

As the enemy emerged from the woods the regiments of my second line stopped him with a well-directed and rapid fire. . . . The enemy was gaining rapidly on the left of the One hundred and nineteenth, which was then exposed to a very severe enfilading fire.

The line fell back step by step to the neighborhood of the church grove, facing about and firing as it yielded. Meanwhile the batteries of Captains Dilger and Wiedrich had kept up a rapid fire, first with spherical case, upon the enemy's columns as they descended from Talley's farm, and then with grape and canister. In and on both sides of the church grove the regiments halted, to make another stand. . . .

The Eighty-second Ohio was directed to draw farther to the right and to occupy the projecting angle of the woods on the right and rear of the church grove; but, while executing this order, one of [General Howard's] aides directed him to occupy the right of the north and south rifle-pit [Stop 14], where the regiment established itself.

About that time one of Colonel Krzyzanowski's aides came to me asking for re-enforcements, as the Twenty-sixth Wisconsin, being nearly enveloped on all sides, could no longer maintain its position. Having no re-enforcements to send, I gave the order to fall back to the border of the woods east of the open ground. The . . . regiment then marched in retreat in good order, facing about and firing as often as possible.

Meanwhile the enemy, after having forced back the One hundred and nineteenth New York by his enfilading fire, gained rapidly on the left of Captain Dilger's battery. This battery and that of Captain Wiedrich remained in position until the very last moment. Captain Dilger limbered up only when the enemy's infantry was already between his pieces. His horse was shot under him, as well as the two wheel horses and one lead horse of one of his guns. After an ineffectual effort to drag this piece along with the dead horses still hanging in the harness, he had to abandon it to the enemy. . . .

The enemy was now pouring in great force upon our right and left, and the position in and near the church grove could no longer be held. The two regiments still remaining there gave several discharges and then fell back in good order. [O.R., XXV, Part 1, pp. 654–56.]

The Eighty-second Illinois held the ground on the ridge immediately to the west—and perhaps one hundred yards north—of the Wilderness Church.

Report of Lieut. Col. Edward S. Salomon, USA, Eighty-second Illinois Infantry, First Brigade, Third Division, Eleventh Army Corps, Army of the Potomac

The regiment arrived with the brigade at a place near Hawkins' farm on the 30th of April, between 6 and 7 p.m. On the 1st of May, at 10 p.m., a working party consisting of 200 men, with a guard of 100 men for protection, under the command of Major Rolshausen, were ordered out to blockade the road in our front and south of the Plank Road. This work was completed about 1 a.m. of the 2d . . . when the major, with his command, returned to the regiment. In the forenoon of the same day the regiment was ordered out on a reconnaissance. . . . After it had proceeded in a southerly direction *as far as Carpenter's farm* we received your order to join the brigade, which order we immediately complied with.

We arrived there between 12 and 1 p.m., and took position in the rear of the One hundred and fifty-seventh New York Volunteers, in column. Between 5 and 6 p.m. the colonel received the order that his men should make themselves comfortable, but soon afterward we heard a heavy fire on our right. The brigade signal to assemble was immediately sounded, and our regiment fell in. At the same time horses, mules, and ambulances of the First Division came running in the greatest confusion and disorder from the right, and passed in the rear of the regiment. We immediately formed line of battle, facing to the west, during the formation of which 2 of our men fell. We then marched in line of battle and in good order to the top of a little hill in our rear, and there faced the enemy. During these movements, men of the First Division continued to run in the greatest confusion on our right. We commenced firing and the regiment fired at least 6 rounds from this position.

The enemy advanced with a steady and heavy fire, in compact masses. Through his advance from the right he drove the troops on the right of the regiment to our rear, exposing us to a heavy front and flank fire. [General Schimmelfennig] then personally ordered the colonel to fall back a little from the top of the hill. The regiment fell back 15 yards in good order, leaving about 70 killed and wounded on the ground it had occupied. Colonel Hecker then took the flag in his hand, cheering his men to make a charge as soon as the enemy should arrive at the proper distance, but, observing that the right of the regiment, which had been exposed to a heavy flank fire, gave way, he returned the flag to the color bearer, and hastened to the right, but, before he arrived there, received a shot through the left thigh. He rode behind the center of the regiment, where he fell from his horse. The major, who went to his assistance, was wounded . . . immediately afterward. The regiment fell back to the woods in its rear, having received your orders to do so. [*O.R.*, XXV, Part 1, pp. 663–64. Emphasis added.]

Drive out to **ROUTE 3. TURN RIGHT** and immediately move into the left lane. **TURN LEFT** at the next crossover and then **TURN LEFT** again so that you are going **EAST** on **ROUTE 3**. Drive about 0.3 mile and **PULL OFF ONTO THE RIGHT SHOULDER**, positioning your car so that you are short of the trees in the median, since much of the terrain described is north of the road. You will be just beyond the crossover you used to get back to the Wilderness Church.

STOP 14, DOWDALL'S TAVERN: THE BUSCHBECK LINE

Here, a few yards east of Dowdall's Tavern—which before the Turnpike became a dual lane highway, was situated a few yards to your right and rear—a line of earthworks described as the "north and south rifle-pit" had been constructed. This "Buschbeck Line" ran at right angles to Howard's main earthworks, which were located in the woods to the south.

The shallow rifle pits . . . had been dug in the morning by Barlow's brigade, and . . . were unfinished when Barlow was ordered down into the woods below the Furnace. This line of earthworks was so slight that it would protect the soldier only when kneeling or lying down. It was constructed without provision for the use of artillery, and when the pit was occupied by the infantry, all of the artillery was ordered to the rear excepting Dilger's guns. . . . The shallow rifle pit was completely filled with soldiers, and more than it could properly hold. [Augustus Choate Hamlin, *The Battle of Chancellorsville* (Bangor, Maine: published by the author, 1896), p. 75.] A segment of this "cross-trench" remains near the white house about 100 yards to your right.

When *Jackson* rolled up the flanks of Devens' division and drove Schurz's regiments from the position near Wilderness Church, Buschbeck's brigade "was faced about, and, lying on the other side of the rifle-pit embankment, held on with praiseworthy firmness." [*O.R.*, XXV, Part 1, p. 630.]

*Report of Maj. Gen. Carl Schurz, USA, Commanding Third
Division, Eleventh Army Corps, Army of the Potomac*

Arriving near the north and south rifle-pit, General Schimmelfennig ordered the Eighty-second Illinois to charge into the projecting
corner of the woods on the right [your left], the border of which was
already in possession of the enemy. The One hundred and fifty-
seventh [New York] was directed to fall back along the Plank Road,
so as to clear the front of the rifle-pit, which seemed to be well filled
with men, and to take position on the border of the woods behind.
. . . I rejoined [General Howard] behind the rifle-pit, which was
manned in the center by some of Colonel Buschbeck's regiments; on
the left by several companies of the Seventy-fourth Pennsylvania,
Sixty-first Ohio, and One hundred and nineteenth New York, and on
the extreme right by the Eighty-second Ohio. Several pieces of the
Reserve Artillery were still firing.

Behind the rifle-pit there was a confused mass of men belonging
to all divisions, whom we made every possible effort to rally and
reorganize, a thing extremely difficult under the fire of the enemy. I
succeeded once in gathering a numerous crowd, and, placing myself
at its head, led it forward with a hurrah. It followed me some
distance, but was again dispersed by the enemy's fire. . . . I tried the
same experiment two or three times, but always with the same result.
[*O.R.*, XXV, Part 1, pp. 656–57.]

*Report of Brig. Gen. Alexander Schimmelfennig, USA,
Commanding First Brigade, Third Division,
Eleventh Army Corps, Army of the Potomac*

The first division which gave way on that day (because attacked
in front and from the flank and rear) was that of General Devens,
Colonel von Gilsa's brigade firing one round per man and General
McLean's not firing at all; . . . it was the second line of your division,
which, though overrun by the First Division, changed front from the
south to the west in less than two minutes' time, the brigade battery,
that of Captain Dilger, being on the left, and checked the heavy
column of the enemy pouring in upon us from the front and both
flanks. . . . The first line of your division, in conjunction with
Colonel Buschbeck's brigade, formed in the rear of two of my regiments—the Eighty-second Illinois . . . and the One hundred and fifty-
seventh New York . . . and manned the rifle-pits, the Second Brigade

of the Second Division being, at that critical moment, detached from the corps by order of Major General Hooker.

[General Schurz's] two brigades and that of Colonel Buschbeck, numbering together not quite 4,000 muskets, were the men who stood the brunt of the battle and held at bay the enemy's masses for at least one hour. . . . These three brigades, though outflanked on both wings, firmly stood their ground until sufficient time had elapsed for the corps behind to come to their support and take up a position in the rear. This is all that under the circumstances could be expected from your command. . . .

My brigade and the Third Division did everything possible to avert the catastrophe which followed. The only reconnaissances undertaken were those made by my brigade, and the enemy's movements were reported by me fully two hours before the battle commenced.

General, I am an old soldier. To this hour I have been proud to command the brave men of this brigade; but I am sure that unless these infamous falsehoods (circulated through the papers . . . as if a nest of vipers had but waited for an auspicious moment to spit out their poisonous slanders) be retracted and reparations made, their good-will and soldierly spirit will be broken, and I shall no longer be at the head of the same brave men whom I have heretofore the honor to lead. [*O.R.*, XXV, Part 1, pp. 662–63.]

Report of Lieut. Col. Adolph von Hartung, USA, Seventy-fourth Pennsylvania Infantry, First Brigade, Third Division, Eleventh Corps, Army of the Potomac

At about 5.30 p.m. the regiments on our right were suddenly attacked in very great force by the enemy, and his attack was directed on our right flank and back. The regiment on our right broke through the ranks of the Seventy-fourth Regiment in such a manner that the regiment got at once thrown in such disorder that a restoring of order was an utter impossibility. The first we ever knew of the enemy was that our men, while sitting on their knapsacks and ready to spring to their arms, were shot from the rear and flank. A surprise in broad daylight . . . was so complete that the men had not even time to take their arms before they were thrown in the wildest confusion. The different regiments on our right were in a few minutes all mixed up with the Seventy-fourth. The enemy pressed heavily. Some guns of Dieckmann's battery in front, without firing a single shot, broke through the whole mixed crowd, and the regiment could, under such circumstances, do nothing else but retreat through the woods.

Preserving as much order as possible, I led the regiment back behind a rifle-pit near the old headquarters of Major-General Howard. About 50 paces in front of this rifle-pit, right near the road, I found Major-General Howard, who was crying, "Stop; face about; do not retreat any farther." This was well said, but impossible to be done. The troops were entirely mixed up, the panic was great, the enemy pressed heavily, the rifle-pits in the rear was already glittering with bayonets, and occasional shots from behind were showing the greatness of the danger of trying to rally the troops in front of the pit. To obey the order of Major-General Howard at this moment and at this place would have been certain useless destruction to every man of the regiment.

The rifle-pit alone and nowhere else was the right place for rallying the troops. There the greatest order was soon restored, and the regiment awaited calmly the approach of the enemy. Different regiments were on our right and left. On our right I remember the One hundred and nineteenth and Sixty-eighth New York Regiments, all well rallied again.

We were soon furiously attacked, but the enemy was handsomely checked and driven back. The men stuck to their colors and fought bravely, but renewed attacks of superior forces and flank movements of the enemy made all the troops on our left fall back. Our artillery, too, retreated, and broke through the rifle-pits and through our ranks. The troops on our right, too, withdrew, and the Seventy-fourth Regiment, nearly left alone, could not keep up the defense any longer, and consequently retreated. A part of the men, as it does always happen, got separated from the main part of the regiment and retreated on their own hook. The main part of the regiment retreated in the greatest order up to a point near Major General Hooker's headquarters, where the whole Eleventh Corps was rallied again. [O.R., XXV, Part 1, p. 665.]

Report of Maj. Gen. Oliver O. Howard, USA, Commanding
Eleventh Army Corps, Army of the Potomac

Now as to the causes of this disaster to my corps:

1. Though constantly threatened and apprised of the moving of the enemy, yet the woods was so dense that he was able to mass a large force, whose exact whereabouts neither patrols, reconnaissances, nor scouts ascertained. He succeeded in forming a column opposite to and outflanking my right.

2. By the panic produced by the enemy's reverse fire, regiments and artillery were thrown suddenly upon those in position.

3. The absence of General Barlow's brigade, which I had previously located in reserve and *en echelon* with Colonel von Gilsa's, so as to cover his right flank. This was the only general reserve I had. [*O.R.*, XXV, Part 1, p. 630.]

Report of Brig. Gen. R. E. Rodes, CSA, Commanding D. H. Hill's
Division, Second Army Corps, Army of Northern Virginia

On reaching the ridge at Melzi Chancellor's, which had an extended line of works facing in our direction, an effort was made [by the enemy] to check the fleeing columns. For a few moments they held this position, but once more my gallant troops dashed at them with a wild shout, and, firing a hasty volley, they continued their headlong flight. . . . It was at this point that *Trimble's* division, which had followed closely in my rear, headed by the brave and accomplished *Colston*, went over the works with my men, and from this time until the close of the engagement the two divisions were mingled together in inextricable confusion. . . . During this glorious victory and pursuit of more than two miles, I had only three brigades really engaged. *General Colquitt*, soon after starting, was misled by the appearance of a small body of the enemy's cavalry, and, notwithstanding the instructions to himself and *General Ramseur*, halted his brigade to resist what he supposed to be an attack on his flank. This error was discovered too late to enable him to do more than follow the victorious troops of *Doles* over the field they had won. *Ramseur*, being ordered to follow *Colquitt* and watch his flank, was necessarily deprived of any active participation. [*O.R.*, XXV, Part 1, pp. 941–42.]

Report of Brig. Gen. R. E. Colston, CSA, Commanding Trimble's Division, Second Army Corps, Army of Northern Virginia

About 5 p.m. . . . . I received orders to form line of battle near the Luckett house, perpendicular to a road which passes on by Wilderness Church and merges into the Plank Road leading to Chancellorsville. After receiving several orders and counter orders, which caused some delay, my line was finally formed—my three brigades being nearly all on the left of the road, *Colston's* brigade being on the right, under *Colonel [E. T. H.] Warren*, *Jones'* brigade next, and *Nicholls'* on the extreme left. My line was about 200 yards in the rear of *General Rodes*, who was in the first line, and orders were received that when any portion of the first line needed re-enforcements, the officer commanding the position would call for and receive aid from the portion of the line in his rear without referring the order to division commanders.

Orders to advance were received at 6 o'clock precisely, and the troops moved on with enthusiasm against the enemy. In a few moments the action opened with a tremendous fire of musketry, two pieces of *Stuart's* Horse Artillery in the road supporting our infantry with their fire. Notwithstanding the tangled and very difficult character of the woods and the resistance of the enemy, our troops advanced with great rapidity, driving the enemy like chaff before them, but not without loss to themselves.

The division had advanced but a short time (not more than ten or fifteen minutes), and the battle had hardly more than commenced, when *General Rodes* called upon *Colonel Warren* to support him. The troops of my division had pressed on so ardently that they were already within a few steps of the first line, and in some places mixed up with them. The second and third brigades, commanded by *General J. R. Jones* and *Colonel Warren*, pushed on with and through the first line, and they were the first to charge upon and capture the first line of intrenchments of the enemy, which were in an open field beyond the Wilderness Church. This they did under a heavy fire of artillery and musketry. A large number of prisoners and two pieces of artillery were taken here by the Second Brigade, *Capt. W. S. Hannah*, of the Fifteenth Virginia Regiment, being the first to lay his hands upon these pieces, and *Color Sergeant [Joseph H.] Pickle*, of the same regiment, planted his colors over them. At the same time three pieces of artillery and a number of prisoners were taken by the Third Brigade, whose gallant commander (*Colonel Warren*) had fallen, severely wounded, a few minutes before. . . .

We continued to drive the enemy before us until darkness prevented our farther advance. The firing had now ceased. Owing to the very difficult and tangled nature of the ground over which the troops had advanced, and the mingling of the first and second lines of battle, the formation of the troops had become very much confused, and different regiments, brigades, and divisions were mixed up together. In order to be ready to renew the conflict at daylight, it was necessary to reform them in proper order, and a portion of *General A. P. Hill's* troops having moved to the front, I ordered the different brigades of my division to form near the log hospital [Stop 15], which was occupied by the enemy's wounded, and to draw a fresh supply of ammunition. The Fourth Brigade was formed on the left of the Plank Road, the others on the right. The First *[Paxton]*, which had been detached in the evening, not having yet rejoined, was some distance in the rear. [*O.R.*, XXV, Part 1, pp. 1004–5.]

Report of Lieut. Oscar Hinrichs, CSA, Chief Engineer, Trimble's Division, Second Army Corps, Army of Northern Virginia

The advance was ordered at 6 p.m. precisely. Two pieces of *Stuart's* Horse Artillery occupied a position in the road, and opened simultaneously with our first line on the enemy. The first discharge was very heavy—so much so that *General Rodes'* men, who occupied the first line on our division front, apparently faltered and were overrun by our division, owing, first, to the eagerness of the men, and secondly, to the probable fact of *General Jackson's* having ordered the attack to be vigorous. The men, now mixed up with those of *General Rodes*, pushed forward at a double-quick, which was only checked into a quick-step by the enemy and the natural difficulties of the ground. In this manner several miles of ground were passed over, the enemy being speedily dispossessed of their intrenched positions.

The general and staff turned off the dirt road about 1½ miles from the point of starting, to the right, into and across a cleared field, when, on seeing *Colonel Warren* being carried out, I was directed . . . to carry the order to take command of the brigade to the first ranking field officer of that brigade that could be found. *Lieutenant-Colonel [S. D.] Thruston*, commanding Third North Carolina troops, was the first officer found, and to him was the order communicated. Finding him on the point of falling from exhaustion, I gave my horse to him, and followed the regiment, up to that time nearly entire and well kept together, for about an hour, when I took my horse again and rejoined the general. I found him about 4 miles from our point of starting, on the Plank Road near a small Yankee hospital, endeavoring to reform the division into regiments and brigades. It was now nearly 9 o'clock, quite dark, and all firing ceased, except an occasional musket and gun. [*O.R.*, XXV, Part 1, pp. 1009–10.]

Union entrenchments across the Plank Road about one mile west of Chancellorsville. (USAHMI)

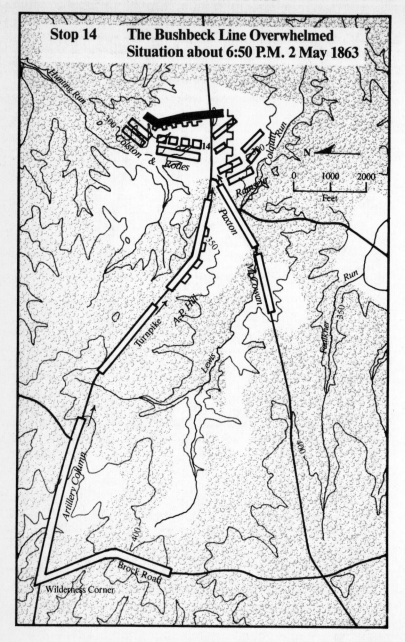

**Stop 14   The Bushbeck Line Overwhelmed
Situation about 6:50 P.M. 2 May 1863**

Continue in the same direction on **ROUTE 3** for slightly more than 0.6 mile. Pull off on the right shoulder just beyond the entrance to **WILDERNESS RESORT.** The building variously described as a shop, school house, or 'log hospital,' was located here.

STOP 15, JACKSON'S FINAL ACT

Report of Brig. Gen. R. E. Rodes, CSA, Commanding D. H. Hill's Division, Second Army Corps, Army of Northern Virginia

Pushing forward as rapidly as possible, the troops soon entered a second piece of woods thickly filled with undergrowth. The right, becoming entangled in an abatis near the enemy's first line of fortifications, caused the line to halt, and such was the confusion and darkness that it was not deemed advisable to make a farther advance. I at once sent word to *Lieutenant-General Jackson*, urging him to push forward the fresh troops of the reserve line, in order that mine might be reformed.

Riding forward on the Plank Road, I satisfied myself that the enemy had no line of battle between our troops and the heights of Chancellorsville, and on my return informed *Colonel [S.] Crutchfield*, chief of artillery of the corps, of the fact, and he opened his batteries on that point. The enemy instantly responded by a most terrific fire, which silenced our guns, but did but little execution on the infantry, as it was mainly directed down the Plank Road, which was unoccupied except by our artillery. When the fire ceased, *General [A. P.] Hill's* troops were brought up, and as soon as a portion were deployed in my front as skirmishers I commenced withdrawing my men, under orders from the lieutenant-general. . . .

On withdrawing my troops, I was directed to see that *Jones'* brigade, of *Colston's* division, was so placed as to guard a road coming in from the direction of the furnace on the right, and to relieve, with one of my brigades, *McGowan's* brigade, of *[A. P.] Hill's* division, then guarding a second road from the same direction, which entered the Plank Road farther up [your present location.]

While preparing to make these dispositions, a sudden and rapid musketry fire was opened in front, which created a little confusion among the troops. Order was speedily restored, however. Apparently this firing proceeded entirely from our own men, as not a ball from the enemy came within sound. There being no place but the open ground at Melzi Chancellor's suitable for such a purpose, I withdrew all my troops excepting *Colquitt's* brigade, then on guard, to reform them at that point. Finding the intrenchments partially occupied by *Paxton's* brigade, I formed line of battle in connection with him.

At this time the enemy opened a terrific fire of artillery similar to that which had taken place just before my withdrawal, which caused much confusion and disorder, rendering it necessary for me to place guards across the road to stop stragglers. Shortly after this occurrence I was informed that *Lieutenant-General Jackson* was wounded, and also received a message from *Major-General [A. P.] Hill* that he likewise was disabled, and that the command of the corps devolved on me. Without loss of time, I communicated with *Brigadier-Generals Heth* and *Colston*, commanding, respectively, the divisions of *A. P. Hill* and *Trimble*, and made the necessary arrangements for a renewal of the attack in the morning, it being agreed that the troops were not in condition to resume operations that night. Just at this time (about 12 o'clock) the enemy made an attack on our right, but being feeble in its character and promptly met, it lasted but a short time. [*O.R.*, XXV, Part 1, pp. 941–42.]

A CAVALRY CHARGE

Your present location is also the site of one of the rare mounted cavalry charges against infantry to occur during the Civil War, an unexpected encounter that struck at least one Confederate present as "being as unlikely as an attack from a gunboat." [Bigelow, *Chancellorsville*, p. 317 n.]

Report of Brig. Gen. A. Pleasonton, USA, Commanding First Cavalry Division, Army of the Potomac

On the 2d, the command moved gradually to the front, when, about 4 o'clock in the afternoon, I received orders from Major-General Hooker to proceed down the Plank Road and turn to the south after a number of trains the enemy were moving in the direction of Orange Court House, Major-General Sickles, with the Third Army Corps, having already started after them.

I joined General Sickles in about an hour's time, and found him sharply engaged with the enemy, but driving them about 2 miles south of the Plank Road leading toward Orange Court-House. Finding I could not advance just then in that direction, and after consultation with Major-General Sickles, I prepared to return to the plateau at the head of Scott's Run. While doing so, I heard heavy firing and rebel yells in the direction of Hunting Run, and an aide-de-camp of General Warren's, of Major General Hooker's staff, rode up to say the Eleventh Corps was falling back rapidly and a regiment of cavalry was needed to check the movement. I immediately ordered the Eighth Pennsylvania Cavalry to proceed at a gallop, attack the rebels, and check them until we could get the artillery in position. This service was splendidly performed by the Eighth, but with heavy loss, and I gained some fifteen minutes to bring Martin's battery into position, reverse a battery of Sickles' corps, detach some cavalry to stop runaways, and secure more guns from the retreating column. Every moment was invaluable. [*O.R.*, XXV, Part 1, pp. 774–75.]

Narrative of Maj. Pennock Huey, USA, Eighth Pennsylvania Cavalry, Second Brigade, First Cavalry Division, Army of the Potomac

Just as we reached Hazel Grove, at Scott's Run Crossing, at half-past 6 o'clock p.m. . . . a staff-officer rode up in a state of great excitement and reported to General Sickles that the enemy had flanked General Howard's corps, and that he had been sent for a regiment of General Pleasonton's cavalry. General Sickles immediately ordered General Pleasonton to send a regiment. General Pleasonton then ordered me to report with my regiment as quickly as possible to General Howard, whom I would probably find near the old Wilderness Church. There were no other orders given to me or to any officer of my regiment.

I found the regiment, standing to horse, on the opposite or north side of Hazel Grove, near the road. The wood in front was so thick with underbrush that a bird could scarcely fly through it; much less could a cavalry charge have been made. On inquiring for the adjutant of the regiment, and on being informed by some of the men where he was, I rode to the point designated and found Major Peter Keenan, Captain William A. Dailey, Adjutant J. Haseltine Haddock, and Lieutenant Andrew B. Wells playing cards under a tree. When I ordered them to mount their commands they were all in high spirits about the game, Keenan remarking: "Major, you have spoiled a good game."

After mounting the regiment I rode off at its head in my proper place, followed by four other officers, all of whom belonged in front except Lieutenant Carpenter, who commanded the second company of the first squadron, and might properly have been in the rear of the first company, where he undoubtedly would have been had I supposed there was danger ahead. . . .

We rode through the wood toward the Plank Road; there was no unusual stir or excitement among the men or officers of the regiment, the impression being that the enemy were retreating, and all who had not heard of General Howard's disaster felt happy with the thought that the battle was almost over. No one in the regiment, with the exception of myself, knew where we were going or for what purpose.

From the information I had received from General Pleasonton, and from hearing the aide make his report before I started, I had no idea that we would meet the enemy till after I had reported to General Howard. Therefore the surprise was as great to us as to the enemy, as we were entirely unprepared, our sabers being in their scabbards.

When we arrived almost at the Plank Road, we discovered that we had ridden right into the enemy, the Plank Road in our front being occupied by them in great force, and that we were completely

Chancellorsville House 1884. (USAMHI)

surrounded, the woods at that point being filled with flankers of *Jackson's* columns, who were thoroughly hidden from our view by the thick undergrowth. It was here that I gave the command to "draw sabers and charge," which order was repeated by Major Keenan and other officers. The charge was led by the five officers . . . who were riding at the head of the regiment when we left Hazel Grove. On reaching the Plank Road it appeared to be packed about as closely with the enemy as it possibly could be.

We turned to the left, facing the Confederate column, the regiment crowding on, both men and horses in a perfect frenzy of excitement, which nothing but death could stop. We cut our way through, trampling down all who could not escape us, and using our sabers on all within reach, for a distance of about 100 yards, when we received a volley from the enemy which killed Major Keenan, Captain Arrowsmith, and Adjutant Haddock . . . besides a large number of men. . . .

MOST of the regiment came out of the wood on the north or opposite side of the Plank Road. I immediately reformed as much of it as I could get together (which included almost every mounted man and officer left) in rear of the artillery that was then going into line on the left of the Plank Road, and just in the rear of the thick wood which had completely obscured us from their view while we were making our charge. The object in re-forming there was to support the

artillery, and also to prevent them from opening fire till after our men had come out of the wood.

Our charge had such a telling effect on the enemy that they did not advance farther on the Plank Road than the point where we struck them, and very few of them crossed the narrow road over which we had passed (that road being parallel with the two lines of battle.)

Our artillery opened fire first at the Plank Road, not at Hazel Grove, as soon as they knew that we were out and were reforming in their rear.

Dusk was now coming on. As we could be of no further service there, we fell back a short distance to the Chancellorsville House, where we arrived before the artillery at Hazel Grove opened fire. . . . I formed the regiment across the plain, covering the road that led toward the river and the fords, where the regiment did service all night in stopping the stampeded and scattered soldiers, and assisted in re-forming them. Here we remained all night.

About four o'clock on the morning of the 3d I went to General Hooker's headquarters to report and to receive orders. . . . Just as I arrived there General Pleasonton rode up. . . . He expressed great surprise and pleasure on seeing me, and said "that he was afraid we had all been captured or killed," and "that it was almost miraculous that we had been able to extricate ourselves from the perilous position;" it being very evident that he thought we *had* been surrounded and captured, and that he lost a regiment from his small command. Nor was he aware that we had made a charge on the enemy, or . . . had done anything toward stopping the advance of *Stonewall Jackson's* column as it came rushing up the plank . . . till he learned it from me at that time and place.

My verbal report to him seemed to change the whole tenor of his thoughts, and to quicken his idea of making a glowing report redounding to his own glory. The imaginative orders to the regiment and his own after-conceived heroic exploits (as reported by him) were after-thoughts. . . .

Brevet Brig. Gen. Huey, "The Charge of the Eighth Pennsylvania Cavalry," *Battles and Leaders*, III, p. 186; Beginning with "MOST," the rest of this narrative is taken from Pennock Huey, *A True History of the Charge of the Eighth Pennsylvania Cavalry at Chancellorsville* (Philadelphia: Porter and Coates, 1885), p. 19. Huey reported losses of "about 30 men and about 80 horses."

Narrative of Captain Andrew B. Wells, USA, Company F,
Eighth Pennsylvania Cavalry, Second Brigade, First Cavalry
Division, Army of the Potomac

I was under the impression, and believe that the other officers also were, that we were on our road to report to General Howard. Anyhow, I fell in with the second squadron, Captain William A. Corrie being in command, and he and I rode together at the head of it. When we passed out of the clearing there were no officers or men on our flank, all was in order ahead, and the command was moving at a walk. The command entered the woods and was still moving on a walk, when, at the distance of about one mile from where we had mounted, Captain Corrie and myself saw the first squadron take the trot, leaving a space between us of about twenty-five yards. At the same time we heard the command, "Draw sabers," and saw the first squadron draw them. We then heard the musketry-firing. It was given in continuous but distant volleys.

We of the second squadron knew that our time was at hand, and Captain Corrie gave the order to draw sabers and charge. Taking a trot, we found that the road took a bend as we proceeded. When we turned the corner of the wood-road [about 300 yards to your right] a sight met our eyes that it is impossible for me to describe. After charging over the dead men and horses of the first squadron we charged into *Jackson's* column, and, as luck would have it, found them with empty guns—thanks to our poor comrades ahead. The enemy were as thick as bees, and we appeared to be among thousands of them in an instant.

After we reached the Plank Road we were in columns of fours and on the dead run, and when we struck the enemy there occurred a "jam" of living and dead men, friends and enemies, and horses, and the weight of the rear of our squadron broke us into utter confusion, so that at the moment every man was for himself.

The third squadron . . . was in our rear, and came thundering along after us, but as to the balance of the regiment I do not know how they came in or got out.

The enemy were as much surprised as we were, and thought, no doubt . . . that the whole cavalry of the Army of the Potomac was charging them. I distinctly remember hearing a number of them call out, "I surrender, I surrender." We did not stop to take any prisoners for fear of being captured ourselves, (I had been caught once and was just out of Libby prison and did not want to be captured again) but made for our lines as best we could.

The whole affair was accidental. . . . The officers who were at the head of our column, seeing the situation, had only an instant to determine what was to be done. We could not turn around and get out in the face of the enemy, and the only thing left for us was to go through them, "sink or swim."

Can any man who was a soldier for one moment imagine an officer deliberately planning a charge by a regiment of cavalry, strung out by twos in a column half a mile long in a thick wood? [*Battles and Leaders*, III, pp. 187–88.]

An officer on *General Paxton's* staff later recalled that rumors of cavalry attacks, undoubtedly a reference to the charge of the Eighth Pennsylvania, had impressed the army "making the men supersensitive on the subject." Word that Yankee cavalry were loose in the woods may well explain why the men of the advance line appeared to be unusually jumpy. (Bigelow, *Chancellorsville*, p. 317.)

JACKSON'S DEATH

Narrative of Captain James Power Smith, CSA,
Assistant Adjutant General, Second Army Corps,
Army of Northern Virginia

[I] was ordered to remain at the point where the advance began, to be a center of communication between the general *[Jackson]* and the cavalry on the flanks, and to deliver orders to detachments of artillery still moving up from the rear. . . . About 8 p.m., in the twilight . . . I gathered my couriers about me and went forward to find *General Jackson.* The storm of battle had swept far on to the east and become more and more faint to the ear, until silence came with night over the fields and woods. As I rode along that old turnpike, passing scattered fragments of Confederates looking for their regiments, parties of prisoners concentrating under guards, wounded men by the roadside and under the trees at Talley's and Chancellor's, I had reached an open field on the right, a mile west of Chancellorsville, when, in the dusky twilight, I saw horsemen near an old cabin in the field. Turning toward them I found *Rodes* and his staff engaged in gathering the broken and scattered troops. . . . "*General Jackson* is just ahead on the road, Captain," said *Rodes;* "tell him I will be here at this cabin if I am wanted."

I had not gone a hundred yards before I heard firing, a shot or two, and then a company volley upon the right of the road, and another upon the left. A few moments farther on I met *Captain Murray Taylor*, an aide of *A. P. Hill's*, with tidings that *Jackson* and *Hill* were wounded, and some around them killed, by the fire of their own men.

Spurring my horse into a sweeping gallop, I soon passed the Confederate line of battle, and, some three or four rods in its front, found the general's horse beside a pine sapling on the left, and a rod beyond a little party of men caring for a wounded officer. The story of the sad event . . . came to me from the lips of the wounded general himself, and [is] . . . confirmed and completed by those who were eye-witnesses. . . .

When *Jackson* had reached the point where his line now crossed the turnpike. . . . not half a mile from a line of Federal troops, he had found his front line unfit for the farther and vigorous advance he desired, by reason of the irregular character of the fighting, now right, now left, and because of the dense thickets, through which it was impossible to preserve alignment. Division commanders found it more and more difficult as the twilight deepened to hold their broken brigades in hand. Regretting the necessity of relieving the troops in front, *General Jackson* had ordered *A. P. Hill's* division, his third and reserve line, to be placed in front.

While this change was being effected, impatient and anxious, the general rode forward on the turnpike, followed by two or three of his staff and a number of couriers and signal sergeants. He passed the swampy depression [perhaps 300 yards in your front] and began the ascent of the hill toward Chancellorsville, when he came upon a line of Federal infantry lying on their arms. Fired at by one or two muskets (two musket-balls from the enemy whistled over my head as I came to the front), he turned and came back toward his line, upon the side of the road to his left. As he rode near to the Confederate troops, just placed in position and ignorant that he was in the front, the left company began firing to the front, and two of his party fell from their saddles dead. . . . Spurring his horse across the road to his right, he was met with a second volley from the right company of *Pender's [Lane's]* North Carolina brigade. Under this volley, when not two rods from the troops, the general received three balls at the same instant. One penetrated the palm of his right hand and. . . . a second passed around the wrist of the left arm and out through the left hand. A third ball passed through the left arm half-way from shoulder to elbow. The large bone of the upper arm was splintered to the elbow-joint, and the wound bled freely.

His horse turned quickly from the fire, through the thick bushes which swept the cap from the general's head, and scratched his forehead, leaving drops of blood to stain his face. As he lost his hold upon the bridle-rein, he reeled from the saddle, and was caught by the arms of *Captain Wilbourn*, of the Signal Corps. Laid upon the ground, there came at once to his succor *General A. P. Hill* and members of his staff. [I] . . . reached his side a minute after, to find *General Hill* holding the head and shoulders of the wounded chief. Cutting open the coat-sleve from wrist to shoulder, I found the wound in the upper arm, and with my handkerchief I bound the arm above the wound to stem the flow of blood. Couriers were sent for *Dr. Hunter McGuire*, the surgeon of the corps and the general's trusted friend, and for an ambulance. . . . With difficulty litter-bearers were brought from the line near by, and the general was placed upon the litter and carefully raised to the shoulder, I myself bearing one corner.

A moment after, artillery from the Federal side was opened upon us; great broadsides thundered over the woods; hissing shells searched the dark thickets through, and shrapnels swept the road along which we moved. Two or three steps farther, and the litter bearer at my side was struck and fell, but, as the litter turned, *Major Watkins Leigh*, of *Hill's* staff, happily caught it. But the fright of the men was so great that we were obliged to lay the litter and its burden down upon the road. As the litter-bearers ran to the cover of the trees, I threw myself by the general's side and held him firmly to the ground. . . . Over us swept the rapid fire of shot and shell—grape-shot striking fire upon the flinty rock of the road all around us, and sweeping from their feet horses and men of the artillery just moved to the front.

Soon the firing veered to the other side of the road, and I sprang to my feet, assisted the general to rise, . . . and with the wounded man's weight thrown heavily upon me, we forsook the road. Entering the woods, he sank to the ground from exhaustion, but the litter was soon brought, and again rallying a few men, we essayed to carry him farther when a second bearer fell at my side. This time . . . the litter careened, and the general fell to the ground with a groan of deep pain. . . . Raising him again to his feet, he was accosted by *Brigadier-General Pender*: "Oh, General, I hope you are not seriously wounded. I will have to retire my troops to re-form them, they are so much broken by this fire."

But *Jackson*, rallying his strength, with firm voice said: "You must hold your ground, *General Pender*; you must hold your ground, sir!"

and so uttered his last command on the field. [*Battles and Leaders*, III, pp. 209–12.]

Jackson was carried in a field ambulance to the Wilderness Tavern, where the Second Corps Hospital had been established. Later that night his arm was amputated, and two days later he was removed by way of Todd's Tavern and Spotsylvania Court House to Guiney's Station, on the Richmond, Fredericksburg and Potomac Railroad—twenty-seven jarring miles in an ambulance. He died of pneumonia on May 10.

Report of Brig. Gen. Henry Heth, CSA, Commanding Brigade and Ambrose P. Hill's Division, respectively, Second Army Corps, Army of Northern Virginia

I put my brigade in motion and advanced, passing Melzi Chancellor's house, and entered the thick oak woods on the left of the Plank Road. On entering these woods, the enemy opened upon my command a heavy fire of artillery, doing us some damage. It was now becoming quite dark. The undergrowth was so thick and entangled that it was impossible to advance in any order. I ordered the brigade to reform on the Plank Road, which had scarcely been done when orders were received from *General Hill* to move down the road by the flank. On reaching the position in the road occupied by *General Hill*, he directed me to deploy two regiments, one on the right, the other on the left of the road, to check the enemy, who were advancing. These movements had not been completed before the enemy opened heavily upon the Fifty-fifth Virginia. . . . Soon after, *General Hill* informed me that he was wounded, and directed me to take command of the division. [*O.R.*, XXV, pt. 1, p. 890.]

Report of Brig. James H. Lane, CSA, Commanding Brigade, A. P. Hill's Division, Second Army Corps, Army of Northern Virginia

General A. P. Hill ordered me (at dark) to deploy one regiment as skirmishers across the road, to form line of battle in rear with the rest of the brigade, and to push vigorously forward. In other words, we were ordered to make a night attack and capture the enemy's batteries in front, if possible. Just then they opened a terrific artillery fire, which was responded to by our batteries. As soon as this was over, I deployed the Thirty-third North Carolina troops forward as skirmishers, and formed line of battle to the rear—the Seventh and Thirty-seventh to the right, the Eighteenth and Twenty-eighth to the left, the left of the Thirty-seventh and the right of the Eighteenth resting on the road. I had moved forward the Eighteenth and Twenty-eighth to within a short distance of our line of skirmishers, and I was about to move the Seventh and Thirty-seventh to a corresponding position before ordering the whole line forward, when Lieutenant-Colonel [Levi H.] Smith, of a Pennsylvania regiment [the One hundred and twenty-eighth] entered our lines with a white flag and wished to know if we were Confederate or Union troops. Considering this an illegitimate use of the white flag, as he expressly stated it was not his object to surrender, and not wishing to let him return, I sent *Lieutenant [O.] Lane* to *General A. P. Hill* to know what I should do. Our skirmishers on the right soon after fired upon a few of the enemy who had approached tolerably near, and a few random shots were fired by the Seventh and Thirty-seventh Regiments without orders, which appears to have drawn the enemy's artillery and infantry fire. I understand from the official report of the commanding officer of the Eighteenth North Carolina troops that *General A. P. Hill,* staff and couriers were in the road in advance of them at this time, and to avoid the enemy's fire some of them dashed into the woods over the Eighteenth Regiment, which fired into them, mistaking them in the dark for the enemy's cavalry. . . .

General A. P. Hill being wounded, the night attack was not made as at first contemplated. I withdrew the left wing of the Thirty-third, which formed on the right of the Seventh, and extended our line still farther to the right, with the Eighteenth and Twenty-eighth Regiments, the right of the Twenty-eighth resting on a road running obliquely to the Plank Road, with two of its companies broken back, to guard against a flank movement. [*O.R.,* XXV, Part 2, p. 916.]

According to Douglas Southall Freeman, the fatal shots fired at *Jackson* and his party came from the Eighteenth North Carolina of Lane's brigade. (Douglas Southall Freeman, *Lee's Lieutenants: A Study in Command* [3 vols., New York: Charles Scribner's Sons, 1946), II, p. 567 n.)]

Report of Lieut. Col. Forney George, CSA, Eighteenth North Carolina, Lane's Brigade, A. P. Hill's Division, Second Army Corps, Army of Northern Virginia

About dark of the 2d . . . [we] came upon the right flank and to the rear of the enemy, and for a short time were exposed to very severe shelling, by which we lost several killed and wounded. We were then drawn up in line of battle on the left of the turnpike, our right resting on the road, and ordered to charge the enemy's battery, some distance in our front. We had not advanced far (being informed that there was no one but the enemy in front of us) before *General A. P. Hill* and staff, who had been fired upon by the enemy, rushed upon our line in order to effect their escape, when our men, thinking it was a cavalry charge from the enemy, fired several rounds at them,

South side of the Plank Road near the site of Jackson's mortal wounding. Note the trees shattered by artillery fire. (USAMHI)

doing some damage before the mistake was discovered. Very soon the enemy opened fire upon us, killing and wounding several of our men. We were then ordered across and to the right of the turnpike, and formed about 300 yards from and perpendicular to the road.

During the night the enemy advanced upon us twice, and each time he was repulsed in handsome style. [*O.R.*, XXV, Part 1, p. 920.]

A NIGHT ATTACK

Night attacks, like mounted cavalry charges against infantry, were rare in the Civil War—usually for good reasons, as the following reports make clear. Advancing by the light of the moon, with bayonets fixed and pieces uncapped, two brigades from Birney's division, Sickles' Third Corps, plunged into the gap between the Union and Confederate lines which were astride the Turnpike. The right of this line charged against a *Union* battery from the neighboring Twelfth Corps; the Union left hit *Lane's* brigade a short distance to your right. Like the reports involving the Eighth Pennsylvania, the following extracts also illustrate how much more organized and purposeful a Civil War action can be in the official report of the commander giving the orders than in accounts submitted by subordinates stuck with executing the mission.

Report of Brig. Gen. David B. Birney, USA, Commanding First Division, Third Army Corps, Army of the Potomac

At midnight I received an order from Major-General Sickles to make necessary dispositions to drive the enemy from the woods in our front and retake the Plank Road and earthworks on it. I placed Ward's brigade in front line, with Hayman's in second line, 100 yards in rear, and gave orders that the pieces were to be uncapped and not discharged until the Plank Road and earthworks were reached; that the movement was to be by right of companies to the front until the enemy's line was reached. Upon the left of the line of battle a wide road had been cut through the woods [to your immediate right], perpendicular to the Plank Road. Upon this I sent in, by column of companies at full distance, the Fortieth New York, Seventeenth Maine, and Sixty-third Pennsylvania. The movement was successfully executed amid most terrific musketry and artillery fire.

In moving through the thick undergrowth of these close woods at midnight, there was necessarily some disorder, but the object was successfully gained. [*O.R.*, XXV, Part 1, p. 409.]

Report of Brig. Gen. J. H. Hobart Ward, USA, Commanding
Second Brigade, First Division, Third Army Corps,
Army of the Potomac

The advance started about 11.30 p.m., my brigade in line of battle, the other brigades of the division in support. The Seventeenth Maine, from the Third Brigade, and the Sixty-third Pennsylvania Volunteers, from the First Brigade, were assigned to me, in addition to my own command, the Twentieth Indiana not having yet arrived from the extreme front. The advance in the moonlight across the field was a brilliant sight.

On arriving at the wood in which the enemy were lodged, the command advanced most gallantly. They soon encountered the enemy in our old barricades, drove them out and occupied them, completely taking the enemy by surprise, who at once retired, permitting one of our batteries to advance up the Plank Road, but which, in the darkness of the dense woods, our troops took to be a battery of the enemy, and charged and captured it accordingly. . . . In the meantime the Fortieth New York and Seventeenth Maine, advancing up the road on the left, recaptured two field-pieces and five caissons from the enemy, taken by them that afternoon. The enemy were so completely surprised that they immediately fell back, thus opening our communication with the main body. [*O.R.*, XXV, Part 1, pp. 429–30.]

Report of Col. Samuel B. Hayman, USA, Commanding Third
Brigade, First Division, Third Army Corps, Army of the Potomac

At about 10 p.m. my command was formed into a column of attack, to support General Ward in an attack upon the enemy occupying our rifle-pits in our present front. The Seventeenth Maine was formed in column to support the Fortieth New York, moving upon a road leading to the Plank Road we had held in the morning. My brigade was directed to take the caps from the rifles and rely upon the bayonet alone. The troops, after advancing some quarter of a mile, encountered a fire from the front and both flanks. The rifle-pits were carried in the face of a terrible fire from both friend and foe; at least such is the opinion entertained by the officers and enlisted men of my command. The prevalence of this opinion no doubt checked the ardor induced by the excitement of the charge, yet a sufficient number advanced to ascertain the fact that the Plank Road was occupied by the enemy in force. The Third and Fifth Michigan with other troops occupied the rifle-pits during the night, and the brigade reorganized as well as possible before daylight. [*O.R.*, XXV, Part 1, p. 433.]

Report of Lieut. Col. Charles B. Merrill, USA, Seventeenth Maine Infantry, Third Brigade, First Division, Third Army Corps, Army of the Potomac

By orders from superior headquarters, the regiment under my command was placed, with a portion of Ward's brigade, in a column under the command of Colonel Egan, of the Fortieth New York Volunteers, to take part in a night attack upon the enemy in order to regain the position lost by our forces during the afternoon.

The column was formed at 9 p.m., and marched on the left of the line, supporting the general line advanced at that time by the Third Army Corps. Our course led us into a narrow road through dense woods. The enemy soon opened upon us a severe musketry fire in front and on both flanks. The regiment in advance and the head of our regiment were thrown into temporary confusion, but the left wing remained firm. When we were formed into column we had received orders not to fire until a line of battle was arranged, and the Fortieth New York had wheeled into line. In this position we could do nothing, and were forced back for a short distance.

The column was reformed and again advanced, meeting with a fire from the enemy concealed in the woods. No one knew the exact position of the enemy's forces, and we were ordered by Colonel Egan to form a line of battle facing to the right, but as it was thought that our own forces were in that direction, the line of the Seventeenth was formed facing to the left. The formation was scarcely completed before we received a volley of musketry from our front, which we returned with vigor. Soon after, by order from General Ward, the forces with which we acted were withdrawn, and our regiment bivouacked on the field near the woods. [*O.R.*, XXV, Part 1, p. 435.]

Report of Col. Byron R. Pierce, USA, Third Michigan Infantry, Third Brigade, First Division, Third Army Corps, Army of the Potomac

My position was in the second line, the First New York Volunteers on my left and the Thirty-seventh New York Volunteers on my right, with instructions to use the bayonet only, the first line to do the firing, to take the guide on the left, and advance by the right of companies to the front. I gave the order to my company officers that, as soon as the firing commenced, to bring their companies into line, thinking that amid the din of battle the order might not be heard, as the lines were but a few feet apart. Advancing into the woods, the order repeatedly came down from the left to take ground to the right, which brought us in an oblique direction to the right. We advanced about 500 yards into the woods, when the fire opened in front.

In the confusion of an attack of this kind in the night, it was only through the greatest exertions of my officers that the line was formed. Once formed, the men dashed on with a yell, taking an oblique direction to the right, dashed over a breastwork, and received a fire of musketry and grape from the right. Still they dashed on to within a few yards of the battery, when it was discovered that we were charging the Twelfth Army Corps, of our own troops. I collected together what I could find of my regiment, which had become very much scattered, and received orders to place it in the breastwork that we had already charged, in front of the Twelfth Corps, where we remained until daylight. . . . [O.R., XXV, Part 1, p. 437. Emphasis added.]

Report of Brig. Gen. James H. Lane, CSA, Commanding Brigade, A. P. Hill's Division, Second Army Corps, Army of Northern Virginia

Between 12 and 1 o'clock that night, the enemy could be heard marshaling their troops along our whole front, while their artillery was rumbling up the road on our right. Soon after, their artillery opened right and left, and Sickles' command rushed upon us with loud and prolonged cheering. They were driven back on the left by our skirmishers, but the fight was more stubborn on the right, which was their main point of attack. The Eighteenth, Twenty-eighth, and left wing of the Thirty-third engaged them there, and gallantly drove them back, although they had outflanked us, and encountered the two right companies of the Twenty-eighth, which had been deflected in anticipation of such a movement. A subsequent attack made about half an hour later was similarly repulsed. The Twenty-eighth captured a staff officer. The colors of the Third Maine Volunteers were taken by *Captain [Niven] Clark's* company of the same regiment. The Eighteenth also captured an aide to General [A. S.] Williams. A number of field and company officers and a large number of men were captured along our whole line. After the enemy were repulsed, *General McGowan* was ordered forward with his brigade, and took position on our right. [O.R., XXV, Part 1, pp. 916–17.]

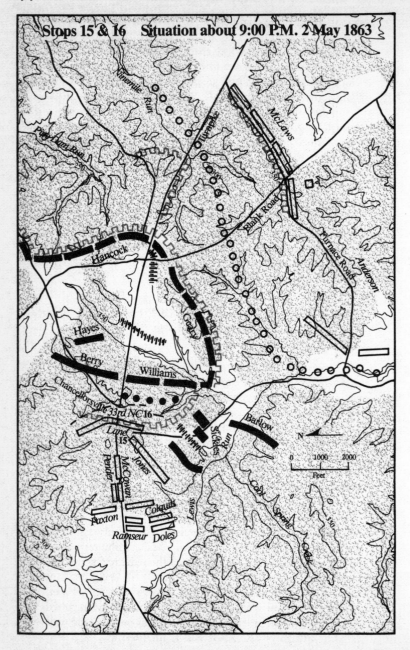

Stops 15 & 16   Situation about 9:00 P.M. 2 May 1863

Continue driving the same direction on **ROUTE 3** until you are opposite the road leading to the Chancellorsville Visitor Center. **TURN RIGHT** on **STUART DRIVE.** Drive about 0.1 mile to the **PAXTON MONUMENT** on your right. Pull off and stop there. If you want to look at the remains of the log breastworks, face the woods with the Paxton Monument at your back. Walk into the woods at the "Ten o'clock" direction about 50 yards. When you find the shallow trench and breastworks trace, you can follow it back to your left until it intersects the road (less than 100 yards) and then walk back to your car along Stuart Drive.

STOP 16, "THE LOG WORKS"

Here "a substantial breastwork was constructed of logs and earth in rear of the abatis" by men of Williams' division, Twelfth Army Corps, after the skirmish with *Wright's* Confederate brigade and a battery of *Stuart's* horse artillery late in the afternoon of May 1 [O.R., XXV, Part 1, p. 708]. Sometime later Sickles' corps arrived to fill in the gap between the Twelfth Corps, the right flank of which rested on the Plank Road at the end of these breastworks, and the Eleventh Corps, which occupied similar works parallel to and south of the Plank Road in the vicinity Dowdall's Tavern (the Melzi Chancellor house).

The next morning, when Sickles' corps moved forward to attack the rear of *Jackson's* column near Catharine's Furnace, Williams' was ordered to make a wide turning movement two or three miles "to the left and front", so as to envelop the temporary works of *Anderson's* Confederate division along the Furnace Road; and then, upon reaching the Plank Road, to sweep both sides of that road in the direction of Chancellorsville. On moving forward through the woods Williams endeavored to maintain contact with the left of Whipple's division, Third corps, and his brigades were "penetrating the dense evergreen thickets" of Scott's Run valley when Slocum ordered him to reoccupy his log works at once.

Report of Brig. Gen. Alpheus S. Williams, USA, Commanding First Division, Twelfth Army Corps, Army of the Potomac

On reaching the open fields to the front of our original position, I saw the ravine and ridge in the vicinity of Fairview swarming with fugitives of the Eleventh Corps. I rode as rapidly as possible with my staff to the Plank Road, where Lieutenant-Colonel Dickinson, of General Hooker's staff, and other officers were engaged in trying to stop and form the fleeing troops. The attempt was practically fruit-less, and I returned to meet Ruger's and Knipe's brigades, which came at a double quick, and moving by flank along the entire line of the woods south of the Plank Road, through which the fugitives were passing, were faced to the front, and, with a loud cheer, pushed into the woods. The movement checked at once all farther advance of the enemy. Ross' (Second) brigade took up its original position on the left, and Ruger's brigade immediately reoccupied a portion of its barricades.

By orders of the major-general commanding the corps, I directed General Knipe to attempt to reoccupy his original line of rifle-pits, which extended diagonally through the woods to the Plank Road. It was now quite dark; the woods were thick with underbrush, and a marsh near the center made it necessary to detach one regiment to the right. It was not known that the enemy had driven the Eleventh Corps from the north side of the Plank Road. Orders were given to advance cautiously, with skirmishers well out; but in spite of all precaution the One hundred and twenty-eighth Pennsylvania, Colonel Mathews, on the right of our line, found itself partly enveloped on its right and rear, and before it could be extricated its colonel and lieutenant-colonel, with at least 150 of the men, fell into the hands of the enemy. . . . The Forty-sixth Pennsylvania and Fifth Connecticut undoubtedly fell under the heavy fire of the enemy, concealed in the woods on our right and in our own rifle-pits, on the extreme right of our line. . . .

On the first appearance in our rifle-pits of the men of the Eleventh Corps falling back from the attack on the right, four companies of the Twenty-eighth New York Volunteers, Lieutenant-Colonel Cook commanding (six companies being on detached duty), left as guard in camp, were deployed across the woods, and for a while successfully stopped the fugitives. It is estimated that nearly 2,000 formed behind our barricades, but they fled at almost the first approach of the enemy, breaking through our thin line of skirmishers. Lieutenant-Colonel Cook attempted to resist the enemy's advance, but, passing our flank on the north side of the Plank Road, they succeeded in placing themselves in his rear, and making prisoners of Lieutenant-Colonel Cook, 2 captains, and about 60 men of his command.

Finding that our original line of intrenchments could not be reoccupied, and that from the direction of the enemy's attack it would furnish little, if any, defense to our own troops, with the approval of the major-general commanding the corps I ordered a new line to be taken up along the interior edge of the woods, in front of the ravine near Fairview, connecting near the Plank Road with the left of Berry's division, of the Third Corps, which had come up to take position on the right of the Plank Road. On consultation with General Berry, I decided to relieve, by two regiments of the Second Brigade of my division, two regiments of his command which were on the left of the Plank Road. The night was passed in throwing up along my whole line such defenses of logs and earth as was possible from the scarcity of tools at hand. The ammunition was also fully replenished to all the regiments from the division pack train.

During the evening a staff officer of General Sickles' corps communicated to me the intention of attacking the enemy on his right flank, in the woods, with at least one brigade of that corps. On account of the position of most of my line, at right angles to the position of General Sickles' troops on the left, and from the evident danger of confusion and mishap in the darkness of the night, I asked this officer to have the attack deferred until I could communicate with General Slocum, who was then at the headquarters of the army.

The attack, however, began before I could see General Slocum, and, if without important results, yet, I think, without injury inflicted by our own guns upon our own troops, as was at first feared. I used all endeavors to communicate to my line the nature and locality of the attack, and to prevent firing in the direction of the attacking party. The infantry on the right of my line, finding itself threatened during this attack, opened a brisk fire, and the artillery shelled the woods in advance with a vigor that must have been very destructive to the enemy's masses in the woods. [*O.R.*, XXV, Part 1, pp. 678–79.]

Report of Maj. Gen. James E. B. Stuart, CSA, Commanding Second Army Corps, Army of Northern Virginia

It was already dark when I sought *General Jackson*, and proposed, as there appeared nothing else for me to do, to take some cavalry and infantry over and hold the Ely's Ford Road. He approved the proposition, and I had already gained the heights overlooking the ford, where was a large number of camp fires, when *Captain Adams*, of *General A. P. Hill's* staff, reached me post-haste and informed me of the sad calamities which for the time deprived the troops of the leadership of both *Jackson* and *Hill*, and the urgent demand for me to come and take command as quickly as possible. I rode with rapidity back 5 miles, determined to press the pursuit already so gloriously begun . . . *General A. P. Hill* was still on the ground, and formally turned over the command to me. I sent also a staff officer to *General Jackson* to inform him that I would cheerfully carry out any instructions he would give, and proceeded immediately to the front, which I reached at 10 p.m.

I found, upon reaching it, *A. P. Hill's* division in front, under *Heth*, with *Lane's, McGowan's, Archer's,* and *Heth's* brigades on the right of the road, within half a mile of Chancellorsville, near the apex of the ridge, and *Pender's* and *Thomas'* on the left. I found that the enemy had made an attack on our right flank, but were repulsed. The fact, however, that the attack was made, and at night, made me apprehensive of a repetition of it, and necessitated throwing back the right wing, so as to meet it. I was also informed that there was much confusion on the right, owing to the fact that some troops mistook friends for the enemy and fired upon them. Knowing that an advance under such circumstances would be extremely hazardous, much against my inclination, I felt bound to wait for daylight. . . . The commanding general was with the right wing of the army, with which I had no communication except by a very circuitous and uncertain route. I nevertheless sent a dispatch to inform him of the state of affairs, and rode around the lines restoring order, imposing silence, and making arrangements for the attack early next day. I sent *Col. E. P. Alexander,* senior officer of artillery, to select and occupy with artillery positions along the line bearing on the enemy's position, with which duty he was engaged all night.

At early dawn, *Trimble's* division composed the second line and *Rodes'* division the third. The latter had his rations on the spot, and, as his men were entirely without food, was extremely anxious to issue. I was disposed to wait a short time for this purpose; but when, as preliminary to an attack, I ordered the right of the first line to swing around and come perpendicular to the road, the order was misunderstood for an order to attack, and that part of the line became engaged. I ordered the whole line to advance and the second and third lines to follow. As the sun lifted the mist that shrouded the field, it was discovered that the ridge on the extreme right [Hazel Grove] was a fine position for concentrating artillery. I immediately ordered thirty pieces to that point, and, under the happy effects of the battalion system, it was done quickly. The effect of this fire upon the enemy's batteries was superb.

In the meantime the enemy was pressing our left with infantry, and all the re-enforcements I could obtain were sent there. *Colquitt's* brigade, of *Trimble's* division, ordered first to the right, was directed to the left to support *Pender. Iverson's* brigade, of the second line, was also engaged there, and the three lines were more or less merged into one line of battle, and reported hard pressed. Urgent requests were sent for re-enforcements, and notices that the troops were out of ammunition, etc. I ordered that the ground must be held at all hazards; if necessary, with the bayonet. About this time also our right connected with *Anderson's* left, relieving all anxiety on that subject. I was now anxious to mass infantry on the left, to push the enemy there, and sent every available regiment to that point.

About 8 a.m. the works of the enemy directly in front of our right were stormed, but the enemy's forces retiring from the line facing *Anderson,* which our batteries enfiladed, caused our troops to abandon these works, the enemy coming in their rear. It was stormed a second time, when I discovered the enemy making a flank movement to the left of the road, for the purpose of dislodging our forces, and hastened to change the front of a portion of our line to meet this attack, but the shortness of the time and the deafening roar of artillery prevented the execution of this movement, and our line again retired. The third time it was taken. . . . Artillery was pushed forward to the crest, sharpshooters were posted in a house in advance [probably Van Wert's] and in a few moments Chancellorsville was ours (10 a.m.) The enemy retired toward Ely's Ford, the road to United States Ford branching one-half mile west of Chancellorsville. . . .

This region . . . is known as the "Wilderness." Rapid pursuit in such a country is an impossibility where the enemy takes care to leave his trains beyond the Rappahannock, and avails himself . . . of the appliances of art, labor, and natural obstacles to delay his pursuers. In this battle, in which the enemy's main force was attacked in chosen positions, he was driven entirely from the field and finally fled across the river. Our troops behaved with the greatest heroism.

I was called to the command, at 10 o'clock at night, on the battlefield, of the corps . . . in the midst of a night attack made by the enemy, without any knowledge of the ground, the position of our forces, or the plans thus far pursued, and without an officer left in the corps above the rank of brigadier-general. Under these disadvantages the attack was renewed the next morning, and prosecuted to a successful issue. [*O.R.*, XXV, Part 1, pp. 887–89.]

Report of Brig. Gen. Henry Heth, CSA, Commanding
Brigade and Ambrose P. Hill's Division, respectively,
Second Army Corps, Army of Northern Virginia

Major General Stuart now ordered me to prepare to advance. I ordered *General McGowan* and *Archer* to move forward, as the line formed by their brigades was not perpendicular to the Plank Road, but inclined to the right and rear. *Archer's* brigade only advanced a short distance before it became hotly engaged, the enemy being strongly posted behind breastworks making an angle with the Plank Road. I now gave the order for a general advance. . . . *Pender* and *Thomas*, on the left, found the enemy posted behind a breastwork of logs and brush, immediately in their front, at a distance of about 150 yards. The breastworks were charged and carried, the men never hesitating for a moment, driving the enemy before them and pursuing him until a second line was reached, which was in like manner broken. A third line . . . was now encountered. After a desperate and prolonged fight, without supports or a piece of artillery to aid them, but on their part subjected to heavy artillery fire of from ten to twelve pieces, these gallant brigades fell back in order to the breastworks from which the enemy had been driven, and which they held until re-enforcements were brought up, when again the attack was renewed and the enemy driven from this part of the field. . . .

Lane's brigade, supported by the Fortieth and Forty-seventh Virginia Regiments (*Heth's* brigade), and *McGowan's* brigade advanced and charged the enemy behind his breastworks, who was supported by twenty-nine pieces of artillery. I cannot conceive of any body of men ever being subjected to a more galling fire than this force. The brigades . . . drove the enemy from his works and held them for some time, but were finally compelled to fall back, which was unavoidable from the course that affairs had assumed on the right of the line. . . . Under the murderous fire of artillery to which they were particularly exposed, no officers or men could have done better. [*O.R.*, XXV, Part 1, pp. 891–92.]

Report of Brig. James H. Lane, CSA, Commanding Brigade,
A. P. Hill's Division, Second Army Corps, Army
of Northern Virginia

On Sunday morning, about sunrise, the whole brigade was wheeled a little to the left, that the line might be perpendicular to the Plank Road, and then, in obedience to orders, moved gallantly forward, with shouts, driving in the enemy's skirmishers, and handsomely charging and carrying their breastworks . . . on a hill commanded by the Chancellorsville Hill, which was fortified with a line of earthworks for twenty-eight pieces of artillery, running nearly parallel to our position, and between 400 and 500 yards distant, with a stream of water intervening. As soon as we had dislodged their infantry, these guns, with others, opened a murderous fire of shell, grape, and canister upon us, a fresh column of their infantry was thrown against us, and, with our right flank completely turned, we were forced back with the loss of about one-third of the command. . . .

As soon as the . . . brigade was reformed and replenished with ammunition, they were taken back into the woods to the left of the Plank Road, to the support of *General Colquitt's* command, which was then nearly out of ammunition. The woods which we entered were on fire; the heat was excessive, the smoke arising from burning blankets, oilcloths, etc., very offensive. The dead and dying of the enemy could be seen on all sides enveloped in flames, and the ground on which we formed was so hot as at first to be disagreeable to our feet. . . . The men took their positions without a murmur, and notwithstanding their previous hard marching, desperate fighting, and sleepless nights, remained under arms again the whole of Sunday night in the front line, while heavy skirmishing was going on. Never have I seen men fight more gallantly and bear fatigue and hardship more cheerfully. I shall always feel proud of the noble bearing of my brigade in the battle of Chancellorsville – the bloodiest in which it has ever taken a part. . . . The brigade loss is . . . 909. [*O.R.*, XXV, Part 1, 917–18.]

Report of Col. J. M. Brockenbrough, CSA, Fortieth Virginia Infantry, Commanding Heth's Brigade, A. P. Hill's Division, Second Army Corps, Army of Northern Virginia

During the night the enemy was not idle, but worked like beavers in erecting the most formidable barricades and breastworks, thus partially relieving themselves of the panic of the previous evening and determining them to give battle.

Early on the morning of the 3d, the brigade . . . was again deployed in line of battle extending on either side of the road, the Fortieth and Forty-seventh Virginia Regiments on the right, following *General Lane's* brigade; the Fifty-fifth and Twenty-second Virginia on the left, supporting *General Pender*. The advance of our leading line became irregular, and the turnpike, which separated the brigade, being much more elevated than the ground upon either side, the interval between the two portions became so considerable as not to be seen the one by the other. Being in close proximity to the enemy, our advance line in a few minutes became hotly engaged, and we were exposed to the most deadly fire I have ever experienced. Very soon the troops in advance were forced back through our lines, leaving us without support on either flank. The two regiments on the left of the road had by this time moved within 100 yards of the enemy's intrenchments, and, while fiercely engaging them, had their left turned and were compelled to retire. The two regiments on the right remained in their position, awaiting support to charge the enemy's works.

Finding no one disposed to move, though many thousands had taken shelter behind the barricade, our line was formed, and, being joined by about 1,200 troops of different brigades, we led the second charge. Upon reaching the edge of the field, these troops, with a yell, increased their speed to a double-quick, and such was the impetuosity of the charge that the enemy's resistance, though fierce and bloody, was of short duration.

We soon triumphantly mounted their intrenchments, completely routing them from a position from which it is almost impossible to conceive how an army could be driven. On gaining these works, we discovered the field literally crowded with men fleeing in every direction, and poured into them a deadly fire. Occupying this position about two minutes, we discovered troops advancing through the woods upon our left, and supposed they were friends until a volley fired into our left and rear removed the delusion. Their numbers and position being vastly superior to ours, and being unsupported on our left, we were again forced to retire.

As soon as our artillery shelled this piece of woods, we advanced a third time, and held the position. Artillery now coming to our support, soon silenced the enemy's batteries (which had harassed us during the entire day), and forced them to abandon in great confusion their strong and well-selected position, to take shelter in the Wilderness and retreat toward the river. [*O.R.*, XXV, Part 1, pp. 894–95.]

Continue to drive in the same direction on **STUART DRIVE** for about 0.4 mile until you come to the cleared area and artillery position at **HAZEL GROVE**. Pull off to the **LEFT** and **PARK** in front of the sign. You can read the accounts at this site if you wish, but you will get a far better appreciation of the significance of the terrain at Hazel Grove if you walk about 100 yards into the woods. To do this, dismount and walk to the opposite side of the road, cross the clearing and enter the woods at the corner of the clearing that was at your right rear when you parked your car. Follow the faint trail and the remnants of an old barbed wire fence into the woods about 60 yards to the trace of the old breastworks, and then follow that line another 40 yards. **TURN LEFT**, crossing in front of the defensive line, and move at a right angle to that line until you come to a steel cable marking the Park boundary. You now have a good view of the open ground toward Lewis Run, the watercourse that has been dammed to form the lake to your left front. If you cannot see the lake, move a few yards along the cable until your line of sight is clear of obstructions.

British officers at Hazel Grove with Branch Spaulding lecturing August 20, 1941. (NPS)

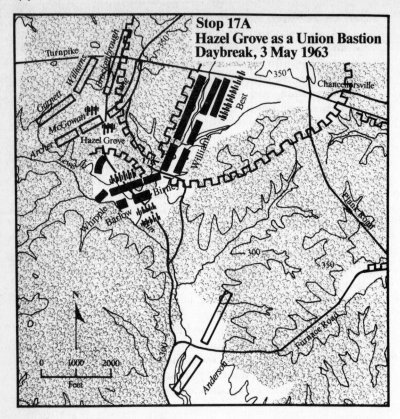

Stop 17A
Hazel Grove as a Union Bastion
Daybreak, 3 May 1963

STOP 17A, HAZEL GROVE

The first troops to occupy Hazel Grove were men of the Third Corps, who reached here about sunset on May 1. From here Union observers had spotted *Jackson's* column marching the following morning to the southwest, and guns on this elevation, about 300 yards to the west, fired upon *Jackson's* men and trains. It was also from here that Sickles had pushed two divisions forward that afternoon to harrass *Jackson's* rear guard at Catharine Furnace.

After *Jackson* drove the Eleventh Corps from its positions, Hazel Grove became key terrain, not only because it was one of the few commanding pieces of ground in the area suitable for artillery but also because as long as this position remained under Union control, it would be difficult for the forces under *Lee* and *Stuart* to reunite.

Hazel Grove was the name given to a large plateau that extended along Scott's Creek to the north. At the time of the battle the cleared area formed an irregular rectangle running nearly northeast and southwest, perhaps a quarter of a mile in extent, "but was in no place farther than two hundred yards from the woods. . . . On the south and east it sloped off into a marsh and a creek" which today form Cool Spring Lake. [*Battles and Leaders*, III, p. 179.] A farm house and outbuildings stood in the southern portion of the clearing, where the large resort buildings now stand. A road that connected the Plank Road (at Stop 15) with Catharine Furnace passed through that farmstead, following the same trace used by the main road through Wilderness Resorts, and at the time of the battle there was apparently some kind of path that extended from the house to Fairview. Your car is parked on the extreme eastern tip of Hazel Grove: the cleared plateau extended some 400 yards from that point, across the land you view from this position.

The works you followed to reach this position were thrown up by the Twenty-seventh Indiana and the Third Wisconsin, of Ruger's brigade, Williams' division, Twelfth Corps, on the night of 1 May, after the skirmish involving *Wright's* Confederate brigade in the vicinity of the Hazel Grove farm house. Ruger was ordered specifically to "construct breastworks in the edge of the wood, completely covering by their . . . cross-fire the open ground in front of the position of the brigade and also a portion of the line then occupied by General Birney's division," Third Army Corps. [*O.R.*, XXV, Part 1, p. 708.]

At noon on May 2, Sickles ordered Birney's division to move forward, pierce *Jackson's* column, and seize possession of the road over which it was passing. Crossing Scott's Run, which "was some 5 feet deep, with high banks," Birney encountered no opposition until he reached Catharine Furnace, which was quickly seized by Berdan's Sharpshooters. "After an exciting artillery duel" with a battery posted near the Welford House, Birney sent two regiments to support the Sharpshooters who were engaged with the Twenty-third Georgia, posted in the unfinished railroad cut near the Welford House. Meanwhile Sickles ordered Birney to await the arrival of Whipple's division and a brigade from the Twelfth Corps to support his left, and of Barlow's brigade from the Eleventh Corps to protect his right, before continuing his advance.

At 6.30 p.m. Birney received orders from Hooker "to advance rapidly." Two brigades were sent against "the retreating column of the enemy," while a third kept open the communication to Catharine Furnace. Finding Confederates "in some force on three sides," Birney then assumed a defensive posture and was preparing to bivouac when he received word that the Eleventh Corps had given way "in entire disorder," and he was ordered to return at once to Hazel Grove. But before Sickles' infantry could reach this location, where two cavalry regiments were in bivouac and the reserve ammunition train of the Third Corps was parked, along with many other trains and batteries, Brig. Gen. Pleasanton had already organized his defense. [*O.R.*, XXV, Part 1, p. 408.]

Report of Maj. Gen. Daniel E. Sickles, USA, Commanding Third Corps, Army of the Potomac

Regarding the moment opportune for the advance of General Pleasanton with his cavalry and horse battery [to Catharine Furnace], I was about to dispatch a staff officer to bring him forward when it was reported to me that the Eleventh Corps had yielded the right flank of the army to the enemy, who was advancing rapidly, and, indeed, was already in my rear. . . . I did not credit his statement until an aide-de-camp of General Warren, of General Hooker's staff, confirmed the report, and asked for a regiment of cavalry to check the movement. The Eighth Pennsylvania Cavalry was immediately sent by General Pleasonton. . . . I had only time to despatch staff officers to recall Birney and Whipple, when the enemy's scouts and some dragoons disclosed themselves as I rode toward the bridge [built earlier that day] across Scott's Run for the purpose of making disposition to . . . arrest this disaster. Meeting General Pleasanton, we hastened to make the best available disposition to attack *Jackson's* columns on their right flank.

I confided to Pleasanton the direction of the artillery—three batteries of my reserve . . . and his own horse battery. The only supports at hand comprised two small regiments of cavalry and one regiment of infantry, of Whipple's division. Time was everything. The fugitives of the Eleventh Corps swarmed from the woods and swept frantically over the cleared fields, in which my artillery was parked. The exulting enemy at their heels mingled yells with their volleys, and in the confusion . . . it seemed as if cannon and caissons, dragoons, cannoneers, and infantry could never be disentangled from the mass in which they were suddenly thrown. Fortunately there was only one obvious outlet for these panic-stricken hordes after rushing between and over our guns, and this was through a ravine crossed in two or three places by the headwaters of Scott's Run. This was soon made impassable by the reckless crowd choking up the way. . . .

A few minutes was enough to restore comparative order and get our artillery in position. The enemy showing himself on the plain [the high ground east of Dowdell's Tavern] Pleasanton met the shock at short range with the well-directed fire of twenty-two pieces, double-shotted with canister. The rebels pressed up the Plank Road rapidly. . . . and our batteries opened on the advancing columns with crushing power. The heads of the columns were swept away to the woods, from which they opened a furious but ineffectual fire of musketry. Twice they attempted a flank movement, but the first was checked by our guns, and the second and most formidable was baffled by the advance of Whipple and Birney, who were coming up rapidly, but in perfect order, and forming in lines of brigades in rear of the artillery, and on the flanks. My position was now secure in the adequate infantry support which had arrived; the loud cheers of our men as twilight closed the combat vainly challenged the enemy to renew the encounter.

While these movements were in progress on the flank, the First and Second Brigades of the Second Division (Berry's), which had been held in reserve at Chancellorsville, were ordered by the general-in-chief to take a position perpendicular to the Plank Road and check the enemy's advance. . . . These dispositions were made without the steadiness of these veteran troops being in the least disturbed by the torrents of fugitives breaking through their intervals. The regiments of the first line, covered by their skirmishers, immediately threw up a strong breastwork of logs and abatis. Prisoners captured (among them an aide of *General Stuart's*, who had come forward with a party to remove a caisson left by the Eleventh Corps) disclosed to us the enemy's lines of battle, about 300 yards in front, in the woods. Osborn, Berry's chief of artillery . . . placed Dimick's and Winslow's batteries on the crest of the hill [about 700 yards west of Chancellorsville] perpendicular to the road and 300 or 400 yards in rear of the line of battle. These admirable dispositions, promptly made, the splendid fire of the artillery, and the imposing attitude of an iron wall of infantry co-operated with our flank attack to check the enemy's advance, which was effectually accomplished before dark. . . .

After dark, the enemy's line could only be defined by the flash of his musketry, from which a stream of fire occasionally almost enveloped us. As often as these attacks were renewed . . . they were repulsed by our guns. . . . Ascertaining the enterprise of cutting us off from the army to be hopeless, the enemy sullenly withdrew to the line of rifle-pits and breastworks formerly held by the Eleventh Corps. . . . To quote the felicitous observations of General Pleasanton—

Such was the fight at the head of Scott's Run—artillery against infantry at 300 yards; the infantry in the forest, the artillery in the clearing. War presents many anomolies, but few so strange in its results as this. [*O.R.*, Part 1, pp. 386–89.]

The abortive night attack that followed has already been described at Stop 15.

Report of General Robert E. Lee, CSA, Commanding Army of Northern Virginia

As soon as the sound of cannon gave notice of *Jackson's* attack on the enemy's right, our troops in front of Chancellorsville were ordered to press him strongly on the left, to prevent re-enforcements being sent to the point assailed. They were directed not to attack in force unless a favorable opportunity should present itself, and, while continuing to cover the roads leading from their respective positions toward Chancellorsville, to incline to the left so as to connect with *Jackson's* right as he closed in upon the center. These orders were well executed, our troops advancing up to the enemy's intrenchments, while several batteries played with good effect upon his lines until prevented by the increasing darkness.

Early on the morning of the 3d, *General Stuart* renewed the attack upon the enemy, who had strengthened his right during the night with additional breastworks, while a large number of guns, protected by intrenchments, were posted so as to sweep the woods through which our troops had to advance. *Hill's* division [now commanded by *Heth*] was in front, with *Colston* in the second line and *Rodes* in the third. The second and third lines soon advanced to the support of the first, and the whole became hotly engaged. [*O.R.*, Part 1, p. 799.]

Report of Brig. Gen. Henry Heth, CSA, Commanding Brigade and A. P. Hill's Division, Second Army Corps, Army of Northern Virginia

General Archer advanced with his brigade. Conforming his line of battle to that of the enemy, he charged the works in his front, and, without the least halt or hesitation, carried them, driving the enemy before him, who outnumbered him five to one. *General Archer* succeeded in capturing a battery of four guns. By his gallant attack he secured the key to the enemy's position, clearing a hill [your present location] and open space in his front, and thus gaining for our artillery a position from which they were enabled to silence the 29-gun battery of the enemy, which had inflicted so much loss upon our lines. From this position our artillery had also a raking fire on the enemy's works on our right. *General Archer*, after carrying the hill . . . advanced beyond the open space and attacked the enemy on his right. He was joined by *Major-General Anderson*. [*O.R.*, XXV, Part 1, pp. 891–92.]

Report of Brig. Gen. J. J. Archer, CSA, Commanding Brigade,
A. P. Hill's Division, Second Army Corps, Army of
Northern Virginia

About sunrise we moved forward to the attack, through dense pine timber, driving before us the enemy's skirmishers, and, at a distance of 400 yards, emerging into the open field in front of a battery, which was placed on an abrupt hill near a spring-house. We advanced at double-quick, and captured 4 pieces of artillery and about 100 prisoners, driving the infantry supports in confusion before us.

From this position the enemy could be seen in heavy force in the woods, which commenced about 600 yards diagonally to the right and front, and in the high open ground to the front. . . . My brigade, which was at the beginning only 1,400 strong and entirely unsupported, attacked with great intrepidity; but the position was strongly intrenched and manned by vastly greater numbers, and we were forced to retire from within 70 yards of the intrenchments. We again formed and advanced to the attack, and were again forced to retire. I now moved the brigade to the point where we had captured the batteries, to await the arrival of re-enforcements. Soon after, *Major [W.J.] Pegram* came up and occupied the position with artillery. *Colonel [John T.] Mercer* came up on the left with three regiments of *Doles'* brigade, and *General Anderson* came up from the rear on my right with his division. He soon after moved to the right, leaving me in support of the artillery, which had opened a heavy and effective fire upon the enemy, which was hotly returned, although with little effect.

In a few minutes *General [R. E.] Lee* rode up, and soon directed me to move forward with my own brigade and the three regiments of *Doles'*. . . . After advancing 400 or 500 yards, *Colonel Mercer* requested a short halt until the ammunition, which had just arrived, could be distributed to his regiments. During this halt I received an order through one of *General Stuart's* staff not to advance farther until I received the order from him; but other troops coming up on *Colonel Mercer's* left and on my right, I moved slowly forward and soon came, on ascending the hill in front of Chancellorsville, in full view and range of the enemy's cannon, which opened a heavy fire upon us. [*O.R.*, XXV, Part 1, p. 925.]

Archer could not have known it, but had he delayed his attack for an half hour or so he could have seized Hazel Grove with scarcely a fight, for at daylight Hooker had ordered Sickles to withdraw from this position and occupy a new line of intrenchments at Fairview, placing his guns in field-works on the crest of the hill in rear of his infantry. [*Official Records*, XXV, Part 1, p. 390.]

> *Report of Brig. Gen. Charles K. Graham, USA,*
> *Commanding First Brigade, First Division, Third Army Corps,*
> *Army of the Potomac*
>
> Early on the morning of May 3, I was ordered to send a regiment to repair the bridges over the swampy ground on our right flank, to enable the artillery to move off in safety. I sent the One hundred and fifth Pennsylvania. . . . At this time the enemy opened a brisk fire on our whole line. The troops that had been in my front, and which I was ordered to follow from the field, were now retiring hastily, leaving my lines exposed to a galling fire from the rapid advance of the enemy. I now commenced retiring, having first given them a few volleys from the Fifty-seventh, One hundred and forty-first, and Sixty-third Pennsylvania Volunteers, which formed my left, and were most exposed. This served to check the enemy to some extent, and enabled me to bring off my command in better order than I other-wise could have done. We now retired rapidly, closely followed, and subjected to a hot fire. We followed the rear of Whipple's division, passing to the right of the batteries on the hill, and forming again to the left of the Plank Road, and directly behind the graveyard near Fairview. My formation was in close column of regiments. [*O.R.*, XXV, Part 1, p. 414.]

Now return to the area where your car is parked and position yourself near the guns. As you view the cleared ground to the north-east you can visualize the famous artillery duel with Union guns in position at Fairview.

STOP 17B

When ordered to evacuate Hazel Grove, Sickles fell back upon Fair-view, the high ground that you can see over the sights of these Confeder-ate guns. Here a new line of breastworks had been constructed. From 30 to as many as 50 Confederate guns crowned these heights to wage a memorable duel with 40 guns at Fairview. The numbers vary because not all were in action at any one time: there were always batteries that had been relieved or sent to the rear to refill ammunition chests.

Report of Col. E. P. Alexander, CSA, Commanding Artillery Battalion, First Army Corps, and Acting Chief of Artillery, Second Army Corps, Army of Northern Virginia

Being called to the command of the artillery on the field by the wounding of *Colonel [S.] Crutchfield*, I reported to *(General Stuart)* at 10 p.m. on the night of the 2d, and was directed to reconnoiter the ground during the night and post the necessary guns by dawn for an early attack. A careful examination showed that our attack must be made entirely through the dense wood in front of us, the enemy holding his edge of it with infantry protected by abatis and breastworks, supported by a numerous and powerful artillery in the fields behind, within canister range of the woods.

There were but two outlets through which our artillery could be moved—one the Plank Road, debouching within 400 yards of twenty-seven of the enemy's guns, protected by breastworks and enfiladed for a long distance by a part of them, as well as by two guns behind a breastwork thrown up across the road abreast of their line of abatis and infantry cover; the second outlet was a cleared vista or lane through the pines (a half mile to the south of the Plank Road), some 200 yards long by 25 wide. This opened upon a cleared ridge, held by the enemy's artillery, about 400 yards distant. This vista was reached from the Plank Road by two small roads, No. 1 leaving the Plank Road near our infantry lines [Stop 15] and running parallel with and close behind them to the head of the vista, where it crossed them and went perpendicularly down the vista to the enemy's position; thence it bore to the left or north, and, crossing a ravine, came up on the plateau in front of Chancellorsville, at the south end of the enemy's line of artillery breastworks. Road No. 2 left the Plank Road a half mile behind our lines, and ran into road No. 1 at the head of the vista.

At dawn I posted seventeen guns as follows:

Captain E. A. Marye, of *Walker's* battalion, with two Napoleons and two rifles, in the Plank Road where it was crossed by our advanced lines of infantry;

Captain [E. B.] Brunson, of *Walker's* battalion, with four rifles, also in the Plank Road a short distance in rear of *Captain Marye*, to fire over his head and to his right and left over our infantry (in no other way could sufficient fire be thrown down the Plank Road);

Captain [R. C. M.] Page, of *Carter's* battalion, with three Napoleons, was placed in thin woods on road No. 1, 300 yards south of Plank Road, to fire upon their infantry lines until the enemy were started from their cover, when he was to advance down road No. 1 through the vista and join the artillery force which would operate there;

Lieutenant [John H.] Chamberlayne, with two Napoleons, was masked in the pines at the head of the vista, to assist the infantry in forcing a passage through it and to advance with them;

Major [W. J.] Pegram, of *Walker's* battalion, was placed with four Napoleons on Road No. 2, 400 yards in rear of the vista, on a small cleared knoll, to fire over the pines at enemy's smoke, and advance down road No. 2 through the vista as soon as a start was made in front.

The rest of the artillery (*Alexander's, Carter's, Jones', McIntosh's,* and part of *Walker's* battalion) was held in reserve in rear.

About daylight the attack was commenced vigorously. Within ninety minutes the enemy were driven from the ridge in front of the vista, and the guns designated for this work (under *Pegram, Page,* and *Chamberlayne*) at once moved out and occupied it, having a fine field of fire, both at the enemy's breastworks and artillery, and somewhat of a flank fire upon those of their guns which commanded the Plank Road. These guns were immediately re-enforced by ten guns of my own battalion. . . . Their fire was assisted by *Jordan's* battery, of *Alexander's* battalion, which here came in on the right with *Anderson's* division. *Capt. O. B. Taylor,* with four Napoleons and part of *Colonel Jones'* battalion, was shortly afterward advanced upon the Plank Road to re-enforce our fire down it and into the woods on the right and left.

About 9 a.m. the magnificent fire of our guns on the right, and the steady advance of our infantry, which had routed the enemy from the abatis lines, and was beginning to fire upon his intrenched artillery and forming for a charge, proved too much for the enemy's nerve, and with one accord his entire artillery limbered up and abandoned their breastworks and retreated to the immediate vicinity of the Chancellorsville house, whence they again opened heavily. Our infantry meanwhile followed and occupied their works, firing on their retreat, while all the artillery on the right limbered up and moved forward, taking position under their abandoned breastworks and in the field to the south of them, and reopened upon the position of Chancellorsville, assisted by the artillery on the Plank Road. This was accomplished successfully under a hot and enfilading fire, and our guns, when opened, speedily drove the enemy from this his third position. His guns having taken refuge behind the houses, our guns were for a while directed on them, and the large brick tavern was set on fire and burned, General Hooker, who had taken shelter in it, being wounded there.

At 10 a.m. the enemy retreated down the road toward the United States Ford, and took refuge behind the heavy works, which served as a *tete-de-pont* to his crossing, and eventually covered his retreat. This assault must ever be memorable for its fierceness, vigor, and success, against superior numbers and a position that might well be deemed impregnable, and I consider the part borne by the artillery, in its prompt and thorough co-operation with the gallant assaults of the infantry, as the most brilliant page of its history. Its loss was heavy, but I cannot now specify it for the lack of reports of subordinate officers. [*O.R.*, XXV, Part 1, pp. 822–24.]

Writing forty years after the event, *General Alexander* saw the events described above in a somewhat different perspective.

The battle was still Hooker's, had he fought where he stood. But about dawn he made the fatal mistake of recalling Sickles from the Hazel Grove position, which he was holding with Whipple's and Birney's divisions, and five batteries. There has rarely been a more gratuitous gift of a battle-field. Sickles had a good position and force enough to hold it, even without reinforcements, though ample reinforcements were available. The Federal line was longer and overlapped ours on its right, and our only opportunity to use artillery was through the narrow vista . . . which was scarcely sufficient for four guns, and had but a very restricted view. . . . A Federal battery, supported by two regiments, had been designated as a rear-guard, and it alone occupied the plateau when our advance was made, though the rear of the retiring column was still near. [*Military Memoirs of a Confederate*, p. 345.]

Stops 17B, 18, 19

Hazel Grove as a Confederate Fire Base in Stuart's Attack. Situation about 7:00 A.M. 3 May 1863

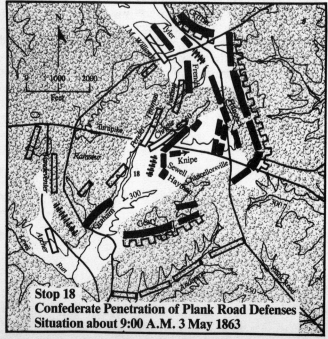

Stop 18

Confederate Penetration of Plank Road Defenses Situation about 9:00 A.M. 3 May 1863

Continue driving in the same direction on STUART DRIVE. When you reach the fork in the road, TURN LEFT on BERRY-PAXTON DRIVE and drive about 0.5 mile to the turnaround. Park there, dismount, and walk out toward the guns at FAIRVIEW. When you reach the epaulements, TURN LEFT, and walk down to the treeline.

STOP 18, FAIRVIEW

Report of Capt. Thomas W. Osborn, U.S.A., First New York Light Artillery, Chief of Artillery, Third Army Corps

At 4 p.m. [May 2] we realized a heavy attack was being made on the left, and the varying direction of the sound showed us too plainly our forces were giving way. The division [Berry] was soon ordered to the front, the batteries following. . . . As we passed General Hooker's headquarters, a scene burst upon us which, God grant, may never again be seen in the Federal Army. . . . The Eleventh Corps had been routed, and were fleeing to the river like scared sheep. The men and artillery filled the roads, its sides, and the skirts of the field, and it appeared that no two of one company could be found together. Aghast and terror-stricken, heads bare and panting for breath, they pleaded like infants at the mother's breast that we would let them pass to the rear unhindered. The troops in the old division, unwavering, and the artillery, reckless of life or limb, passed through this disorganized mass of men. Reaching the crest of the hill, I left the batteries of Dimick and Winslow on the brow, taking position perpendicular to the road, Dimick taking the right, excepting one section . . . which I took about 400 yards to the front, on a line with the front of the woods, and only a few yards in the rear of our line of battle.

At this time (a little after sunset), a rebel battery opened fire on the batteries on the brow of the hill, and less than 1,000 yards from them. Winslow and Mason, in command of two section of Dimick's battery, accepted the challenge, and almost immediately silenced them.

All was now quiet, excepting that we could constantly hear the enemy, from 300 to 1,000 yards in our front, massing their troops and moving their artillery. It was now evident that their force was large, as the swearing of officers and giving orders sounded like the chattering of a multitude. This continued until 9.30 o'clock, during which time several commissioned officers rode within our lines of pickets and were captured. At this time, I distinctly saw the head of a column moving down the road, it being a beautiful moonlight night. The column seemed to cover the entire breadth of the road, and moved very cautiously until within 150 yards of us, when it began to deploy in line of battle. At this moment, I directed Lieutenant Dimick to open with canister, clearing the road almost instantly. The batteries on the crest opened, at the signal, upon the road beyond, and, taking the reports of prisoners as reliable, the havoc in their ranks was fearful.

This same movement of the enemy occurred at 10.30 and at 12 midnight, excepting he did not move his forces upon the open road, but in the woods, and the challenge to open fire was given by the enemy's infantry against our own, but the results were each time the same, the enemy being at each assault repulsed. He used his artillery considerably, but to no great effect, only wounding a few artillery-men and killing a few horses. The practice of the artillery this evening was the most splendid I ever saw. The lines of battle at several times became closely engaged, but the batteries on the crest varied their elevation most admirably, keeping precisely the time of fuse required and the exact elevation necessary to strike the rebel line of battle, and I have yet to learn that one Federal soldier was struck by one of our shots or a premature explosion of a shell; yet we repeatedly tore the rebel lines to fragments, and assisted our gallant infantry to drive them, shattered, to the rear. . . .

During the night, Captain Squier, chief engineer of General Berry's staff, threw up small works in front of the guns, which were of great benefit during the engagement of the following day.

At 5 o'clock in the morning, the enemy attacked us in force, and, after a very severe fight . . . the Federal line began to fall back. From the first moment I learned the position of the enemy, I played upon him with the artillery, the section in the road using very short fuse and canister as the enemy moved to and fro. In the movement of this section, securing and defending the front of our line from the persis-tent attacks of the enemy, notwithstanding its own exposed condi-tion, and under a most galling fire from the rebel sharpshooters and line of battle, Lieutenant Dimick showed the skill and judgment of an accomplished artillery officer and the intrepid bravery of the truest soldier. After holding this position for upward of an hour, his men fighting bravely, but falling rapidly around him (his horse being shot under him), and our infantry crowding back until his flanks were exposed, I gave him the order to limber and fall back. In doing this

his horses became entangled in the harness, and in freeing them he received a shot . . . in the spine. . . .

The division artillery was now confined entirely to the brow of the hill. . . . The battle was now beginning with almost unparalleled fury, the enemy throwing his troops upon us in double and triple lines, and then in solid masses. The infantry of the division fought with stubborn desperation, and the contending forces surged backward and forward like two huge waves, mingling and unmingling as the one or the other gained a momentary advantage. It was at this time that the artillery carried the most fearful havoc among the enemy's forces. . . .

During the heat of the battle, I perceived the firing of my guns began to slacken, and learning the ammunition was giving out, I applied for another battery of Captain Randolph, chief of corps artillery, and though he gave me orders for Captain von Puttkammer's Eleventh New York Independent Battery, I could not get him to the front, and I was compelled to withdraw my guns, and thus caused the gallant old division to fall back before the rebel masses. [*O.R.*, XXV, Part 1, pp. 483–5.]

Report of Lieut. George B. Winslow, USA, Battery D, First New York Light Artillery, Second Division, Third Army Corps, Army of the Potomac

I . . . placed my battery in the first eligible position I could find, which was upon the brow of the hill some 500 or 600 yards in rear of our advance line, my right resting upon the Plank Road. The position, as the battle developed, proved an admirable one. . . .

During the night, I threw my battery into *echelon*, at about two-thirds the usual intervals and distances, the better to command the slope of the hill and both flanks, and, when not engaged in firing, had my men throw up earthworks in front of the guns, which proved of great service in the next morning's engagement. Toward morning, Captain Squier, of Major-General Berry's staff, who had a pioneer company under his command, relieved my men of this duty.

At the first glimmer of day on Sunday, the 3d instant, the battle opened furiously upon our left and front, the enemy driving our lines back upon their supports after a brief but brisk engagement. Our artillery fired upon the enemy's infantry until the two lines were so near each other that our fire was alike dangerous to friend and foe. Berry's division, in our front at the time, repulsed the enemy handsomely, as it did repeatedly during the morning, aided by the artillery.

Our left having fallen back, our troops in front were exposed to a heavy fire both in front and flank, and finally fell back a short distance, but in good order, the batteries keeping the enemy in check while our infantry rallied and advanced, regaining their former position.

Four or five times our infantry retired a short distance, and again obstinately advanced, driving the enemy, who seemed to outnumber them two to one. At each successive attack, the enemy's numbers increased. As they came down the hill in almost solid masses, our artillery greeted them with shot and shell, causing a fearful destruction in their ranks.

Just before the last charge of the New Jersey Brigade, in front of my battery, the enemy came down in solid masses, covering, as it were, the whole ground in front of our lines, with at least a dozen stand of colors flying in their midst. I immediately ordered my guns loaded with solid shot, and, as our infantry fell back and wheeled to the left, unmasking the battery, fired at about 1½ degrees' elevation. The effect was most terrible. A few rounds sufficed to drive the enemy in great confusion up the hill, whereupon our infantry again charged and took several stand of colors.

The enemy then crossed the road and came down in the woods upon our right. Just before this, the section of Dimick's battery in front had been compelled to retire, and, soon after, his guns upon my right also withdrew. Meanwhile the enemy continued to advance, our own troops slowly retiring before him. In a few moments, the former came out of the woods not more than 100 yards from the muzzle of my guns, planted their colors by the side of the road, and commenced picking off my men and horses. When a sufficient number had rallied around their colors, my guns having been previously loaded with canister, I gave the order to fire. In this way they were repeatedly driven back. They were, however, rapidly closing around us in the woods upon our right, not more than 25 or 30 yards from my right gun, when I received your orders to limber up and retire; besides, my ammunition was exhausted. I limbered from the left successively, continuing to fire until my last piece was limbered. [*O.R.*, XXV, Part 1, pp. 487–88.]

Report of Brig. Gen. Joseph B. Carr, USA, Commanding Second Division, Third Army Corps, Army of the Potomac

On the morning of May 3, at 7.30 o'clock, I was informed by Lieutenant Freeman, aide-de-camp, of the division staff, that Major-General Berry had fallen, mortally wounded, and . . . command of the division devolved on me. . . . At this time my second line was about to engage the enemy, my first line being compelled to fall back in consequence of an injudicious retreat of a Maryland regiment, belonging to General Knipe's brigade [Twelfth Army Corps], jeopardizing my left flank, as well as a section of Dimick's battery, then in position on the Plank Road. On making this discovery, I at once ordered the Eleventh New Jersey Volunteers, Colonel McAllister, to support the artillery, which it did, until the battery was removed to the rear, in a manner highly creditable.

On going to the left of the road, I found the Third [the New Jersey] Brigade advancing on the enemy in two lines. This command maintained its position until forced back by overwhelming masses of the rebels. Subsequently this brigade made several charges with the bayonet, capturing eight stands of colors . . . and over 1,000 prisoners, adding fresh laurels to its almost universal fame. . . .

The division held its position for over four hours against a force of the enemy three times as great as its own, and until its ammunition was entirely expended, when, receiving no support, it retired. I immediately reformed the balance of the First and Third Brigades . . . in the rear of the Chancellor house, but, in consequence of a galling fire from the enemy's artillery, was compelled to move down the road to the opening opposite the white house [at the apex of the final Union position, Stop 22]. Here I . . . [was] ordered to support General Whipple's division, on the left of the road leading to the Chancellor house. [*O.R.*, XXV, Part 1, pp. 445–46.]

Report of Col. William J. Sewell, USA, Fifth New Jersey Infantry, Commanding Third Brigade, Second Division, Third Army Corps, Army of the Potomac

At 4.30 a.m., May 3, the brigade was under arms, and immediately afterward was placed in position in the second line, its right resting on the Plank Road, and connecting with the First Brigade of this division.

At 6 a.m. skirmishing commenced on the left, and soon extended along the whole front, accompanied by a hot artillery fire from the enemy, which was very destructive to the regiments in the second line.

At 6.30 a.m. the enemy advanced to the attack, driving in our skirmishers, and soon afterward a part of the first line nearest the road. The position vacated by the first line was taken by the Fifth and Eighth New Jersey Regiments, of this command, when the engagement became general, the enemy advancing in such strength that the second line became engaged in fifteen minutes after the first line was attacked.

It has been the fortune of this brigade to have participated in many hard-fought actions, but former experience was nothing in comparison to the determination of the enemy to carry this position. Battalion after battalion was hurled against our ranks, each one to lose its colors and many of its men taken prisoners. The Seventh New Jersey here took five of the enemy's colors; the Fifth New Jersey took three. The brigade took at least 1,000 prisoners.

At 8.30 a.m. I was informed by Capt. T. W. Eayre, assistant adjutant-general, of General Mott being wounded, as also Colonels Burling and Park, which left me in command of the brigade. General Mott up to this time had been wherever his presence was necessary, his gallantry in this as in previous actions inspiring confidence in all.

I now rode to the right of my line, and, crossing the Plank Road in search of General Berry, found that he had been killed some time previous. My ammunition was nearly out and the enemy on my right flank. I here found the Eleventh New Jersey, of the First Brigade, and requested Colonel McAllister to advance for the protection of my flank, to which he very gallantly responded, driving the enemy and relieving me from an enfilading fire, but to hold the position longer required reinforcements. I sent Captain Eayre to Major General Sickles to state my condition, but did not receive any encouragement. Immediately afterward I went to him myself, but with the same result: there were no reserves at his disposal.

The enemy still advancing in great force, I fell back slowly in rear of the line of batteries, where, under the orders of General Sickles . . . I reformed the remnant of the brigade. Previous to this time, Colonel Francine had retired from the field (unwell), having fought his regiment gallantly up to that time, but inopportunely now taking with him some 400 of the brigade, under the impression that I had been wounded, which left me with about 300 men and the twelve colors of the brigade.

The batteries soon retired, their positions being immediately occupied by the enemy's infantry. The fire became so hot that to remain in that position would be only to sacrifice my men, and, having no orders to retire, I advanced once more on the double-quick, again driving the enemy, taking possession of the small works thrown up for the protection of our guns, and planting the colors of the brigade on the parapets. My last round was fired here, and, no signs of support coming up, I retired from the field under a severe fire from the enemy's artillery and infantry, losing men at every step. . . . Most of the officers and men are supposed to have been killed or wounded when falling back.

Total killed 55; wounded 420; missing 48 . . . Total 523. [*O.R.*, XXV, Part 1, pp. 473–74. Col. L. R. Francine "through exhaustion," his voice having left him "entirely," and "being scarcely able to speak in a whisper," left the field upon the advice of his surgeon. *Ibid.*, p. 478.]

Report of Maj. Gen. Henry W. Slocum, USA, Commanding Twelfth Army Corps, Army of the Potomac

At daybreak on Sunday, May 3, the enemy commenced the attack on Williams' and Berry's divisions. The troops of Birney's division . . . occupying the hill [Hazel Grove] in prolongation of Geary's line, soon retired. A battery belonging to the same division, which was with these troops, was, I am informed, captured by the enemy. I know that immediately after the infantry had retired from this position a battery was used on this point against Geary's line with fearful effect, as it enfiladed his position completely. The efforts of the enemy for three hours were directed mainly against the divisions of Generals A. S. Williams and Berry.

Repeated efforts were made by heavy columns of the enemy to break these lines, but without effect; our troops held their ground with a determined bravery seldom equaled. Our artillery was advantageously posted and handled with great skill and effect.

At 8 a.m. I informed the commanding general of the fact that our small-arm ammunition was nearly exhausted, and that a new supply was necessary or that my troops must be relieved. As there was no ammunition on hand, a brigade of Birney's division was ordered to relieve a portion of Williams', which was done, but too late to prevent the advance of the enemy. Our artillery, also, which had been firing constantly for about three hours, was nearly exhausted of ammunition.

At about 9 a.m. the troops on the right of my command fell back, which was soon followed by a portion of my line. The enemy at once gained a position which enabled him to use his infantry against our batteries. The artillery, however, held its position until two battery commanders . . . were killed beside their pieces, until 63 cannoneers were killed or wounded, and until 80 horses had been shot in the harness. The batteries were then retired to a position in rear of our second line without the loss of a single piece. The infantry also retired in much better order than could reasonably have been anticipated, and formed in rear of the new line. At 9 p.m. on Sunday, I was ordered to take a position on the extreme left of the line, which was done at once, and every hour was occupied in strengthening our position until we were ordered to recross the river. [*O.R.*, XXV, Part 1, pp. 670–71.]

Report of Capt. Clermont L. Best, USA, Fourth U.S. Artillery, Chief of Artillery, Twelfth Army Corps, Army of the Potomac

Here I beg leave to offer an opinion. Our position could not have been forced had the flanks of our line of guns been successfully maintained. An important point—an open field about a mile to our left and front, guarded by a brigade of our troops (not of the Twelfth Corps) and a battery—was seemingly taken by a small force of the enemy and the battery captured and turned on us with fearful effect . . . and enfilading General Geary's line. It was most unfortunate. My line of guns, however, kept to its work manfully until about 9 a.m., when, finding our infantry in front withdrawn, our right and left turned, and the enemy's musketry already so advanced as to pick off our men and horses, I was compelled to withdraw my guns to save them. We were also nearly exhausted of ammunition. [*O.R.*, XXV, Part 1, p. 675.]

Report of Brig. Gen. Alpheus S. Williams, USA, Commanding First Division, Twelfth Army Corps, Army of the Potomac

On the morning of May 3, my line was as follows: Connecting with the left of Berry's division, on the Plank Road . . . just in advance of Fairview, were two regiments of the Second Brigade (the One hundred and twenty-third New York and Third Maryland Volunteers), having been transferred from the left during the early morning. Ruger's brigade completed the line along the inner edge of the woods to the angle of our breastworks, where it crossed the ravine eastward, to connect with Geary's division in the woods in front of Chancellorsville. Two regiments of the Second Brigade (the One hundred and forty-fifth New York and Twentieth Connecticut Volunteers) were placed in the rifle-pits in this line. Three broken regiments of Knipe's brigade (all the field officers but one having been captured or disabled the previous night) were placed in reserve in rifle-pits about 200 yards in rear of my right. These regiments were, soon after the attack began, moved to the breastworks, where General Knipe assumed command of the regiments of the Second Brigade, Colonel Ross having left the front, reported wounded.

The lines thus formed with Geary's division presented two sides of a square, with the angle toward some cleared fields and a farmhouse on elevated ground [Hazel Grove], not over 600 yards distant to the left and front, as seen from Fairview. . . . It was an important position, as it nearly enfiladed our infantry lines and commanded our artillery position at Fairview.

The enemy commenced his attack at the earliest dawn, pushing his column through the woods in our front with wonderful vigor and obstinacy. He was successfully resisted at all points of my lines, and although his attacks were almost without cessation, he was repeatedly driven back in confusion during three to four hours, always, however, replacing his broken columns with fresh troops.

In the meantime the enemy either by the withdrawal of our troops or their retreat from the open elevated ground to our left and front before described, had seized upon that important position, and with a strong force attempted to carry our breastworks beyond the angle on the left. They were successfully resisted by the Twentieth Connecticut, One hundred and forty-fifth New York, and a portion of Ruger's brigade. A number of the enemy who had penetrated our lines were taken prisoners.

At the same time the enemy placed several batteries in position on this open hill . . . and opened a most vigorous fire upon our batteries at Fairview and our lines of infantry both right and left of this position.

This desperate struggle in front and flank by artillery and infantry continued almost without cessation until about 8.30 a.m. My regiments had literally exhausted their ammunition. Some of them had been twenty-four hours without food, and most of them several nights with but little sleep, while engaged in intrenching. My regiments had several times crossed the breastworks to attack the enemy's repulsed columns, but the nature of the ground, the thickness of the underbush, the heavy columns of the enemy always at hand, as well as their position on either flank of my line, admonished me to act on the defensive until a more favorable moment for the offensive should present itself.

Finding it was impossible to bring up my ammunition pack train under the tremendous fire of artillery and infantry, or to replenish my ammunition in any other way, I reported to the major-general commanding the corps that my regiments must be replaced with fresh troops, and that it would be impossible for me longer to resist the heavy attacks of the enemy. Soon after, meeting General Sickles on the field, he assured me that troops of his corps had already been sent to replace my line.

I immediately sent orders to the brigadiers to withdraw their troops in order as soon as relieved. It was not too soon. The enemy were pressing forward on both flanks of my north and south line. The artillery on our front was already mostly withdrawn with empty chests. The troops sent to my relief were checked before they reached our breastworks, and the whole line finally fell back in good order under a severe artillery and infantry fire, which swept the open field as far back as the Chancellor house. At this point my brigades were halted behind the rifle-pits fronting down the Wilderness Plank Road, and after awhile, by order of the major-general commanding the corps, moved down the road toward the United States Ford, behind our second line. . . . [*O.R.*, XXV, Part 1, pp. 679–81.]

Brig. Gen. Alpheus S. Williams to his daughter, May 18, 1863

I think the heaviest attack was against me, but as I was nearer and could see my own position best, and *hear* there the most, I may be mistaken. At any rate, the fire of musketry was incessant for quite four hours, almost without cessation or intermission. But in all that time they were never able to reach my front line. Three times they were driven back and their masses (in column) thrown into great confusion, but almost immediately replaced with fresh troops. Our batteries on the ridge a few hundred yards behind my line opened through the entire line of thirty-four pieces, I believe, and for a while Sickles kept up the fire with great animation. Soon, however, his division began to give way and some of his troops came back diagonally through our lines in great confusion. . . . The din of war was never more violent than for the next two hours. . . .

No man can give any idea of a battle by description nor by

painting. If you can stretch your imagination so far as to hear, in fancy, the crashing roll of 30,000 muskets mingled with the thunder of over a hundred pieces of artillery; the sharp bursting of shells and the peculiar whizzing sound of its dismembered pieces, traveling with a shriek in all directions; the crash and thud of round shot through trees and buildings and into the earth or through columns of human bodies; the "phiz" of the Minie ball; the uproar of thousands of human voices in cheers, yells, and imprecations; and see the smoke from all the engines of war's inventions hanging sometimes like a heavy cloud and sometimes falling down like a curtain between the combatants; see the hundreds of wounded limping away or borne to the rear on litters; riderless horses rushing wildly about; now and then the blowing up of a caisson and human frames thrown lifeless into the air; the rush of columns to the front; the scattered fugitives of broken regiments and skulkers making for the rear. If you can hear and see all this in a vivid fancy, you may have some faint idea of a battle. . . . But you must stand in the midst and feel the elevation which few can fail to feel, even amidst its horrors, before you have the faintest notion of a scene so terrible and yet so grand.

My personal experiences . . . were these: As soon as the battle opened I rode to the right to consult with Gen. Berry, for the maintenance of his line was my safety. Poor man! He was probably dead within fifteen minutes after I left him, killed by a rifle ball. . . . Leaving Gen. Berry, I rode down my line, giving such instructions as seemed necessary to my brigades. My line was well sheltered behind logs and a slight depression of the ground behind the woods. This artificial and natural protection saved me hundreds of lives.

I then took position on a knoll which overlooked my whole division from the left of the battery. Of course I remained stationary nowhere, as the changing tide of affairs kept me moving from right to left to see that all was firm and safe. In one of these movements I had a most extraordinary escape. . . . when a shell struck in the mud directly under my horse and exploded. . . .

At length, after four hours or so of this incessant strife and turmoil, it was reported to me that every regiment was nearly out of ammunition. I sent a staff officer to Gen. Hooker or to Gen. Slocum, who was at general headquarters, with the report that I should soon be flanked on both sides unless fresh troops came to my support and to replace my exhausted regiments, half of whom had been without food for nearly twenty-four hours. Hooker replied that I must furnish my own ammunition, which, of course, was not possible through that volcano of flame and roar with a mule pack-train. At length I saw Sickles not far in the rear, and as he had, or ought to have had, two divisions which had been but little engaged, I went to him and was told that he had just sent forward his troops to replace mine.

I hurried to the front to order my regiments to withdraw as soon as other troops came up, but the relieving troops never reached my line. The right (Berry's division) was giving way. The artillery was already nearly gone with empty chests. The Rebels had already occupied the woods far in front of my line on my left flank. There was no time for delay if I would save anything of my command. Oh! but for *one* of the four corps which lay behind me unengaged. . . .

The getting away was worse than the staying. Our line of retreat was over the ravine, up an exposed slope, and then for three-quarters of a mile over an open plain swept by artillery and infantry of the Rebels as they pressed forward. There was no shelter on our side of the Chancellorsville House. . . . The infantry pursuit was feeble, but the artillery thundered its best—or worst—upon us. . . . Many a poor fellow lost his life or limb in this fearful transit. . . .

Reaching Chancellors House, I formed line behind some rifle pits made by the Rebels [two brigades of Anderson's divisions, after the evacuation of United States Ford on April 29] . . . facing down the Plank Road toward Germanna. Here I was ordered by a staff officer of Gen. Hooker to hold this place at all hazards, who to my protestation that I had no ammunition, replied with immense pomposity, "Use the bayonet"! As we were suffering hugely from artillery shells thrown from a half mile to a mile distant, I didn't exactly see how my bayonets were to be effective. . . .

I have written you a hurried and yet, so far as I can, a faithful account of this campaign. You will see how poorly it agrees with newspaper stories, which so far as I have seen are mainly fictions. Indeed, most of the pretended writers see nothing. They are safely in the rear. At least it was so with one who pretended to report for the 11th and 12th corps for the New York *Herald*. He went over the river on Friday and never appeared, so far as I could learn, on the south side again. . . .

Of thirty-one field officers engaged in these operations, fourteen are numbered with the casualties. . . . All the adjutant generals are wounded or missing. . . . My aggregate of casualties in the division is nearly 1,700. I had less than 5,000 in the Sunday battle, consequently I have lost more than one man in three! The absence of many intimate friends and the sad results of our promising campaign have made me almost melancholy. . . . [Milo M. Quaife, ed., *From the Cannon's Mouth* (Detroit: Wayne State University Press, 1959), pp. 195–202 *passim*.]

Return to your car. Drive back down BERRY-PAXTON DRIVE slightly more than 0.1 mile to a monument on the right side of the road. Pull over to the right and stop there.

STOP 19, *THE TWENTY-SEVENTH INDIANA*

Ruger's brigade was posted on the left of Williams' division, his left resting on the "substantial breastwork of logs and earth" that had been constructed two days previously. His brigade thus formed an angle between Williams' line of battle astride the Plank Road and Geary's division in its original intrenchments facing south. When Sickles' Third Corps was ordered to fall back from Hazel Grove, this position and much of Geary's line to the east was exposed to an enfilading fire from Confederate artillery and persistent attacks from Confederate infantry.

Report of Col. Silas Colgrove, USA, Twenty-seventh Indiana Infantry, Third Brigade, First Division, Twelfth Army Corps, Army of the Potomac

Shortly after sunrise on Sunday morning, the 3d, the enemy, having obtained possession of our breastworks on the right, advanced on our line and opened fire.

In a very short time the whole line became engaged. The enemy advanced steadily, delivering their fire with telling effect. Our whole line stood firm. No part of the line yielded an inch or wavered. The enemy poured in regiment after regiment of fresh troops, determined to break the line, but whenever and wherever they made their appearance they found our fire so deadly that they were forced to halt and seek shelter behind the timber and rises in the ground.

After the battle had progressed an hour or more, my officers notified me that the ammunition was running out. I immediately rode up to the right of the line to find [General Ruger]. I found that all the other regiments were also running short of ammunition. I could not see [him], and was informed that Captain Scott, assistant adjutant-general, had been wounded and had left the field. I immediately ordered the whole line to fix bayonets and charge, which was done in gallant style. The rebels fled before us like sheep, and took refuge behind the breastworks and reopened fire upon us.

After delivering a few rounds, I ordered a second charge. Our men charged to the breastworks on the extreme left of our line. In some instances a regular hand-to-hand fight took place. The enemy soon gave way, and, being in our abatis, they were soon thrown into the utmost confusion. While endeavoring to retreat through the brush and tree-tops, they became mixed up in a perfect jam, our men all the time pouring in the most deadly fire. . . . I have never witnessed on any other occasion so perfect a slaughter. Many of them made no attempt to get away, but threw down their arms and came into our lines. . . . We took from 150 to 200 prisoners, and sent them to the rear. . . .

All this time there was very heavy firing going on on our right, and was fast gaining our rear. I soon ascertained that our forces were being driven back. I immediately ordered our line to fall back, which it did in good order, and formed again on the original line of battle.

By this time many of our men were entirely out of ammunition, and but a few rounds remained to any. The enemy were still advancing on our right and our forces falling back. At this critical moment I received orders from you to fall back in good order, which was done. [*O.R.*, XXV, Part 1, pp. 711–12.]

Continue driving in the same direction on **BERRY-PAXTON DRIVE** to the "Y" intersection with **STUART DRIVE**. Take the **LEFT** fork, away from **HAZEL GROVE**. At the next "Y" intersection, take the **RIGHT** fork onto **SICKLES DRIVE** for a short detour down to **CATHARINE FURNACE**. You will drive nearly 1.0 mile before you come to familiar territory around the furnace. **TURN LEFT** into the same parking lot you used for the stop here (Stop 9). Then reverse your route to return on **SICKLES DRIVE**. This excursion allows you to get a better feel for the terrain and distances in this part of the field. When you reach the "Y" intersection where **SICKLES DRIVE** originates, take the **RIGHT** fork and proceed on **SLOCUM DRIVE** for about 0.3 mile. A trench will begin to become visible on your right at about 0.1 mile past the intersection. After driving along that trench for about 0.2 mile, pull off to the right wherever you find a good spot.

STOP 20, SLOCUM'S POSITION

This line of intrenchments on your right marks the position taken by Geary's division, Twelfth Army Corps, upon arriving at Chancellorsville on April 30. That evening the command constructed abatis by cutting down the small brushwood and trees along the front and barricaded the Plank Road with large timbers. When the division advanced early the next afternoon through the dense thicket and underbrush and became engaged in a skirmish with a part of *Anderson's* division, it was ordered to fall back to this position.

During the night of May 1, these earthworks were thrown up along the whole line, the scarcity of intrenching tools forcing many men to use "their saber-bayonets, tin-plates, pieces of boards, and, in some cases, merely their hands to scrape up the dirt."

The next morning *Jackson's* columns of infantry and artillery were

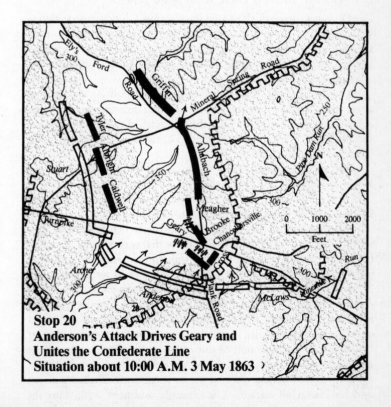

Stop 20
Anderson's Attack Drives Geary and
Unites the Confederate Line
Situation about 10:00 A.M. 3 May 1863

observed moving southwesterly along a ridge about 1¾ miles away, and Knap's battery opened fire. Late in the afternoon Geary was ordered to send troops forward along the Plank Road to cut off *Jackson's* trains. Moving forward about 500 yards with less than half of his command, he discovered the Confederates posted behind similar breastworks, and after a brief engagement he was ordered back to his original line of battle.

You are about where Greene's brigade was posted, on the left of Geary's line. The remnants of the intrenchment that you see immediately to your right was described as "a breastwork of logs and earth, with a trench in the rear, making a very good defensive work." An abatis of slashed trees covered the line "200 or 300 feet in front." [*O.R.*, XXV, Part 1, p. 758] Most of the action described below took place in the woods ahead, and to your left and rear.

Report of Brig. Gen. John W. Geary, USA, Commanding Second Division, Twelfth Army Corps, Army of the Potomac

During a panic which ensued shortly after this occurrence among some troops of another corps upon our right, our men nobly stood their ground, notwithstanding the fact that numbers of the panic-stricken men . . . came directly into our lines, almost bearing down all opposition in their flight.

During the night heavy and continuous picket firing was kept up along the front, and numbers of prisoners and deserters were brought in by our skirmishers, by whom the character of the coming contest was disclosed. These were forwarded to headquarters for examination by the commanding general.

Shortly after daylight on the morning of the 3d instant, the action commenced at a distance from our line on the right and rear of the army, and within half an hour it had reached my division and become general along the whole front.

About 8 o'clock the division was in the trenches, exposed to a terribly raking and enfilading fire from the enemy, who had succeeded in turning the right flank of the army, leaving us exposed to the full fury of his artillery. At the same time attacks were made upon us in front and flank by his infantry. Thus hemmed in, and apparently in danger of being cut off, I obeyed an order to retire and form my command at right angles with the former line of battle, the right resting at or near the brick house, the headquarters of General Hooker.

While in the execution of this order, and having withdrawn the command and in the act of forming my new front, General Hooker came up and in person directed me to resume my original position and hold it at all hazards. I accordingly advanced again into the trenches with the First Brigade, Greene's and Kane's having, in the confusion of the moment and the conflict of orders, become separated from the command and retired to a line of defense in a woods to the north of the Chancellor house. Upon regaining the breastworks, I found the Sixtieth and One hundred and second New York Volunteers, of Greene's brigade, had been left behind when the command had retired, and were now hotly engaged with the enemy, who were attempting breaches throughout the whole length of my line, and in many places actually occupied it. These two regiments had captured some 30 prisoners and a battle-flag of the enemy, the One hundred and second having captured that of the Twelfth Georgia [*Doles'* brigade, *D. H. Hill's* division]. Our men here, after a fierce struggle, took a number of prisoners who had advanced into our works under the impression that we had abandoned them.

The fire upon our lines was now of the most terrific character I ever remember to have witnessed. Knap's and Hampton's batteries had been ordered to take part in the engagement in another part of the field. Two brigades of my command were separated from me, and, had I even known their locality, could not hope to have them reach my position. I was thus left with but Candy's brigade and two regiments of Greene's, and Lieutenant Muhlenberg with two sections of Bruen's battery and one of Best's. Against this comparatively small body the whole fury and force of the enemy's fire seemed to be concentrated. Three of his batteries engaged Lieutenant Muhlenberg in direct fire at about 1 mile range. A heavy battery completely enfiladed our works from the right; that constructed by them in the woods directly in our front, which had been discovered by me in the engagement of the previous day, played upon us at short range with destructive effect, while under cover of their guns the infantry, becoming emboldened by the near approach of what seemed to them our utter and total annihilation, charged upon us repeatedly and were as often repulsed.

At this stage of the action the enemy suffered severely at our hands. Candy's brigade seemed animated by a desire to contest single-handed the possession of the field, and before the deadly aim of our rifles rank after rank of the rebel infantry went down. . . .

When the order was given by me to retire by the left flank, the movement was executed in excellent order, and even at that time the parting volleys of this brigade . . . showed their determination to avenge the death of their comrades if they could not avert the issue of the day; but the odds against us were too fearful to render the contest one of long duration, and, finally, after suffering very severe loss, and finding the enemy almost entirely enveloping my front, right, and rear, the order of General Slocum to retire was obeyed in a soldierly and masterly manner. We took position in the woods in the rear of Chancellorsville. . . .

The losses and casualties in the division are not so numerous nor so serious as might be supposed, when account is taken of the murderous nature of the fire to which a great portion of the command was so long exposed. This is to be attributed in some measure to the admirable self-control and discipline shown by the men under such trying circumstances, and the prudence of the officers in keeping them well covered.

The following is a summary of the entire loss in killed, wounded, and missing.

Killed 124
Severely wounded 329
Slightly wounded 308
Missing 448
Total 1,209

[*O.R.*, XXV, Part 1, pp. 730–33.]

Report of Brig. Gen. George Doles, CSA, Commanding Brigade, D. H. Hill's Division, Second Army Corps, Army of Northern Virginia

Sunday morning, May 3, at 6 o'clock, the command was ordered forward as follows: Forty-fourth, Twenty-first, Twelfth, Fourth [Georgia], the left of the Forty-fourth connecting with the right of *General Ramseur's* brigade. The march to the front was through a very dense pine wood and swamp. During the march the left of the brigade lost its connection with the right of *General Ramseur*, and moved off by the right flank, passing in rear of the regiments to its right, while four companies of the Twenty-first Georgia and the Twelfth Georgia, with portions of the Forty-fourth and Fourth, moved to the front. The right portion of the brigade was ordered by *General [J. E. B.] Stuart* to support a battery to its right, while the left moved forward, assaulting the enemy and assisting in driving him from his position from behind a strong work of logs. He was dislodged, after a very stubborn resistance, by a charge. This portion of the command kept up the pursuit, driving him through the woods back on his batteries on the heights near Chancellorsville.

While moving to assault him in his position on the hill, I discovered the enemy in large force to my right. *Colonel [Edward] Willis,* commanding Twelfth Georgia, was ordered to wheel his regiment to the right and engage him, the other companies coming up promptly to *Colonel Willis'* support. The enemy, after the first fire, fled; a large number threw down their arms and surrendered; they were ordered to the rear.

Being protected by a crest of a hill to the left of the enemy's batteries, we moved by the flank, getting in his rear, when he abandoned seven pieces of artillery on the hill and fled. We were attacked in our rear by his infantry force from the wood; we faced to the rear, charged the wood, and, after a few minutes' resistance, he withdrew.

After he withdrew, his batteries at the Chancellor house opened a very destructive fire on us with grape, canister, and shrapnel. We were within about 400 yards of his batteries. We did not have force enough to carry his position, and seeing no support on the field, and the enemy moving a large infantry force to our right, we withdrew to the woods where we first engaged him. That portion of the brigade ordered to support our battery was under command of *Col. J. T. Mercer*, Twenty-first Georgia. They were afterward ordered forward, and to conform to the movements of *General Archer's* brigade. After advancing to the woods from which we were forced to retire, they were also forced to retire. The brigade was reformed, and, by order from *General [R. E.] Lee*, ordered to the spring to our right, to act as provost-guard over a large number of prisoners collected there. [*O.R.*, XXV, Part 1, pp. 967–8.]

Report of Maj. Gen. Richard H. Anderson, CSA, Commanding Division, First Army Corps, Army of Northern Virginia

At daylight on the 3d, *Perry's* brigade was directed to gain the Catharpin Road and move toward the furnace. At sunrise, when it was supposed that *General Perry* had had time to reach the vicinity of the furnace, *General Posey's* skirmishers were pushed forward toward it, and it was discovered that the enemy had retired. Soon afterward, in obedience to the directions of the commanding general, my whole force was advanced toward Chancellorsville, *Mahone's* brigade having its right on the Plank Road, and *Wright's, Posey's,* and *Perry's* successively forming a line of battle on the left of and nearly perpendicular to that portion of the Plank Road between us and Chancellorsville. The troops pressed forward with spirited impetuosity and with as much rapidity as was permitted by the dense thickets and tangled abatis through which they were obliged to force their way. After a short and sharp encounter, they drove the enemy from his intrench-ments. *Wright's* brigade was the first to reach Chancellorsville, at which place it captured a large number of prisoners. The other brigades coming up immediately afterward, the division was placed in line along old turnpike to the east of Chancellorsville. [*O.R.*, XXV, Part 1, 851.]

Report of Brig. Gen. E. A. Perry, CSA, Commanding Brigade, Anderson's Division, First Army Corps, Army of Northern Virginia

Some time before daylight of the morning of May 3, I moved my command, by direction of *Major-General Anderson*, down the Cathar-pin Road, for the purpose of scouring the country to the left . . . and rear of . . . *Anderson's* line. I found the country clear, and moved up by the [Catharine] furnace on the left of the line, and came up with the other brigades of the division near to the enemy's works. I at once formed my line of battle, and pushed forward upon the right flank of the enemy's works, on the left of the . . . division. The fire was quite brisk here from a line of the enemy thrown back at right angles to this front to protect his flank and rear. This line soon gave way, and, pushing forward, I found myself inside of his breastworks.

Having no knowledge of the ground, and the woods being so thick as to entirely obstruct the view, I was at a loss for some time as to the direction of the enemy's next line. Their musket-balls soon gave me the proper direction, and I changed front, and, sending out skirmishers, soon found their line on the thickly wooded hill in the rear of their breastworks, and to their right of the field in front of Chancellor's. I ordered a charge, and the enemy, after one or two rounds, broke in the utmost confusion, throwing down arms, knap-sacks, etc., great numbers of them running into our lines.

No sooner had the enemy's line vanished than their batteries poured a most terrific fire of grape and canister into my lines. The men lying down, and being partially protected by a small ridge, the fire was not as fatal as I had reason to fear. Upon going to the front, I found no infantry in my front between me and the Turnpike Road, and that I could not lead my men against the enemy's battery without encountering the range of our own battery on the left of the rear of my line, which was then clearing out the enemy in double-quick time.

While making this charge, portions of two other brigades, who were lying down in the woods, and whom a portion of my line had charged over, rushed back from the sudden and terrific fire poured into us before the enemy gave way, and the Eighth Florida Regiment, which had not then passed over them, mistaking them for the left of their own brigade, allowed themselves to be swept back a short distance by them. They were not, however, at all panic-stricken, but were rallied at once, their *morale* and spirit in no manner impaired. . . .

I remained in that position until the rest of the division was marched up by *General Anderson*, and moved by the right flank with them to the Turnpike Road, where the division halted. Soon after, I was directed . . . to occupy the works on the right of the Pike Road, to prevent the enemy from throwing a force into them. I remained in these works until ordered to follow the division toward the United States Ford. [*O.R.*, XXV, Part 1, p. 875.]

Report of Brig. Gen. A. R. Wright, CSA, Commanding Brigade, Anderson's Division, First Army Corps, Army of Northern Virginia

Early on Sunday morning, I received orders to advance my brigade through the woods in the direction of Chancellorsville, connecting my right with *General Mahone's* left and my left with *General Posey's* right. This gave me a line of over a mile to cover with less than 1600 men. I soon found that this was entirely impracticable, and I pushed forward through the woods, endeavoring to keep equidistant from *Mahone* and *Posey*, keeping my flanks protected by a strong line of skirmishers and flankers. In this order I moved steadily on, my right about three-fourths of a mile to the left of the Plank Road, until I fell upon a strong body of Yankee infantry posted in the woods, about one-half mile in the front (as I afterward discovered) of a strong line of rifle-pits, protected by abatis formed by the felling of the thick forest timber for some distance in front of their intrenchments. Quickly engaging the enemy with vigor, he gave way, and I pursued him up and into his strong works. Here my small command encountered the most terrible fire of artillery and musketry I have ever witnessed, and our farther advance was temporarily checked.

About this time firing on my left was heard, and I felt assured *Posey* was up to his work. Not having heard from or of *General Mahone*, I dispatched an officer of my staff to seek him and inform him of my position, and beg him to move forward to my support. Immediately after this messenger left me, *Major Taylor* . . . in command of *General Mahone's* line of skirmishers, approached me and informed me that he knew nothing of the locality of *General Mahone's* brigade, except when last heard from it was very far in the rear, and that he should wait or fall back with his skirmishers until he could be brought near to his brigade. I urged him not to do so. . . . *Major Taylor* left me, and I saw no more of him or *General Mahone's* forces during the day.

Being thus without support on my right, I determined to move a little toward the left, where I continued to hear *Posey's* fire. . . . About this time the firing far on the left . . . became heavy, and I felt assured that *Jackson [Stuart]* was advancing there. *Major Jones* moved his regiment rapidly up to within a few rods of the enemy's works, where, pressed by *Posey* and *Perry* on my immediate left, and *Jackson* farther on, the Yankees gave way, and fled from their intrenchments. We pressed forward, and immediately occupied them, although on my right the enemy still retained possession of their works and opened a pretty sharp fire of shell and musketry upon us as we took possession. . . . I was then ordered by *Major General Anderson* to move up the Third Georgia Regiment and dislodge the enemy's sharpshooters on our right, and then push forward for the enemy's battery which was so incessantly playing upon us. The order was given, and the Third Georgia commenced its movement . . . toward the Plank Road, led by *Major Jones*. In a few minutes he received a severe wound . . . and the command devolved upon *Captain Andrews*, who continued to advance until, having reached the Plank Road, about 200 yards from Chancellorsville, I ordered him to charge the enemy, then in some confusion around and in the rear of the brick house. This charge was made with spirit, and the enemy fled, leaving us in entire possession of his strong position. . . . My loss during this day was pretty severe, amounting to 17 killed and 163 wounded. [*O.R.*, XXV, Part 1, pp. 867–69.]

TO STOP 21

Continue driving in the same direction on SLOCUM DRIVE until you come to a STOP sign at a "T" intersection. TURN LEFT on ROUTE 610 (ORANGE PLANK ROAD), and drive about 0.1 mile to the STOP sign at the intersection with Route 3. DRIVE STRAIGHT ACROSS ROUTE 3 and then TURN LEFT into the parking lot at the site of the Chancellor House. You may wish to dismount to read the signs and consider the terrain.

STOP 21, THE CHANCELLOR HOUSE

You are now at the scene of the auspicious beginning of Hooker's campaign, when three days earlier the Union commander not only expected a victory but had crowed to a newspaper correspondent standing nearby: "The Rebel army is now the legitimate property of the Army of the Potomac."

What a different sight now! The original house that served as Hooker's headquarters had been set on fire by Confederate shells earlier in the morning, and Confederate infantry had emerged from the Wilderness and were advancing across the fields.

Narrative of Major Charles Marshall, CSA, serving on the staff of General R. E. Lee

On the morning of May 3 . . . the final assault was made upon the Federal lines at Chancellorsville. *General Lee* accompanied the troops in person, and as they emerged from the fierce combat they had waged in the depths of that tangled wilderness, driving . . . the enemy before them across the open ground, he rode into their midst.

The scene is one that can never be effaced from the minds of those who witnessed it. The troops were pressing forward with all the ardour and enthusiasm of combat. The white smoke of musketry fringed the front of the line of battle, while the artillery on the hills in the rear . . . shook the earth with its thunder, and filled the air with the wild shrieks of the shells that plunged into the masses of the retreating foe. To add greater horror and sublimity to the scene, Chancellor House and the woods surrounding it were wrapped in flames.

In the midst of this awful scene, General Lee . . . rode to the front of his advancing battalions. His presence was the signal for one of those outbursts of enthusiasm which none can appreciate who have not witnessed them. The fierce soldiers with their faces blackened with the smoke of battle, the wounded crawling with feeble limbs from the fury of the devouring flames, all seemed possessed with a common impulse. One long, unbroken cheer, in which the feeble cry of those who lay helpless . . . blended with the strong voices of those who still fought, rose high above the roar of battle, and hailed the presence of the victorious chief.

He sat in the full realization of all that soldiers dream of— triumph; and as I looked upon him in the complete fruition of the success which his genius, courage, and confidence in his army had won, I thought that it must have been from such a scene that men in ancient days rose to the dignity of gods. [Maurice, ed., *Aide-de-Camp of Lee*, pp. 172–73.]

Hooker made a less dignified exit. In 1876, accompanied by his literary executor, Hooker made his only visit to the battlefield. When they reached the Chancellor House, which by this time had been rebuilt, he recalled:

> I was standing on this step of the portico on the . . . morning of the 3d of May, and was giving direction to the battle, which was now raging with great fury, the cannon-balls reaching me from both the east and the west, when a solid shot struck the pillar near me, splitting it in two, and throwing one-half . . . against me, striking my whole right side, which soon turned livid. For a few moments I was senseless, and the report spread that I had been killed. But I soon revived, and, to correct the misapprehension, I insisted on being lifted upon my horse, and rode back toward the white house, which subsequently became the center of my new position. Just before reaching it, the pain . . . became so intense that I was likely to fall, when I was assisted to dismount, and was laid upon a blanket spread out upon the ground, and was given some brandy. This revived me, and I was assisted to remount. Scarcely was I off the blanket when a solid shot, fired by the enemy at Hazel Grove, struck in the very center of that blanket . . . and tore up the earth in a savage way."

As he ended this recital, General Hooker turned to Major Chancellor, who was standing by, and said, "Ah, Major! Your people were after me with a sharp stick on that day." [Samuel P. Bates, "Hooker's Comments on Chancellorsville," *Battles and Leaders*, III, pp. 220–21.]

Report of Maj. Gen. Darius Couch, USA, Commanding Second Army Corps, Army of the Potomac

By 9 a.m. the only point contested by the two armies was the salient, Chancellorsville. On our side the woods in front were held by a part of the Twelfth Corps, under Geary; the open ground by a few regiments of Hancock's division and about eighteen pieces of artillery. The enemy succeeded in planting their batteries, most of them well covered, to the west, on our right; to the east, on our left, and southerly, on our front, concentrating their fire on this point with great accuracy, and terrible execution. . . .

About 9.45 a.m. I was called to the Chandler house [known also to Union soldiers as the white house] to briefly take command of the army, simply acting as executive officer to General Hooker in fulfilling his instructions, which were to draw in the front and make some new dispositions. On leaving Chancellorsville to see General Hooker, General Hancock was left in command . . . withdrawing successfully upon receiving the orders. I express my thanks to this officer for his gallantry, energy, and his example of marked personal bravery. [O.R., XXV, Pt. 1, p. 307.]

Report of Maj. Gen. Winfield S. Hancock, USA, Commanding First Division, Second Army Corps, Army of the Potomac

The battle was renewed at 5.30 a.m. Previous to that time, expecting to meet the enemy on my main line of battle, I had not held a very heavy force on my first line [astride the Turnpike facing east], but now, knowing the danger and confusion that would arise from the musket-balls of the enemy crossing our line of communication at Chancellorsville. . . . I strengthened the advance position [which] . . . was frequently assaulted during the morning . . . the enemy [McLaws] marching their regiments up to the abatis. . . .

Later in the morning I was directed by Major General Couch to face to the rear with my men on the second line, excepting Colonel Cross' command, and march to the road running between Chancellor's house and the United States Ford, and to be ready to advance against the enemy, who were then threatening that line of communication from my rear.

Having arrived at that point, General Hooker directed me to leave one brigade there, subject to his orders . . . and to return to my first line of battle, commanding the old turnpike road, with the remainder of my troops. I obeyed the order, closing the regiments to the right to connect again with Colonel Cross, on the turnpike. . . . The enemy threatening General Geary's right, I was directed to face Colonel Cross' command about, establishing a line of battle to protect that point. Shortly afterward Colonel Cross was ordered back, by General Couch, to occupy his original line.

General Sickles' command had now retired from the position west of Chancellorsville, and, seeing the enemy advancing in line of battle in the open plain toward the Chancellor house, I immediately faced my line about, and took position on the Plank Road, in line with Colonel Cross' command, his right resting on the turnpike, . . .

supporting Pettit's battery, a half battery of Thomas' . . . in Colonel Cross' front, and Leppien's battery, on the right of Chancellor's house.

The enemy, who had threatened to advance, was soon dispersed by the fire of the artillery. He, however, immediately planted several batteries in the open plain, about 900 yards to my front, and, with the batteries on the Fredericksburg Road [Turnpike], immediately in my rear, and those near the Plank Road to my left, opened a tremendous fire upon my lines.

An infantry assault was made at the same time on General Geary's command, of the Twelfth Corps, on my left; success alternating from one side to the other, my artillery assisting our forces, until finally that command was forced to quit its ground and retire from the field. Its resistance was stern, but unsuccessful.

I was now fighting in opposite directions, one line faced toward Fredericksburg, the other toward Gordonsville . . . being about half a mile apart. Projectiles from the enemy's artillery . . . passed over both lines, while other pieces . . . enfiladed both. . . . The Chancellor house, which was being used as a hospital, was fired by shells. . . . Leppien's battery, of five guns . . . on the right of the Chancellor house, having lost all its officers, cannoneers, and horses for the guns, I made a detail of men, who removed the pieces by hand to a place of safety. . . .

I next received an order that, after General Sickles' troops had retired, I would also be ordered to withdraw. . . . I first sent orders to the batteries to retire. After that had been accomplished, I marched my command in good order and without molestation, save by artillery, to a point about half a mile to the rear, toward the United States Ford, where a new line was established. . . . This movement was completed about 11 a.m. At the same time . . . I sent directions to my line [facing] toward Fredericksburg to retire in a direction which would enable them to join me. A portion of this command, deflecting too far to their left, was intercepted by a column of the enemy and captured.

Rifle pits were immediately thrown up on our new front, abatis felled, and the position made as strong as practicable. I have no doubt that we could have successfully resisted any assault. During our stay there we suffered from artillery, and also lost a few men by the enemy's sharpshooters. [O.R., XXV, Pt. 1, p. 313–14.]

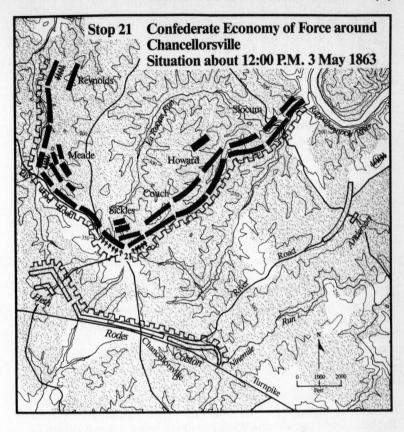

Stop 21   Confederate Economy of Force around
Chancellorsville
Situation about 12:00 P.M. 3 May 1863

TO STOP 22

When you have finished, drive back to ROUTE 3 and TURN RIGHT. Drive west on ROUTE 3 about 0.8 mile and then follow the signs to the parking lot at the CHANCELLORSVILLE VISITOR CENTER. Again, you may want to dismount to view the displays. Then continue through the parking lot, TURN RIGHT at the YIELD sign, and drive about 0.75 mile. Park in the vicinity of the historical sign on the left side of the road. Dismount and walk forward to the STOP sign.

STOP 22, THE APEX

You are now at the apex of Hooker's new line. The "White House," mentioned in reports, stood in the angle formed by these roads—the Ely's Ford Road to the left, and the old Mineral Spring Road in your front, which at the time of the battle was an extension of the Bullock Road (where you are parked). About one quarter of a mile to your left another road that led to the United States Ford branches off to the north. As Union forces withdrew from the salient at Chancellorsville, they would have marched from your right, by the flank, up the Ely's Ford Road in front of you.

The new Union position was in effect a fortified bridgehead shaped like an irregular U, with both flanks resting on high ground near the Rappahannock. Because Confederate artillery could fire into both sides of this apex, the Union troops threw up sections of parapets known as *traverses* to protect themselves against enfilade fire. If you have any interest in seeing this new wrinkle in field fortification, which Longstreet had already learned to appreciate at Fredericksburg [Stop 5], you may wish to take a brief walking tour.

To see the trenches, cross the road and negotiate the cable barrier that blocks vehicular traffic from the trace of the old Mineral Springs Road. Follow the old road about 200 yards, then walk a few yards into the woods on your right and you will find first-class earthworks. If you have the time or the inclination to follow this line for another 100 yards or so, you will see Hooker's original intrenchments coming on from the right. You will also see why traverses could offer good protection from enfilading artillery fire.

Report of Maj. Gen. Daniel E. Sickles, USA, Commanding
Third Army Corps, Army of the Potomac

I moved to the front of the new lines near the white house, connecting with General Meade on the right and General Couch on the left. Here we intrenched, and, after throwing forward strong lines of supports for the artillery in my front (thirty cannon in position, under the direction of . . . my chief of artillery), I massed my reserves in the woods in columns by divisions, opening *debouches* in all directions. These works were begun under an annoying fire of the enemy's sharpshooters, who were soon handsomely driven by Berdan, to whom the outposts were confided, but not until the brave and accomplished Brig. Gen. A. W. Whipple, commanding Third Division, had fallen . . . while directing in person the construction of fieldworks in his front.

These dispositions continued until Wednesday morning, a deluging rain-storm intervening, which caused a great and sudden rise in the Rappahannock and its tributaries, endangering our bridges and making the roads impracticable for trains. The supply of rations had become so reduced as to render an advance impossible without our trains.

During Tuesday afternoon and night, my pioneers . . . made a road 2 rods wide, through 3 miles of forest, to the United States Ford. [*O.R.*, XXV, Pt. 1, pp. 393–94.]

Major General Daniel Butterfield, USA, Chief of Staff, to Major
General Sedgwick, May 2, 1863 – 12 midnight.

From the statement brought by General Hooker's aide, it seems to be of vital importance that you should fall upon *Lee's* rear with crushing force. He will explain all to you. Give your advance to one who will do all that the urgency of the case requires. [*O.R.*, XXV, Pt. 2, p. 366.]

Major General Joseph Hooker, USA, to His Excellency Abraham
Lincoln, May 3, 1863 – 3.30 p.m.

We have had a desperate fight yesterday and today, which has resulted in no success to us, having lost a position of two lines, which had been selected for our defense. It is now 1.30 o'clock, and there is still some firing of artillery. We may have another turn at it this p.m. I do not despair of success. If Sedgwick could have gotten up, there could have been but one result. As it is impossible for me to know the exact position of Sedgwick as regards his ability to advance and take part in the engagement, I cannot tell when it will end. We will endeavor to do our best. My troops are in good spirits. We have fought desperately to-day. No general ever commanded a more devoted army. [O.R., XXV, Pt. 2, p. 379.]

Narrative of Maj. Gen. Joseph Hooker, USA, Commanding Army of the Potomac

My object in ordering General Sedgwick forward . . . was to relieve me from the position in which I found myself at Chancellorsville on the night of the 2d of May. I was of the opinion that if that portion of the army advanced on *Lee's* rear, sooner than allow his troops to remain between me and Sedgwick, Lee would take the road that *Jackson* had marched over on the morning of the 2d, and thus open for me a short road to Richmond, while the enemy, severed from his depot, would have to retire by way of Gordonsville.

In my judgment General Sedgwick did not obey the spirit of my order, and made no sufficient effort to obey it. His movement was delayed so long that the enemy discovered his intentions, and when that was done he was necessarily delayed in the further execution of the order.

This . . . was while the battle was being fought on the morning of the 3d on the right, and while I was endeavoring to hold my position until I could hear of his approach. . . . General Warren returned on the morning of the 4th, and reported to me verbally that, in his judgment, General Sedgwick would not have moved at all if he (General Warren) had not been there; and that when he did move, it was not with sufficient confidence or ability on his part to manoeuvre his troops.

As General Gibbon was directed to cross [his division, First Army Corps] at the same time that General Sedgwick did, and to hold the city, it gave the latter the use of his whole corps with which to make the advance.

On General Warren reporting to me the condition of General Sedgwick, and informing me that the enemy in his front appeared to have been re-enforced, I directed General Warren to address him the following letter.

May 3, 1863 – 12 midnight

I find everything snug here. We contacted the line a little and repulsed the last assault with ease. General Hooker wishes them to attack him to-morrow. If they will, he does not desire you to attack them again in force unless he attacks him at the same time. He says you are too far away for him to direct. Look well to the safety of your corps, and keep up communication with . . . Banks' Ford and Fredericksburg. You can go to either place you think it best. To cross at Banks' Ford would bring you in supporting distance of the main body, and would be better than falling back to Fredericksburg. [*Report of the Joint Committee on the Conduct of the War*, 1865, Vol. I, pp. 130–31.]

Narrative of Maj. Gen. Joseph Hooker, USA, Commanding the Army of the Potomac

During the 3d and 4th, reconnoissances were made on the right from one end of the line to the other, to feel the enemy's strength and find a place and way to attack him successfully; but it was ascertained that it could only be made on him behind his defences and with slender columns, which I believed he could destroy as fast as they were thrown on to his works. . . .

Being resolved on recrossing the river, on the night between the 4th and 5th I called the corps commanders together, not as a council of war, but to ascertain how they felt in regard to making what I considered a desperate move against the enemy in our front. There were present Generals Meade, Reynolds, Howard, Couch, and Sickles, and for a portion of the time my chief of staff, General Butterfield. I showed them my instructions, stated our circumstances, as clearly as I could, and explained to them the only means that was left, in my judgment, for extricating myself. General Slocum was not present, for the reason that the messenger who was despatched for him failed to find him. He, however, came up after the other corps commanders had dispersed.

After stating . . . the condition of affairs, and what measures I proposed to take if we advanced, I said I would withdraw for a time and let them confer among themselves. . . . When I returned, I called upon them individually for their opinions. General Meade stated that he was for an advance, for the reason that he did not believe we could recross the river in the presence of the enemy. General Reynolds had thrown himself on a bed, being very tired that night from hard work, and had gone to sleep, saying, before he did so, that his opinion would be the same as General Meade's. General Howard voted for an advance, assigning as a reason that he felt as though the army had been placed in the position in which it was by the conduct of his corps, and he had to vote for an advance under any circumstances. His opinion was received for what it was worth. General Couch and General Sickles were of the opinion that the army should recross the river. I stated to General Meade that the army could be withdrawn, without loss of men or material, and that I had no idea that a gun would be fired by the enemy as we did so.

Subsequently, on learning that General Meade was saying that he was unconditionally for an advance, and that he wished the bridges had been carried away so as to have prevented our return, I sent for him soon after our return to camp, and asked him if he had made such a report. He told me that he had. [*Report of the Joint Committee on the Conduct of the War*, 1865, Vol. I, pp. 130–35.

Narrative of Maj. Gen. Darius M. Couch, USA, Second Army Corps, Army of the Potomac

At 12 o'clock on the night of the 4th–5th General Hooker assembled his corps commanders in council. . . . Hooker stated that his instructions compelled him to cover Washington, not to jeopardize the army, etc. It was seen by the most casual observer that he had made up his mind to retreat. We were left by ourselves to consult, upon which Sickles made an elaborate argument, sustaining the views of the commanding general. Meade was in favor of fighting, stating that he doubted if we could get off our guns. Howard was in favor of fighting, qualifying his views by the remark that our present situation was due to the bad conduct of his corps, or words to that effect. Reynolds . . . was in favor of an advance. I had similar views to those of Meade as to getting off the guns, but said I "would favor an advance if I could designate the point of attack". . . . Meade, Reynolds, and Howard voted squarely for an advance, Sickles and myself squarely no; upon which Hooker informed the council that he should take upon himself the responsibility of retiring the army to the other side of the river. As I stepped out of the tent Reynolds, just behind me, broke out, "What was the use of calling us together at his time of night when he intended to retreat anyhow?" [*Battles and Leaders*, III, p. 171.]

Ruins of the Chancellorsville house. (USAMHI)

Return to your car. Drive forward to the STOP sign and TURN RIGHT on ROUTE 610. This road will take you back past the Chancellor House site to ROUTE 3. CROSS THE MEDIAN and TURN LEFT on ROUTE 3 and drive about 5.7 miles. As you near this mark, drive in the RIGHT LANE, and TURN RIGHT on ROUTE 639. About 100 yards down ROUTE 639 TURN RIGHT into the Park Service Parking Area for OLD SALEM CHURCH. Dismount and use the marked crosswalk to enter the church grounds. Then follow the path to the historical marker between the church and the highway.

Salem Church, 1884. (USAHMI)

STOP 23, SALEM CHURCH

You may want to review Union accounts of the action here by turning to the material for Stop 3.

Report of Maj. Gen. Lafayette McLaws, CSA, Commanding Division, First Army Corps, Army of Northern Virginia

I . . . found *General Wilcox* with his brigade in line across the Plank Road at Salem Church, *General Kershaw* forming on his right, and *General Mahone* on the left. I directed *General Mahone* still more to his left, as he was acquainted with the country, and placed *General Semmes* to the immediate left of *General Wilcox*. *General Wofford* was . . . placed on the right of *General Kershaw*. The batteries which I had brought with me had been engaged all the morning and had but little ammunition left. They had been ordered back in such haste that there was no time for them to replenish their chests, but they engaged the enemy until their supplies were nearly exhausted, and then withdrew. . . . The batteries of the enemy were admirably served and played over the whole ground.

Before my command was well in position, the enemy advanced, driving in our skirmishers, and, coming forward with loud shouts, endeavored to force the center *(Wilcox)* and left center *(General Semmes)*, extending the attack somewhat to *Mahone's* brigade. [O.R., XXV, Part 1, p. 827.]

Report of Brig. Gen. Cadmus M. Wilcox, CSA, Commanding Brigade, Anderson's Division, First Army Corps, Army of Northern Virginia

Two regiments of my brigade (the Eleventh and Fourteenth Alabama) were on the left of the road . . . the Tenth Alabama on the right next to the road, and the Eighth Alabama on the right of the Tenth. There was an interval of 75 or 80 yards between the left of the Tenth and the right of the Eleventh. In this interval on the road four pieces of artillery were in battery. The Ninth Alabama was in rear of the Tenth, one company of the Ninth being stationed in the schoolhouse, to the right of the church, and in front some 60 yards. A second company of this regiment was placed in the church, with orders to fire from the windows . . . (this church being occupied with furniture of refugees from Fredericksburg). . . . The principal attack was made at the church and its immediate vicinity. *Kershaw's* brigade was on the right of my brigade; *Semmes* and *Mahone* on the left. . . .

The brigades had not been in position long before the enemy were seen advancing up the Plank Road in line of battle. Their lines crossed the road at right angles. A field battery accompanied their advance. This was halted at the gate, about 1,000 yards distant, and soon opened with a brisk fire of shells upon our battery near the church. The two batteries fired some fifteen or twenty minutes, when ours was withdrawn for the want of ammunition.

The enemy then threw shells to the right and left of the church, through the woods, endeavoring to reach our infantry. These latter were well protected while lying down, and no casualties occurred from explosions of shells.

The enemy's artillery ceased to fire near 5 p.m. Their skirmishers then advanced; a spirited fire ensued between the skirmishers for some fifteen or twenty minutes. Ours then retired, firing as they fell back. The enemy's skirmishers pursued, followed by their solid lines of infantry and still a third line in rear. On either side of the road, as they advanced . . . were open fields, and the ground slightly ascending. These fields continued to within about 250 yards of the church, and then woods, thick, but of small growth.

When the front line of the enemy reached this wood, they made a slight halt; then, giving three cheers, they came with a rush, driving our skirmishers rapidly before them. Our men held their fire till their men came within less than 80 yards, and then delivered a close and terrible fire upon them, killing and wounding many and causing many of them to waver and give way. The enemy still press on, surround the school-house, and capture the entire company of the Ninth Alabama stationed in it, and, pressing hard upon the regiment in rear of the school-house, throw it in confusion and disorder, and force it to yield ground.

The Ninth Alabama, in rear of this regiment, spring forward as one man, and, with the rapidity of lightning, restore the continuity of our line, breaking the lines of the enemy by its deadly fire and forcing him to give way, and, following him so that he could not rally, retake the school-house, free the captured company, and in turn take their captors. The entire line of the enemy on the right of the road is repulsed, and our men follow in rapid pursuit. The regiment that had given way to the first onset of the enemy now returned to the attack and joined in the pursuit. The enemy did not assail with the same spirit on the left of the road, and were more easily repulsed, and now are followed on either side of the road, which is crowded with a confused mass of the discommited enemy. With a good battery to play upon this retreating mass, the carnage would have been terrific. There was no rallying or reforming of this line. Another line came up the Plank Road at a double-quick, and, filing to the right and left, formed line in front of my brigade. This line was scarcely formed before they were broken by the fire of my men, and fled to the rear. The pursuit continued as far as the toll-gate. . . .

Thus ended this spirited conflict at Salem Church; a bloody repulse to the enemy, rendering entirely useless to him his little success of the morning at Fredericksburg. The rear of our army at Chancellorsville was now secure and free from danger, and the Sixth Army Corps of the enemy, and a part of the Second were now content to remain on the defensive. . . .

This success . . . was dearly earned by the sacrifice of the lives of 75 of the noble sons of Alabama, and the wounding of 372, and 48 missing, an aggregate of 495. [*O.R.*, XXV, Part 1, pp. 858–59.]

Report of Brig. Gen. Paul J. Semmes, CSA, Commanding Brigade, McLaws' Division, First Army Corps, Army of Northern Virginia

Arriving on the field, this brigade, by order, took position on the left of that of *General Wilcox*. . . . Marching by the right flank, the most rapid mode of forming — being on the right by file into line — was executed under the fire of the enemy, who were pressing forward his lines to the attack. The fire, at first slight, soon became severe. The two regiments of my left, the Fifty-third and Fiftieth Georgia, took position under a storm of bullets. Position was never more gallantly taken or more persistently and heroically held. The battle of Salem Church raged from this time without intermission on my front for two hours, the enemy's main attack being directed against my left . . . re-enforcement after re-enforcement being pressed forward by him during the . . . fight.

This battle was one of the most severely contested of the war. . . . The brunt of the battle fell upon this brigade. Beyond my left there was only desultory firing, and beyond my right much firing did not extend far beyond and to the right of the road, whilst the roar of musketry raged furiously along my front.

The Tenth and Fifty-first Georgia made a most gallant charge in support of a charge made by . . . *Wilcox's* regiments, driving the enemy in confusion 500 or 600 yards back upon his reserves, the men pressing forward with enthusiastic shouts, and shooting the enemy's men down at almost every step, attaining a position within 100 yards of his reserves. . . . Finding my handful of men left entirely without supports, I at length gave the order to retire to the line of battle, which was done with deliberation.

The Fifty-third and Fiftieth Georgia did not join in this charge. The order was sent to them, but they failed to receive it. During this time these regiments were . . . under repeated assaults of greatly superior numbers, driving the enemy entirely from the field and closing the fight, the Fifty-third Georgia capturing the national colors of the Second Rhode Island Volunteers. . . .

The loss of the brigade in this battle was severe. [*O.R.*, XXV, Part 1, pp. 835–36.]

Report of General R. E. Lee, CSA, Army of Northern Virginia

The next morning *General Early* advanced along the Telegraph Road and recaptured Marye's and the adjacent hills without difficulty, thus gaining the rear of the enemy's left. He then proposed to *General McLaws* that a simultaneous attack should be made by their respective commands, but the latter officer not deeming his force adequate to assail the enemy in front, the proposition was not carried into effect.

In the meantime the enemy had so strengthened his position near Chancellorsville that it was deemed inexpedient to assail it with less than our whole force, which could not be concentrated until we were relieved from the danger that menaced our rear. It was accordingly resolved still further to re-enforce the troops in front of General Sedgwick, in order, if possible, to drive him across the Rappahannock.

Accordingly, on the 4th, *General Anderson* was directed to proceed with his remaining three brigades to join *General McLaws*, the three divisions of *Jackson's* corps holding our position at Chancellorsville. *Anderson* reached Salem Church about noon, and was directed to gain the left flank of the enemy and effect a junction with *Early*. *McLaws'* troops were disposed as on the previous day, with orders to hold the enemy in front, and to push forward his right brigades as soon as the advance of *Anderson* and *Early* should be perceived, so as to connect with them and complete the continuity of our line. Some delay occurred in getting the troops into position, owing to the broken and irregular nature of the ground, and the difficulty of ascertaining and disposition of the enemy's forces.

The attack did not begin until 6 p.m., when *Anderson* and *Early* moved forward and drove General Sedgwick's troops rapidly before them across the Plank Road in the direction of the Rappahannock. The speedy approach of darkness prevented *General McLaws* from perceiving the success of the attack until the enemy began to recross the river a short distance below Banks' Ford, where he had laid one of his pontoon bridges. His right brigades, under *Kershaw* and *Wofford*, advanced through the woods in the direction of the firing, but the retreat was so rapid that they could only join in the pursuit. A dense fog settled over the field, increasing the obscurity, and rendering great caution necessary to avoid collision between our own troops. Their movements were consequently slow. *General Wilcox*, with *Kershaw's* brigade and two regiments of his own, accompanied by a battery, proceeded nearly to the river, capturing a number of prisoners. . . . *General McLaws* also directed *Colonel Alexander's* artillery to fire upon the locality of the enemy's bridge, which was done with good effect.

The next morning it was found that General Sedgwick had made good his escape and removed his bridges. Fredericksburg was also evacuated. . . . *McLaws* and *Anderson*, being directed to return to Chancellorsville. . . . reached their destination during the afternoon, in the midst of a violent storm, which continued throughout the night and most of the following day.

Preparations were made to assail the enemy's works at daylight on the 6th, but, on advancing our skirmishers, it was found that under cover of the storm and darkness of the night he had retreated over the river. . . .

To the skillful and efficient management of the artillery the successful issue of the contest is in great measure due. The ground was not favorable for its employment, but every suitable position was taken with alacrity, and the operations of the infantry supported and assisted with a spirit and courage not second to their own. It bore a prominent part in the final assault which ended in driving the enemy from the field at Chancellorsville, silencing his batteries, and by a destructive enfilade fire upon his works opened the way for the advance of our troops. [*O.R.*, XXV, Part 1, pp. 801–4.]

Narrative of Maj. Gen. Darius N. Couch, USA, Second Army Corps, Army of the Potomac

On the morning of May 5th, corps commanders were ordered to cut roads, where it was necessary, leading from their positions to the United States Ford. During the afternoon there was a very heavy rainfall. In the meantime Hooker had in person crossed the river, but, as he gave orders for the various corps to march at such and such times during the night, I am not aware that any of his corps generals knew of his departure. Near midnight I got a note from Meade informing me that General Hooker was on the other side of the river, which had risen over the bridges, and that communication was cut off from him. I immediately rode over to Hooker's headquarters and found that I was in command of the army, if it had any commander. General Hunt . . . had brought the information as to the condition of the bridges, and from the reports there seemed to be danger of losing them entirely. After a short conference with Meade I told him that the recrossing would be suspended, and that "we would stay where we were and fight it out," returning to my tent with the intention of enjoying what I had not had since the night of the 30th ultimo—a good sleep; but at 2 a.m. communication having been reestablished, I received a sharp message from Hooker, to order the recrossing of the army as he had directed, and everything was safely transferred to the north bank of the Rappahannock.

POST MORTEM

In looking for the causes of the loss of Chancellorsville, the primary ones were that Hooker expected *Lee* to fall back without risking battle. Finding himself mistaken he assumed the defensive, and was outgeneraled and became demoralized by the superior tactical boldness of the enemy. [*Battles and Leaders*, III, p. 171.]

Diary of Col. Charles S. Wainwright, USA, Chief of Artillery, First Army Corps, Army of the Potomac

May 24. The papers and the army continue to discuss the battle. . . . Some of the papers are very severe on Hooker, and insist upon it that he was drunk, which I do not believe. Others go quite as far the other way and try to screen him from all blame, seeking to throw it on one or the other of his subordinates. The attacks on

General Howard are outrageous. He had been in command of the Eleventh Corps but a month before the fight, and was previously unknown to its officers and men. On the Peninsula he won the name of an excellent officer and brave man. . . . I know that he was very anxious to attack *Lee* on Monday. . . .

May 31 General Hooker has just left us. . . . The General sat with us for an hour, and spent that time in an attempt to justify himself as to the result of Chancellorsville. . . . He based his defense for not attacking *Lee* on Monday, [May 4] first that he expected *Lee* would attack his own right. . . . The second excuse . . . was worse than the first, being an attempt to throw the whole blame on General Sedgwick. He was very bitter against "Uncle John," accusing him of being slow and afraid to fight; also of disobeying orders directly. Now for a general to make such charges against an absent subordinate, in defending himself before a lot of young staff officers, while he takes no official notice of it, is—well, I hope Hooker was drunk while here, for his own sake. . . . My feelings were divided between shame for my commanding general, and indignation at the attack on so true, brave, and modest a man as Sedgwick. . . . That Sedgwick did not do what Hooker wanted him to there is no doubt . . . but this was more from Hooker's fault than his, owing as it was to the indistinct, even non-sensical wording of the orders recieved, and the fact that they were delivered from twelve to twenty-four hours later than they should have been. . . . I got my information on both sides as direct as possible. . . .

May 6 The opinion was universal [at Army Headquarters] that we might have done better, and that the failure would doubtless cost Hooker his place. Some half dozen of us, in talking over his successor, all agreed on Meade as the fittest man in this army, with Warren as chief of staff. From what I had seen of Meade during the three days I was at Chancellorsville, and from my previous knowledge of him, I had given him the preference, and was glad to find that there were others, good judges, who agreed with me. [Allan Nevins, ed., *A Diary of Battle: the Personal Journals of Colonel Charles S. Wainwright 1861–1865* (New York: Harcourt, Brace and World, Inc., 1962), pp. 202, 210, 212–14.]

Narrative of Private John O. Casler, CSA, Company A,
Thirty-third Virginia Infantry, Stonewall [Paxton's] Brigade,
Trimble's Division, Second Army Corps, Army of Northern Virginia

Our pioneer corps then went to work burying the dead, when I witnessed the most horrible sight my eyes ever beheld. On the left of our line, where the Louisiana Brigade had fought the last evening of the battle, and where they drove the enemy about one mile through the woods and then in turn fell back to their own position, the scene beggers description. The dead and badly wounded from both sides were lying where they fell. The woods, taking fire that night from the shells, burnt rapidly and roasted the wounded men alive. As we went to bury them we could see where they had tried to keep the fire from them by scratching the leaves away as far as they could reach. But it availed not; they were burnt to a crisp. The only way we could tell to which army they belonged was by turning them over and examining their clothing where they lay close to the ground. There . . . we could see whether they wore the blue or grey.

We buried them all alike by covering them up with dirt where they lay. It was the most sickening sight I saw during the war, and I wondered whether the American people were civilized or not, to butcher one another in that manner; and I came to the conclusion that we were barbarians, North and South alike. [John O. Casler, *Four years in the Stonewall Brigade* (2nd edition: reprinted Marietta, Georgia: Continental Book Company, 1951), p. 151.]

INTELLIGENCE IN THE
CHANCELLORSVILLE CAMPAIGN

In his official *Report* of the Chancellorsville campaign, Lee attributed his success "to the skillful and efficient management of the artillery" and to the initiative and skill of his chief subordinates. Had it not been for the need to maintain secrecy, however, he surely would have given highest credit to his intelligence service, for as one of his division commanders appropriately noted, "every day Lee had information of Hooker's movements."[1] In contrast Hooker, who recently had overhauled his intelligence service, found himself frequently groping in the dark, unable to penetrate the designs of his enemy, sort out contradictory information, or even to get an accurate assessment of enemy numbers. In studying Chancellorsville, therefore, it is especially appropriate to look at the way in which both commanders acquired and made use of intelligence, for as the foremost authority on the campaign has observed, "one of the most important qualifications of a commander is the ability to sift truth from conflicting rumors and reports, and deduce therefrom the dispositions movement, and intentions of the enemy."[2]

When Hooker was given command of the Army of the Potomac, one of his first moves was to overhaul his intelligence service. Heretofore the man responsible for acquiring military information for the Army of the Potomac was Allan Pinkerton, who had come from Chicago in the wake of the fiasco at Bull Run in July 1861, accompanied by his entire detective force. Used initially to tighten security, Pinkerton arrested a number of people suspected of sending information secretly to Richmond, but soon his skilled operatives "were traveling between Richmond and Washington, bringing "valuable information" about enemy plans. "Major Allan," as Pinkerton was then known, was in almost daily contact with the President, Secretary of War, the provost-marshal general and the general in charge of the Union armies. He served as Major General G. B. McClellan's chief of intelligence in both the Peninsular and the Maryland campaigns. There is a picture of "Major Allan" in Miller's *Photographic History of the Civil War*, taken before Richmond. He is sitting in the yard of a frame house with several of his "intrepid" scouts and guides around a table, smoking a pipe and apparently lost in thought; his three operators look as though they might be contemplating the dangers of their next mission.

> He must send his men into the Confederate lines to find out how strong is the opposing army. Probably some of them will never come back.

Since they are all new to this kind of work they have yet to learn how to approximate the size of enemy forces, so there is an inevitable tendency to exaggerate enemy numbers—which is one reason why McClellan would always insist that he faced overwhelming numbers. When McClellan was relieved from command a month after the battle of Antietam, Pinkerton became indignant at his treatment and refused to continue longer at Washington.[3]

According to one authority, the successful secret-service agent must be "keen-witted, observant, resourceful, and possessing a small degree of fear, yet realizing the danger and consequences of detection."

> His work . . . lay, in general, along three lines. In the first place all suspected persons must be found, their sentiments investigated and ascertained. The members of the secret service obtained access to houses, clubs, and places of resort, sometimes in the guise of guests, sometimes as domestics. . . . As the well-known and time-honored shadow detectives, they tracked footsteps and noted every action. Agents . . . gained membership in hostile secret societies and reported their meetings, by which means many plans of the Southern leaders were ascertained. The most dangerous service was naturally that of entering the Confederate ranks for information as to the nature and strength of defenses and numbers of troops. Constant vigilance was maintained for the detection of Confederate spies, the interception of mail-carriers, and the discovery of contraband goods. All spies, "contrabands," deserters, refugees, and prisoners of war found in or brought into Federal territory were subjected to a searching examination and reports upon their testimony forwarded to the various authorities.[4]

When Hooker took over the Army of the Potomac, he could find no document of any kind at headquarters that contained information about the Confederate forces in his immediate front. "There was no means, no organization, and no apparent effort, to obtain such information."[5] He immediately established an organization for that purpose, and soon he was able to acquire "correct and proper" information of the strength and movements of the enemy. On 30 March he named Colonel G. H. Sharpe, of the 120th New York Volunteers, his new deputy provost-marshal-general, in which capacity he was placed in charge of the separate and special Bureau of Military Information. Sharpe remained at the head of this bureau for the rest of the war and supervised the secret service work in the East.[6]

Amidst these organizational changes Hooker planned his campaign. His directive specified only that he assume the offensive without any unnecessary delay and that his operations not uncover Washington. He thought first of crossing the river some distance to the south, where he could turn the Confederate right flank and possibly interpose his army between the Confederate forces under General Robert E. Lee and Richmond, but the rugged terrain, the expanding width of the river in that direction, and the ability of Lee's men to extend their breastworks as rapidly as his own troops could construct practicable roads caused him to set aside this plan in favor of a movement against the other flank. He would send his cavalry corps upstream to cross the rivers, then strike southward, with the primary object of cutting Confederate communications between Fredericksburg and Richmond. Then he would move three infantry corps 30 miles upstream to cross the Rappahannock at Kelly's Ford, with orders to descend the river and take Confederate fortifications at the United States and Banks' Fords in reverse. This would enable him to send two additional corps across the United States Ford to reinforce the marching column, and together they would move directly against the rear of Lee's lines at Fredericksburg. Lee would then either have to come out in the open to fight or else retreat in the direction of Richmond. Hooker left two corps under Major General John Sedgwick to demonstrate against the Confederates at Fredericksburg, with orders to pursue the enemy "with the utmost vigor" if he seemed to be falling back in the direction of Richmond.

Meanwhile Lee made his own preparations. As he worked to improve his own limited logistical capability the troops labored to strength the river defenses.[7] When scouts informed Lee on 12 February that the Union IX Corps had embarked at Belle Plain, on the Potomac some seven or eight miles behind Hooker's lines, Lee promptly countered by directing two divisions from Longstreet's corps to Richmond, where they could help block any Union advance south of the James River. Although Longstreet's divisions had left by the 15th, it was ten days before Hooker's intelligence could piece together enough information "from deserters, contrabands, and citizens" to learn of the movement, and then he had a faulty idea as to the size, location or distribution of the detachment.

> The general tenor of the statements received make it appear that Jackson's corps is left to guard the passage of the river. Ransom's division, of Longstreet's corps, is one mentioned as gone to Tennessee or South Carolina. Pickett's division is one gone to Charlestown.[8]

This disparity in the assessment of the size as well as the destination of enemy detachments and also in the time required for the news to filter back to headquarters was typical of most of the strategical intelligence that reached Lee and Hooker in the weeks ahead. With the departure of Longstreet, Lee had barely 60,000 men to guard the river line—his enemy could muster nearly 134,000.

A week after Longstreet's departure, Stonewall Jackson summoned his topographical engineer and gave him secret orders to prepare a map of the Shenandoah Valley "extended to Harrisburg, Pa., and then on to Philadelphia—wishing the preparation to be *kept* a profound secret."[9] On 9 April, Lee suggested to James A. Seddon, Secretary of War, that the enemy had probably decided to confine the operations of the Army of the Potomac and of forces south of the James to the defensive while reinforcing Union armies in the west: the recent transfer of Burnside's IX Corps to Kentucky raised this as a distinct possibility. "Should General Hooker's army assume the defensive," Lee suggested, "the readiest method of relieving the pressure upon General Johnston and General Beauregard would be for this army to cross into Maryland." For that he would require more provisions and suitable transportation. He would also need a pontoon bridge and two days later he requested the Engineer Bureau to send a pontoon bridge train to Orange Court House, where it could be added to his army once he could seize the initiative and invade Pennsylvania.[10] The immediate problem, however, was to prevent Hooker from maneuvering him out of his lines and driving him back to the defense of Richmond.

> If I am able to determine the enemy's disposition while at the same time I conceal my own, then I can concentrate and he must divide.[11]

These words are provided by Sun Tzu, but Lee made the thought his own.

*   *

The two armies went about gathering intelligence in much the same way. During the preparation, before the commencement of active operations, the chief source of information was probably a loose network of spies and scouts. The terms were often used interchangeably, but in the parlance of that day "spies" were individuals located permanently within enemy lines or territory who were actively involved in collecting information valuable to their military leaders. Here the Confederacy had a natural advance in that the border states, particularly Maryland, contained many southern sympathizers and even in the North there were many who denied the right of the Federal Government to invade the south. This advantage was greater still in the occupied portion of the Confederacy, where nearly every inhabitant was a potential spy willing to provide military information to those fighting for southern independence. As the war went on, the use and number of Union spies were greatly increased, "and in the last year the system reached a high degree of efficiency, with spies constantly at work in all the Confederate armies and in all the cities of the South. Only the names of a few "have been rescued from obscurity."[12]

To the Civil War soldier, however, most of what were loosely termed 'spies' would be considered 'scouts': Scouts were organized under a chief who directed their movements, and their duties were to serve as couriers between the network of spies and their own military leaders. Because their duties involved bearing despatches, locating enemy units, and acquiring precise information about the terrain that would facilitate the march of the army, it was inevitable that scouts would often function as spies. Scouts became "the real eyes and ears of the army" as they probed forward as far as the enemy picket line and then used their trained powers of observation to find out what was happening on the other side. In the Confederate armies these men came primarily from the cavalry, while initially the Union commanders depended more upon civilian spies, detectives, and deserters for information. After Sharpe became head of Hooker's Bureau of Military Information, he turned increasingly to scouts drafted from the army, although at the time of Chancellorsville Lee's intelligence system still enjoyed a decided edge. The *Official Records* contain few references to reports from Union scouts until Hooker's army was actually on the move, whereas Lee frequently received vital information from this source as revealed in the following letter from Lee to President Jefferson Davis a month before the battle.

> All the reports from our scouts on the Potomac indicate that General Hooker's army has not been diminished, and is prepared to cross the Rappahannock as soon as the weather permits. Various days have been specified for him to advance, but that has been prevented by the occurrence of storms. The 17th ultimo was one of the days stated, and on the 22d three days rations had been cooked and placed in the haversacks of the men.[13]

Two days later Lee heard from a scout he had sent into Maryland to watch the Baltimore and Ohio Railroad. This man confirmed what Lee had already heard from other reports, that Burnside's IX Corps was indeed being shipped west on the railroad. The scout had counted five divisions.

They were all infantry, transportation for the whole force requiring forty-seven trains. The troops had been encamped for several days in the neighborhood of Baltimore previous to their departure west, and he was able to converse with them at stopping places on the road. He reports that the men were unwilling to be transferred . . . to the Western Department (and) that they were tired of the war. . . .[14]

In contrast the reports Hooker received from his scouts often were misleading. In late February, for example, a Union scout named Yager reported from Fairfax Station that "Jackson and his army are at Staunton, with the intention of making a raid in Maryland with the help of General Stuart. A week later "our scout" brought in information that "Jackson was going up the Valley toward Strasburg"—information gleaned from a "reliable" Confederate soldier who came from Warrenton.[15]

Both sides also used the Signal Corps to provide intelligence. The Confederate signal service was first in the field and gave timely warning of the Union advance upon the Confederate flank at the first battle of Bull Run. Meanwhile Major Albert Myer, a former surgeon who had been appointed Signal Officer for the Union Army a few weeks before the battle, conducted a signal camp of instruction in Georgetown for 17 officers selected for signal duty from the Pennsylvania Reserve Corps. Initially all officers except for Myer were simply acting signal officers on detached serve from their regiments, but in March 1863 the Signal Corps was organized and it served Hooker well at Chancellorsville.

In both armies there were two kinds of signal stations—one with the primary mission of signal communication and the other to serve as an observation station from which enemy movements could be studied by trained personnel using a high-power telescope. When he later wrote the doctrine, Myer drew upon his Civil War experience.

If there is a commanding peak near where the enemy offer battle, signal-officers should be hurried to it in advance of the army. The enemy are to be kept constantly in view . . . (for) the knowledge to be gained by witnessing . . . the formation of their forces, by estimating their strength . . . and by witnessing early what preparations are made for the battle may be invaluable.

Signal officers were instructed to observe by what roads their ammunition and supply-trains came, to detect where the cavalry is posted, to note any unusual feature in the terrain, and to report upon enemy preparations or movements.[16] Because the Signal Corps operated often in exposed areas some distance from the field army it was often hazardous duty. The ratio of killed to wounded in the Signal Corps was 150% as compared with the ratio of 20% in other branches of the service.[17]

To judge from messages published in the *Official Records*, Lee's signal corps seems to have rendered its greatest services at the operational level while Hooker's information from this source was limited primarily to movements about the battlefield. On 20 April, Confederate signal stations along the Potomac reported sailing ships and steamers descending the river in greater numbers than usual, although no troops were reported as having been seen on board. A week later a signal officer in Richmond forwarded a report from a special agent in Washington that confirmed previous reports to the effect that "troops from the rear have been moved to the Rappahannock." To Lee this meant that the campaign had begun, although he could not have known that that very day Hooker ordered the V, XI, and XII corps to commence their turning movement.[18]

Newspapers were also helpful in estimating enemy intentions and capabilities. Both headquarters were frequently provided with the latest newspapers from Washington or Richmond.[19]

Since the Civil War was the first to be fully covered by the press, newspapers often revealed important military information. On 17 April, for example, the Washington Morning *Chronicle* published extracts from a letter by the medical director of the Army of the Potomac to Hooker, revealing the sanitary condition of the army by providing the number of sick soldiers and including the ratio of sickness per thousand men. This is all that Lee needed to compute the size of Hooker's forces, and since Lee later referred to these figures in his own correspondence there is every likelihood that he did so.[20] Several days later a circular was published for the Cavalry Corps stating "if there is in this command such a person as the correspondent of the Philadelphia *Inquirer*, he will, by direction of the commanding general of the Army of the Potomac, be immediately sent out of the lines of the army, never to return." The following day Hooker demanded that the New York *Times* and the Philadelphia *Inquirer* be called upon to name their correspondents who had furnished the information on a story about an alleged submarine cable in use by the Confederates between Falmouth and Fredericksburg, threatening to suppress the circulation of both papers in the army and excluding their correspondents from his lines if the names were not supplied. And finally Hooker's headquarters issued a general order requiring all correspondents to publish their communications over their own signatures, which would at least identify the men responsible for a serious breach in security.[21]

Although Union generals had frequent access to Southern papers, there is little evidence in the published reports to indicate that this was a source of much useful information. A study of newspapers and the problem of maintaining military secrecy during the war suggests that the Southern press perhaps exercised greater discretion and also was under stricter control, while the logic of the situation would suggest that the southern press was less active in the field because resources were much more limited.[22]

Perhaps it was the Confederate generals—who as a group were far less active in politics—who acted with great discretion. One of Jackson's staff officers recorded in April 1863 how Jackson, after agonizing over writing his after-action reports, would cross out entire passages that he had written with great care "saying that it would not do to publish to the enemy the reason that induced one to do certain things and thus enable them to learn your mode of doing."[23] In sharp contrast we find the Secretary of War writing to Hooker scarcely a month later to complain of an officer who had recently been assigned to his staff:

> We cannot control intelligence in relation to your movements while your generals write letters giving details. A letter from General van Alen to a person not connected with the War Department describes your position as intrenched at Chancellorsville. Can't you give his sword something to do, so that he will have less time for the pen.[24]

It was basically a problem of security. Hooker went to great lengths to restrict the leakage of military information by taking special pains to prevent communication across the river, whether by private citizens or bored pickets, and to restrict—but gradually—access of visitors to his camps. The sudden stoppage of all visitors, he wrote, would serve notice that the army was about to move. He even went so far as to ask the Postmaster in Washington on one occasion to detail mail from his army for a period of 24 hours, stating only that he had "very urgent reasons" for making this request.[25]

Perhaps the greatest damage caused by the frequent breaches of security was the impact that it had upon Hooker and his command style. "I have communicated to no one what my intentions are," he confided to the Union commander at Suffolk the day before he commenced his operations.

> If you were here, I could properly and willingly import them to you. So much is found out by the enemy in my front with regard to movements, that I have concealed my designs from my own staff, and I dare not intrust them to the wires, knowing as I do that they are so often tapped.[26]

Throughout the campaign both commanders made extensive use of cavalry to provide news of enemy activities, and here again the Confederates enjoyed a decided advantage. Some of the best regiments in Lee's cavalry originally came from that part of Virginia that now comprised the theater of operations, and they could always count upon the enthusiastic support of the local population. Maj. Gen. J. E. B. Stuart, the flamboyant Confederate cavalry commander, was still master of the field and so excelled in reconnaissance that when he was killed a year later, Lee's first agonizing words were "He never brought me a piece of false information."[27] Although Hooker had recently consolidated his mounted arm into a separate corps, he needed time before the new division and corps commanders could inspire their men, rebuild morale, and learn to succeed in combat. There was a series of small cavalry engagements in March that enhanced the self confidence of the Union cavalry, but not much in the way of useful intelligence filtered back to army headquarters.

Hooker compounded the problem by sending his new cavalry corps, less one brigade, on a controversial raid against Lee's supply line to Richmond, but the movement, originally ordered for 12 April, had to be postponed because of rampaging waters and it was not until the 29th that the floods had subsided enough to permit Stoneman's mounted corps to cross the Rappahannock. For the next ten days—during which time the army fought and lost the battle of Chancellorsville—the Union cavalry was out of touch and Hooker's army moved blindfolded into the wilderness.

In one area only did a Union instrument of intelligence enjoy a clear advantage—the observation balloon. Thought had been given to the military possibilities of the balloon as early as the previous century, for a treatise written by an Englishman in the final year of the American Revolution suggested that:

> On the first report of a country being invaded, an *Air Balloon* would save the expenses of messengers, posts, etc., from the coasts to the main army, as at the height it ascends, with the assistance of glasses, the number of the enemy, together with their place of landing, might be communicated with great dispatch. . . . A general likewise in the day of battle would drive singular advantage by going up in one of these machines: he would have a bird's eye view of not only everything that was doing in his own, but in the enemy's army.[28]

During the wars of the French Revolution a regular balloon company, the *Ier Compagnie d'Aerostiers* was created to assist in reconnaissance and observation, facilitate signalling between French divisions in the field, and spread revolutionary propaganda leaflets from the air, and for the next few years there was a growing interest in military aeronautics. This soon declined, however, and Napoleon, who relied upon his cavalry for information, showed little interest in the project. Other armies experimented with balloons spasmodically during the first half of the 19th century, but not until the Civil War was there any serious effort to use captive balloons for military purposes. By that time "balloons and aeronauts were no longer rarities: they had become part of American life."[29]

From the first President Lincoln had demonstrated an interest in the military potential of the captive balloon. Within days of the Union defeat at the first battle of Bull Run, he summoned Professor Thaddeus Lowe, a pioneer aeronaut who had offered his services to the government, to the White House. Convinced that the recent defeat "might have been averted if someone in a balloon could have observed the movements of the Confederate forces," Lincoln engaged Lowe as a civilian balloonist at pay equivalent to that of an army colonel. Thanks in large measure to Professor Lowe's efforts, the Aeronautical Corps did useful service throughout the Peninsular campaign, and at the battle of Fredericksburg Hooker's future chief of staff, then a corps commander, made a short ascent to obtain "a view of the topography, ravines, streams, road, etc., that was of great value in making dispositions and movements of the troops." Significantly, although there were three balloons in use at Fredericksburg, none of the printed reports reveals that those who had gone aloft had observed the position of the famous stone wall at Marye's Heights.[30]

The Confederates had no balloons at Chancellorsville. Although a Confederate balloon had been reported visible across the Potomac from Washington in 1861 and several months later in the vicinity of Leesburg, Virginia, this was not a source of intelligence available to Confederate commanders. As Confederate General James Longstreet confessed to Professor Lowe after the war:

> At all times we were fully aware that you Federals were using balloons to examine our positions and we watched with envious eyes their beautiful observations as they floated high in the air, well out of range of our guns. . . . We were longing for balloons that poverty denied us.

During the Seven Days Campaign some Confederates did manage to patch together a balloon made of silk dresses, but because the only gas available was in Richmond, and balloons had to be filled there and then towed either by ship or by rail. On one of its infrequent appearances, when it was attached to a steamer in the James River, the tide went out and both ship and balloon were left stranded high and dry on a bar and subsequently fell into Union hands. "This capture," Longstreet later assured Professor Lowe, "was the meanest trick of the war and one I have never yet forgiven."[31]

In the Chancellorsville campaign Union balloons frequently were in the air, a thousand feet above the ridge that lines the left bank of the Rappahannock, but any intelligence from this source was limited to what could be seen within six to eight miles and thus would be useful only at the tactical level—unless of course Lee should decide to withdraw from his lines above Fredericksburg to conduct operations elsewhere, in which case the balloons would have provided timely intelligence of the movement.

*   *   *

Except for the balloons, in the Chancellorsville campaign the Confederates enjoyed a distinct advantage in all of the methods of gathering intelligence of enemy strength, capabilities, and intentions.

Lee had accurate information of the strength of the Army of the Potomac on the eve of active operations thanks to the untiring efforts of his cavalry, reports from scouts and messages intercepted by his signal corps, and the accommodating Washington newspapers, although he was inclined to think that the numbers reported were "much exaggerated."[32] Hooker, on the other hand, received conflicting reports about the strength and location of Lee's forces. There were persistent rumors of a Confederate build-up to the west, aimed probably at the Shenandoah Valley, and on the eve of battle "deserters" reported that Hood's and Pickett's divisions, of Longstreet's command, had arrived from the vicinity of Richmond. These reports—all of them from deserters purporting to be from these two divisions—were so persistent that it cannot have been mere coincidence, and the camp rumor to the effect that Lee had been overheard saying that this "was the only time he should fight equal numbers" reinforces the suspicion that the Confederate commander was a master of deception.[33] Although the Union commander at Suffolk correctly insisted as late as the second day of the battle that Longstreet was in his front, Hooker's information was that Longstreet had already rejoined Lee.[34]

Lee also had a much clearer perception of enemy intentions than did Hooker. As early as 12 March he received information from citizens at Falmouth "that the enemy will, as soon as roads permit, cross at United States Ford, Falmouth, and some point below, the attempt at Falmouth to be a feint." Accordingly he ordered the commander at the United States Ford:

> If your position can be strengthened, have all needful work done. Have the road repaired. Learn all that you can about United States Ford. This may be effected by inducing one of the enemy's cavalry pickets to come over to exchange papers or to trade. Let me have timely notice of any movements of the enemy.[35]

Throughout April Lee was kept informed by Stuart of enemy activity along the upper Rappahannock, although it was not clear whether Hooker intended to cross at the upper fords or to send his cavalry to the Shenandoah. As Stuart kept probing, Lee gained the impression that Hooker "is rather fearful of an attack from us than preparing to attack"—a perception that may well have reinforced some chancy decisions that he felt compelled to make during the battle.[36] By this time Lee had already decided to assume the offensive by 1 May, "when we may expect General Hooker's army to be weakened by the expiration of the term of service of many of his regiments, and before new recruits can be received"—an assumption that almost certainly was based upon his reading of the Washington papers.[37]

Hooker had a far less acute perception of his opponent's intentions. Obviously he could not establish signal stations deep in enemy territory, as the Confederates could do from the Maryland bank of the upper Potomac, for by the very nature of things, signal stations were more effective to the army on the strategic defensive. Nor could his cavalry systematically penetrate the Confederate cavalry screen or cross the upper Rappahannock except with a considerable force. Scouts were active in rear of the Confederate lines, but often this was a mixed blessing: Lee was well aware that the "chief source of information to the enemy is through our negroes," who could be "easily deceived by proper caution," and he therefore pursued a policy of secrecy which, *"aided by rumor,"* could mask his intentions by planting misleading reports. Lee's policy was to "send no dispatches by telegraph relative to . . . movements, or they will become known."[38] Hooker's intelligence was therefore limited to what could be inferred from information obtained from deserters, slaves (or contrabands) and local inhabitants in enemy territory, and even when the intelligence was accurate Hooker often misinterpreted it.

On 11 April, for example, Lee requested that a pontoon train of 350 feet span, with rigging and everything complete, be sent to Orange Court House, obviously in anticipation of his projected operations in Maryland and Pennsylvania. Ten days later Hooker confided to President Lincoln:

> Deserters inform me that the talk in the rebel camp is that when we cross the river it is their intention to fall in our rear and attack our depots at Aquia. The recent arrival of a pontoon train at Hamilton's Crossing lends plausibility to these reports.[39]

Occasional Confederate reinforcements to the Shenandoah Valley or a regiment or two invariably were enlarged to a division or even a corps by the time the news reached Union headquarters, and when Hooker decided to turn Lee's left and sever his communications with Richmond, he was apprehensive that Lee would fall back once Union forces had crossed the Rappahannock and would retreat over the shortest line to Richmond.[40]

On 14 April, Lee received intelligence that Union cavalry was concentrating on the Upper Rappahannock, where Stuart's cavalry prevented them from establishing a bridgehead on the south bank of the river. A week later small bodies of infantry appeared at Rappahannock Bridge and Kelly's Ford, and two days later some Union infantry crossed the river about 20 miles *south* of Fredericksburg at Port Royal. Lee assumed that these movements were intended to conceal Hooker's designs, "but, taken in connection with the reports of scouts," they indicated that Hooker's army "was about to resume active operations." On 28 April Union troops crossed the Rappahannock in boats near Fredericksburg, drove off Confederate pickets, and proceeded to lay down a pontoon bridge, and the following morning the three corps that Hooker had sent up river commenced to cross at the Rappahannock at Kelly's Ford.[41]

Couriers kept Lee informed of the progress of this massive turning movement. On the 29th Lee learned that enemy cavalry had crossed the Rapidan at Germanna and Ely's Fords, removing any doubt that Hooker's intention was to turn his left "and probably to get into our rear."[42] He immediately requested that the remainder of Longstreet's corps be sent to him and alerted his troops in the lines behind Fredericksburg to make preparatory arrangements to move to strengthen his left. The following day Lee was informed that turning movement comprised the V, XI and XII corps and he ordered the rest of his army, except for one division and a brigade from a second, to march west into the wilderness "and make arrangements to repulse the enemy."[43]

The battle began on 1 May, when Hooker advanced along the three roads leading from Chancellorsville toward Fredericksburg, hoping to uncover Banks' Ford, where bridges were to be thrown across the river, thus shortening significantly the line of communication between the two wings of his army. A Confederate division attacked the center column and drove it back, causing Hooker, who had assumed personal command of his forces at Chancellorsville, to withdraw to a defensive position that had been prepared the previous night. This was done, according to the chief of topographical engineers, Army of the Potomac, because of "information received since the advance began."[44]

The information came from Hooker's observation balloons, hovering high above the hills across the river from Fredericksburg and at Banks' Ford. For when Lee decided to move out of his trenches at Fredericksburg to attack Hooker near Chancellorsville, there was ample and timely warning from "Balloons in the Air" that this was his response. On the 29th there had been reports of Confederate infantry and wagon trains moving to the west. The next day it was noted that "all of the camps west of the railroad have been struck save one small one," and although the telegraph was not in working order and vision was obscured by an early morning fog, by noon on 1 May Hooker was informed that the largest enemy column was moving on the road toward Chancellorsville, leaving the Confederate strength at Fredericksburg "considerably diminished."[45] Shortly before the Confederates attacked he was informed by his chief of staff, at army headquarters across the river from Fredericksburg:

> The enemy will meet you between Chancellorsville and Hamilton's Cross-ing. He cannot, I judge, from all reports, have detached over 10,000 or 15,000 men from Sedgwick's front since sun cleared fog.[46]

This timely intelligence, coupled with the planted reports that "Hood's division arrived yesterday from Richmond," was certainly the reason why Hooker suspended his attack and fell back to defensive lines around Chancellorsville. At the time he made his decision only one division had yet been engaged: two others were within sight of Confeder-ate works guarding Banks' Ford, which he recognized was critical terrain for the success of his operations, and yet Hooker recalled his forces because of news he had just received "from the other side of the river."

> Hope the enemy will be emboldened to attack me. I did feel certain of success. If his communications are cut, he must attack me. I have a strong position. All the enemy's cavalry are on my flanks . . . which I trust will enable Stoneman to do a land-office business in the interior.[47]

When he suspended his own attack Hooker instructed Sedgwick, who commanded 40,000 men at Fredericksburg, "to keep a sharp lookout, and attack if you can succeed." But Sedgwick, who received a steady flow of reports from "balloons in the air" to the effect that the Confederates had withdrawn many troops from their lines at Fredericksburg to meet Hook-er's advance from the west, decided not to attack. Major General John F. Reynolds, who commanded I Corps, cautioned against making an attack and speculated that the Confederates

> have been . . . showing weakness, with a view of delaying Hooker, in tempting us to make an attack on their fortified position, and hoping to destroy us and strike for our depot over our bridges.[48]

In sharp contrast, Lee made the best possible use of his intelligence.

Having won the initiative when Hooker fell back to his fortified lines about Chancellorsville, Lee decided to assume the offensive. Acting on reports from his cavalry that Hooker's right flank rested on no natural obstacle and thus was "in the air," he decided to send Jackson's entire corps to attack the Union right flank and rear. It is possible that Lee and Jackson erred somewhat in their estimation of the exact location of the Union right flank, for in executing the movement Jackson was forced to take a longer route than anticipated to avoid marching across the front of the intrenched XI Corps. Major General Fitzhugh Lee's cavalry brigade, which covered Jackson's marching column, provided the timely intelligence that enabled Jackson's attack to succeed—and Lee to win the most brilliant victory of his career.

Jackson's march did not go unobserved. The balloons at Fredericksburg were too far off to detect the movement through the thick woods, but Jackson's column was observed by Union lookouts in the treetops at Hazel Grove and fired upon by a battery nearby, and about 9:30 a.m. Hooker sent word to the commander of XI Corps, Major General O. O. Howard: "We have good reason to suppose that the enemy is moving to our right." Major General Daniel Sickles, commander of III Corps, likewise saw the continuous column of infantry, artillery, trains and ambulances moving across his front in a southerly direction "toward Orange Court-House, on the Orange and Alexandria Railroad, or Louisa Court-House, on the Virginia Central," but Sickles was uncertain whether this portended a retreat on Gordonsville or an attack upon the Union right flank. Later Howard's scouts and cavalry sent back "the unvarying report" that "The enemy is crossing the Plank Road and moving toward Culpeper."[49] Hooker had assumed all along that once he could maneuver his army across the rivers and astride Lee's line of communications, the Rebels "may as well pack up their haversacks and make for Richmond."[50] It seemed logical to assume, therefore, that the long column was probably headed for the Orange and Alexandria Railroad. Hooker and his subordinates were guilty of "making pictures."

There is no need to devote more attention to the battle. Jackson's flank attack succeeded brilliantly, although Jackson himself was mortally wounded. The following day, after bitter fighting, the Confederates united to drive Hooker's larger forces into defensive lines north of Chancellorsville, enabling Lee later to send desperately needed reinforcements to the tiny force that fought to delay Sedgwick's advance from Fredericksburg. On 4 May Lee concentrated against Sedgwick, driving him back upon Banks' Ford, and two days later Hooker's army, which still significantly outnumbered that of Lee, withdrew to the northern bank of the Rappahannock.

Jackson's biographer considered Chancellorsville, where 60,000 men defeated 130,000, "as much the tactical masterpiece of the nineteenth century as was Leuthen of the eighteenth," and most students of the Civil War would agree that it was Lee's most brilliant achievement.[51] And in searching for the reasons why Lee had been able to outmaneuver superior numbers in this week's fighting in the wilderness of Virginia, high on the list would be his superior use of intelligence, both at the operational and the tactical level.

Ironically, while Hooker was hampered in acquiring strategic intelligence, his tactical intelligence was more than adequate. Thanks to his "balloons in the air," he knew early in the afternoon of 1 May that Lee was moving out from Fredericksburg to attack before there had been any contact on the ground. But instead of utilizing this information, Hooker seemed overwhelmed by it, while Sedgwick convinced himself that this must be a trap. The next day Hooker also had ample warning that a substantial Confederate column was moving toward his flank or rear, and again he did not take appropriate action.

Several weeks after the battle the Balloon Corps was disbanded. In part this was a bureaucratic decision made to resolve a conflict between Professor Lowe and a captain of engineers who was placed in over-all command of the Balloon Corps: protocol, accountability, and the amount of pay Lowe received were the issues. And since Hooker's chief of staff later claimed that he could not recall uses "of any value" during the battle[52] it almost appears as if the decision was made to make the balloons the scapegoat for the battle! The message traffic from the aeronauts published in the *Official Records*, however, suggests that the problem was not in the quality of the intelligence, but in the ability of the Union commanders to make use of it. Had the Union forces in their next battle possessed a balloon in addition to the signal station on Little Round Top, the course of the battle, particularly on the second day, would have been far different.[53] Instead the balloons soon would be sold as government surplus.

APPENDIX II
ORDER OF BATTLE

Organization of the Army of the Potomac, at the battle of Fredericksburg, Va., December 11–15, 1862, Maj. Gen. Ambrose E. Burnside, USA, commanding

RIGHT GRAND DIVISION (Maj. Gen. Edwin V. Sumner)
SECOND ARMY CORPS (Maj. Gen. Darius N. Couch)

First Division (Brig. Gen. Winfield S. Hancock)

First Brigade (Brig. Gen. John C. Caldwell)
(Col. George W. von Schack)
5th New Hampshire
7th New York
61st New York
64th New York
81st Pennsylvania
145th Pennsylvania

Second Brigade (Brig. Gen. Thomas F. Meagher)
28th Massachusetts
63d New York
69th New York
88th New York
116th Pennsylvania

Third Brigade (Col. Samuel K. Zook)
27th Connecticut
2d Delaware
52d New York
57th New York
66th New York
53d Pennsylvania

Artillery
1st New York Light, Battery B
4th United States, Battery C

Second Division (Brig. Gen. Oliver O. Howard)

First Brigade (Brig. Gen. Alfred Sully)
19th Maine
15th Massachusetts
Massachusetts Sharpshooters, 1st Company
1st Minnesota
Minnesota Sharpshooters, 2nd Company
34th New York
82d New York (2d Militia)

Second Brigade (Col. Joshua T. Owen)
69th Pennsylvania
71st Pennsylvania
72d Pennsylvania
106th Pennsylvania

Third Brigade (Col. Norman J. Hall)
(Col. William R. Lee)
19th Massachusetts
20th Massachusetts
7th Michigan
42d New York
59th New York
127th Pennsylvania

Artillery
1st Rhode Island Light, Battery A
1st Rhode Island Light, Battery B

Third Division (Brig. Gen. William H. French)

First Brigade (Brig. Gen. Nathan Kimball)
(Col. John S. Mason)
14th Indiana
24th New Jersey
28th New Jersey
4th Ohio
8th Ohio
7th West Virginia

Second Brigade (Col. Oliver H. Palmer)
14th Connecticut
108th New York
130th Pennsylvania

Third Brigade (Col. John W. Andrews)
Lieut. Col. William Jameson
Lieut. Col. John W. Marshall
1st Delaware
4th New York
10th New York
132d Pennsylvania

Artillery
1st New York Light, Battery G
1st Rhode Island Light, Battery G

Artillery Reserve
(Capt. Charles H. Morgan)
1st United States, Battery I
4th United States, Battery A

NINTH ARMY CORPS (Brig. Gen. Orlando B. Willcox)

First Division (Brig. Gen. William W. Burns)

First Brigade (Col. Orlando M. Poe)
- 2d Michigan
- 17th Michigan
- 20th Michigan
- 79th New York

Second Brigade (Col. Benjamin C. Christ)
- 29th Massachusetts
- 8th Michigan
- 27th New Jersey
- 46th New York
- 50th Pennsylvania

Third Brigade (Col. Daniel Leasure)
- 36th Massachusetts
- 45th Pennsylvania
- 100th Pennsylvania

Artillery
- 1st New York Light, Battery D
- 3d United States, Batteries L and M

Second Division (Brig. Gen. Samuel D. Sturgis)

First Brigade (Brig. Gen James Nagle)
- 2d Maryland
- 6th New Hampshire
- 9th New Hampshire
- 18th Pennsylvania
- 7th Rhode Island
- 12th Rhode Island

Second Brigade (Brig. Gen. Edward Ferrero)
- 21st Massachusetts
- 35th Massachusetts
- 11th New Hampshire
- 51st New York
- 51st Pennsylvania

Artillery
- 2d New York Light, Battery L
- Pennsylvania Light, Battery D
- 1st Rhode Island Light, Battery D
- 4th United States, Battery E

Third Division (Brig. Gen. George W. Getty)

First Brigade (Col. Rush C. Hawkins)
- 10th New Hampshite
- 13th New Hampshite
- 25th New Jersey
- 9th New York
- 89th New York
- 103d New York

Second Brigade (Col. Edward Harland)
- 8th Connecticut
- 11th Connecticut
- 15th Connecticut
- 16th Connecticut
- 21th Connecticut
- 4th Rhode Island

Artillery
- 2d United States, Battery E
- 5th United States, Battery A

CAVALRY DIVISION (Brig. Gen. Alfred Pleasonton)

First Brigade (Brig. Gen. John F. Farnsworth)
8th Illinois
3d Indiana
8th New York

Second Brigade (Col. David McM. Gregg)
(Col. Thomas C. Devin)
6th New York
8th Pennsylvania
6th United States

Artillery
2d United States, Battery M

CENTER GRAND DIVISION (Maj. Gen. Joseph Hooker)
THIRD ARMY CORPS (Brig. Gen. George Stoneman)

First Division (Brig. Gen. David B. Birney)

First Brigade (Brig. Gen. John C. Robinson)
20th Indiana
63d Pennsylvania
68th Pennsylvania
105th Pennsylvania
114th Pennsylvania
141st Pennsylvania

Second Brigade (Brig. Gen. J. H. Hobart Ward)
3d Maine
4th Maine
38th New York
40th New York
55th New York
57th Pennsylvania
99th Pennsylvania

Third Brigade (Brig. Gen. Hiram G. Berry)
17th Maine
3d Michigan
5th Michigan
1st New York
37th New York
101st New York

Artillery
1st Rhode Island Light, Battery E
3d United States, Batteries F and K

Second Division (Brig. Gen. Daniel E. Sickles)

First Brigade (Brig. Gen. Joseph B. Carr)
1st Massachusetts
11th Massachusetts
16th Massachusetts
2d New Hampshire
11th New Jersey
26th Pennsylvania

Second Brigade (Col. George B. Hall)
70th New York
71st New York
72nd New York
73d New York
74th New York
120th New York

Third Brigade (Brig. Gen. Joseph W. Reymon)
　5th New Jersey
　6th New Jersey
　7th New Jersey
　8th New Jersey
　2d New York
　115th Pennsylvania

Artillery
　New Jersey Light, 2d Battery
　New York Light, 4th Battery
　1st United States, Battery H
　4th United States, Battery K

Third Division (Brig. Gen. Amiel W. Whipple)

First Brigade (Brig. Gen. A. Sanders Piatt)
　(Col. Emien Franklin)
　86th New York
　124th New York
　122d Pennsylvania

Second Brigade (Col. Samuel S. Carroll)
　12th New Hampshire
　163d New York
　84th Pennsylvania
　110th Pennsylvania

Artillery
　New York Light, 10th Battery
　New York Light, 11th Battery
　1st Ohio Light, Battery H

FIFTH ARMY CORPS (Brig. Gen. Daniel Butterfield)

First Division (Brig. Gen. Charles Griffin)

First Brigade (Col. James Barnes)
　2d Maine
　Massachusetts Sharpshooters,
　　2d Company
　18th Massachusetts
　22d Massachusetts
　1st Michigan
　13th New York
　25th New York
　118th Pennsylvania

Second Brigade (Col. Jacob B. Sweitzer)
　9th Massachusetts
　32d Massachusetts
　4th Michigan
　14th New York
　62d Pennsylvania

Third Brigade (Col. T. B. W. Stockton)
20th Maine
Michigan Sharpshooters
16th Michigan
12th New York
17th New York
44th New York
83d Pennsylvania

Artillery
Massachusetts Light, 3d Battery (C)
Massachusetts Light, 5th Battery (E)
1st Rhode Island Light, Battery C
5th United States, Battery D

Sharpshooters
1st United States

Second Division (Brig. Gen. George Sykes)

First Brigade (Lieut. Col. Robert C. Buchanan)
3d United States
4th United States
12th United States, 1st Battalion
12th United States, 2d Battalion
14th United States, 1st Battalion
14th United States, 2d Battalion

Second Brigade (Maj. George L. Andrews)
(Maj. Charles S. Lovell)
1st and 2d United States (battalion)
6th United States
7th United States (battalion)
10th United States
11th United States
17th and 19th United States (battalion)

Third Brigade (Brig. Gen. Gouverneur K. Warren)
5th New York
140th New York
146th New York

Artillery
1st Ohio Light, Battery L
5th United States, Battery I

Third Division (Brig. Gen. Andrew A. Humphreys)

First Brigade (Brig. Gen. Erastus B. Tyler)
91st Pennsylvania
126th Pennsylvania
129th Pennsylvania
134th Pennsylvania

Second Brigade (Col. Peter H. Allabach)
123d Pennsylvania
131st Pennsylvania
133d Pennsylvania
155th Pennsylvania

Artillery
1st New York Light, Battery C
1st United States, Batteries E and G

CAVALRY BRIGADE (Brig. Gen. William W. Averill)

1st Massachusetts
3d Pennsylvania
4th Pennsylvania
5th United States

Artillery
2d United States, Batteries B and L

LEFT GRAND DIVISION (Maj. Gen. William B. Franklin)
FIRST ARMY CORPS (Maj. Gen. John F. Reynolds)

First Division (Brig. Gen. Abner Doubleday)

First Brigade (Col. Walter Phelps, Jr.)
22d New York
24th New York
30th New York
84th New York (14th Militia)
2d U.S. Sharpshooters

Second Brigade (Col. James Gavin)
7th Indiana
76th New York
95th New York
56th Pennsylvania

Third Brigade (Col. William F. Rogers)
21st New York
23d New York
35th New York
80th New York (20th Militia)

Fourth Brigade (Brig. Gen. Solomon Meredith)
(Col. Lysander Cutler)
19th Indiana
24th Michigan
2d Wisconsin
6th Wisconsin
7th Wisconsin

Artillery
New Hampshire Light, 1st Battery
1st New York Light, Battery L
4th United States, Battery B

Second Division (Brig. Gen. John Gibbon)
(Brig. Gen. Nelson Taylor)

First Brigade (Col. Adrian R. Root)
16th Maine
94th New York
104th New York
105th New York
107th Pennsylvania

Second Brigade (Col. Peter Lyle)
12th Massachusetts
26th New York
90th Pennsylvania
136th Pennsylvania

Third Brigade (Brig. Gen. Nelson Taylor)
(Col. Samuel H. Leonard)
13th Massachusetts
83d New York (9th Militia)
97th New York
11th Pennsylvania
88th Pennsylvania

Artillery
Maine Light, 2d Battery
Maine Light, 5th Battery
Pennsylvania Light, Battery C
1st Pennsylvania Light, Battery F

Third Division (Maj. Gen. George G. Meade)

First Brigade (Col. William Sinclair)
(Col. William McCandless)
1st Pennsylvania Reserves
2d Pennsylvania Reserves
6th Pennsylvania Reserves
13th Pennsylvania Reserves (1st Rifles)
121st Pennsylvania

Second Brigade (Col. Albert L. Magilton)
3d Pennsylvania Reserves
4th Pennsylvania Reserves
7th Pennsylvania Reserves
8th Pennsylvania Reserves
142d Pennsylvania

Third Brigade (Brig. Gen. C. Feger
Jackson)
(Col. Joseph W. Fisher)
(Lieut. Col. Robert Anderson)
5th Pennsylvania Reserves
9th Pennsylvania Reserves
10th Pennsylvania Reserves
11th Pennsylvania Reserves
19th Pennsylvania Reserves

Artillery
1st Pennsylvania Light, Battery A
1st Pennsylvania Light, Battery B
1st Pennsylvania Light, Battery G
6th United States, Battery C

SIXTH ARMY CORPS (Maj. Gen. William F. Smith)

First Division (Brig. Gen. William T. H. Brooks)

First Brigade (Col. Alfred T. A. Torbert)
1st New Jersey
2d New Jersey
3d New Jersey
4th New Jersey
15th New Jersey
23d New Jersey

Second Brigade (Col. Henry L. Cake)
5th Maine
16th New York
27th New York
121st New York
96th Pennsylvania

Third Brigade (Brig. Gen. David A. Russell)
18th New York
31st New York
32d New York
95th Pennsylvania

Artillery
Maryland Light, Battery A
Massachusetts Light, 1st Battery (A)
New Jersey Light, 1st Battery
2d United States, Battery D

Second Division (Brig. Gen. Albion P. Howe)

First Brigade (Brig. Gen. Calvin E. Pratt)
6th Maine
43d New York
49th Pennsylvania
119th Pennsylvania
5th Wisconsin

Second Brigade (Col. Henry Whiting)
26th New Jersey
2d Vermont
3d Vermont
4th Vermont
5th Vermont
6th Vermont

Third Brigade (Brig. Gen. Francis L. Vinton)
(Col. Robert F. Taylor)
(Brig. Gen. Thomas H. Neill)
21st New Jersey
20th New York
33d New York
49th New York
77th New York

Artillery
Maryland Light, Battery B
New York Light, 1st Battery
New York Light, 3d Battery
5th United States, Battery F

Third Division (Brig. Gen. John Newton)

First Brigade (Brig. Gen. John Cochrane)
65th New York
67th New York
122d New York
23d Pennsylvania
61st Pennsylvania
82d Pennsylvania

Second Brigade (Brig. Gen. Charles Devens, Jr.)
7th Massachusetts
10th Massachusetts
37th Massachusetts
36th New York
2d Rhode Island

Third Brigade (Col. Thomas A. Rowley)
(Brig. Gen. Frank Wheaton)
62d New York
93d Pennsylvania
98th Pennsylvania
102d Pennsylvania
139th Pennsylvania

Artillery
1st Pennsylvania Light, Battery C
1st Pennsylvania Light, Battery D
2d United States, Battery G

CAVALRY BRIGADE (Brig. Gen. George D. Bayard)
(Col. David McM. Gregg)

District of Columbia, Independent
Company
1st Maine
1st New Jersey
2d New York

10th New York
1st Pennsylvania

Artillery
3d United States, Battery C

VOLUNTEER ENGINEER BRIGADE (Brig. Gen. Daniel P. Woodbury)

15th New York
60th New York

BATTALION UNITED STATES ENGINEERS (Lieut. Charles E. Cross)

Artillery (Brig. Gen. Henry J. Hunt)

Artillery Reserve (Lieut. Col. William
Hays)
New York Light, 5th Battery
1st Battalion New York Light,
Battery A
1st Battalion New York Light,
Battery B
1st Battalion New York Light,
Battery C
Unattached Artillery (Maj. Thomas S.
Trumbull)
1st Connecticut Heavy, Battery B
1st Connecticut Heavy, Battery M

1st Battalion New York Light,
Battery D
1st United States, Battery K
2d United States, Battery A
4th United States, Battery G
5th United States, Battery K
32d Massachusetts Infantry,
Company C

Organization of the Army of Northern Virginia, General Robert E. Lee, commanding, December 11–15, 1862

FIRST CORPS (Lieut. Gen. James Longstreet)

McLaws' Division (Maj. Gen. Lafayette McLaws)

Kershaw's Brigade (Brig. Gen. Joseph B. Kershaw)
- 2d South Carolina
- 3d South Carolina
- 7th South Carolina
- 8th South Carolina
- 15th South Carolina
- 3d South Carolina Battalion

Barksdale's Brigade (Brig. Gen. William Barksdale)
- 13th Mississippi
- 17th Mississippi
- 18th Mississippi
- 21st Mississippi

Cobb's Brigade (Brig. Gen. T. R. R. Cobb)
- (Col. Robert McMillan)
- 16th Georgia
- 18th Georgia
- 24th Georgia
- Cobb Legion
- Phillips' Legion

Semmes' Brigade (Brig. Gen. Paul J. Semmes)
- 10th Georgia
- 50th Georgia
- 51st Georgia
- 53d Georgia

Artillery (Col. H. C. Cabell)
- Manly's (North Carolina) Battery
- Read's (Georgia) Battery
- Richmond Howitzers (1st), McCarthy's Battery
- Troup (Georgia) Artillery

Anderson's Division (Maj. Gen. Richard H. Anderson)

Wilcox's Brigade (Brig. Gen. Cadmus M. Wilcox)
- 8th Alabama
- 9th Alabama
- 10th Alabama
- 11th Alabama
- 14th Alabama

Featherston's Brigade (Brig. Gen. W. S. Featherston)
- 12th Mississippi
- 16th Mississippi
- 19th Mississippi
- 48th Mississippi (5 companies)

Mahone's Brigade (Brig. Gen. William Mahone)
- 6th Virginia
- 12th Virginia
- 16th Virginia
- 41st Virginia
- 61st Virginia

Wright's Brigade (Brig. Gen. A. R. Wright)
- 3d Georgia
- 22d Georgia
- 48th Georgia
- 2d Georgia Battalion

Perry's Brigade (Brig. Gen. E. A. Perry)
  2d Florida
  5th Florida
  8th Florida

Artillery
  Donaldsonville (Louisiana) Artillery
  Huger's (Virginia) Battery
  Lewis' (Virginia) Battery
  Norfolk (Virginia) Light Artillery Blues

Pickett's Division (Maj. Gen. George E. Pickett)

Garnett's Brigade (Brig. Gen. Richard B. Garnett)
  8th Virginia
  18th Virginia
  19th Virginia
  28th Virginia
  56th Virginia

Kemper's Brigade (Brig. Gen. James L. Kemper)
  1st Virginia
  3d Virginia
  7th Virginia
  11th Virginia
  24th Virginia

Armistead's Brigade (Brig. Gen. Lewis A. Armistead)
  9th Virginia
  14th Virginia
  38th Virginia
  53d Virginia
  57th Virginia

Jenkins' Brigade (Brig. Gen. M. Jenkins)
  1st South Carolina (Hagood's)
  2d South Carolina (Rifles)
  5th South Carolina
  6th South Carolina
  Hampton Legion
  Palmetto Sharpshooters

Corse's Brigade (Brig. Gen. Montgomery D. Corse)
  15th Virginia
  17th Virginia
  30th Virginia
  32d Virginia

Artillery
  Dearing's (Virginia) Battery
  Fauquier (Virginia) Artillery
  Richmond (Fayette) Artillery

Hood's Division (Maj. Gen. John B. Hood)

Law's Brigade (Brig. Gen. E. M. Law)
  4th Alabama
  44th Alabama
  6th North Carolina
  54th North Carolina
  57th North Carolina

Anderson's Brigade (Brig. Gen. George T. Anderson)
  1st Georgia (Regulars)
  7th Georgia
  8th Georgia
  9th Georgia
  11th Georgia

Robertson's Brigade (Brig. Gen. J. B. Robertson)
  3d Arkansas
  1st Texas
  4th Texas
  5th Texas

Toombs' Brigade (Col. H. L. Benning)
  2d Georgia
  15th Georgia
  17th Georgia
  20th Georgia

Artillery
  German (South Carolina) Artillery
  Palmetto (South Carolina) Light Artillery
  Rowan (North Carolina) Artillery

Ransom's Division (Brig. Gen. Robert Ransom, Jr.)

Ransom's Brigade (Brig. Gen. Robert Ransom, Jr.)
24th North Carolina
25th North Carolina
35th North Carolina
49th North Carolina
Branch's (Virginia) battery

Cooke's Brigade (Brig. Gen. J. R. Cooke)
(Col. E. D. Hall)
15th North Carolina
27th North Carolina
46th North Carolina
48th North Carolina
Cooper's (Virginia) Battery

First Corps Artillery

Washington (Louisiana) Artillery
(Col. J. B. Walton)
1st Company
2d Company
3d Company
4th Company

Alexander's Battalion (Lieut. Col. E. Porter Alexander)
Bedford (Virginia) Artillery
Eubank's (Virginia) Battery
Madison Light Artillery (Louisiana)
Parker's (Virginia) Battery
Rhett's (South Carolina) Battery
Woolfolk's (Virginia) Battery

SECOND CORPS (Lieut. Gen. Thomas J. Jackson)

D. H. Hill's Division (Maj. Gen. Daniel H. Hill)

First Brigade (Brig. Gen. R. E. Rodes)
3d Alabama
5th Alabama
6th Alabama
12th Alabama
26th Alabama

Second (Ripley's) Brigade (Brig. Gen. George Doles)
4th Georgia
44th Georgia
1st North Carolina
3d North Carolina

Third Brigade (Brig. Gen. A. H. Colquitt)
13th Alabama
6th Georgia
23d Georgia
27th Georgia
28th Georgia

Fourth Brigade (Brig. Gen. Alfred Iverson)
5th North Carolina
12th North Carolina
20th North Carolina
23d North Carolina

Fifth (Ramseur's) Brigade (Col. Bryan Grimes)
2d North Carolina
4th North Carolina
14th North Carolina
30th North Carolina

Artillery (Maj. H. P. Jones)
Hardaway's (Alabama) Battery
Jeff. Davis (Alabama) Artillery
King William (Virginia) Artillery
Morris (Virginia) Artillery
Orange (Virginia) Artillery

A. P. Hill's Division (Maj. Gen. Ambrose P. Hill)

First (Field's) Brigade (Col. J. M. Brockenbrough)
- 40th Virginia
- 47th Virginia
- 55th Virginia
- 22d Virginia Battalion

Second Brigade (Brig. Gen. Maxcy Gregg)
(Col. D. H. Hamilton)
- 1st South Carolina
- 1st South Carolina Rifles
- 12th South Carolina
- 13th South Carolina
- 14th South Carolina

Third Brigade (Brig. Gen. E. L. Thomas)
- 14th Georgia
- 35th Georgia
- 45th Georgia
- 49th Georgia

Fourth Brigade (Brig. Gen. J. H. Lane)
- 7th North Carolina
- 18th North Carolina
- 28th North Carolina
- 33d North Carolina
- 37th North Carolina

Fifth Brigade (Brig. Gen. J. J. Archer)
- 5th Alabama Battalion
- 19th Georgia
- 1st Tennessee
- 7th Tennessee
- 14th Tennessee

Sixth Brigade (Brig. Gen. William D. Pender)
(Col. A. M. Scales)
- 13th North Carolina
- 16th North Carolina
- 22d North Carolina
- 34th North Carolina
- 38th North Carolina

Artillery (Lieut. Col. R. L. Walker)
- Branch (North Carolina) Artillery
- Crenshaw (Virginia) Battery
- Fredericksburg (Virginia) Artillery
- Johnson's (Virginia) Battery
- Letcher (Virginia) Artillery
- Pee Dee (South Carolina) Artillery
- Purcell (Virginia) Artillery

Ewell's Division (Brig. Gen. Jubal A. Early)

Lawton's Brigade (Col. E. N. Atkinson)
(Col. C. A. Evans)
- 13th Georgia
- 26th Georgia
- 31st Georgia
- 38th Georgia
- 60th Georgia
- 61st Georgia

Early's Brigade (Col. J. A. Walker)
- 13th Virginia
- 25th Virginia
- 31st Virginia
- 44th Virginia
- 49th Virginia
- 52d Virginia
- 58th Virginia

Trimble's Brigade (Col. R. F. Hoke)
  15th Alabama
  12th Georgia
  21st Georgia
  21st North Carolina
  1st North Carolina Battalion

Hays' (First Louisiana) Brigade
(Brig. Gen. Harry T. Hays)
  5th Louisiana
  6th Louisiana
  7th Louisiana
  8th Louisiana
  9th Louisiana

Artillery (Capt. J. W. Latimer)
  Charlottesville (Virginia) Artillery
  Chesapeake (Maryland) Artillery
  Courtney (Virginia) Artillery
  First Maryland Battery
  Louisiana Guard Artillery
  Staunton (Virginia) Artillery

Jackson's Division (Brig. Gen. William B. Taliaferro)

First Brigade (Brig. Gen. E. F. Paxton)
  2d Virginia
  4th Virginia
  5th Virginia
  27th Virginia
  33d Virginia

Second Brigade (Brig. Gen. J. R. Jones)
  21st Virginia
  42d Virginia
  48th Virginia
  1st Virginia Battalion

Third (Taliaferro's) Brigade (Col. E. T. H. Warren)
  47th Alabama
  48th Alabama
  10th Virginia
  23d Virginia
  37th Virginia

Fourth (Starke's) Brigade (Col. Edmund Pendleton)
  1st Louisiana (Volunteers)
  2d Louisiana
  10th Louisiana
  14th Louisiana
  15th Louisiana
  Coppens' (Louisiana) Battalion

Artillery (Capt. J. B. Brockenbrough)
  Carpenter's (Virginia) Battery
  Danville (Virginia) Artillery
  Hampden (Virginia) Artillery
  Lee (Virginia) Artillery
  Lusk's (Virginia) Battery

RESERVE ARTILLERY (Brig. Gen. W. N. Pendleton)

Brown's Battalion (Col. J. Thompson
Brown)
  Brooke's (Virginia) Battery
  Dance's Battery, Powhatan Artillery
  Hupp's Battery, Salem Artillery
  Poague's (Virginia) Battery, Rockbridge
    Artillery
  Smith's Battery, Third Howitzers
  Watson's Battery, Second Howitzers

Cutts' (Georgia) Battalion
  Lane's Battery
  Patterson's Battery
  Ross' Battery, Capt. H. M. Ross

Nelson's Battalion (Maj. William Nelson)
  Kirkpatrick's (Virginia) Battery,
    Amherst Artillery
  Massie's (Virginia) Battery, Fluvanna
    Artillery
  Milledge's (Georgia) Battery

Miscellaneous Batteries
  Ells' (Georgia) Battery
  Nelson's (Virginia) Battery, Hanover
    Artillery

CAVALRY (Maj. Gen. James E. B. Stuart)

First Brigade (Brig. Gen. Wade
Hampton)
  1st North Carolina
  1st South Carolina
  2d South Carolina
  Cobb (Georgia) Legion
  Phillips' (Georgia) Legion

Second Brigade (Brig. Gen. Fitzhugh Lee)
  1st Virginia
  2d Virginia
  3d Virginia
  4th Virginia
  5th Virginia

Third Brigade (Brig. Gen. W. H. F. Lee)
  2d North Carolina
  9th Virginia
  10th Virginia
  13th Virginia
  15th Virginia

Artillery (Maj. John Pelham)
  Breathed's (Virginia) Battery
  Chew's (Virginia) Battery
  Hart's (South Carolina) Battery
  Henry's (Virginia) Battery
  Moorman's (Virginia) Battery

Organization of the Army of the Potomac, May 1–6, 1863, Maj. Gen. Joseph Hooker commanding

GENERAL HEADQUARTERS
COMMAND OF THE PROVOST-MARSHAL-GENERAL
(Brig. Gen. Marsena R. Patrick)

93d New York Infantry
6th Pennsylvania Cavalry, Companies E
and I
8th U.S. Infantry, Companies A, B, C,
D, F, and G
Detachment Regular Cavalry

Patrick's Brigade (Col. William F. Rogers)
  Maryland Light Artillery, Battery B
  21st New York Infantry
  23d New York Infantry
  35th New York Infantry
  80th New York Infantry (20th Militia)
  Ohio Light Artillery, 12th Battery

Engineer Brigade (Brig. Gen. Henry W. Benham)
  15th New York
  50th New York
  Battalion United States

Signal Corps (Capt. Samuel T. Cushing)

Ordnance Detachment (Lieut. John R. Edie)

Artillery (Brig. Gen. Henry J. Hunt)

Artillery Reserve (Capt. William M. Graham)
  (Brig. Gen. Robert O. Tyler)
  1st Connecticut Heavy, Battery B
  1st Connecticut Heavy, Battery M
  New York Light, 5th Battery
  New York Light, 15th Battery
  New York Light, 29th Battery
  New York Light, 30th Battery
  New York Light, 32d Battery
  1st United States, Battery K
  3d United States, Battery C
  4th United States, Battery G
  5th United States, Battery K
  32d Massachusetts Infantry, Company C

FIRST ARMY CORPS (Maj. Gen. John F. Reynolds)

First Division (Brig. Gen. James S. Wadsworth)

First Brigade (Col. Walter Phelps, Jr.)
22d New York
24th New York
30th New York
84th New York

Second Brigade (Brig. Gen. Lysander Cutler)
7th Indiana
76th New York
95th New York
147th New York
56th Pennsylvania

Third Brigade (Brig. Gen. Gabriel R. Paul)
22d New Jersey
29th New Jersey
30th New Jersey
31st New Jersey
137th Pennsylvania

Fourth Brigade (Brig. Gen. Solomon Meredith)
19th Indiana
24th Michigan
2d Wisconsin
6th Wisconsin
7th Wisconsin

Artillery (Capt. John A. Reynolds)
New Hampshire Light, 1st Battery
1st New York Light, Battery L
4th United States, Battery B

Second Division (Brig. Gen. John C. Robinson)

First Brigade (Col. Adrian R. Root)
16th Maine
94th New York
104th New York
107th Pennsylvania

Second Brigade (Brig. Gen. Henry Baxter)
12th Massachusetts
26th New York
90th Pennsylvania
136th Pennsylvania

Third Brigade (Col. Samuel H. Leonard)
13th Massachusetts
83d New York (9th Militia)
97th New York
11th Pennsylvania
88th Pennsylvania

Artillery (Capt. Dunbar R. Ransom)
Maine Light, 2d Battery (B)
Maine Light, 5th Battery (E)
Pennsylvania Light, Battery C
5th United States, Battery C

Third Division (Maj. Gen. Abner Doubleday)

First Brigade (Brig. Gen. Thomas A. Rowley)
121st Pennsylvania
135th Pennsylvania
142d Pennsylvania
151st Pennsylvania

Second Brigade (Col. Roy Stone)
143d Pennsylvania
149th Pennsylvania
150th Pennsylvania

Artillery (Maj. Ezra W. Matthews)
1st Pennsylvania Light, Battery B
1st Pennsylvania Light, Battery F
1st Pennsylvania Light, Battery G

SECOND ARMY CORPS (Maj. Gen. Darius N. Couch)

First Division (Maj. Gen. Winfield S. Hancock)

First Brigade (Brig. Gen. John C. Caldwell)
  5th New Hampshire
  61st New York
  81st Pennsylvania
  148th Pennsylvania

Second Brigade (Brig. Gen. Thomas F. Meagher)
  28th Massachusetts
  63d New York
  69th New York
  88th New York
  116th Pennsylvania (battalion)

Third Brigade (Brig. Gen. Samuel K. Zook)
  52d New York
  57th New York
  66th New York
  140th Pennsylvania

Fourth Brigade (Col. John R. Brooke)
  27th Connecticut
  2d Delaware
  64th New York
  53d Pennsylvania
  145th Pennsylvania

Artillery (Capt. Rufus D. Pettit)
  1st New York Light, Battery B
  4th United States, Battery C

Second Division (Brig. Gen. John Gibbon)

First Brigade (Brig. Gen. Alfred Sully)
  (Col. Henry W. Hudson)
  (Col. Byron Laflin)
  19th Maine
  15th Massachusetts
  1st Minnesota
  34th New York
  82d New York (2d Militia)

Second Brigade (Brig. Gen. Joshua T. Owen)
  69th Pennsylvania
  71st Pennsylvania
  72d Pennsylvania
  106th Pennsylvania

Third Brigade (Col. Norman J. Hall)
  19th Massachusetts
  20th Massachusetts
  7th Michigan
  42d New York
  59th New York
  127th Pennsylvania

Artillery
  1st Rhode Island Light, Battery A
  1st Rhode Island Light, Battery B

Sharpshooters
  1st Company Massachusetts

Third Division (Maj. Gen. William H. French)

First Brigade (Col. Samuel S. Carroll)
14th Indiana
24th New Jersey
28th New Jersey
4th Ohio
8th Ohio
7th West Virginia

Second Brigade (Brig. Gen. William Hays)
(Col. Charles J. Powers)
14th Connecticut
12th New Jersey
108th New York
130th Pennsylvania

Third Brigade (Col. John D. MacGregor)
(Col. Charles Albright)
1st Delaware
4th New York
132d Pennsylvania

Artillery
1st New York Light, Battery G
1st Rhode Island Light, Battery G

Reserve Artillery
1st United States, Battery I
4th United States, Battery A

THIRD ARMY CORPS (Maj. Gen. Daniel E. Sickles)

First Division (Brig. Gen. David B. Birney)

First Brigade (Brig. Gen. Charles K. Graham)
(Col. Thomas W. Egan)
57th Pennsylvania
63d Pennsylvania
68th Pennsylvania
105th Pennsylvania
114th Pennsylvania
141st Pennsylvania

Second Brigade (Brig. Gen. J. H. Hobart Ward)
20th Indiana
3d Maine
4th Maine
38th New York
40th New York
99th Pennsylvania

Third Brigade (Col. Samuel B. Hayman)
17th Maine
3d Michigan
5th Michigan
1st New York
37th New York

Artillery (Capt. A. Judson Clark)
New Jersey Light, Battery B
1st Rhode Island Light, Battery E
3d United States, Batteries F and K

Second Division (Maj. Gen. Hiram G. Berry)
(Brig. Gen. Joseph B. Carr)

First Brigade (Brig. Gen. Joseph B. Carr)
(Col. William Blaisdell)
1st Massachusetts
11th Massachusetts
16th Massachusetts
11th New Jersey
26th Pennsylvania

Second Brigade (Brig. Gen. Joseph W. Revere)
(Col. J. Egbert Farnum)
70th New York
71st New York
72d New York
73d New York
74th New York
120th New York

Third Brigade (Brig. Gen. Gershom Mott)
  (Col. William J. Sewell)
  5th New Jersey
  6th New Jersey
  7th New Jersey
  8th New Jersey
  2d New York
  115th Pennsylvania

Artillery (Capt. Thomas W. Osborn)
  1st New York Light, Battery D
  New York Light, 4th Battery
  1st United States, Battery H
  4th United States, Battery K

Third Division (Maj. Gen. Amiel W. Whipple)
(Brig. Gen. Charles K. Graham)

First Brigade (Col. Emlen Franklin)
  86th New York
  124th New York
  122d Pennsylvania

Second Brigade (Col. Samuel M. Bowman)
  12th New Hampshire
  84th Pennsylvania
  110th Pennsylvania

Third Brigade (Col. Hiram Berdan)
  1st U.S. Sharpshooters
  2d U.S. Sharpshooters

Artillery (Capt. Albert A. von Puttkammer)
  (Capt. James F. Huntington)
  New York Light, 10th Battery
  New York Light, 11th Battery
  1st Ohio Light, Battery H

FIFTH ARMY CORPS (Maj. Gen. George G. Meade)

First Division (Brig. Gen. Charles Griffin)

First Brigade (Brig. Gen. James Barnes)
  2d Maine
  18th Massachusetts
  22d Massachusetts
  2d Co. Massachusetts
  1st Michigan
  13th New York (battalion)
  25th New York
  118th Pennsylvania

Second Brigade (Col. James McQuade)
  (Col. Jacob B. Sweitzer)
  9th Massachusetts
  32d Massachusetts
  4th Michigan
  14th New York
  62d Pennsylvania

Third Brigade (Col. Thomas B. W. Stockton)
  20th Maine
  Michigan Sharpshooters
  16th Michigan
  12th New York
  17th New York
  44th New York
  83d Pennsylvania

Artillery (Capt. Augustus P. Martin)
  Massachusetts Light, 3d Battery (C)
  Massachusetts Light, 5th Battery (E)
  1st Rhode Island Light, Battery C
  5th United States, Battery D

Second Division (Maj. Gen. George Sykes)

First Brigade (Brig. Gen. Romeyn B. Ayres)
   3d United States, Companies B, C, F, G, I, and K
   4th United States, Companies C, F, H, and K
   12th United States, Companies A, B, C, D, and G (First Battalion), and A, C, and D (Second Battalion)
   14th United States, Companies, A, B, D, E, F, and G (First Battalion), and F and G (Second Battalion)

Second Brigade (Col. Sidney Burbank)
   2d United States, Companies B, C, F, I, and K
   6th United States, Companies D, F, G, H, and I
   7th United States, Companies A, B, E, and I
   10th United States, Companies D, G, and H
   11th United States, Companies B, C, D, E, F, and G (First Battalion), and C and D (Second Battalion)
   17th United States, Companies A, C, D, G, and H (First Battalion), and A and B (Second Battalion)

Third Brigade (Col. Patrick H. O'Rorke)
   5th New York
   140th New York
   146th New York

Artillery (Capt. Stephen H. Weed)
   1st Ohio Light, Battery L
   5th United States, Battery I

Third Division (Brig. Gen. Andrew A. Humphreys)

First Brigade (Brig. Gen. Erastus B. Tyler)
   91st Pennsylvania
   126th Pennsylvania
   129th Pennsylvania
   134th Pennsylvania

Second Brigade (Col. Peter H. Allabach)
   123d Pennsylvania
   131st Pennsylvania
   133d Pennsylvania
   155th Pennsylvania

Artillery (Capt. Alanson M. Randol)
   1st New York Light, Battery C
   1st United States, Batteries E and G

SIXTH ARMY CORPS (Maj. Gen. John Sedgwick)

First Division (Brig. Gen. William T. H. Brooks)

First Brigade (Col. Henry W. Brown)
   (Col. William H. Penrose)
   (Col. Samuel L. Buck)
   (Col. William H. Penrose)
   1st New Jersey
   2d New Jersey
   3d New Jersey
   15th New Jersey
   23d New Jersey

Second Brigade (Brig. Gen. Joseph J. Bartlett)
   5th Maine
   16th New York
   27th New York
   121st New York
   96th Pennsylvania

Third Brigade (Brig. Gen. David A. Russell)
  18th New York
  32d New York
  49th Pennsylvania
  95th Pennsylvania
  119th Pennsylvania

Artillery (Maj. John A. Tompkins)
  Massachusetts Light, 1st Battery (A)
  New Jersey Light, Battery A
  Maryland Light, Battery A
  2d United States, Battery D

Second Division (Brig. Gen. Albion P. Howe)

Second Brigade (Col. Lewis A. Grant)
  26th New Jersey
  2d Vermont
  3d Vermont
  4th Vermont
  5th Vermont
  6th Vermont

Third Brigade (Brig. Gen. Thomas H. Neill)
  7th Maine
  21st New Jersey
  20th New York
  33d New York
  49th New York
  77th New York

Artillery (Maj. J. Watts de Peyster)
  New York Light, 1st Battery
  5th United States, Battery F

Third Division (Maj. Gen. John Newton)

First Brigade (Col. Alexander Shaler)
  65th New York
  67th New York
  122d New York
  23d Pennsylvania
  82d Pennsylvania

Second Brigade (Col. William H. Browne)
  (Col. Henry L. Eustis)
  7th Massachusetts
  10th Massachusetts
  37th Massachusetts
  36th New York
  2d Rhode Island

Third Brigade (Brig. Gen. Frank Wheaton)
  62d New York
  93d Pennsylvania
  98th Pennsylvania
  102d Pennsylvania
  139th Pennsylvania

Artillery (Capt. Jeremiah McCarthy)
  1st Pennsylvania Light,
    Batteries C and D
  2d United States, Battery G

  Light Division (Col. Hiram Burnham)
    6th Maine
    31st New York
    43d New York
    61st Pennsylvania
    5th Wisconsin
    New York Light Artillery, 3d Battery

ELEVENTH ARMY CORPS (Maj. Gen. Oliver O. Howard)

First Division (Brig. Gen. Charles Devens, Jr.)
(Brig. Gen. Nathaniel C. McLean)

First Brigade (Col. Leopold von Gilsa)
41st New York
45th New York
54th New York
153d Pennsylvania

Second Brigade (Brig. Gen. Nathaniel C. McLean)
(Col. John C. Lee)
17th Connecticut
25th Ohio
55th Ohio
75th Ohio
107th Ohio

Unattached
8th New York (one company)

Artillery
New York Light, 13th Battery

Second Division (Brig. Gen. Adolph von Steinwehr)

First Brigade (Col. Adolphus Buschbeck)
29th New York
154th New York
27th Pennsylvania
73d Pennsylvania

Second Brigade (Brig. Gen. Francis C. Barlow)
33d Massachusetts
134th New York
136th New York
73d Ohio

Artillery
1st New York Light, Battery I

Third Division (Maj. Gen. Carl Schurz)

First Brigade (Brig. Gen. Alexander Schimmelfennig)
82d Illinois
68th New York
157th New York
61st Ohio
74th Pennsylvania

Second Brigade (Col. W. Krzyzanowski)
58th New York
119th New York
75th Pennsylvania
26th Wisconsin

Unattached
82d Ohio

Artillery
1st Ohio Light, Battery I

Reserve Artillery (Lieut. Col. Louis Schirmer)
New York Light, 2d Battery
1st Ohio Light, Battery K
1st West Virginia Light, Battery C

TWELFTH ARMY CORPS (Maj. Gen. Henry W. Slocum)

First Division (Brig. Gen. Alpheus S. Williams)

First Brigade (Brig. Gen. Joseph F. Knipe)
5th Connecticut
28th New York
46th Pennsylvania
128th Pennsylvania

Second Brigade (Col. Samuel Ross)
20th Connecticut
3d Maryland
123d New York
145th New York

Third Brigade (Brig. Gen. Thomas H. Ruger)
27th Indiana
2d Massachusetts
13th New Jersey
107th New York
3d Wisconsin

Artillery (Capt. Robert H. Fitzhugh)
1st New York Light, Battery K
1st New York Light, Battery M
4th United States, Battery F

Second Division (Brig. Gen. Oliver O. Howard)

First Brigade (Col. Charles Candy)
5th Ohio
7th Ohio
29th Ohio
66th Ohio
28th Pennsylvania
147th Pennsylvania

Second Brigade (Brig. Gen. Thomas L. Kane)
29th Pennsylvania
109th Pennsylvania
111th Pennsylvania
124th Pennsylvania
125th Pennsylvania

Third Brigade (Brig. Gen. George S. Greene)
60th New York
78th New York
102d New York
137th New York
149th New York

Artillery (Capt. Joseph M. Knap)
Pennsylvania Light, Battery E
Pennsylvania Light, Battery F

CAVALRY CORPS* (Brig. Gen. George Stoneman)

First Division (Brig. Gen. Alfred Pleasonton)

First Brigade (Col. Benjamin F. Davis)
8th Illinois
3d Indiana
8th New York
9th New York

Second Brigade (Col. Thomas C. Devin)
1st Michigan, Company L
6th New York
8th Pennsylvania
17th Pennsylvania

Artillery
New York Light, 6th Battery

Second Division (Brig. Gen. William W. Averell)

First Brigade (Col. Horace B. Sargent)
1st Massachusetts
4th New York
6th Ohio
1st Rhode Island

Second Brigade (Col. John B. McIntosh)
3d Pennsylvania
4th Pennsylvania
16th Pennsylvania

Artillery
2d United States, Battery A

Third Division (Brig. Gen. David McM. Gregg)

First Brigade (Col. Judson Kilpatrick)
1st Maine
2d New York
10th New York

Second Brigade (Col. Percy Wyndham)
12th Illinois
1st Maryland
1st New Jersey
1st Pennsylvania

Regular Reserve Cavalry Brigade (Brig. Gen. John Buford)
6th Pennsylvania
1st United States
2d United States
5th United States
6th United States

Artillery (Capt. James M. Robertson)
2d United States, Batteries B and L
2d United States, Battery M
4th United States, Battery E

*The Second and Third Divisions, First Brigade, First Division, and the Regular Reserve Brigade, with Robertson's and Tidball's batteries, on the "Stoneman Raid," April 29 – May 7.

Organization of the Army of Northern Virginia, General Robert E. Lee, commanding,
May 1–6, 1863

FIRST CORPS*

McLaws' Division. (Maj. Gen. Lafayette McLaws)

Wofford's Brigade (Brig. Gen. W. T. Wofford)
16th Georgia
18th Georgia
24th Georgia
Cobb's Georgia Legion
Phillips' Georgia Legion

Kershaw's Brigade (Brig. Gen. Joseph B. Kershaw)
2d South Carolina
3d South Carolina
7th South Carolina
8th South Carolina
15th South Carolina
3d South Carolina Battalion

Semmes' Brigade (Brig. Gen. Paul J. Semmes)
10th Georgia
50th Georgia
51st Georgia
53d Georgia

Barksdale's Brigade (Brig. Gen. William Barksdale)
13th Mississippi
17th Mississippi
18th Mississippi
21st Mississippi

Artillery (Col. H. C. Cabell)
Carlton's (Georgia) Battery (Troup Artillery)
Fraser's (Georgia) Battery
McCarthy's (Virginia) Battery (1st Howitzers)
Manly's (North Carolina) Battery

Anderson's Division (Maj. Gen. Richard H. Anderson)

Wilcox's Brigade (Brig. Gen. C. M. Wilcox)
8th Alabama
9th Alabama
10th Alabama
11th Alabama
14th Alabama

Mahone's Brigade (Brig. Gen. William Mahone)
6th Virginia
12th Virginia
16th Virginia
41st Virginia
61st Virginia

Wright's Brigade (Brig. Gen. A. R. Wright)
3d Georgia
22d Georgia
48th Georgia
2d Georgia Battalion

Posey's Brigade (Brig. Gen. Carnot Posey)
12th Mississippi
16th Mississippi
19th Mississippi
48th Mississippi

---

*Lieutenant-General Longstreet, with Hood's and Pickett's divisions and Dearing's and Henry's artillery battalions, in Southeastern Virginia.

Perry's Brigade (Brig. Gen. E. A. Perry)
  2d Florida
  5th Florida
  8th Florida

Artillery (Lieut. Col. J. J. Garnett)
  Grandy's (Virginia) Battery
  Lewis' (Virginia) Battery
  Maurin's (Louisiana) Battery
  Moore's [formerly Huger's] (Virginia) Battery

Artillery Reserve

Alexander's Battalion (Col. E. P. Alexander)
  Eubank's (Virginia) Battery
  Jordan's (Virginia) Battery
  Moody's (Louisiana) Battery
  Parker's (Virginia) Battery
  Rhett's (South Carolina) Battery
  Woolfolk's (Virginia) Battery

Washington (La.) Artillery (Col. J. B. Walton)
  Eshleman's 4th Company
  Miller's 3d Company
  Richardson's 2d Company
  Squires' 1st Company

SECOND CORPS (Lieut. Gen. Thomas J. Jackson)
(Maj. Gen. Ambrose P. Hill)
(Brig. Gen. R. E. Rodes)
(Maj. Gen. J. E. B. Stuart)

Hill's Division (Maj. Gen. A. P. Hill)
(Brig. Gen. Henry Heth)
(Brig. Gen. W. D. Pender)
(Brig. Gen. J. J. Archer)

Heth's Brigade (Brig. Gen. Henry Heth)
  (Col. J. M. Brockenbrough)
  40th Virginia
  47th Virginia
  55th Virginia
  22d Virginia Battalion

McGowan's Brigade (Brig. Gen. S. McGowan)
  (Col. O. E. Edwards)
  (Col. A. Perrin)
  (Col. D. H. Hamilton)
  1st South Carolina
  1st South Carolina
  12th South Carolina
  13th South Carolina
  14th South Carolina

Thomas' Brigade (Brig. Gen. E. L. Thomas)
  14th Georgia
  35th Georgia
  45th Georgia
  49th Georgia

Archer's (Fifth) Brigade (Brig. Gen. J. J. Archer)
  (Col. B. D. Fry)
  13th Alabama
  5th Alabama Battalion
  1st Tennessee
  7th Tennessee
  14th Tennessee

Lane's (Fourth) Brigade (Brig. Gen.
J. H. Lane)
  7th North Carolina
  18th North Carolina
  28th North Carolina
  33d North Carolina
  37th North Carolina

Pender's Brigade (Brig. Gen.
W. D. Pender)
  13th North Carolina
  16th North Carolina
  22d North Carolina
  31st North Carolina
  38th North Carolina

Artillery (Col. R. L. Walker)
  Brunson's (South Carolina) Battery
  Crenshaw's (Virginia) Battery
  Davidson's (Virginia) Battery
  McGraw's (Virginia) Battery
  Marye's (Virginia) Battery

D. H. Hill's Division (Brig. Gen. R. E. Rodes)
(Brig. Gen. S. D. Ramseur)

Rodes' Brigade (Brig. Gen. R. E. Rodes)
  (Col. E. A. O'Neal)
  (Col. J. M. Hall)
  3d Alabama
  5th Alabama
  6th Alabama
  12th Alabama
  26th Alabama

Doles' Brigade (Brig. Gen. George Doles)
  4th Georgia
  12th Georgia
  21st Georgia
  44th Georgia

Colquitt's Brigade (Brig. Gen.
A. H. Colquitt)
  6th Georgia
  19th Georgia
  23d Georgia
  27th Georgia
  28th Georgia

Iverson's Brigade (Brig. Gen. Alfred
Iverson)
  5th North Carolina
  12th North Carolina
  20th North Carolina
  23d North Carolina

Ramseur's Brigade (Brig. Gen. S. D.
Ramseur)
  (Col. F. M. Parker)
  2d North Carolina
  4th North Carolina
  14th North Carolina
  30th North Carolina

Artillery (Lieut. Col. T. H. Carter)
  Reese's (Alabama) Battery
    Carter's (Virginia) Battery (King
    William Artillery)
    Fry's (Virginia) Battery (Orange
  Artillery)
    Page's (Virginia) Battery (Morris
  Artillery)

Early's Division (Maj. Gen. Jubal A. Early)

Gordon's Brigade (Brig. Gen. John B. Gordon)
- 13th Georgia
- 26th Georgia
- 31st Georgia
- 38th Georgia
- 60th Georgia
- 61st Georgia

Smith's Brigade (Brig. Gen. William Smith)
- 13th Virginia
- 49th Virginia
- 52d Virginia
- 58th Virginia

Hoke's Brigade (Brig. Gen. Robert F. Hoke)
- 6th North Carolina
- 21st North Carolina
- 54th North Carolina
- 57th North Carolina
- 1st North Carolina Battalion

Hays' Brigade (Brig. Gen. Harry T. Hays)
- 5th Louisiana
- 6th Louisiana
- 7th Louisiana
- 8th Louisiana
- 9th Louisiana

Artillery (Lieut. Col. R. S. Andrews)
- Brown's (Maryland) Battery
- Carpenter's (Virginia) Battery
- Dement's (Maryland) Battery
- Raine's (Virginia) Battery

Trimble's Division (Brig. Gen. R. E. Colston)

Paxton's (First) Brigade (Brig. Gen. E. F. Paxton)
(Col. J. H. S. Funk)
- 2d Virginia
- 4th Virginia
- 5th Virginia
- 27th Virginia
- 33d Virginia

Colston's (Third) Brigade (Col. E. T. H. Warren)
(Col. T. V. Williams)
(Lieut. Col. S. T. Walker)
(Lieut. Col. S. D. Thruston)
(Lieut. Col. H. A. Brown)
- 1st North Carolina
- 3d North Carolina
- 10th Virginia
- 23d Virginia
- 37th Virginia

Jones' (Second) Brigade (Brig. Gen. J. R. Jones)
(Col. T. S. Garnett)
(Col. A. S. Vandrventer)
- 21st Virginia
- 42d Virginia
- 44th Virginia
- 48th Virginia
- 50th Virginia

Nicholls' (Fourth) Brigade (Brig. Gen. F. T. Nicholls)
(Col. J. M. Williams)
- 1st Louisiana
- 2d Louisiana
- 10th Louisiana
- 14th Louisiana
- 15th Louisiana

Artillery (Lieut. Col. H. P. Jones)
Carrington's (Virginia) Battery
(Charlottesville Artillery)
Garber's (Virginia) Battery (Staunton
Artillery)
Latimer's (Virginia) Battery (Courtney
Artillery)
Thompson's Battery (Louisiana Guard
Artillery)

Artillery Reserve (Col. S. Crutchfield)

Brown's Battalion (Col. J. Thompson
Brown)
Brooke's (Virginia) Battery
Dance's (Virginia) Battery (Powhatan
Artillery)
Graham's (Virginia) Battery
(Rockbridge Artillery)
Hupp's (Virginia) Battery (Salem
Artillery)
Smith's Battery (3d Richmond
Howitzers)
Watson's Battery (2d Richmond
Howitzers)

McIntosh's Battalion (Maj.
D. G. McIntosh)
Hurt's (Alabama) Battery
Johnson's (Virginia) Battery
Lusk's (Virginia) Battery
Wooding's (Virginia) Battery (Danville
Artillery)

RESERVE ARTILLERY (Brig. Gen. William N. Pendleton)

Sumter (Ga.) Battalion (Lieut. Col.
A. S. Cutts)
Patterson's Battery (B)
Ross' Battery (A)
Wingfield's Battery (C)

Nelson's Battalion (Lieut. Col.
W. Nelson)
Kirkpatrick's (Virginia) Battery
(Amherst Artillery)
Massie's (Virginia) Battery (Fluvanna
Artillery)
Milledge's (Georgia) Battery

CAVALRY (Maj. Gen. James E. B. Stuart)

First Brigade* (Brig. Gen. Wade Hampton)
- 1st North Carolina
- 1st South Carolina
- 2d South Carolina
- Cobb's Georgia Legion
- Phillips' Georgia Legion

Second Brigade (Brig. Gen. Fitzhugh Lee)
- 1st Virginia
- 2d Virginia
- 3d Virginia, Col. Thomas H. Owen
- 4th Virginia, Col. Williams C. Wickham

Third Brigade* (Brig. Gen. W. H. F. Lee)
- 2d North Carolina
- 5th Virginia
- 9th Virginia
- 10th Virginia
- 13th Virginia
- 15th Virginia

Fourth Brigade* (Brig. Gen. William E. Jones)
- 1st Maryland Battalion
- 6th Virginia
- 7th Virginia
- 11th Virginia
- 12th Virginia
- 34th Virginia Battalion
- 35th Virginia Battalion

Horse Artillery (Maj. R. F. Beckham)
- Lynchburg Beauregards
- Stuart Horse Artillery
- Virginia Battery
- Washington (S. C.) Artillery

*On detached service.

An early post-war photo of Fairview. (NPS)

The pontoon bridge site as it appears today. This photo is taken from the east bank of the
Rappahannock just below Chatham House. (HWN)

APPENDIX III

Burial of soldiers killed at Fredericksburg. (USAMHI)

Estimates of numbers engaged in Civil War battles vary, and statistics on killed, wounded, captured and missing are incomplete. Participants attempted to fill gaps as they wrote their official reports, and historians have tried to refine the data. The tabulation that follows is drawn from the *Official Record*, Vol. 21, pp. 129–142, 558–562 and Vol. 25, Pt. 1, pp. 172–191, 806–809, and from Thomas L. Livermore, *Numbers and Losses in the Civil War in America*, 1861–1865 (New York: Houghton, Mifflin and Company, 1901).

RECAPITULATION OF CASUALTIES

Battle of Fredericksburg
December 13, 1862

	Engaged	Killed	Wounded	Captured or Missing	Aggregate
Army of the Potomac	113,687	1,284	9,600	1,769	12,653
Army of Northern Virginia	72,497	595	4,061	653	5,309

Battle of Chancellorsville
May 1–4, 1863

	Engaged	Killed	Wounded	Captured or Missing	Aggregate
Army of the Potomac	104,891	1,575	9,559	4,684	15,818
Army of Northern Virginia	48,080	1,581	8,700	2,018	12,299

NOTES TO APPENDIX I

1. Major General R. E. Colston, "Lee's Knowledge of Hooker's Movements," Robert Underwood Johnson and Clarence Clough Buel, eds., *Battles and Leaders of the Civil War* (4 volumes: New York, The Century Co., 1888), III, p. 233.

2. John Bigelow, Jr. *The Campaign of Chancellorsville: A Strategic and Tactical Study* (New Haven: Yale University Press, 1910), p. xii.

3. George H. Casamajor, "The Federal Secret Service," in Francis Trevelyan Miller, ed., *The Photographic History of the Civil War* (10 vols., New York: The Review of Reviews Co., 1911), VIII, 269–76.

4. *Ibid.*, p. 276.

5. Francis A. Lord, *They Fought for the Union* (New York: Bonanza Books, 1950, p. 133; Bigelow, *Chancellorsville*, p. 47).

6. Lord, *They Fought for the Union*, p. 133.

7. *Official Records*, XXV, pt. 1, pp. 194–95.

8. *Ibid.*, pt. 2, pp. 99–100, 630–31.

9. Archie P. McDonald, ed., *Make me a Map of the Valley: The Civil War Journal of Stonewall Jackson's Topographer* (Dallas: Southern Methodist University Press, 1973), p. 116.

10. *Official Records* XXV, pt. 2, pp. 713–15.

11. Robert Debs Heinl, Jr., *Dictionary of Military and Naval Quotations* (Annapolis: United States Naval Institute, 1966), p. 160.

12. Casamajor, "The Federal Secret Service," p. 284; John W. Headley, "The Confederate Secret Service," *Miller's Photographic History.* VIII, 286.

13. *Official Records*, XXV, pt. 2, pp. 700–701.

14. *Ibid.*, pp. 702–3. For other specific reports that clarified Lee's picture of what was happening on the other side of the river, see *ibid.*, pp. 598, 642, 646, 691, 724–25.

15. *Ibid.*, pp. 101, 114.

16. Bvt. Brig. Gen. Albert J. Myer, *A Manual of Signals for the Use of Signal Officers in the Field* (Washington: Government Printing Office, 1877).

17. A. W. Greely, "The Signal Service," *Photographic History of the Civil War*, VIII, p. 309.

18. *Official Records*, XXV, pt. 2, 738, 752.

19. On 21 May 1863 Hooker's chief of staff forwarded a Richmond newspaper "of yesterday," *ibid.*, p. 333.

20. *Official Records*, XXV, pt. 2, pp. 239–41, 790.

21. *Ibid.*, pp. 258, 269–70, 316.

22. Lord, *They Fought for the Union*, p. 135.

23. McDonald, *Make me a Map of the Valley*, p. 125.

24. *Official Records*, XXV, pt. 2, 351.

25. *Ibid.*, pp. 153–54, 209, 267, 269.

26. *Ibid.*, pp. 257–58.

27. Douglas Southall Freeman, *R. E. Lee: A Biography* (4 vols., New York: Charles Scribner's Sons, 1936), III, 327. For an account of the role played by Union cavalry throughout the Chancellorsville campaign, see Stephen Z. Starr, *The Union Cavalry in the Civil War. I. From Fort Sumter to Gettysburg, 1861–1863.*

28. Eugene B. Block, *Above the Civil War: the Story of Thaddeus Lowe, balloonist, inventor, railway builder* (Berkeley: Howell-North Books, 1966), pp. 2–3.

29. F. Stansbury Haydon, *Aeronautics in the Union and Confederate Armies, with a survey of Military Aeronautics prior to 1861* (Baltimore: The Johns Hopkins Press, 1941), vol. 1, pp. 1–38 *passim*.

30. Captain W. Z. Glassford, "The Balloon in the Civil War," *Journal of the Military Service Institution of the United States*, XVIII (March, 1896), p. 265.

31. Longstreet is quoted in Block, *Above the Civil War*, p. 96.

32. *Official Records*, XXV, Pt. 2, p. 752. According to Bigelow, "throughout the operations . . . Lee underestimated the strength of Hooker's army, and Hooker overestimated that of Lee's." *Campaign of Chancellorsville*, p. 158 n.

33. *Official Records*, XXV, pt. 2, pp. 198, 322, 327, 322–33.

34. *Ibid.*, p. 371.

35. Lee to Stuart, 12 March 1863, *Ibid.*, pp. 664, 669.

36. Lee to Stuart, 16 April 1863, *Ibid.*, p. 737.

37. Lee to Davis, 16 April, 1863, *Ibid.*, pp. 724–25. "If there are any two-years' men that you consider unreliable, in consequence of the near expiration of their term of service, you will leave them on duty with the division left behind." S. Williams, Assistant Adjutant-General, to Commanding Officer, Second Corps, 27 April, 1863. *Ibid.*, p. 267.

38. *Ibid.*, pp. 679, 701, 826.

39. *Ibid.*, pp. 238, 715.

40. See *ibid.*, pp. 114, 253, 728; Bigelow, *Chancellorsville*, p. 139.

41. *Official Records*, XXV, pt. 1, p. 796; pt. 2, 744–45.

42. Lee to Davis, 29 April 1863, *ibid.*, pt. 2, p. 756.

43. *Ibid.*, pp. 761–62. These "arrangements" included constructing a defensive line at Zoar Church, about 3 miles east of Chancellorsville.

44. *Ibid.*, pt. 1, p. 199; pt. 2, p. 306.

45. *Ibid.*, pt. 2, pp. 277–78, 288, 301, 324, 333, 336.

46. *Ibid.*, p. 330. For reports of the arrival of Hood's division, see *ibid.*, p. 332–33.

47. *Ibid.*, pp. 328, 330, 332–33.

48. *Ibid.*, p. 337.

49. *Ibid.*, pt. 1, pp. 386, 628.

50. Hooker as quoted in Bigelow, *Chancellorsville*, jp. 126.

51. G. F. R. Henderson, *Stonewall Jackson and the American Civil War* (2 vols., London: Longmans, Green and Co., 1906), II, 470.

52. Glassford, "Balloon in the Civil War," p. 265; Block, *Above the Civil War*, pp. 101–102.

53. General E. P. Alexander, *Military Memoirs of a Confederate* (Bloomington: Indiana University Press, 1962), p. 352.

INDEX

A modern view of Fredericksburg from the east bank of the Rappahannock from Chatham House. (HWN)

Chancellorsville, the old road near Catharine Furnace as it appears today. This is the site of Jackson's flank march. (HWN)